France on Trial

France on Trial

The Case of Marshal Pétain

JULIAN JACKSON

The Belknap Press of
Harvard University Press
Cambridge, Massachusetts
2023

First published in the United Kingdom by Allen Lane, an imprint
of Penguin Books Ltd, Penguin Random House, London, 2023
Set in 10.5/14 pt Sabon LT Std
Typeset by Jouve (UK), Milton Keynes

First Harvard University Press edition, 2023

Library of Congress Cataloging-in-Publication Data

Names: Jackson, Julian, 1954– author.
Title: France on trial : the case of Marshal Pétain / Julian Jackson.
Description: First Harvard University Press edition. | Cambridge,
Massachusetts : The Belknap Press of Harvard University Press, 2023. |
Includes bibliographical references and index.
Identifiers: LCCN 2023002544 | ISBN 9780674248892 (hardback)
Subjects: LCSH: Pétain, Philippe, 1856–1951—Trials, litigation, etc. |
Trials (Treason)—France—Paris. | France—History—German occupation,
1940–1945.
Classification: LCC DC342.8.P4 J34 2023 | DDC 944.081/6—dc23/eng/20230208
LC record available at https://lccn.loc.gov/2023002544

In memory of Michael Sibalis

Contents

List of Illustrations

Every effort has been made to contact all copyright holders. The publisher will be pleased to amend in future printings any errors or omissions brought to their attention.

17. Pierre Laval, 4 August 1945. Photograph: Keystone / Hulton Archive / Getty Images.
18–21. Courtroom sketches by André Galland, from *Le Procès Pétain* by Frédéric Pottecher (ed. J. C. Lattès, Paris: 1980). Copyright © Société de la Propriété Artistique des Dessins et Modèles.
22. Tract threatening the jurors. Archives Nationales (F7/15549).
23. Jacques Isorni addresses the court. Photograph: AFP / Getty Images.
24. *France-Soir*, 14 August 1945, BNF.
25. *L'Humanité*, 19 August 1945, BNF.
26. Pro-Pétain tract. Archives Nationales (F7/15488).
27. *Le Maréchal*, new series 42, June/July 1964. Reproduced with permission from Association pour défendre la mémoire du maréchal Pétain (ADMP).
28. ADMP tract. Archives de la Préfecture de Police, Paris (BA/1979).
29. 'The Trial of Marshal Philippe Pétain'. Photograph: copyright © LAPI/Roger-Viollet.
30. Author's photograph.
31. Jeune Nation advert, 2021. Source: www.jeune-nation.com

Pétain's last journeys

Legend:
- ← 26 August – 6 September 1944: Vichy – Belfort – Sigmaringen
- ← - - 21 – 26 April 1945: Sigmaringen – Wangen – Bregenz – Wessen – Vallorbe – Montrouge
- ← · — 15 August 1945: Paris – Portalet
- ← · · · 14 November 1945: Portalet – Île d'Yeu

Calais

Dieppe

NORMANDY

Paris
Montrouge

Verdun

GERMANY

Nancy

Sigmaringen

Montoire-sur-le-Loir

Wangen

Belfort

Bregenz

Île d'Yeu

Wessen

Vallorbe

SWITZERLAND

Vichy
Riom

FRANCE

ITALY

Bordeaux

Hendaye

Toulouse

Perpignan

Portalet

Port-Vendres

Mediterranean Sea

SPAIN

N
W E
S

Paris

Arc de Triomphe

Champs-Élysées

Place de la République

Père-Lachaise Cemetery

Gare d'Orsay

Palais de Justice

Île de la Cité

Notre Dame

Boulevard Saint-Michel

River Seine

Montrouge

0   100 miles

0   100   200 km

0   2 miles

0   2 km

Acknowledgements

The writing of every book has its own story. In this case, research was initially disrupted in December 2019 by a wave of French strikes protesting against pension reforms. As a result, to visit archives or libraries, if they were open, involved long walks across Paris. No sooner were the strikes over than Covid struck. This ruled out a planned visit to the State Department archives in Washington. Instead, I wish to thank Sahand Yazdanyar for researching in those archives on my behalf once they had reopened. My visit to Pétain's grave on the Île d'Yeu was also delayed by a year, but it is a pleasure to thank Sam, Merry and family for organizing that trip, and making it so pleasurable when it finally took place in the summer of July 2021.

Visiting the courtroom where Pétain's trial took place was complicated by the fact that the Palais de Justice had become a no-go zone during the interminable trial of the Bataclan terrorists. My visit finally took place thanks to the magistrate Marie-Luce Cavrois, who showed me round the Palais. She also introduced me to her colleague and friend Jean-Paul Jean, who generously shared with me his extensive knowledge of the French magistrature at the time of the *épuration*.

My dear friend Carol Piketty, although now sadly retired from the Archives Nationales, was nonetheless able to give me many useful tips, and put me in touch with her former colleague Olivier Chosalland, who helpfully guided me through the papers of Louis-Dominique Girard, which he had recently catalogued.

Many friends and colleagues read the book in various stages. The first was Colin Jones, who also, at the very beginning of the project, found me my title. Patrick Higgins, who read a long version of the book, commented as robustly and perceptively as he always does.

Marc-Olivier Baruch, Robert Paxton and Antoine Prost were all kind enough to read the almost finished text very closely. They collectively saved me from many mistakes. Robert Gildea, who read the manuscript for Penguin, offered very helpful suggestions on a somewhat raw version; as did the anonymous reader for Harvard.

My agent Andrew Gordon was, as always, supportive, and his gently incisive comments on an early draft succeeded in the delicate task of making it clear that much work remained to be done while not terminally depressing me. The team at Allen Lane have once again been a joy to work with. Richard Mason was a superb copy-editor; and Alice Skinner an efficient solver of many problems. I feel once again privileged to have as my Penguin editor the deservedly legendary Stuart Proffitt, who devotes such care and thought to his manuscripts. Over the final three weeks, my editor at Harvard, Joy de Menil, gave the book an extraordinarily close reading. I have never previously lived such an intensive, enriching and stimulating collaboration with an editor on a book manuscript.

Most of the book was written in the wonderful surroundings of the Cévennes during the two Covid lockdowns which I spent there with Douglas, my partner. Douglas is always hoping each new book will take less time and cause less mess (papers and books strewn on the floor) than the previous one. He is always disappointed but without his love and support the books would not be written at all.

Boisset-et-Gaujac, November 2022

Dramatis Personae

The Defendant
Marshal Philippe Pétain (1856–1951): military hero; head of the
  Vichy *État français*, 1940–1944.

The Prosecution
Pierre Bouchardon (1870–1950): *juge d'instruction* (examining
  magistrate) in many First World War treason trials, and for the
  trial of Pétain.
André Mornet (1870–1955): *procureur* (prosecutor) in many First
  World War treason trials, and for the trial of Pétain.

The Judge
Pierre Mongibeaux (1879–1950).

The Jurors
Parliamentary Jurors: Bèche, Émile (1898–1977); Bender, Émile
  (1871–1953); Bloch, Jean-Pierre (1905–1999); Delattre, Gabriel
  (1891–1984); Dupré, Léandre (1871–1951); Faure, Pétrus (1891–
  1985); Lévy-Alphandéry, Georges (1862–1948); Mabrut, Adrien
  (1901–1987); Prot, Louis (1889–1972); Renoult, René (1867–
  1946); Sion, Paul (1886–1959); Tony-Révillon, Michel
  (1891–1957). Reserves (*suppléants*): Catalan, Camille
  (1889–1951); Chassaing, Eugène (1876–1968); Rous, Joseph
  (1881–1974); Schmidt, Jammy (1872–1959).
Resistance Jurors: Bergeron, Marcel (1899–1972); Gervolino, Roger
  (1909–1991); Guérin, Maurice (1887–1969); Guy, Jean (n.d.);
  Lecompte-Boinet, Jacques (1905–1974); Lescuyer, Roger

(1919–1971); Loriguet, Marcel (1913–1983); Meunier, Pierre (1908–1996); Perney, Ernest (1873–1946); Yves Porc'her (1887–1969); Seignon, Henri (1899–1973); Stibbe, Pierre (1912–1967). Reserves (*suppléants*): Destouches, Gilbert (1909–2005); Lévêque, Marcel (1924–?); Poupon, Georges (1911–1974); Worms, Jean ('Germinal') (1894–1974).

The Defence Lawyers

Jacques Isorni (1911–1995): defence lawyer in the purge trials of Robert Brasillach and Pétain; devoted much of his life to the defence of Pétain's reputation.

Jean Lemaire (1904–1986): a member of the defence team and later a President of the Association to Defend the Memory of Marshal Pétain (ADMP).

Fernand Payen (1872–1946): civil lawyer and senior defence lawyer.

Witnesses for the Prosecution*

Léon Blum (1872–1950): Socialist politician; head of the left-wing Front Populaire government in 1936. Tried and imprisoned by Vichy.

Édouard Daladier (1884–1970): French premier, 10 April 1938–21 March 1940; tried and imprisoned by Vichy.

Albert Lebrun (1871–1950): President of the French Republic in 1940.

Jules Jeanneney (1864–1957): President of the Senate (upper house of parliament) in 1940.

Louis Marin (1871–1960): Conservative French politician; member of Paul Reynaud's government in 1940.

Édouard Herriot (1872–1957): President of the Chamber of Deputies (lower house of parliament) in 1940.

Paul Reynaud (1878–1966): French premier, 21 March–16 June 1940; interned by Vichy.

François Charles-Roux (1879–1961): Head of the Quai d'Orsay (French Foreign Ministry), May–October 1940.

Paul-André Doyen (1881–1974): General and French representative on the Armistice Commission until July 1941.

* In total, eighteen witnesses were called for the prosecution and forty-one for the defence.

Witnesses for the Defence

Jean Berthelot (1897–1985): Engineer; Vichy Minister of Transport, December 1940–April 1942.

Henri Bléhaut (1889–1962): Admiral; Vichy Naval and Colonial Minister from March 1943; accompanied Pétain to Sigmaringen.

Jacques Chevalier (1882–1962): Catholic philosopher; Vichy Minister of Education, December 1940–February 1941.

Victor Debeney (1891–1956): General; head of Pétain's secretariat from August 1944; accompanied him to Sigmaringen.

Marcel Peyrouton (1887–1983): Vichy Minister of the Interior, July 1940–February 1941.

Bernard Serrigny (1870–1954): General; old friend of Pétain.

Jean Tracou (1891–1988): Head of Pétain's *cabinet civil* in 1944.

Maxime Weygand (1867–1965): General; appointed commander-in-chief of the French Army, 28 May 1940; Vichy Delegate to North Africa, September 1940–November 1941; arrested by the Germans in November 1942.

Other Witnesses Called to Testify by the Judge

Fernand de Brinon (1885–1947): Vichy delegate to the Occupied Zone; head of Sigmaringen government, 1944–1945.

Joseph Darnand (1897–1945): Founder and leader of the *Milice*; Vichy Minister of the Interior in 1944.

Pierre Laval (1883–1945): Leading politician of the Third Republic; Vichy prime minister, July–December 1940 and April 1942–August 1944.

Georges Loustaunau-Lacau (1894–1955): French army officer; anti-Communist right-wing conspirator.

Pétainists Who Did Not Testify in the Trial

Raphaël Alibert (1987–1963): Right-wing activist; Vichy Minister of Justice, July 1940–February 1941; condemned to death in absentia 1947.

Gabriel Paul Auphan (1894–1982): Admiral: Vichy Naval Minister, April–November 1942; went into hiding at the Liberation and sentenced to hard labour in absentia in 1946.

Jean Borotra (1898–1994): Tennis champion in the 1920s (twice Wimbledon singles champion); Vichy Commissioner for Sport, 1940–1942.

Louis-Dominique Girard (1911–1990): Deputy head of Pétain's *cabinet civil* in 1944; married Pétain's great grand-niece in 1949 and wrote several books defending Pétain.

Bertrand Ménétrel (1906–1947): Pétain's doctor and close adviser; accompanied him to Sigmaringen.

Louis Rougier (1889–1982): Philosopher who claimed to have negotiated an agreement with Churchill in 1940; indefatigable pro-Pétain polemicist after 1945.

Introduction: The Fateful Handshake

October 1940 was a busy month for Adolf Hitler. In the early hours of Tuesday 22nd he set off from Munich in his special train, 'Amerika', to meet the Spanish leader Francisco Franco. Passing through France, he stopped at the small town of Montoire-sur-le-Loir for a brief meeting with the French prime minister, Pierre Laval. On Wednesday the train reached Hendaye, on the Spanish frontier. This was where Hitler had to meet Franco, as the gauge width of Spanish railways prevented him from going any further. The next day, on the return journey, he stopped again at Montoire in the afternoon. This time he was meeting the French Head of State, Marshal Philippe Pétain, before rounding off his railway tour with a visit to Benito Mussolini in Florence.

Behind this flurry of railway diplomacy lay an uncomfortable truth: Germany had just lost the Battle of Britain. Hitler's mind now turned to destroying British naval power in the Mediterranean. Such a strategy would require the support of the three Mediterranean powers: Spain, France, Italy. Hitler's ten-hour encounter with Franco was a disaster. 'I would rather have three or four teeth extracted than go through that again,' he told Mussolini. He had hoped that the Spanish leader might join the war or at least open Gibraltar to German troops, but Franco had asked to be rewarded with French territories in North Africa coveted by Spain, which would have jeopardized any chance of Hitler rallying France to his Mediterranean plans. Hitler needed to square the competing interests of the French and Spanish and, if that proved impossible, to decide which country had more to offer him. That was his purpose in sounding out Pétain.

Venerated as a hero of the Great War, the eighty-four-year-old Marshal had become head of government in June 1940 after a six-week campaign in which France's armies had been humiliatingly routed by the Germans. Believing that further resistance was futile, Pétain had signed an armistice with Germany. This allowed the Germans to occupy two-thirds of French territory while leaving an unoccupied 'Free Zone' in the South. Since Paris was in the Occupied Zone, Pétain's government installed itself at the town of Vichy in central France. Famous as a spa resort, Vichy was a curious choice of capital city – rather as if the British had moved their government to Harrogate in North Yorkshire. But the town's numerous hotels provided ready accommodation for the influx of officials and ministers who replaced its habitual clientele of valetudinarians and holiday-makers. This setting imparted a somewhat surreal character to France's new government: 'a banana Republic with no bananas', as one observer described it.[1] But Vichy was not really a Republic either, as Pétain's government had suspended France's democratic institutions and installed a quasi-dictatorship. The motto of the former Republic, 'Liberty, Equality, Fraternity', was replaced by 'Work, Family, Fatherland'.

No one expected the French government to remain in Vichy for long. Most assumed the armistice would be a short-lived arrangement pending a full peace treaty after Britain's defeat. When that defeat failed to materialize, the terms of the armistice started to weigh heavily on France: they contained no provision for the release of over one million French soldiers taken prisoner in June 1940 who remained incarcerated in Germany. The demarcation line imposed by the armistice between the Free and Occupied Zones paralysed the French economy and disrupted daily life, and the French were required to pay a daily indemnity to cover German occupation costs. In short, the armistice was a noose around France's neck. The Vichy government was desperate to loosen the knot. Thus Pétain had his own reasons for wanting to meet Hitler when the unexpected opportunity arose.

Why Montoire-sur-le-Loir? The town was conveniently located on a branch line just off the main railway route from Paris to Spain. Security considerations also played a part. Hitler's 'Amerika' was a fortress on wheels, with sumptuous accommodations, a state-of-the-art communications centre, and its own anti-tank gun batteries. But this was not enough. Every stopover had to be close to a tunnel in case of aerial attack. Montoire was near to the tunnel of Saint-Rémy, where heavy iron doors were hastily installed in preparation for the visit. The town's 2,800 inhabitants were instructed to stay home and to keep their shutters closed. The mayor was seized as a potential hostage and designated as food taster to forestall any attempt to poison his visitor. The station was decked out with tropical plants from the Botanical Gardens of nearby Tours and a red carpet was commandeered from Montoire's church. A certain solemnity was required for the occasion.

Pétain's party, which included Pierre Laval, drove up from Vichy on the afternoon of 24 October. It was the first time Pétain had set foot in the Occupied Zone since the signing of the armistice. Any outing was a welcome relief from the monotony of Vichy. The meeting took place in Hitler's saloon car. Also present were the German Foreign Minister, Joachim von Ribbentrop, and Hitler's interpreter, Paul Schmidt. Hitler, who had served as an ordinary soldier in the Great War, was impressed to find himself in the presence of the last surviving titan of that conflict. On meeting Pétain he said in German: 'I am happy to shake the hand of a Frenchman who was not responsible for this war.' Since there was no interpreter present at that moment, Pétain replied evasively, in French: 'Splendid, splendid; thank you.'

While Pétain and Laval were ensconced with Hitler, other members of the French party, including Pétain's doctor and adviser Bernard Ménétrel, exchanged pleasantries and *petits fours* with Hitler's doctor and a German diplomat. The two doctors discussed the health of their respective patients – Pétain's more robust than Hitler's. The Führer treated his guest with deference, accompanying him to his car once the meeting was over. He certainly found Pétain more agreeable than 'that Jesuit cur' Franco. As for Pétain, always susceptible to flattery, he was more favourably impressed by the former Austrian corporal than he had expected. It was Laval who commented afterwards that Hitler's ill-fitting uniform made him look like a hotel porter.[2]

The encounter, which lasted about two hours, was inconclusive, but its symbolic impact was incalculable. Soon afterwards the Germans produced a short newsreel of the event. It shows Pétain stepping out of his car to a line of German soldiers standing at attention. He shakes hands with von Ribbentrop and Field Marshal Wilhelm Keitel. Then, accompanied by the latter, he crosses the railway track (the potted

1. The handshake: Pétain and Hitler, 24 October 1940.

plants in evidence) where Hitler, wearing a cap that seems oddly too big, is waiting for him. The two men shake hands. The photograph of that handshake with the interpreter standing between them, and Ribbentrop slightly to the side, would be reproduced innumerable times over the next four years.[3] After the war, Pétain told one of his lawyers that it had not been a proper handshake. Since Hitler had held out his hand, he could hardly ignore it – 'but I only took his fingers'. This feeble claim was tested by Pétain's post-war judges, who blew up reproductions of the photograph.[4] On another occasion Pétain said: 'He held his hand out to me; I could hardly spit in it! All the more so since I was there to see if I could get the return of our prisoners.'[5]

Whatever kind of handshake it was, the photograph was a propaganda coup for the Nazi regime, headline news throughout the world, and a shock to French public opinion. It was a shock because the armistice did not signify that France was formally at peace with Germany. An armistice is merely a suspension of hostilities. France was no longer fighting Germany, but she was technically neutral. Many people wanted to believe that, behind the scenes, Pétain was secretly working against Hitler with France's former ally Britain, or with General de Gaulle, who was continuing the fight from London. Was it still possible to believe this after the handshake? In a radio speech on 30 October, explaining the Montoire meeting to the French public, Pétain made things worse:

> Last Thursday I met the Chancellor of the Reich. This meeting has aroused hopes and provoked concerns: I owe you some explanations . . . It was entirely of my own volition that I accepted the Führer's invitation. There was no Diktat and no pressure. A collaboration is envisaged between our two countries. I have accepted the principle of it. The details will be discussed later . . . He who has taken into his hands the destiny of France has a duty to create the atmosphere most favourable to safeguard the interests of the country. It is in honour, and to maintain French unity . . . in the framework of the active construction of a new European order that I enter today down the road of collaboration . . . This collaboration must be sincere.[6]

This was not the first time the word 'collaboration' had been used to describe the relations between France and Germany since the defeat. It appeared in clause 3 of the armistice requiring French authorities in the Occupied Zone to 'collaborate' with the Germans. But this related to technical cooperation on routine matters of administration; it had no political connotations. The word 'collaboration' had also appeared obliquely in a speech by Pétain on 11 October suggesting that France needed to 'free herself from her so-called traditional enmities and friendships' in order 'to seek collaboration in all fields with *all* her neighbours [i.e. Germany]'. But on 30 October, in one short speech, Pétain used the word three times, presenting it as a bold new direction of French foreign policy. He was aware of the gravity of his words: 'This is my policy. My ministers are responsible to me. It is I alone who will be judged by History.'

TRIAL OF THE CENTURY

That hour of judgement came almost five years later when Pétain was brought before a High Court to answer for his conduct. The court had been set up by the provisional government of General de Gaulle after the Liberation of France in the summer of 1944. De Gaulle had left France for London four years earlier because he refused to accept the armistice with Germany. In a famous radio broadcast on the BBC on 18 June 1940 he had sounded the call to resistance, and soon afterwards he also raised the spectre of retribution. In another broadcast in July 1940 he declared that France would 'punish . . . the artisans of her servitude'.[7] He gave no names but his speeches over the next four years never held back from direct attacks on Pétain, whom he referred to as 'le Père la Défaite' – Father of Defeat – an ironic inversion of the soubriquet applied to Georges Clemenceau, France's prime minister during the Great War, who had been dubbed 'le Père la Victoire' – Father of Victory.

Vichy leaders at first had little reason to be seriously worried about these hollow threats from a minor general across the Channel – soon to be 'ex-General' when they stripped him of his title and sentenced him to death in absentia. But de Gaulle's broadcasts on the BBC gradually transformed him into the embodiment of resistance. In May 1943, after the Allies had secured North Africa, he moved his base of operations to Algiers and became head of the French Council for National Liberation (CFLN). On 3 September 1943 this proto-government in exile issued a decree stating that France would bring to trial 'Pétain and those who belonged or belong to the pseudo-government created by him, which capitulated, destroyed the constitution, collaborated with the enemy, delivered French workers to the Germans'.[8]

The trial of Pétain finally opened in Paris on 23 July 1945 (ending on 15 August). Sandwiched between the celebrations for VE Day on 8 May, marking the end of the war in Europe, and VJ Day on 15 August, marking the end of the war in the Far East, Pétain's trial was the news event of the summer. 'The greatest trial in history', as the headlines grandiloquently proclaimed, was front-page news of every French newspaper every day for three weeks. Despite chronic shortages, the paper allowance was temporarily increased to allow newspapers to publish four pages instead of two. Even this left little space for other news. Only a few international events, such as Winston Churchill's surprising electoral defeat or the dropping of the atom bomb on Hiroshima, displaced the trial from the headlines. The trial attracted worldwide attention, especially in Britain and America, but also in Scandinavia, Canada and Spain.[9] Most foreign embassies sent an observer every day. It was attended by the most celebrated journalists of the day and discussed in the press by France's most famous writers – François Mauriac, Albert Camus, Georges Bernanos.

This was obviously a 'political' trial. It was inconceivable that Pétain would not be found guilty. The only uncertainty was the penalty. As Camus wrote in April 1945: 'If Pétain is absolved, it would mean that all those who fought against the occupier were in the wrong. Those who were shot, tortured, deported would have suffered in vain.'[10] This was only one of many trials that took place in the aftermath of the Axis defeat. The most famous of these, the Nuremberg trials, opened in September 1945, a month after Pétain's trial ended, and they were followed by the Tokyo trials in April 1946. Yet in both these cases the defendants were being tried by an International Tribunal, whereas in Pétain's case a *French* court was judging a *French* leader. Perhaps more comparable might be the trial of the Norwegian collaborationist leader Vidkun Quisling, which started on 20 August, five days after Pétain's trial closed. But Quisling was a fanatical Nazi sympathizer with no popular support. Pétain, on the other hand, had been revered and loved by the French, and the Vichy regime had been recognized by governments throughout the world, including the United States. Another comparison might be the trial of the Romanian leader Ion Antonescu in May 1946, but this was undertaken primarily to assert the legitimacy of the new Communist regime.[11] In all trials of this kind, many factors are at play: retribution and revenge for the victors, consolation and closure for the victims. They are also exercises in national pedagogy, enabling the new political authorities to deliver their version of history.[12]

All this was true of the Pétain trial. One can understand why a historian has written that this was less a trial than 'an elaborate ceremony aimed at symbolically condemning a policy'.[13] But despite many irregularities, what took place in the courtroom was not a charade. Pétain's defence lawyers were allowed to interrogate witnesses and consult documents. Over the course of three weeks, sixty-three witnesses were called to testify in the crowded and stiflingly hot courtroom. They included a former President of the Republic and five former prime ministers; generals and admirals, diplomats and civil servants; former resisters and former collaborators; even a Bourbon prince.

The trial of a Marshal of France was by definition an extraordinary event. In France, the title 'Marshal' is an honour rather than a military rank. It is awarded to generals in recognition of exceptional service in wartime only. Eight Marshals had been created after the Great War. Pétain was the only one alive in 1945. An aura surrounds any French Marshal, but Pétain had become a semi-divinity due to his command of France's armies at the Battle of Verdun, February–December 1916, the longest battle of the war. Since the French Revolution, only two other Marshals had been put on trial. Marshal Ney, one of Napoleon's most famous generals, was tried under the Bourbon monarchy in December 1815, and Marshal François Bazaine, commander of the French Army during the Franco-Prussian War, was tried in 1873 for surrendering to the Germans in 1870. Ney was executed; Bazaine sentenced to life imprisonment. Bazaine is forgotten today, but in 1945 comparisons between him and Pétain were frequently made. On the first page of his war memoirs General de Gaulle recalled his mother's shock at seeing her parents, in tears, as they cried out: 'Bazaine has capitulated'.[14]

Bazaine was accused of only a single act of military dereliction, surrender to the enemy. Pétain was being tried for his role as Head of State during the four most controversial years in French history. To express the immensity of what was at stake, his trial was often compared to that of Louis XVI or Charles I of England – even that of Joan of Arc. The trial of Pétain was in some sense putting France on trial: few people had not at some moment believed in him. He may have been a sacrificial victim in the national catharsis of the Liberation, but complicity in the actions of his regime was widely shared.

The trial also promised to be an opportunity for self-education. In June 1940, when France's armies were collapsing, millions of French men and women were on the roads with their families fleeing the advancing Germans. They knew nothing of the behind-the-scenes political machinations leading to that fateful radio speech when Pétain announced that his government was seeking an armistice. Once the new regime took power in Vichy, it offered its own partisan version of events, setting up a High Court at the town of Riom, near Vichy, to try the politicians it blamed for having dragged France into war and causing her defeat. One of Pétain's most famous slogans had been: 'I hate the lies that have done you so much harm.' Meanwhile in London, French broadcasters on the BBC coined the jingle *Radio Paris ment, Radio Paris est allemand* ('Radio Paris lies, Radio Paris is German').

So who was telling the truth? Who was lying? For four years the French had survived on vague rumours and desperate hopes. They had constructed their own version of events by sifting through the distortions and half-truths of Vichy propaganda, the news they heard on the BBC, the broadcasts of de Gaulle, the resistance tracts they stumbled upon. Now, for the first time, they had an opportunity to hear these painful and confusing events being presented, debated and explained.

PÉTAIN'S CRIME

This book does not seek to 're-open' the trial or to argue that Pétain was treated too harshly or not harshly enough. That has been done several times over the years, mostly by nostalgic Pétainists trying to rehabilitate Vichy.[15] These are now a diminishing band and if the trial were re-opened today, it would not be by defenders seeking to rehabilitate their hero but by those eager to convict him for Vichy's role in the deportation of 75,000 Jews. In the courtroom in 1945 that terrible event attracted less attention than a telegram that Pétain might or might not have sent to Hitler on 25 August 1942, after a failed Anglo-American landing in Dieppe. This is not only because the persecution of the Jews was a less central issue then, but also because of the way in which the case against Pétain had been framed. He was tried for treason, which is described in the French Penal Code as '*intelligence* [collusion] with the enemy'. Today he would be tried for 'crimes against humanity', a category of crime that was developed at Nuremberg just after Pétain's trial had finished. It is also true that we know much more about Vichy's role in the deportation of the Jews than the court in 1945. But there was also much else the court did not know it knew: the judge who took over the High Court after Pétain's trial even wrote a book (in English, *The Real Trial of Marshal Pétain*), because he was shocked how much of the evidence collected for the trial had not been exploited.[16]

Revisiting Pétain's trial is not the same as re-opening it. It offers a fascinating opportunity to watch the French debating their history. Through the arguments in the courtroom we can explore choices that were made and paths that were taken; but also paths that were not taken and choices that were rejected. We can hear the historical actors of both sides explaining their decisions, see how Vichy's defenders justified their actions, and understand what the regime's accusers considered to be its main crimes.

The shorthand term 'Vichy' encompasses a dense period of four years during which events moved disconcertingly fast. After the armistice on 22 June, France's parliament was convened hastily at Vichy on 10 July to grant Pétain full powers to draft a new constitution. The very next day he issued a series of 'Constitutional Acts' which effectively made him a dictator and put parliament into abeyance. The Republic was not formally abolished, but Pétain was now described as 'Head of State' – leaving it ambiguous what kind of state he headed.

Using these new powers, Pétain's government proceeded to implement what it described as a 'National Revolution', issuing a string of new ordinances, which included measures of persecution against Jews. It also set up a special court at Riom near Vichy to try those it blamed for the defeat. The real head of the government in this period was the former prime minister, Pierre Laval, who was officially anointed as Pétain's successor in one of the Constitutional Acts. This monarchical touch made Laval Pétain's dauphin. But on 13 December 1940 Laval was summarily sacked by Pétain for reasons that remain obscure. The presumption that Laval was sacked because Pétain disapproved of 'collaboration' with Germany is weakened by the fact that his successor, Admiral Darlan, pushed that policy even further, offering Germany the use of French air bases in Syria in May 1941.

Although Darlan could hardly be accused of being a lukewarm collaborator, the Germans never forgave Pétain for sacking Laval. In April 1942 they forced Pétain to recall him. Laval was now Vichy's uncontested strongman until the end, but his freedom of manoeuvre in relation to Germany was shrinking. In his first period in power, Laval had envisaged collaboration as a way of preparing the ground for a general settlement with a victorious Germany. When he was recalled, it was more a matter of interminable wrangling with the Germans, whose demands became ever more insatiable as the war turned against them. They demanded that French workers be recruited for their war factories, that Jews be rounded up for deportation, and that the Vichy government step up its repression of the Resistance.

Laval's ability to manoeuvre was fatally weakened in November 1942 when American forces landed in French North Africa. Almost immediately the Germans retaliated by occupying the whole of France. The armistice had originally allowed Vichy a large Unoccupied Zone and left her in control of her North African colonies. Now, at a stroke, Vichy France had lost those two important assets. This was a major turning point for the regime. Pétain might have taken the opportunity to resign or join the Allies in North Africa. He opted instead to remain in place, linking his fate irrevocably to the Vichy regime until its demise in August 1944.

Negotiating its way through the thickets of this complicated history, the trial had to answer many questions. Was the armistice itself treason? Was there a realistic alternative? Was the vote granting powers to Pétain in 1940 legal? Had he abused the powers he had been granted? Could collaboration be defended? Had Pétain supported it? Why did Pétain hang on to power even after November 1942? What were the respective responsibilities of Pétain and Laval in this tragic history?

Beyond debating these specific issues, the trial confronted broader moral and philosophical questions. Where did patriotic duty lie after the defeat? Does a legal government necessarily have legitimacy? Are there times when conscience overrides the duty to obey laws? Are there times when the immediate well-being of the people of a nation can conflict with that nation's higher interests?

The answers to these questions were not self-evident. We can see this by considering the contrasting views of three contemporary observers who opposed Vichy. The first was General de Gaulle himself. Writing ten years after the event, de Gaulle did not disguise his displeasure at the conduct of the trial:

For me, the supreme fault of Pétain and his government was to have concluded . . . the so-called 'armistice'. Certainly, on the date when it was signed, the battle in mainland France was undeniably lost. Ending the fighting . . . in order to put an end to the rout, would have been a totally justified local military decision . . . Then the government would have gone to Algiers taking with it the treasure of French sovereignty, which for fourteen centuries had never been handed over, continuing the struggle to the end. But to have taken out of the war our untouched Empire, our intact fleet, our colonial troops . . . to have reneged on our alliances, and above all to have submitted the State to the discretion of the Reich – that is what should have been condemned . . .

The handing over to Hitler of French political prisoners, of Jews, of foreigners that had taken refuge with us . . . all these stemmed ineluctably from the poisoned well [i.e. the armistice] . . . So I was annoyed to see the High Court, the politicians, the newspapers, refrain from stigmatizing 'the armistice' and, instead, concentrating on facts accessory to it.[17]

Raymond Aron, who would become one of France's most celebrated intellectuals after the war, left for London in 1940. As editor of the journal *France Libre*, a publication unremitting in its attacks on the Vichy regime, Aron wrote excoriating attacks on collaboration. He could not be accused of any kind of sympathy for Pétain. But when he published his articles in book form two months before the Pétain trial, he attached a note nuancing his original judgements. The problem when judging Vichy, he suggested, was 'that the consequences of the acts had almost nothing in common with the intentions of the actors'. He went on:

It is not impossible that the armistice and Vichy, for two and half years, attenuated the rigours of the occupation. In interposing the French administrative apparatus between the Gestapo and the French population, the policy . . . procured for the 40 million French who found themselves hostages, multiple although mediocre advantages that are as difficult to quantify as to deny . . . Recognized by Russia until the spring of 1941, and by the United States until the Liberation of North Africa [in November 1942], the government of Vichy could be seen in the eyes of the mass of civil servants, and above all army officers, as a legitimate government. Once an armistice had been signed, France and France's allies had a significant interest in saving the French fleet and Empire.[18]

For Aron, the point after which Pétain could no longer be defended was November 1942 when Vichy lost North Africa and the Germans occupied the whole of France.[19]

Simone Weil, another brilliant intellectual who went into exile, took a still different line. In November 1942, from New York, she wrote to a friend denying rumours that, as a former pacifist, she had any sympathy for the armistice:

> In June 1940 I ardently desired the defence of Paris . . . It was with con-sternation . . . that I heard the news of the armistice, and I immediately decided to get to England . . . Until then, I participated in the distribu-tion of clandestine literature . . . What has given rise to these rumours [of being indulgent towards Pétain] is that I do not like people who are living perfectly comfortably here treating as cowards and traitors those in France who are struggling as best they can in a terrible situation . . . The armistice was a collective cowardice, a collective treason; the entire nation shares some responsibility . . . At the time, from what I wit-nessed, the entire nation welcomed the armistice with a sense of relief; and that resulted in an indivisible national responsibility. Moreover, I think that Pétain has done more or less everything that his physical and mental state allowed to limit the damage. One should not use the word 'traitor' except for those people whom one is certain desired the victory of Germany.[20]

Weil was a figure of exceptional moral rigour. This letter was a re-action to the 'resisters of Fifth Avenue', those self-righteous exiles who, from the safe distance of a Manhattan cocktail party or a com-fortable New York hotel, denounced as traitors those who had remained in France. Arriving in England to join the Gaullists, she died in 1943 as a result of health complications caused by the near-starvation diet she had adopted to share the sufferings of the French. Subsequent events might have led her to revise her judgements, at least on Pétain – but probably not her view that the armistice was a collective fault. This opinion was shared by the philosopher Jean Wahl, the recipient of her letter. Wahl had escaped from the Drancy internment camp outside Paris, and managed to reach New York, where he became a prominent figure in the intellectual community of exiles. Although he was opposed to Vichy – a regime which had imprisoned him – he too refused to see Pétain as a traitor and even believed that the armistice could be justified.[21]

De Gaulle, Aron and Weil all opposed Vichy – but each took a different view of Pétain's crime. For de Gaulle, the crime was the armistice and nothing but the armistice; for Aron the armistice was defensible and Pétain's crime came two years later, when he remained in France even after the Germans had flouted the armistice by occupying the entire country; Weil condemned the armistice as an act of collective cowardice which could not be blamed on Pétain alone.

The events that took place in the stiflingly hot courtroom over three weeks in the summer of 1945 did not settle the matter. As the American historian of Vichy Robert Paxton wrote in the 1980s, 'The controversy over whether Pétain had been a traitor or a canny realist after the French defeat of June 1940 remains the bitterest French family quarrel since the Dreyfus affair.'[22] Pétain's main defence lawyer, Jacques Isorni, devoted much of his life to arguing that the sentence should be revised and that, instead of mouldering in a grave on the island where he had been imprisoned, Pétain's body should be transported to the Ossuary of Douaumont, near Verdun, to lie alongside the soldiers he had commanded in the Great War. Pétain remained a potent symbol for the extreme right in France, and his name even came up in the French presidential campaign of 2022. All this vindicated the prediction made immediately after the trial by the novelist François Mauriac (1885–1970), a left-wing Catholic who had opposed Vichy: 'For everyone, whatever happens, for his admirers, for his adversaries, Pétain will remain a tragic figure, caught between treason and sacrifice . . . A trial like this one is never over and will never end.'[23]

PART ONE

Before the Trial

I

The Last Days of Vichy

In July 1940 a politician remarked, half-seriously, that Pétain had more power than any other leader since Louis XIV. This was a remarkable outcome for a man who, twenty-five years earlier, had been an obscure colonel heading for retirement. Up to that moment, the army had been the main horizon of his existence, as both a career and a substitute family.

Born in 1856 to a modest peasant family near Calais, Philippe Pétain had lost his mother to childbirth when he was only eighteen months old. After his father's rapid remarriage he and his siblings were farmed out to relatives. He always mourned the mother he had never known: 'My stepmother was a shrew; my father's house was largely closed to me,' he remarked in a rare reminiscence. He explained his notoriously reserved and secretive personality by the absence of family affection, and by his need from an early age to fend for himself. Certainly, the man who later celebrated the virtues of family had no positive memories of his own and retained little contact with his siblings. Though he would later extol the peasant values of rootedness in the soil, he showed no nostalgia for his own roots: the country residence he acquired later in life was on the fashionable Côte d'Azur.

His education was taken in hand by a maternal uncle, a priest who spotted the boy's intelligence. For a young man of his humble background, the army was a classic route to advancement. In the wake of France's defeat by Germany in 1871, the desire for revenge was shared by many boys of his age. Before 1914, his military career was respectable but unremarkable. Promotion was hampered by his scepticism about the prevailing doctrine of the French high command, which advocated an offensive strategy at almost any cost. In lectures at

France's military staff college, the École de Guerre, Pétain had argued that advances in military technology had shifted the advantage to the defence, emphasizing the importance of meticulous tactical preparation before embarking on any offensive. His adage was: '*Le feu tue*' (Firepower kills).

These insights were vindicated when war broke out in 1914. Pétain proved himself an unflappable commander with exceptional organizational skills, leading him, in February 1916, to be given command of the defence of Verdun in north-eastern France. For ten months the French fought off a sustained German assault on the city and its surrounding fortresses. Pétain rotated his forces so that no soldier spent too long in the inferno of the battle. As a result, most French soldiers served at some point at Verdun, making it a battle of the entire French nation. Despite the huge number of casualties, Verdun was not seen by the French as a symbol of futile waste, as the Somme was by the British, but of heroic patriotism.

Pétain was only in direct command at Verdun for the first two months, after which another general, Robert Nivelle, replaced him. This reflected a concern among the high command that he was too reluctant to seize the advantage with a counter-offensive. Pétain's detractors often commented that his prudence tended towards pessimism, even at times defeatism. Yet even doubters were impressed by his handling of a wave of army mutinies that broke out after a suicidal offensive, planned by Nivelle, in the spring of 1917. Now commander of the French armies, he ended the mutinies not only by reimposing discipline through a few exemplary executions but also by improving the conditions for the soldiers. All this won him a reputation as a general who genuinely cared about the welfare of ordinary soldiers. By the end of the war, Pétain combined in his person the aura of all the military heroes of the Great War – Haig in Britain, Hindenburg in Germany, Foch in France.[1] Until his retirement in 1931, he played a leading role in French military planning. His mythic stature was also sustained by his appearance: piercing blue eyes, snow-white hair, and his famous 'marble countenance' (*visage marmoréen*). Pétain cultivated this image. On his appointment to Verdun, journalists had scrambled to procure photographs of him, but soon his portrait was plastered over newspapers throughout the world.

Showered with honours, he was regularly invited to preside over ceremonies, inaugurate monuments and speak at banquets. Elected to the Académie Française in 1929, he was often asked to represent France abroad at funerals and anniversaries. He had acquired the aura of royalty. Even someone impervious to flattery – which Pétain was not – would have been affected by such adulation. Pétain started to conceive of himself as a political sage with views about the world going beyond the military. He was no ideologue (nor was he, for that matter, a great reader) and he never espoused the ultra-reactionary opinions flaunted by other Marshals of the Great War such as Foch. But he developed simple homespun ideas about politics – especially the importance of the family and the need to instil schoolteachers with patriotic and moral values.

Pétain's experience at Verdun had made him suspicious of interfering politicians who visited his headquarters for photo opportunities – though he liked photo opportunities when he was the subject of them – and the mutinies had made him paranoid about threats to social order. The spread of Communism in the interwar years only heightened these fears. When, in 1925, Pétain was sent to command French forces in Morocco and suppress a tribal uprising in concert with the Spanish, he came to admire the Spanish military dictator Primo de Rivera, who embodied his ideal of firm leadership.

In 1934, Pétain became War Minister in a conservative national unity government under Gaston Doumergue. It was a sign of Pétain's growing ambitions that the portfolio he had really coveted was Education. That government lasted only nine months, but it gave him new political contacts and further whetted his ambitions. Conservatives who were turning against the Republic came to see him as a providential figure. All this made it entirely natural that after France's humiliating defeat by Germany in June 1940 Pétain was unanimously viewed as a saviour when he took over as head of the so-called Vichy regime.

FALLEN HERO

Over the next four years, Pétain's power was progressively whittled away by the demands of the German occupiers and the ambitions of

Pierre Laval, prime minister from April 1942 to August 1944. The last act in the drama of Pétain's political emasculation occurred at the end of 1943 when a plot hatched by his closest advisers to reassert his authority ended instead in his complete humiliation. After this Pétain commented ruefully that, far from being Louis XIV, he was more like 'the little king of Bourges' – a reference to Charles VII who, ascending the throne during the Hundred Years War, had controlled only a sliver of French territory until the victories of Joan of Arc.

The abortive plot to save Pétain had been inspired by recent events in Italy. In July 1943 a cabal around King Victor Emmanuel had ousted the fascist dictator Mussolini and replaced him with the less tainted Marshal Pietro Badoglio. The purpose of the Badoglio operation had been to rescue something from the wreckage of Mussolini's regime, sideline the radical forces of the Italian resistance, and do a deal with the Allies. The plan bore fruit. Badoglio signed an armistice with the Allies, taking Italy out of the war. In return the Allies seemed ready, for the moment at least, to leave him and the king in power. Might such a scheme work in France?

In the French version of this scenario, Pétain's advisers schemed to oust his pro-German prime minister, Pierre Laval, and revive the promise Pétain had made in 1940 to draft a new constitution. The plan was for Pétain to make a radio broadcast reminding the French people that 'I incarnate French legitimacy' and informing them that if he were to die before the constitution was ready, power would revert to the parliament he had ignored for four years. Pétain was being billed to play the role of Badoglio or Victor Emmanuel to Laval's Mussolini. This last-ditch attempt to give Vichy a political makeover was about saving the skins – literally – of those who had served it, and of Pétain himself. If this plan had any remote chance of success, it was because President Roosevelt was known to distrust de Gaulle. Might Roosevelt jump at this opportunity to sideline him?

We will never know because the Germans got wind of the plot. When listeners tuned in to hear Pétain's radio speech on 12 November 1943, they were treated instead to the light operetta *Dédé*. Two weeks later, Pétain received a threatening letter from the German Foreign Minister, Joachim von Ribbentrop, insisting that Laval remain in the government and that it be reshuffled to bring in ultra-collaborationist politicians unreservedly committed to Germany. Pétain could now have resigned on the grounds that he had lost any semblance of power, and that his presence only served to disguise ever more repressive German policies. But whether nursing a fantasy that he still had a role to play, or believing he had already burnt his bridges, he chose to remain in his post. It was a fateful decision. The last months of the Vichy regime – between January and August 1944 – witnessed the worst atrocities of the Occupation. Pétain had missed his chance to dissociate himself from them.

To ensure that he did not stray again, the Germans placed Pétain under the strict surveillance of Cecil von Renthe-Fink, a diplomat whom he sarcastically referred to as his 'jailor'. To all intents and purposes, he was now a prisoner – an extraordinary contrast with his position four years earlier.

In these last months of the Vichy regime, under the vigilant scrutiny of Renthe-Fink, Pétain was lonely and isolated. He had lost almost all the advisers who surrounded him in 1940. Some had been removed because the Germans mistrusted them; others had abandoned Vichy's sinking ship. The sole survivor of his first days at Vichy was his doctor and confidant Bernard Ménétrel. Since Pétain was in remarkably good physical shape, looking after his health was not a time-consuming activity. So Ménétrel also acted as political adviser and became the gatekeeper to anyone wanting access to Pétain. Laval once commented: 'I had predicted everything except that France would be governed by a doctor.'[2]

Two other members of Pétain's inner circle in 1944 had not previously played a central role: the one-armed General Victor Debeney, head of Pétain's General Secretariat, and Admiral Henri Bléhaut, appointed Under Secretary of State for the Navy and the Colonies in March 1943 – at a time when Vichy had lost both its navy and its colonies. These two men assumed importance in large measure because almost no one else was left.

The other survivor from the early days at Vichy, along with Ménétrel, was Pétain's wife. Pétain had been a dedicated womaniser for many years, often maintaining several mistresses at the same time. When the war made him a celebrity, he won ever more female admirers. Then, suddenly, in September 1920, having long resisted the ties of marriage, he married his long-term mistress Eugénie-Anne Hardon (usually known as Annie).[3] No one knew for sure when their relationship started. Her romantic version was that they had first met when she was twenty-four but that her family had been shocked by the twenty-year age gap between them. Instead, she married the artist François Dehérain. After her divorce in 1914, she resumed – if it had ever ceased – the relationship with Pétain. He was spending the night with her in a hotel near the Gare du Nord in Paris in February 1916 when he was tracked down to be informed about his appointment to Verdun.

After a life of bachelorhood, Pétain appears to have concluded that his station in life now required him to marry. In the weeks before he proposed to Annie, he made the same offer to at least two other old flames. One turned him down because she was a widow with young children. Another, the Wagnerian soprano Germaine Lubin, refused because she was married and did want to go through a divorce. So on 14 September 1920, Pétain married Annie Hardon in a civil ceremony. The marriage was a discreet affair, as his conservative friends and admirers were shocked that he was marrying a divorcee. Perhaps Pétain resigned himself to Annie because he knew that she would have no illusions about his fidelity.[4] The couple lived in adjoining apartments in Paris and, during the Occupation, in adjoining hotels in Vichy.

In March 1941 their marriage was solemnized in a religious ceremony – her first marriage had been annulled in 1929 – to the relief of the Catholic Church, which was a staunch supporter of the Vichy regime. Having spent half a lifetime trying to pin him down, Annie demanded the respect that went with her new title of *La Maréchale*. Her imperious personality was sharpened by the knowledge that so many people had disapproved of her. She would remain at Pétain's side to the end.

KIDNAPPED

The Vichy regime entered its final death agony after the D-Day landings in Normandy on 6 June 1944. The Allies did not achieve all their initial objectives but within a week they had established a small beachhead on French soil. On 14 June General de Gaulle was permitted by the British to pay a short visit from London to Bayeux, the largest town so far liberated. These were de Gaulle's first steps on metropolitan French soil since his departure almost exactly four years earlier. For de Gaulle, who had so far been only a voice on the radio for most French people, the purpose of the visit was to show himself in person and prove to himself and the Allies that he enjoyed genuine popular support. Having shaken the hand of the local *préfet,* who had hastily removed Pétain's portrait from the wall, de Gaulle made a speech in the main square that was cheered by the population. His mission triumphantly accomplished, de Gaulle returned to Algiers.

On 31 July the American troops finally broke through the German lines at Avranches, in the south of the Cotentin Peninsula in Normandy; two weeks later they had advanced halfway to Paris. On 20 August, De Gaulle was back in Normandy preparing to accompany the Allied armies into Paris. As for the town of Vichy itself, it was only a matter of days before it too was within reach of the Allies after a second Allied landing, on 15 August, on France's Mediterranean coast. The success of this operation exceeded expectations, and Allied troops were soon advancing up the Rhône valley.

On 17 August 1944, Renthe-Fink informed Pétain that, ostensibly for his own protection, he would have to leave Vichy. As long as the Germans held some French territory, Pétain remained useful to them. But he refused to budge. For the next two days Renthe-Fink put increasing pressure on Pétain's advisers, who knew they would be powerless if the Germans insisted on moving him. All that they could hope to do was to establish for posterity that Pétain had been forced to leave against his will. To demonstrate this, he wrote a letter of protest to Hitler:

> In concluding the armistice of 1940 with Germany, I showed my irrevocable decision to link my fate to that of my country and never to leave French territory . . . Today your representatives force me by violence, and despite all the promises I have made, to leave for an unknown destination. I submit a solemn protest against this act of force which prevents me from carrying out my prerogatives as head of the French State.[5]

When, on 19 August, Renthe-Fink returned to the Hotel du Parc with a final ultimatum, Pétain received him frostily with General Debeney and Admiral Bléhaut at his side. An orderly announced that diplomatic representatives of two neutral countries – the Papal Nuncio and the Swiss consul, Walter Stucki – were waiting in the next room. Renthe-Fink shouted that they could not be admitted. Bléhaut shouted back, '*Vous nous emmerdez*' ('You are pissing us off'). Then Ménétrel burst into the room accompanied by the two diplomats so that they could witness the fact that Pétain was acting under duress. The Germans left the hotel but announced that they would return tomorrow to take Pétain away.

At 6 a.m. the next day German tanks arrived outside the hotel. Pétain, having briefly roused himself to look out of the window, returned to bed. An hour later German soldiers broke down the doors of the hotel. The German officer in charge of the operation reported:

> When I arrived in the hotel lobby, Lieutenant Petit of the Marshal's guard stopped me and said that I was in the house of Marshal Pétain . . . and that he forbad me to go any further. I replied that I knew this but I had received an order that I would carry out at any cost. After an exchange of military salutes, Lieutenant Petit let me pass.[6]

When the Germans smashed the glass panels of the door to Pétain's bedroom, they found him dressing. Ménétrel was on hand with a tape recorder and camera to record the kidnapping.[7] He insisted that the Marshal be allowed to eat breakfast before leaving. Pétain descended the staircase, raised his hat to onlookers, and then set off with his advisers in a convoy of six cars.

Progress was painfully slow on roads choked with retreating German military vehicles. Stopping for lunch at the Prefecture of Moulins about 60 kilometres from Vichy, Pétain's advisers made copies of his letter to Hitler, and also of a speech which had been crafted over the last few days. This was Pétain's last message to the French people before the opening declaration at his trial almost a year later:

> When this message reaches you, I will no longer be free . . . For more than four years, having decided to remain among you, every day I have tried to do what best served the permanent interests of France. Loyally,

but without compromises, I have had only one aim: to protect you from the worst. Everything that I have accepted, that I have consented to, that I have been subjected to, whether of my own accord or because I was forced, has been to protect you. For if I could no longer be your sword, I have wanted to be your shield.[8]

This idea of Pétain as a 'shield' was to become a key element in his future defence.

Since he no longer had access to the airwaves, copies of the message were thrown from the car windows. Most of these were dispersed by the wind. Some were picked up by passers-by and a bunch were left at the hotel in Saulieu, where Pétain spent the night.[9] Erratically typed on flimsy paper, this document was intended as evidence if Pétain was ever summoned to account to the French for his actions.

On the evening of 21 August, Pétain's party reached the Prefecture of Belfort where they were amazed to find Pierre Laval, still nominally his prime minister. Two weeks earlier, Laval in Paris had made his own last-ditch attempt to save his skin. Knowing that the Allies' arrival was imminent, he had conceived the idea of reconvening the parliament of the Third Republic. Parliament would provide a source of legitimate French authority which the liberating Americans might be prepared to recognize. Like Pétain's advisers in the previous year, he was gambling on the fact that the Americans were known to distrust de Gaulle: his scheme offered them another way of sidelining him.

The German ambassador, Otto Abetz, gave his benediction and on 12 August Laval drove from Paris to Nancy, where the president of the lower house of parliament, Édouard Herriot, was living under house arrest. The plan had no chance of working without his co-operation. Only three days were enough to establish, with or without Herriot, that the plan was doomed. The Germans turned against it and forcibly removed Laval from Paris on 17 August, as they began to evacuate the city.

Relations between Pétain and Laval had always been execrable, but in Belfort they were for once of the same mind: since both were prisoners, neither would agree to exercise any further governmental responsibility. They would go on 'strike'. After a brief encounter they no longer had to endure each other's physical presence. Pétain took up residence just outside Belfort in the nearby château of Morvillars; Laval remained at the prefecture. Over the next few days they communicated only by letter.

In the meantime, de Gaulle was installing his provisional government in Liberated Paris. He entered the city on 25 August and next day organized a triumphal ceremony on the Champs-Elysées. At least one million people gathered for a glimpse of the Liberator as he processed from the Arc de Triomphe. No one was thinking about Pétain at that moment, but Pétain loyalists tried one last desperate throw of the dice. On the day after his parade, de Gaulle was handed a letter that Pétain had confided to Admiral Auphan, his former Naval Minister. Auphan had been sent to Paris to contact de Gaulle and reach an agreement with him on Pétain's behalf – on condition that 'the principle of legitimacy I represent is respected'. Unsurprisingly de Gaulle, who had no intention of seeking Pétain's benediction, refused even to see Auphan. He later described this moment with priceless contempt in his *Memoirs*:

> What an outcome! What a confession! Thus, as Vichy crumbled, Philippe Pétain turned towards Charles de Gaulle ... In reading this text that was handed over to me, I felt both reinforced and overwhelmed by a terrible sadness. Monsieur le Maréchal! You who had once so honoured our armies, you who had once been my leader, what had you now come to ... Above all, the condition that Pétain put on an agreement with me was precisely the reasons why this agreement was impossible. The legitimacy that he claimed to incarnate was one that the government of the Republic denied absolutely ... The only answer I could give him was my silence.[10]

De Gaulle's predictable refusal to accept his authority from the hands of Pétain confirmed that Pétain *would* have to account to the French people for his actions since 1940 – but first it would be necessary to find him.

2

A Castle in Germany

Some 440 kilometres east of Paris, in Belfort, the Germans were still pondering what to do next with their valuable prisoner. Scattered around the area were a number of former collaborationist politicians who had fled Paris. Four of these were now invited to a meeting with Hitler at his so-called Wolf's Lair in East Prussia. Pierre Laval, who was also invited, refused to go.

The four men who accepted Hitler's invitation – Marcel Déat, Jacques Doriot, Fernand de Brinon and Joseph Darnand – were unconditionally committed to the German cause, although they had reached this radical position by different routes.[1] Déat, a star of the Socialist Party in the 1920s, had drifted to the far right in the 1930s just as Oswald Mosley had in England. In 1941, Déat set up his own French fascist party (the RNP) in occupied Paris. Its membership was too minuscule to allow him to play a significant political role, but his violent newspaper articles attacking Vichy for being too lukewarm about collaboration gave him a certain influence. Living in the pure constructions of his mind, Déat was the type of intellectual who remains shielded from reality by the logic of his arguments.

Jacques Doriot, a former Communist who had broken with the Party in the mid-1930s, was animated above all by a visceral hatred of the Soviet Union. The founder in 1936 of France's most successful fascist party, the Parti Populaire Français (PPF), he was a compelling orator. When, after Germany's attack on the Soviet Union in June 1941, some French ultra-collaborators set up a 'Legion of French Volunteers' (LVF) to fight Bolshevism, Doriot didn't just support the initiative; he actually joined up.

Unlike Déat and Doriot, Joseph Darnand had never been on the left. A brave soldier in the Great War, he had been devoted to the person of Pétain ever since. Active in extreme right-wing circles in the interwar years, believing in order and despising democracy, it was only natural that he should rally to Vichy. In January 1943 he founded Vichy's notorious *Milice*, a paramilitary organization that would use any means necessary, however brutal, to crush the Resistance. A few months later Darnand became an officer in the SS. That such an ardent French nationalist should end his career in German uniform was as strange as Doriot, a rising star of French Communism, ending his career as a fighter against the Soviet Union on the Eastern Front.

The fourth member of this group, Fernand de Brinon, was a journalist long committed to Franco-German reconciliation. Unlike the others, he had no political base, no followers, no charisma. His trump card was that, owing to his extensive German contacts, he had been named Vichy's 'Delegate' to the Occupied Zone in 1940, assuming the strange role of the French government's ambassador to France.

These four men were rivals and enemies. Whether out of ideological conviction, a delusional belief that the Germans had not lost the war, or a recognition that having burnt their bridges they had nothing left to lose, all were ready to pursue the collaborationist adventure to the end. Each hoped their moment had arrived: if there was to be a Nazi *Götterdämmerung*, they were ready to perish in the conflagration. The purpose of their long journey across Germany was to learn Hitler's intentions for France.

In the last week of August, at the castle of Steinhort in East Prussia, Joachim von Ribbentrop had eight meetings with this fractious group. His plan was for a rump French government presided over by Pétain but run by Doriot, who had some political clout thanks to his party, the PPF. The problem was that the three others also wanted to run the government, and that Doriot was hated by Pétain. Brinon probably had the strongest card to play since his role as Vichy's delegate to the Occupied Zone gave him a certain legitimacy. These surreal negotiations finally resulted in an agreement that Brinon would form a government with Pétain's approval. This was intended to be a provisional arrangement, paving the way for a future Doriot government. Brinon had no choice but to accept, hoping later to wriggle out of the commitment to make way for Doriot. The other two, Déat and Darnand, also harboured their own ambitions.

Once this agreement had been reached, the four men were ushered into the presence of the Führer himself, in the very room where he had survived an assassination attempt a month earlier. A trembling wreck, stuffed with drugs, and still visibly suffering the consequences of the attack, Hitler launched into a long monologue which mesmerized his visitors. He even had a kind word for Déat, who had himself survived an assassination attempt in 1941.

One might wonder why Hitler should have cared about these legal niceties, which had taken a week to negotiate. In the immediate future, having a 'French' administration in place might facilitate the German retreat. And in the case of an eventual reconquest of French territory – a fantasy still considered possible – a 'legitimate' French government, however fictitious, would be useful. As Hitler told his four French interlocutors, referring to his own appointment as German Chancellor in 1933 by the respected President von Hindenburg, 'a government always derives some force by being covered by legality'.[2] Or, as Brinon put it more irreverently, Pétain would be the 'cover girl' for a German-controlled ultra-collaborationist operation.[3]

Now it was necessary to secure the cover girl's agreement. But when Brinon returned to France on 5 September, Pétain refused even to receive him. Negotiations were conducted through letters conveyed by General Debeney, who scurried between Brinon in Belfort and Pétain at the château of Morvillars a few kilometres away. Ménétrel urged Pétain to refuse any association with the plot hatched in the Wolf's Lair. But after a few days a compromise was reached. Having reaffirmed in yet another letter that, being on strike, he could not delegate his authority to anyone, Pétain agreed not to 'make objections' to Brinon 'continuing to occupy himself' with issues related to his post as his 'delegate' to the Occupied Zone. It is not clear why Pétain made this concession. Perhaps, obsessed as he was with the fate of the French prisoners of war in Germany, he wanted some French authority to look after their interests. It also seems that, following his seizure by the Germans a few days earlier, Pétain was in a muddled state of mind.[4] Whatever the reason for the concession, it allowed Brinon a foot in the door.

On 6 September 1944, just as this agreement was concluded, the gunfire of advancing Allied armies could be heard in Belfort. Their arrival now imminent, Pétain had to be moved further east. That morning the Germans came to take him away. Some in Pétain's entourage thought their destination might be Baden-Baden, where many French collaborators were hiding out. To move the French government from the spå town of Vichy to the spa town of Baden-Baden offered a certain poetic symmetry. In fact, Pétain's final destination was the castle of the princes of Hohenzollern-Sigmaringen, in southern Germany. The prince had recently been arrested and his family turfed out of the castle. As a cousin of King Carol of Romania, he was suspected of having encouraged Romania's decision to rally to the Allies in August 1944. This was Hitler's revenge.[5]

SIGMARINGEN

Although it was not a spa town, Sigmaringen offered an appropriately Ruritanian setting for the final act of the Vichy drama. Situated in

2. Vichy in exile: the Castle of Sigmaringen.

Baden-Württemberg, on the river Danube, it was less a town over-looked by a castle than a castle with a town attached. The massive structure, with 800 rooms, was big enough to accommodate the war-ring factions of French exiles who had fled the Allied advance without their ever needing to meet – or even see one another. Renovated in the nineteenth century, the castle seemed like a fantasy German palace reimagined by Viollet-le-Duc or Disney. As one of Laval's aides recalled:

> The robber barons of the Teutonic Middle Ages had built it on a rocky point in a curve of the Danube and the victorious plunderers of 1870 had restored and enlarged it. It is an enormous confusion of apart-ments, separate but linked by endless corridors. As if dreamt up by Victor Hugo, it received visitors in an atmosphere of heavy grandeur and faded ostentation, with numerous grand staircases and secret stair-ways, paintings, displays of armour and terrible weapons, statues of hunting trophies, and old furniture. The elevator was almost big enough to hold a Simca motorcar.[6]

The most famous description of Sigmaringen castle comes from the great French novelist Céline. Anti-semitic to the point of derangement, the misanthropic Céline's relations with the Germans in occupied Paris had been as good as they were ever capable of being with any-one. He had left Paris in June 1944, intending to cross through Germany and find refuge in Denmark, with two phials of cyanide in his luggage just in case. But he did not make it to Denmark on this occasion and ended up instead at Sigmaringen. The surrealistic story of this phantom government in its fantastical setting was perfectly suited to Céline's strange hallucinatory prose with its idiosyncratic punctuation (three dots being his favourite). This episode formed the subject of his first post-war novel:[7]

> Stucco, turrets, chimneys, gargoyles . . . ! Super Hollywood! . . .
>   What a picturesque spot! . . . you'd think you were at an operetta . . . a perfect setting . . . you're waiting for the sopranos, the lyric tenors . . . for echoes you've got the whole Black Forest . . . ten, twenty mountains of trees! [. . .] The most amazing is the Castle . . . stucco and papier maché . . . like a wedding cake on top of the town [. . .] the treasures,

the tapestries, the woodwork, the plate, the trophies, armours, banners . . .
every floor a museum . . . not to mention the bunkers under the Danube, the fortified tunnels . . . How many holes, hiding places, had those
princes, dukes and gangsters dug? . . . Fourteen centuries of Hohenzo-
llerns! Secretive diggers! . . . their whole history under the castle, the
doubloons. The slain, hanged, strangled and mummified rivals [. . .] All
the hiding places and labyrinths! the trick tapestries with exits through
goddesses; the apartments, boudoirs, cupboards with triple bottoms,
corkscrew stairways.

Pétain's entourage was housed in the princely apartments on the
seventh floor, accessed by the huge lift. He and his wife lodged at one
end of an immense corridor lined by statues, portraits and hunting
trophies, while Ménetrel, Bléhaut and Debeney were housed at the
other end, along with Pétain's valet and chauffeur. German guards
were never far away. Laval, his wife and entourage were on the floor
below, in the apartments where the princely family had lodged
their guests. Laval's quarters were hardly less grand than Pétain's. His
wife took exception to dining under a huge bust of Kaiser Wilhelm, muttering that if she had the strength she would have thrown
it into the Danube. Laval had been accompanied to Germany by a
number of his former ministers who refused, like him, to play any
role in the Brinon operation. They became known as the 'sleeping
ministers'.

On the first night, Renthe-Fink presented himself to the Pétains as
they were sitting down to dinner. He was told he would not be welcome and had no better luck with Laval on the floor below. Brinon's
pseudo-government was installed in a separate wing on the third
floor, in the former apartments of the prince's children. Another huge
wing was allocated to Otto Abetz, Hitler's ambassador to Paris for
much of the war. Abetz livened up the decoration of his apartments
with Fragonard paintings and Gobelins tapestries pillaged from various Paris collections; spares were loaned to Brinon.

The only countries with diplomatic representation to this parody of
a government were Japan, in the form of its playboy ambassador,
Mitani Takanobu, and the Republic of Salò, the rump fascist state set
up in northern Italy by Mussolini under German patronage after he

was ousted from power in September 1943. Mussolini, housed in a grand villa with splendid views over Lake Garda, was, like Pétain, an impotent prisoner in a gilded cage.

The spatial geography of Sigmaringen was meticulously organized by the Germans with distinctions of hierarchy minutely observed. Only Pétain was allowed to use the lift. Menus were carefully calibrated according to status. On the Pétain floor alone there were three different levels of menu, with only Pétain and his wife accorded the luxury of full-fat cheese (*fromage gras*). Laval, on the floor below, had mostly potatoes and cabbage – although they were served on silver platters.

The castle, while massive, could not house the 1,500 or so French refugees – criminals, black marketeers and ultra-collaborators with their assorted wives, mistresses and hangers-on – who had followed the 'government' of France to Germany. This hoi-polloi had to make do with the overcrowded hotels, school buildings and gymnasia scattered around the town. Céline had arrived with his wife, Lucette, his cat Bébert, and his friend the anti-semitic actor Robert Le Vigan. A trained doctor as well as novelist, Céline was disappointed not to be appointed as doctor in the castle but often visited to treat Laval's ulcer. He was also kept busy in the town, treating the many diseases which spread among the French crowded into insalubrious lodgings.

ÉMIGRÉ POLITICS

Soon after his arrival, Brinon wrote a grovelling letter to thank Hitler for having confidence in him. His hope of establishing the credibility of his 'government' – or *Délégation* as it was initially called – was undermined by Pétain's refusal ever to see him in person. Renthe-Fink advised him to break down the door of the Marshal's apartments if necessary, but Brinon demurred and the two men communicated entirely by letter.[8] On 30 September, Brinon invited Pétain to a ceremony where the French flag was to be raised over the castle and the German guard replaced by a French one. Sigmaringen, granted extraterritorial status, was now a fragment of France on German soil. Pétain did not acknowledge the invitation but the ceremony went

ahead anyway in the presence of Brinon, his team and a few onlookers. Neither Laval nor Pétain were present. This did not stop Brinon
from invoking Pétain's name in his speech:

> We are here today, at the side of the Marshal, the sole legitimate leader
> of the French State ... Our only objective is to continue to serve the
> policy the Marshal has incarnated for all those who have served him
> since the collapse of the warmongering democracy.

He ended with 'Vive la France! Vive le Maréchal!' Although Pétain
responded with a curt note protesting the use of his name, Brinon's
speech was enough to give the Germans the fig leaf of an excuse to
issue a communiqué announcing that Pétain was still head of the government.[9] At the end of October, the first issue of the official newspaper
of the Delegation (now renamed the 'Governmental Commission for
the defence of French interests') carried a huge reproduction of a
photograph of Pétain inscribed with a dedication to his 'faithful
Brinon'. The photo dated back to November 1941, and Pétain sent
another letter of protest, refusing to be Brinon's 'cover-girl'.

Only once did his guard slip. On 29 September, Pétain received
Gabriel Bruneton, the official in charge of looking after the welfare of
French workers in German factories. Bruneton, who harboured a religious devotion to the Marshal, wanted to be sure that he still had
Pétain's backing. Pétain reassured him: 'You are my representative
and the depositary of my thinking.' It is unclear why Pétain breached
his principle of silence. Perhaps it was a residue of his idea that he was
the Father-Protector of the French people. Perhaps his vanity was
pricked by evidence that he could still inspire such devotion. Whatever the motive, the gesture backfired. At the raising of the colours
ceremony, Brinon quoted Pétain's words to Bruneton: 'I remain incontestably and legally the Chef des Français.'

This alarmed the eagle-eyed Ménétrel, who wrote after meeting
with Bruneton:

> We need the courage to tell the Marshal, one last time, what he risks if
> he does not make the situation absolutely clear ... He no longer has the
> possibility to do any more for France ... but he has an absolute duty to
> do nothing that might stain his memory ... Any positive manifestation

by the Marshal will seem like pro-German activity and will destroy the effect produced by the announcement of his captivity . . . The policy of the Marshal is already difficult to defend. His best excuse, over four years, is German pressure and his desire to avoid the worst.[10]

Pétain never again repeated this *faux pas*. He attended Mass at the castle every Sunday, hidden from view in the secret loggia that led to the princely apartments by a special walkway. In good weather, he was allowed to leave the castle in a car and take a walk in the countryside – with Gestapo officers at a discreet distance. Members of the French community sometimes gathered to watch him on these constitutionals. This produced a characteristic rant from Céline:

> You might have expected . . . not at all . . . that they'd chew him out something terrible . . . that it was a shame! A disgrace! Him and his sixteen food cards . . . not at all! . . . everybody knew! . . . and knew he ate them all up! That he didn't leave a crumb for anybody! That his appetite was remarkable . . . not to mention the total comfort . . . housed like a king . . . him who was responsible for everything . . . a whole floor to himself! . . . heated!
>
> You'd have expected that crowd of roughnecks to do something . . . to jump him . . . to disembowel him . . . not at all . . . just a few sighs . . . they step aside . . . they watch him start on his outing . . . he carried his cane . . . and off we go . . . and dignified . . . he answers their greetings . . . men and women . . . little girls' curtseys.[11]

Ménétrel spent his time huddled with Pétain in his quarters, working on his future defence. Since Debeney and Bléhaut were new to the inner circle, they had little light to throw on the early days of the regime. Ménétrel drafted a memorandum on Pétain's activities. The document was divided into two sections: 'Conditions in which the demand for an armistice emerged in June 1940' and 'Events of November 1942'. He was right to think that these two moments would be much discussed at the trial. Since he was working without archives, details were left to be filled in later. When Pétain returned to France, the seventeen typed pages of this document were found in his luggage, with a few marginal corrections (of only stylistic significance) in his own hand.[12]

Ménétrel knew that the Germans were aware of his efforts to thwart them. He also knew that the last thing they wanted was for Pétain to die. As Renthe-Fink wrote to Abetz: 'If we want to continue using the Marshal for our policy we need to be concerned about his health.'[13] So Ménétrel tried to make himself indispensable by writing frequently to Abetz, warning him that conditions in the castle threatened Pétain's (very robust) health. He wrote to the Swiss minister in Berlin asking for warm clothes, since they had left Belfort in such a hurry. His patient was also said to need pipes, a lighter, soap, toothpaste, shaving cream.[14]

This did not stop Brinon from striking against Ménétrel. Returning from an outing with Pétain on 22 November, Ménétrel was seized and put under house arrest. He was detained at a locality only a few kilometres away so that Pétain would feel his absence more acutely. It was hoped that his nerve might crack and that he might cooperate in the hope of being reunited with his doctor and confidant. This tactic failed. Pétain's pleas to have his doctor brought back went unacknowledged, but Ménétrel's removal did not break his resistance to Brinon's attempts to secure his cooperation. Pétain would never see Ménétrel again.

When Céline's name was proposed as a possible replacement as his physician, Pétain allegedly remarked: 'I would prefer to die at once.' Brinon's candidate was Dr Schillemans, a young army doctor languishing in a nearby French POW camp. Schillemans was extracted from captivity and sent to the castle, but Pétain refused to see him. The doctor nonetheless hung around the premises in case the patient might one day need help. Schillemans' own memoir of Sigmaringen could not be more different from that of Céline. His description of sighting Pétain on one of his walks reveals the levels of adulation the Marshal could still inspire:

> His grey eyes gave us a beautiful look, not that of a senile old man, but that beautiful gaze one saw on the posters in 1940 . . . These were eyes that seemed to pierce you, the eyes of an intelligent Leader waiting for the answer to a question he had posed. The look that alighted upon me for a brief moment, just enough time for him to take three or four steps, had a limpidity, an inner flame, such a splendid luminosity, that I could still feel its effect when he had passed by and his silhouette was lost in the wisps of mist floating above the road.[15]

Despite Pétain's non-cooperation, Brinon's Governmental Commission went through the futile motions of 'governing'. One surreal subject of discussion was the interest rate at which the 'government' would eventually reimburse the Germans for their 'generosity' in making Sigmaringen available. Otherwise, pending a reconquest of France, the Commission's only possible *raison d'être* was to look after the interests of the large number of French who found themselves on German soil for different reasons. These included about 1.2 million prisoners of war, 650,000 French workers who had been forcibly sent to German factories and farms, 10,000 fighters of the Milice with their families, 5,000 members of Doriot's PPF party and their families, and 3,500 volunteers from the Legion of Volunteers against Bolshevism (LVF).[16]

Déat, as Secretary for Labour, was supposedly responsible for French workers. He busied himself by perfecting the bureaucratic structures of his imaginary 'ministry'. Since this was not enough to occupy his restless intelligence, he also travelled around the ruins of Germany lecturing at congresses where he was in his element. In Dresden he spoke on 'French thought and history in Germany and France' and in Berlin on 'The Unity of European civilization'. Darnand, as Secretary of the Interior, was responsible for policing. A man of action who had been happiest as a soldier (he often strutted around in his Waffen SS uniform), he was ill at ease among intellectual phrasemakers like Déat. Often absent from the castle, his main worry was the welfare of the *miliciens* who had followed him to Germany.

No member of the Commission was busier than Jean Luchaire, a venal journalist with expensive tastes and Brylcreemed hair. He had arrived in Sigmaringen with a considerable retinue including at least two mistresses, his wife and his daughter Corinne, an actress popular on stage in occupied Paris. Luchaire was in charge of propaganda, which was something he knew about. The fact that there was little the Commission could actually *do* made it all the more important to give the impression of doing something. He set up a radio station, which alternated news bulletins and light operettas, and a newspaper, *France*. To give a flavour of its contents, one article, on 5 November 1944, reporting on the condition of French workers in Germany, was headed 'Auschwitz, model camp'.[17]

Since the Commission had no power, matters of protocol assumed obsessive importance. A mini-crisis exploded when someone was spotted using the staircase reserved for members of the Commission. The violator protested his innocence and, after a full investigation, turned out to be innocent, but he was nonetheless reminded that he must never use the staircase.[18] When not squabbling over protocol, the French sought distraction in self-improvement. The castle had a well-stocked library and its librarian had never been busier. Déat plunged into Voltaire and Goethe; Pétain settled down to the memoirs of Talleyrand – perhaps seeking tips about how to make a transition from one regime to another. The library also had an excellent collection of old maps useful for those planning their eventual escape.

Cultural events were organized in the *salle des fêtes* and in the town. These included readings of plays; a colloquium on 'The Intellectual in Germany'; a Bach recital by the celebrated ultra-collaborationist pianist Lucienne Delforge (whose presence in Sigmaringen caused tensions with Céline's wife since Delforge had been Céline's mistress in the 1930s). The cultural highlight of the autumn was a visit by the Belgian fascist leader Léon Degrelle. Appearing in his SS uniform Degrelle lectured on 'The New Europe and the Recovery of France'. *Le tout Sigmaringen* turned out to hear him including Céline, dressed like a tramp as usual, a pair of moth-eaten mittens strung around his neck and carrying a bag from which protruded the head of his cat Bébert. Increasingly exasperated by the insanely exalted tone of the lecture, Céline left before the end muttering loudly about this '*roi des cons*' (king of idiots).

It was, however, impossible to shut out the real world entirely. *France* warned its readers endlessly about horrors being perpetrated in liberated France. Typical headlines were 'ANARCHY IN FRANCE' and 'FRANCE RAVAGED BY COLD AND POVERTY'. More directly worrying were the reprisals being exacted against collaborators, especially the news in late autumn that formal purge trials were beginning in Paris. The first case to come up before the court was the journalist Georges Suarez, who was executed by firing squad on 9 November. Worryingly for the Sigmaringen exiles, his offences had been incomparably less serious than those of any member of Brinon's pseudo-government.

3

Paris after Liberation

The apocalyptic headlines issuing from Sigmaringen about the parlous state of post-Liberation France bore little relation to reality, but it was true that the euphoria of Liberation had quickly turned sour. Those who had cheered de Gaulle on the Champs-Elysées hoped to be able to put the war behind them. But the fighting was far from over. Initially the German forces had fallen back surprisingly fast, and by the end of November 1944 the Allies had pushed them up to the Vosges mountains in the east. Strasbourg was taken back on 23 November. But the fighting was becoming more gruelling, and in the face of tenacious German resistance in Alsace the Allied offensive stalled. A German counter-offensive in the Ardennes in late December took the Allies by surprise. It briefly looked as if Strasbourg might need to be evacuated.

De Gaulle himself did not regret the continuation of the fighting. As he wrote in his Memoirs:

> That the war was to continue was certainly tragic from the point of view of losses, damages and expenses which we French would still have to endure. But from the viewpoint of France's higher interests – which is something quite different from the immediate interests of the French – I did not regret it. For with the war dragging on, our aid would be necessary.[1]

Despite his efforts, over the previous four years France had been a spectator in the world war. The Resistance had succeded in saving national honour, but it had done so without affecting the outcome of the conflict. The French had endlessly photographed themselves liberating their capital city, but the truth was that the Germans had evacuated it. People returning to Paris immediately after Liberation were struck by the city's eerie beauty– as if nothing had happened. A French journalist who had worked with the BBC in London wrote:

> We found Paris intact. We had for so long been haunted by the fear of savage reprisals against its monuments. All was there, in place, with a serenity that had survived the insurrection and the battle . . . The windows of the Louvre still caught the afternoon sun.[2]

The diplomat Hervé Alphand, who had worked alongside de Gaulle, described the entry into Paris in lyrical terms: 'Every child, every woman, every man, smiling, greets us. Paris! Paris at last! Such beauty with the light of a Corot.'[3] It was as if, with the disappearance of the German street signs desecrating the city's landscape, the scenery of a play had been removed. Now life could return to normal, and the past four years be forgotten.

Yet there was another way of reading this eerie beauty. To one American observer, the city brought to mind less a Corot landscape than a 'Canova death mask'. To another it seemed 'empty and hollow and dead, like an exquisite corpse'.[4]

De Gaulle wanted to summon the 'corpse' back to life. His first priority was to integrate the motley forces of the Resistance into a regular army, but his provisional government also faced the considerable challenge of feeding and housing France's civilian population in conditions of extreme dislocation. Much of the country's infrastructure had been destroyed; German requisitions had drastically reduced France's livestock and agricultural production; coal was scarce, and the transport to move it even scarcer. Homes were only allocated electricity for a few hours a day. The black market had become an ingrained feature of life under occupation, and the only thing that changed after Liberation was that it now functioned less efficiently. These problems were compounded by an exceptionally harsh winter at the end of 1944. Liberated they may have been, but the French people were colder and hungrier than they had been at any time under occupation.

Hervé Alphand may have been reminded of Corot in August, but four months later he told a different story: '31 December 1944: Paris is lugubrious, cold, and as if emptied of its soul. It reminds me a bit of

Vienna at the end of the last war, a splendid décor, empty of people, and without lighting.'[5] Maurice Garçon, a prominent lawyer whose diary gives a vivid picture of Paris at this time, and especially of the workings of the courts, wrote:

> Everything is lacking. No wood, no coal, no electricity and almost no gas. For the first time in my life, I am seriously suffering from cold . . . We all cluster in one room of the apartment in front of a tiny fire . . . Hard to find any food. Of the five years of the war this is the hardest winter, not the coldest but the one where one feels most impotent. After the days of euphoria of the liberation we thought our troubles were over . . .
>
> The Palais de Justice is like a fridge . . . Magistrates wrap themselves in blankets, lawyers wear *cache nez* above their black robes, a female lawyer drapes a fur coat over her shoulders.[6]

Janet Flanner, a seasoned observer of Paris life for *The New Yorker*, reported: 'Little is left even of some of the more orderly high hopes which fluttered in French hearts as the French flag fluttered overhead on the day of liberation. Paris is free, and no one forgets it for a minute, since nothing much else has happened to remember.'[7]

De Gaulle's government had no intention of letting people forget that although they might be cold and hungry, at least they were free. If it could not provide bread, the government would organize circuses. Endless parades, marches and processions were held in Paris, leading the American ambassador to comment that there was something unseemly about spending so much on such events when it was hardly possible to feed the population.[8] On 11 November 1944, Armistice Day, Churchill joined de Gaulle for another massive procession down the Champs-Elysées. On 3 April 1945 there was a grandiose ceremony to award the Cross of the Liberation to the City of Paris. In addition to these official ceremonies, others were organized by resistance associations around the renaming of a street or the unveiling of a plaque to commemorate a resistance hero. Many of these events were organized by the Communist Party, which had ended the war as the dominant force of the Resistance. It endlessly invoked the memory of its '75,000 martyrs', the number of Communist resisters that it claimed, somewhat exaggeratedly, had perished during the Occupation.

During these strange months between liberation and victory, Parisian cultural life had resumed. It was possible, for the first time since 1940, to see Pablo Picasso's paintings. It was also possible to hear the singers Charles Trenet and Edith Piaf, who, despite having performed in occupied Paris, quickly surmounted any difficulties in returning to the stage. The biggest cultural excitement of the moment was the return, after a four-year hiatus, of American films. There was catching up to do with movies starring Cary Grant and Bette Davis. In April 1945, Parisians had a chance to see Charlie Chaplin's anti-Nazi satire, *The Great Dictator*, first released in 1940. But now, as searing images of the recently liberated concentration camps were being projected in cinemas, ridicule no longer seemed an adequate response to Hitler's crimes.

The cinematic event of the Liberation was the release in March 1945 of a French film, not an American one: *Les Enfants du Paradis*. It was a collaboration between the director Marcel Carné and the poet and *scénariste* Jacques Prévert. This duo had created several legendary films in the 1930s and they had continued to work together during the Occupation. *Les Enfants du Paradis* was a celebration of the world of the Paris theatre in the 1830s, with sumptuous sets by Alexandre Trauner. The film's plot centres on four men all fascinated by the enigmatically beautiful courtesan Garance, played by Arletty, the most famous French actress of the day. Three of her admirers – Pierre-François Lacenaire, a raffish criminal who fancies himself as a poet; Frederick Lemaître, a Shakespearean actor; and Baptiste Debureau, a celebrated mime artist – were based on real historical personalities while the fourth admirer, the aristocrat Count Édouard de Montray, was an invention. If Garance enjoys the company of the cynical Lacenaire, sleeps with the loquacious and charming Lemaître, and becomes the mistress of the rich de Montray, it is the dreamily idealistic mime Baptiste whom she secretly loves. When he plucks up the courage to declare his love, it is too late: he is now married with a child. With a rare flash of moral scruple, Garance will not destroy his family. In the last poignant scene of the film, while Paris is celebrating carnival, Garance's carriage drives away after her adieu to Baptiste. He chases desperately after her, but she is lost in the throng of joyous crowds. The film ends on a note of personal melancholy and public celebration which captures something of the mood of the Liberation.

The 'Children of Paradise' of the film's title are the ordinary people of Paris crowding into the cheap upper balcony seats to watch Baptiste. They are the unspoken heroes of the film whose true subject is Paris: the bustle of its streets, the energy of its people, the vitality of its culture. It is easy to see why the film was celebrated as expressing the glory of French civilization, the spirit of Liberation and the recovery of France. Yet in truth it could have been released at any time over the previous four years. During the Occupation, the Paris film scene had been surprisingly vibrant. Filmmakers had taken refuge in escapist romantic comedies, adaptations of French literary classics (there were seven based on Balzac novels alone), or historical costume dramas. In 1942, Jean-Louis Barrault, who played Baptiste in *Les Enfants du Paradis*, had starred in *La Symphonie fantastique*, a biopic about Hector Berlioz, and Arletty in *Les Visiteurs du soir*, a medieval romance written and directed by the same team who created *Les Enfants*. Viewers could read resistance messages into these films. The life of Berlioz might be interpreted as a celebration of French romanticism. In *Les Visiteurs du soir* the devil turns one of the heroes into a statue whose heart continues beating – like the heart of France under Occupation. The films celebrated a France outside time that the Germans could not contaminate.

Les Enfants du Paradis could just as easily have been the last film of the Occupation as the first of the Liberation. Filming started in 1943 but was interrupted by restrictions and power cuts. In January 1944 another hitch arose when one of the main actors, Robert Le Vigan, failed to turn up. A notoriously committed collaborator, he had gone into hiding – joining Céline in Sigmaringen – and a last-minute replacement was found. These delays did not worry Carné, who seized the opportunity to promote his film as the first big post-Liberation production. But, whereas in liberated Italy the post-war cinema of neo-realism pointed to something new, and marked a break with the past, *Les Enfants* is a film that looks backwards, perfectly exemplifying that uneasy moment between liberation and victory when the new France, whatever that might be, had yet to be born – and the shadow of the old remained so present.[9]

Les Enfants du Paradis was still playing when Germany finally surrendered on 8 May 1945. In Paris, bells rang out and loudspeakers broadcast a speech by de Gaulle. All through the night, the crowds swelled. Projectors lit up the Sacré Coeur basilica where thousands assembled to watch the fireworks. But there was something superficial and fragile about the celebrations, as was noted by two very different observers. Maurice Garçon recorded in his journal:

> People are laughing and shouting, but there is no real enthusiasm ... People are happy, but not that happy. The war is over but everyone feels that the difficulties are going to go on ... A real *fête* is one in which one participates as an actor, and in reality this crowd is only made up of spectators. Something is missing.[10]

Simone de Beauvoir registered a similar unease:

> This victory had been won a very long way from us; we had not waited for it, like the Liberation, in a kind of feverish anxiety; we knew it was coming for a long time, and it did not open up new hopes; it simply put a final full stop to the war; in some sense it was like a death; as when a man dies, when times stops for him ... The war was over: it remained in our arms like a huge awkward corpse; and there was no place in the world to bury it.[11]

As if subliminally acknowledging the truth that France's role in Germany's defeat had been minimal, few newspapers carried the word 'victory' in their headlines, proclaiming instead that 'Germany Has Capitulated' or 'The War Is Over'. The exception was the Communist newspaper *L'Humanité*, which carried in huge letters the longest headline of all – perhaps the longest headline ever – where celebration of victory was accompanied by a call to vengeance:[12]

> VICTORY! ACCLAIMED ALL DAY YESTERDAY BY THE PEOPLE OF PARIS IN CELEBRATING THE MILITARY TRI-UMPHS OF THE UNITED NATIONS OVER HITLERISM. IN INNUMERABLE PARADES, IN IMPROVISED MASS MEET-INGS, EVERYWHERE WAS PROCLAIMED THE WISH TO CRUSH THE RESIDUE OF HITLERISM. FROM ONE END OF THE LAND TO THE OTHER, JUST ONE UNANIMOUS CRY: PÉTAIN TO THE GALLOWS!

THE *ÉPURATION*

One notable absentee from the premiere of *Les Enfants du Paradis* in March 1945 was its star, Arletty, who had been arrested in September 1944 owing to her very public affair with a Luftwaffe officer, Hans-Jürgen Soehring. We do not know if she really told her accusers, as legend has it, 'My heart is French, but my ass is international', nor if she ever said 'If you did not want us to sleep with the Germans, you should not have let them in.' Certainly, these quips captured her truculent personality – both in life and on screen. No case was in the end brought against Arletty – it is not true that her head was shaved as happened to many other unfortunate women accused of improper relations with the Germans – but her experience was only one moment in that wave of post-Liberation purges known in French as the *épuration*.

The word *épuration* conveys not only the idea of retribution and revenge but also of purification and cleansing. The purges were intended not only to punish the guilty but to create a morally renewed nation.[13] Imagined as a moment of national catharsis, the *épuration* soon became another source of popular discontent. The government was accused of dragging its feet; the choice of victims seemed too arbitrary. This was a major cause of friction between de Gaulle and the Resistance. If de Gaulle's overriding priority was for France's armies to redeem her reputation by re-entering the war before it was too late, many resistance leaders believed that redemption was impossible without retribution. During the Occupation, resistance publications had compiled blacklists of prominent personalities to be punished after Liberation. The most violent calls for a purge came, unsurprisingly, from the Communist Party.

De Gaulle also supported the punishment of traitors so long as it was done by the state in an orderly fashion. He wanted to avoid an anarchic bloodbath as well as being pragmatically aware that postwar France would need the services of individuals who might have compromised themselves under the Occupation. In a speech after the Liberation, he proclaimed that France had been betrayed only by a 'handful' of traitors who needed to be punished. Others wanted to extend the net wider. The main problem, however, was to avoid the *épuration* taking on the appearance of a victors' justice, or mirroring the dubious practices of the Vichy regime, which had often resorted to retroactive justice and established special courts to act more expeditiously than the existing ones.

The task of finding legally robust procedures was entrusted to a committee of jurists who had been involved in the Resistance. They solved the issue of retroactivity by categorizing collaboration as an act of treason already covered by article 75 of the Penal Code criminalizing '*intelligence* [collusion] with the enemy'.[14] The trouble was that this was hardly applicable to minor cases of misconduct that fell short of treason. To surmount this hurdle a new transgression was invented, that of national 'indignity'. Its punishment was 'national degradation', which included the loss of some civic rights, such as the right to vote or to be employed by the state.[15] This was judged not to breach the non-retroactive principle since *indignité nationale* did not constitute a sanction in the criminal sense. More problematic from a juridical point of view was the requirement that jurors sitting in the courts administering the purges had to be individuals who had 'never ceased to demonstrate their patriotic sentiments', which meant, in effect, that they had to prove some participation in the Resistance. This was a clear breach of the principle of impartiality and was criticized for this reason even by some jurists who had been in the Resistance.[16]

What was to be done about the most prominent figures of the Vichy government, from Pétain downwards? Ever since the French Revolution, all French constitutions had included a provision to judge politicians accused of treason. In the Third Republic, established in 1875, this role was given to the parliamentary upper house – the Senate – sitting in special session as a High Court. But this procedure was impossible to envisage in 1945. It was not even yet decided whether France would keep the same constitution, and most members of the Senate elected under it had voted Pétain full powers in 1940. It was decided instead to create a new High Court, *Haute Cour de Justice*, to try the Vichy leaders.

The next problem was finding untarnished judges to run all these courts, given how compromised the entire French legal establishment had been by the Occupation.[17] Vichy may have been an authoritarian regime that repudiated the practices of the previous Republic, but it had been served loyally by that Republic's civil servants and officials – and by its magistrates. In the French system, judges and public prosecutors are professional magistrates, not political appointees or lawyers arguing a brief. They were vital cogs in the Vichy regime and this was emphasized by the unprecedented formal obligation imposed on them to swear a public oath of loyalty to Pétain. At a solemn ceremony on 1 September 1941, in the presence of the Minister of Justice, all magistrates – that is all judges and public prosecutors – had to proclaim: 'I swear loyalty to the person of the Head of State.' Maurice Garçon's view of this matter was doubtless shared by many of his lawyer colleagues:

> What is there more servile and more cowardly than a magistrate? That famous independence which people talk about is just an illusion, and a dangerous one because it is continuously repeated and everyone believes in it. The truth is much more depressing. Magistrates, in their large majority, are ambitious men who take the view that their careers require a blind obedience to power whoever wields it.[18]

Garçon recognized that even lawyers like himself defending victims of the regime were being sucked into a judicial process which flouted many principles previously held sacrosanct. In 1943 he had taken on the defence of five young men from Poitiers accused of 'terrorism', which was how Vichy described acts of resistance:

> I am mortified that I agreed take on this case. Appearing in court I become complicit in a shameful travesty ... Those who were behind this will exploit the parody of my presence to claim that the rights of the defence have been respected. Unwillingly I become complicit in a machination.[19]

Despite his scruples, Garçon's eloquence did save them from the death penalty.[20]

Such moral dilemmas were even more acute for magistrates than for a defence lawyer like Garçon. Only one, Paul Didier, refused to take the oath. When his name was called out at the swearing-in ceremony, he shouted out to general astonishment: 'I refuse to swear.' He was promptly sacked and interned before being placed under house arrest. This was not the first time in his career that Didier would display such independence of mind. Although he was reinstated soon after the Liberation, his example was not celebrated after the war even by members of the magistrature who had opposed Vichy. He was seen as an embarrassment more than a hero, having challenged the ingrained culture of obedience of the entire corps. Magistrates believed they were there to implement laws, not to judge them.[21]

Only two magistrates were awarded the much-coveted honour of Compagnon de la Liberation by de Gaulle, rewarding those who had played an important role in the Liberation of France. The first, René Parodi, had been executed by the Germans; the second, Maurice Rolland, lived to see the Liberation. Both men had sworn the oath on the grounds that some compromise with the regime might allow them to do more for victims of the regime than open defiance. They did not consider the oath as morally binding. This was also the official position of de Gaulle's Free French in London.[22]

It was still necessary to find some way of dealing with magistrates who had all too zealously carried out Vichy's bidding. This issue was handled by another committee of resistance jurists, who opted in favour of a limited purge. 'To overturn immediately and completely the entire personnel of the judiciary would lead to chaos,' they argued. 'What needs to be done is to remove those who during the Occupation showed themselves unworthy of their office.'[23] As one journalist remarked during the Pétain trial: 'Where else are we going to find magistrates? On the moon?'[24] Re-establishing the credibility of the magistrature was urgent. Until the new courts could start work, France was ruled by a kind of frontier justice. Local resistance groups were carrying out their own summary justice, sometimes covered by the fig leaf of *ad hoc* tribunals, and sometimes by no fig leaf at all. In the early days of the Liberation, when the government turned a blind eye, some 9,000 people lost their lives in this so-called *épuration sauvage*.

To weed out magistrates who had severely compromised themselves a special purge commission was set up at the Liberation.[25] In April 1945, after about sixty sessions, this body had completed its work. The commission had to establish whether magistrates had displayed an excess of zeal or used the margin of manoeuvre available to them. This was a complicated issue. Leniency did not necessarily serve the cause of those who came up before Vichy courts. If the Germans were unhappy about a verdict, they might simply seize the defendants themselves. The purge Commission had to sift justifiable defences from self-serving ones. The prize for casuistry must be awarded to the magistrate who argued that since the oath he had sworn in 1941 was to the 'Head of State', he had really been swearing allegiance to the President of the Third Republic as the Vichy regime had no legitimacy.[26]

Apart from Prefects, not one of whom remained in post, no servants of the state suffered more heavily in the *épuration*. Out of 3,000 French magistrates, 277 were sanctioned and 186 were removed from their post. Only fifteen of the fifty senior magistrates (*procureurs généraux* and *premiers présidents*) remained in place.[27] This was no whitewash. Still, the reputation of the magistrature remained severely compromised, a fact that defence lawyers exploited in the post-war trials. In the trial of the collaborationist writer Robert Brasillach, his lawyer turned the tables on the prosecution:

> Your institution [the Ministry of Justice] today sounds the fanfare of the Resistance. Well and good! . . . But for four years you represented collaboration. You are, whether you like it or not, in solidarity with this institution which, for four years, pursued and condemned Jews, pursued and condemned resisters, pursued and condemned Communists . . . When I think that often the Germans chose their hostages from those whom you had condemned, I do not give you the right to invoke the memory of the victims . . . I have the right to turn to them and ask: from what have you most suffered? The writings of a journalist or the acts of the pitiless prosecutor?[28]

The lawyer who uttered these words was Jacques Isorni, who was to find himself four months later one of the lawyers defending Pétain.

The courts started operating even before the judicial purge was completed. The earliest trials targeted journalists, whose commitment to collaboration was easy to prove because it had been so public. The only evidence needed were newspaper clippings. The first case in Paris was that of the aforementioned journalist Georges Suarez, who was sentenced to death on 23 October 1944 and executed on 9 November. This was the case that had sent a chill down the spine of the Sigmaringen exiles. On 25 October came the turn of Lucien Felgines, a broadcaster working for the Nazi-run Radio Paris, who was sentenced to twenty years in prison; then on 30 October the journalist Stephane Lauzanne, also sentenced to twenty years in prison. The next day the so-called Comte de Puységur was sentenced to death for distributing pro-German tracts.

The seventy-year-old semi-lunatic Puységur, whose visiting cards described him as 'anti-semitic, anti-masonic, anti-bourgeois, anti-capitalist, anti-communist, anti-démocratic and anti-Republican', and who had told the court that fortune tellers had assured him Germany would win the war, was hardly a significant figure. Or, to take another example picked up by the press, was it fair that a typist working for Radio Paris was sentenced to life imprisonment while a few weeks earlier one of the leaders of an ultra-collaborationist party, Georges Albertini, had been jailed for only five years? Other observers were disturbed by the partisan atmosphere of the trials. Maurice Garçon, who had deplored the workings of the courts under the Occupation, was equally disgusted by the Suarez trial:

> The court was full . . . Hardly any room left. I just managed to squeeze in . . . The public was rowdy, they were there for the kill. During a recess, photographers hurried forward, their flash bulbs going off. The defendant was like someone who had been thrown to the wolves. He was alone, abandoned. One knew it was over for him. However ignominious his actions, I felt pity for him . . .
>
> Suarez listened, obviously with regrets, as his newspaper articles were read out. They are abominable. His defence was stupid. One felt that he was destabilized by the implacable atmosphere which surrounded him . . . The mood got nastier. Saurez looked around the hall with terror . . . I would condemn him but not in that way. Nothing feels less like justice than this kind of revolutionary atmosphere.[29]

Garçon did not doubt that Suarez deserved his fate, but others worried about singling out personalities who had sinned only by words. A celebrated exponent of this position was François Mauriac, one of France's most famous novelists and also a brilliant journalist.

Mauriac had been actively involved in the Resistance. He was one of the founders of the *Comité national des écrivains*, a resistance organization that had drawn up a blacklist of writers tainted by collaboration. But when writers started appearing before the courts, Mauriac began to feel qualms about sentencing them to death. He took up the case of the journalist Henri Béraud, who was condemned to death in December 1944; de Gaulle commuted the sentence to life imprisonment.

Newspapers dubbed Mauriac 'St François of the Assizes'. His articles in *Le Figaro* were answered by the rising star Albert Camus in the resistance newspaper *Combat*. 'Every time I speak of justice. M. Mauriac speaks of charity,' wrote Camus in one article – although this was a simplification of Mauriac's position.[30] When the writer Robert Brasillach was sentenced to death in February 1945, Mauriac organized a writers' petition to plead for clemency despite the fact that Brasillach had often attacked him viciously. Fifty-nine writers signed the petition including Paul Valéry and Jean Cocteau; Jean-Paul Sartre and Simone de Beauvoir refused to sign. Camus supported clemency out of a principled opposition to the death penalty. This time, de Gaulle did not commute the sentence. Brasillach was executed by firing squad on 6 February 1945.[31]

Critics of the *épuration* focused on the fact that it had so far tackled none of the big beasts of the Vichy regime. Indeed, it had taken several months even to establish the composition of the High Court that would try them. Only on 18 November, spurred into action by press criticisms, did the government announce how this Court would operate. At the start of December the public prosecutor, André Mornet, announced the names of seventy individuals (in the end it would be 108) who would be judged, but there was still no timetable. The problem was that so few of the potential defendants were on hand to be tried. Some had taken refuge abroad in Spain, others had gone into hiding in France. Pétain was in Germany. Their trials could only take place *in absentia*, but this would not have the same impact as an in-person trial. There would be no speeches by lawyers, no witnesses to hear.

The issue was discussed at the end of the year by the Assemblée Consultative, a body consisting of resisters and former parliamentarians that de Gaulle had created as a temporary parliament until proper elections could be held. The feelings of frustration over the purges focused around the person of Pétain. One speaker lambasted the government for dragging its feet:

> For many who rallied late to the Resistance, it would be enough to replace the portrait of Marshal Pétain by that of de Gaulle . . . We condemn this thesis and cannot accept it. This shadow must be lifted . . . And for this there is only one solution: to prepare without further ado the trial of the traitor Pétain [loud applause]. How do you want us to reply to these . . . high officials, these generals who say to us: 'We only obeyed the orders of Marshal Pétain.' We reply by saying to them: 'It is not about Marshal Pétain. It is about a traitor.' But this traitor still holds the Legion of Honour, he is still a member of the Académie Française. Until we dispel such equivocations, our new regime remains sullied. People might object perhaps that we do not have Pétain here, that he is in Germany. But what does that matter! What matters is not the carcass of this old man, what matters is what he represents.[32]

In the absence of Pétain, the Court set to work on the case of Admiral Esteva, Vichy's senior commander in Tunisia. When the Allies had launched an attack on Morocco and Algeria in November 1942, Esteva had allowed German troops to land in Tunisia, a decision that prolonged the war in North Africa by several months. After a four-day trial that ran from 12 to 15 March, Esteva was sentenced to life in prison. If he escaped the death penalty, it was partly because he could plead in his favour that he had released some resisters from prison before the Germans had arrived. It was also true that no one suspected him of any kind of sympathy for the Axis powers. A man of limited intelligence, Esteva had been motivated by an almost religious devotion to Pétain. This formed a key argument of his defence, which was built around the illogicality of judging Esteva before Pétain. 'If Esteva's treason depends on that of Pétain,' his lawyer Chresteil told the court, 'if it is a corollary of that of Pétain, it is impossible to judge the crime's accomplice before judging its principal author.'[33]

Esteva's trial was followed by that of General Dentz, commander of Vichy military forces in Syria, who had ordered his troops to fire on British and Gaullist troops in June 1941, when they attempted to take Syria back from Vichy. After a three-day trial he was sentenced to death, but the sentence was commuted to life imprisonment by de Gaulle. Dentz's lawyers used the same arguments as Esteva's. André Mornet, the prosecutor in both cases, was only too aware of the force of these arguments. He wrote somewhat defensively to his superior, the Minister of Justice, arguing that his decision to open the proceedings of the High Court with these two cases had been juridically defensible, on the grounds that 'they reveal at the military level the harmful effects of the policy of collaboration followed by the Marshal, at the same time as they show traces of an intervention by him'.[34]

At last, on 23 April, immediately after Dentz's conviction, Mornet announced that the trial of 'Pétain, Henri, Philippe, Benoni, Omer' was ready to begin. It would start *in absentia* on 17 May. Two days later, his plan was thrown into turmoil by the startling news that the defendant had presented himself at the Franco-Swiss border so that he could answer to the French people in person.

4

Pétain's Return

At the end of 1944, as the news from France became ever more alarming, the Sigmaringen exiles had briefly consoled themselves with rumours that the Germans were about to unleash their much-vaunted secret weapons. The V2 rocket attacks on London in the autumn had raised their hopes and then came the news, on 19 December, of the German counter-offensive through the Ardennes. Was this the long-awaited turnaround?

Some imagined themselves exacting bloody revenge on the Gaullist and Communist 'terrorists'. Others had visions of being greeted as liberators by cheering French crowds disappointed in de Gaulle, while still others nursed a fantasy of an alliance with a chastened de Gaulle ready to turn on the Communists. Brinon's Christmas message was upbeat: 'We say that Germany's cause is a sacred cause. We believe in her victory . . . To the French who are suffering under de Gaulle we call out: "understand and act". The power imposed over you is usurped.'[1]

In truth, Brinon's stock was falling with the Germans. Abetz and Renthe-Fink were recalled to Berlin, and Jacques Doriot, who had established himself a few kilometres away from Sigmaringen in a castle near Lake Constance, was encouraged by the Nazis' Propaganda Minister, Joseph Goebbels, to establish his own radio station and his own newspaper, *Le Petit Parisien*. Thanks to German funding, this was a slicker publication than Jean Luchaire's published at Sigmaringen. It had sports pages and carried news of cultural events in Paris – Camille Saint-Saëns' *Samson and Delilah* at the Opéra, Paul Claudel's *Le Soulier de satin* at the Comédie Française – as if preparing its readers for the delights awaiting them once France got rid of de

Gaulle while simultaneously undermining the claims that France was in chaos. On 6 January 1945, Doriot formed his own 'Committee of French Liberation'. If Brinon's Commission was a tragi-comic parody of Vichy, Doriot had now created his own parody of de Gaulle's Free French Committee of Liberation.

There were now on German soil, a few kilometres apart, two rival newspapers, two rival radio stations, and two rival organizations representing 'France'. Brinon and Déat felt they had to bring Doriot on board rather than oppose him. The reconciliation was due to be sealed at a meeting between Déat and Doriot on 22 February, but Doriot never made it. His car was hit by an Allied aerial attack, probably a stray bombing rather than a targeted one. Sigmaringen, secretly delighted, went into mourning.

While Allied bombing intensified, reducing much of Germany to ruins, in the rural backwater of Sigmaringen the only evidence of war was the Allied planes passing overhead to drop their bombs on Munich and Nuremberg. *France* continued to offer its alternative reality to a diminishing band of readers. On 23 February they could read: 'Liberation has Turned France into the Field of Ruins and Death.' That same issue also carried the announcement of a lecture by Déat optimistically entitled 'Programme for a French national socialism'. On 2 March the paper comforted its readers: 'Despite the enemy pressure, the Wehrmacht front continues to hold! Dr Goebbels affirms the will of the German people to go on fighting.' A week later it proclaimed: 'Bolshevik Atrocities: General Guderian Declares that the Red Army has Received the Order to Pillage and Kill.'[2]

At the end of March, the newspaper shifted from a daily to a weekly publication – but not many weeks were left. Despite the bombastic headlines, no one was under any illusion. The exiles were planning their escape. Céline was among the first to leave, at the end of March. He and Lucette managed to enter Denmark, where they were interned. Luchaire crossed the Brenner Pass into Italy, but he was arrested by the Americans on arrival. Déat, more lucky, made the same journey, and took refuge in an Italian monastery, where he died in 1955, having converted to Catholicism. Brinon, refused entry into neutral Switzerland, was eventually arrested by the Americans.

Only Pétain was eager to return to France. Once he had heard the news of the establishment of the High Court at the end of 1944, his consuming obsession was to defend his reputation before it. On 5 April he asked Hitler's permission to return to France:

> As head of the government in Bordeaux in June 1940 I refused to leave France . . . The government of the Reich has forced me to leave France on 20 August 1944 . . . It is only in France that I can account for my actions . . . At my age, one only fears one thing: not having performed one's duty and I want to perform mine.[3]

He received no reply.

By 19 April, Allied forces were about 40 kilometres away from Sigmaringen. The next day, Reinebeck and von Tangstein, the German officials who had replaced Renthe-Fink and Abetz, informed Pétain that he would have to be moved to avoid falling into Allied hands. For Pétain, ending the war under German protection was the worst possible outcome. He produced another letter of protest addressed to Hitler, again asking to be allowed to go back to France. Knowing that Germany's collapse was imminent, von Tangstein was ready to disobey orders. He told Pétain that he would be taking him in the direction of the Swiss border. Pétain had always enjoyed good relations with the Swiss representative to Vichy, Walter Stucki, and the prospect of being allowed to cross into Switzerland was an acceptable option.

At 4 a.m. on 21 April, Reinebeck and von Tangstein arrived to take Pétain away. A few hours later, soldiers of the French First Army reached the castle gates. The commanding officer was met by six Germans in civilian clothes. He addressed the one who seemed to be in charge:

> 'Are you the owner of the Castle?'
> 'No Monsieur. The *valet de chambre* of Marshal Pétain.'
> 'Where is Marshal Pétain?'
> 'I do not know.'

There were no French left in the castle. The liberating soldiers came upon a list of internal telephone numbers including those of 'Frau Pétain' and 'Präsident Laval'. They went up to Pétain's bedroom. The French officer reported back to his superiors: 'The bed was unmade, drawers open, boxes spread out over chairs. On the chest of drawers a bottle of mineral water, half empty, with the Vichy label . . . I am not inventing anything.'[4]

Pétain's wife later wrote a detailed narrative of the events of the next three days. It provides a vivid picture of their journey amid the chaotic collapse of Nazism. Her purpose was to demonstrate his patriotism, but other testimonies confirm its accuracy. Pétain's party set off towards the town of Wangen, she explained, about 120 kilometres to the south-east of Sigmaringen:

> At Wangen no orders had been given, and no one had been alerted to our arrival. It was bitterly cold. We were taken to the Town Hall . . . Then the Mayor arrived in panic. He showed respect to the Marshal and seemed mortified by the lack of a proper welcome. The entire population was gathered in the square looking at us as if we were strange beasts.

In the end they were put up in the nearby castle of Zeil, home of the Prince of Waldburg. Their worry was that the castle was north of Wangen whereas Switzerland lay to the south. At midnight on the next day von Tangstein informed Pétain, since the Allies were getting closer, that it would be necessary to move again:

> VON TANGSTEIN: Monsieur le Maréchal, the military situation requires you to leave. I am coming to ask you to do so.
> PÉTAIN: I refuse to leave . . .
> VON TANGSTEIN: Marshal, I beg you. I have orders. I must obey. I beg you. [The discussion became nastier. The Marshal's tone got harder.]

The screams of the participants in this psychodrama could be heard in the corridor outside the room until Pétain announced he was going to bed:

> At 6.30 a.m. von Tangstein and von Reinebeck arrived in our room . . . The Marshal curled up in a ball in his bed:
> 'Leave me alone; I am tired; I am at the end of my tether; at my age one cannot survive this kind of tiredness. I refuse to get up . . . And anyway you do not have the agreement of the Swiss to let me pass through the country.'

Late the next day, Pétain's German minders secured agreement that the Swiss would allow Pétain into the country. Pétain and his party set off late on the following day for the town of Bregenz:

> Our departure was decided for 22h because during the day Allied planes were bombing the roads. At 22.30 we left Zeil for Bregenz, about 80 km away. We did not get to Bregenz before 3 in the morning: the roads were clogged with people fleeing, ramshackle convoys of lorries pulled by tractors, of horses and of people on foot. Bregenz was glacially cold. We were given a room in a small hotel. The Marshal went to bed.

The next morning they crossed into Switzerland. In Annie Pétain's words: 'At 10.00 the barrier at the frontier was raised. We passed through it. We were in Switzerland. It was 24 April. The Marshal's birthday. He was 89, entering into his 90th year.'

Pétain and his entourage were lodged in a hotel in the village of Weesen while awaiting the response of the French government to his request to be allowed to return to his homeland. The Swiss authorities were relieved that their embarrassing guest did not wish to remain.[5] After the French response had been received, the party set off again and arrived at Vallorbe, on the French frontier, in the late afternoon of 26 April. A room had been reserved for Pétain at the station hotel. While he settled down to his last meal as a free man, a Swiss policeman was sent across the border to work out the arrangements with the French authorities.

Pétain arrived at the frontier post at 7.15 p.m. His car was the first to cross, and the Swiss guard of honour saluted as it passed. On the French side, Pétain got out of his car and saluted the French republican guards lined along the road. Presumably obeying orders, they ignored him.

De Gaulle had sent General Koenig to meet Pétain on behalf of the French government. A mere captain in 1940, Koenig was a hero of the Free French, the commander of French forces at the battle of Bir Hakeim against Rommel in the Western Desert of Libya in June 1942. When Pétain got out of his car, Koenig saluted. Pétain held out his hand but Koenig kept his hands rigidly at his side. Koenig had not planned what to do, but it seemed inappropriate to shake the hand of the man he was arresting. Momentarily taken aback, Pétain was forced to withdraw his hand. When a French police officer asked Pétain to give his name and title, he replied: 'I think I am still Marshal of France.'

For Koenig, this had been an excruciating encounter. Years later he wrote to a friend that 'the most painful duty I ever had to accomplish was to go to the Franco-Swiss frontier to greet a broken (*accablé*) old man who had come to hand himself over to French justice'.[6] Pétain returned to his car, whose chauffeur had now been replaced by a French policeman. He was driven on the short journey to the station where a special train was waiting to take him to Paris.

3. *L'Humanité*, 18 April 1945: 'Somewhere in Germany: Don't you think, Adolf, that the time has come to make the gift of our persons?' An ironic reference to Pétain's famous phrase in 1940 that he was making the 'gift of his person' to the French people.

45

HITLER'S SECRET WEAPON?

The news of Pétain's return caused consternation in France. The following day a government official in Bordeaux reported to his superiors in Paris:

> The announcement ... has provoked stupor. It is a sensation eclipsing all the great international events in the mind of public opinion. The Marshal's gesture is much commented upon in those circles which have remained favourable to the former Head of State but do not openly show themselves. They judge that his decision to give himself up to the French is a wise decision that pleads in his favour. All the arguments inspired by indulgence are put forward. People speak of senility, the noxious influence of his entourage, his desire to avoid sufferings to the French during the Occupation. On the other hand, resistance circles are very worried. It is seen as a piece of 'theatre' and people suspect this is the start of an operation to allow the collaborationists retrospectively to justify themselves as having been in their own way resisters ... In general there is agreement that the political repercussions of the trial will make it the most important judicial event of the century ... The strength of these first reactions leads one to fear that, depending on the evolution of the Pétain case, one can expect quite violent disturbances.[7]

In the end no important disturbances took place, but the government was hearing the same type of news from all across France.

Preparations for the trial were thrown into disarray. As one American newspaper put it, 'Pétain may be a hot potato for de Gaulle. On trial in France he can talk back.'[8] It suddenly became necessary to interrogate the defendant and examine the documents found in his possession. The final defeat of Germany also meant that many French politicians deported to Germany had returned, and they would also have to be interviewed. The trial would have to be postponed for weeks or months. The lawyer Maurice Garçon wrote in his usual dyspeptic manner:

> Apart from a few fanatics, everyone regrets Pétain's return – regrets the fact that he lived on until the end. He has missed the last chance he had

to make the 'gift of his person' to France as he offered to do on taking over in June 1940. Already people are starting to quarrel. This will be worse than the Dreyfus case. This time it is not just quarrels between different political groups. France herself is at stake.[9]

Curiously even those previously clamouring for a Pétain trial were apprehensive. One common reaction in resistance circles was that Pétain's return was a cunning ploy by Hitler to cause dissension in France.[10] Given the circumstances surrounding his return, the idea of Pétain as Hitler's secret weapon was unfounded, indeed paranoid, but it revealed a fear, even among his enemies, that Pétain retained something of his aura. Even British observers wondered if this was not 'the last dirty trick that the Marshal with the connivance of Hitler would play on his country'.[11] An American newspaper headlined: 'Pétain is Germany's V2 against France'.[12] This theory was bolstered by the fact that the formal request to the Swiss to allow Pétain into the country had come from a German official.[13]

It was not only in France that the prospect of a trial caused apprehension. The American government feared revelations about its close relations with Vichy and the British were nervous about stories being put about that there had been a secret agreement between Pétain and Churchill. From Canada there were warnings that the trial might 'resuscitate polemics in Quebec favourable to Pétain who was represented as a champion of the Catholic Church, on one hand, and of an anti-British policy, on the other'.[14]

De Gaulle's archives contain a paper from a jurist offering a way out. It argued that the High Court, as currently constituted, was no longer adequate to carry out such a sensitive trial. It had been set up while France was in a constitutional limbo and therefore unable to respect the tradition that treason trials of political leaders should be carried out by the sovereign nation through parliament. Since the end of the war was imminent, it would soon be possible to elect a new parliament. Why not postpone the trial until then? Such a delay also offered the hope that Pétain might die first.[15] But the last thing that de Gaulle wanted was for the Pétain affair to drag on for months longer.

DE GAULLE AND PÉTAIN

Certainly no one was less enthusiastic about the prospect of a trial in person than Charles de Gaulle. The relationship between the two men went back thirty-six years to 1909 when, before starting at the Saint-Cyr military academy, the nineteen-year-old de Gaulle had served for a year in an infantry regiment commanded by the fifty-three-year-old Colonel Pétain. De Gaulle rejoined the same regiment after graduating three years later. When he was believed to have been killed in combat at Verdun in March 1916, it was Pétain who wrote a posthumous citation commending him for bravery in the field.

Despite their disparity of age and rank, de Gaulle had clearly made an impression on Pétain. In 1925, soon after graduating from the École de Guerre (the training college for senior officers), he was invited to join Pétain's *cabinet*. De Gaulle's year at the École had not been happy. Repeatedly clashing with his superiors, he emerged with low final marks which would have been lower but for Pétain's personal intervention. Pétain wanted de Gaulle to help him on a history of the French Army that he was writing with an eye to election to the Académie Française. He had few literary gifts, and the younger officer seemed a perfect ghostwriter. In 1922 de Gaulle had published a short book, *Discorde chez l'ennemi*, revealing himself to be a stylish writer.

For several years, de Gaulle and Pétain were close – as close as was possible given their respective ranks and the icy reserve of their personalities. They visited the battlefields of Verdun together in 1926 and Pétain dedicated a photo of himself to de Gaulle's son Philippe (although the idea that Pétain was his godfather is a myth). The de Gaulles often dined with the Pétains even if Madame de Gaulle, a devout Catholic, disapproved of the Marshal's marriage to a divorcee. The Maréchale in turn patronized the homely Madame de Gaulle, allegedly complaining she could only talk about making jam.

Relations between the two men soured towards the end of the decade when Pétain brought in other helpers to work on the book. De Gaulle was insulted that 'his' work might be debased by turning it into a collective enterprise. He wrote an aggrieved letter, displaying an extraordinary sense of self-belief – not to say insolence – on the part of a mere captain writing to France's most venerated military figure. The startled Pétain assured de Gaulle that once the book was published his contribution would be acknowledged, but the project was quietly shelved. Perhaps it was no longer necessary, since Pétain had in the meantime been elected to the Académie Française.

In 1938, when de Gaulle decided to publish, under his own name, the book he had been helping him write, Pétain tried to stop him. De Gaulle would have none of it, saying, 'You can give me orders in military matters but not literary ones.' Their relationship was over.[16]

Later in life, de Gaulle would often remark that Pétain was a great man who had 'died' in 1925 – an odd remark since 1925 was the year he had started working for him. What he seems to have meant was that viewing Pétain at close quarters, he realized that he had become a prisoner of his own myth. His ideas about the world – and about warfare – had ossified. De Gaulle, not naturally deferential, found the atmosphere of hushed reverence around Pétain stultifying, and in private correspondence started referring to him irreverently as 'the great personage'. But none of this affected his admiration for the Pétain of the Great War. In his book, ultimately published as *La France et son armée* in 1938, de Gaulle wrote that Pétain had a sense 'of the art of the real and possible', which complemented the more impetuous qualities of Marshal Foch: Pétain was a great tactician, Foch a great strategist.

De Gaulle's papers contain some fragmentary, tantalizing and elusive notes on Pétain, penned in 1938, presumably in preparation for the portrait of Pétain he was drafting for his book:

Cloaks the misery of his solitude in pride . . .
Very sensitive in matters concerning himself . . .
Too assured of himself to give in.
Too ambitious to be a mere arriviste.
Too personal to have any faith in others.
Too prudent not to take risks.
His philosophy is one of adjustment.
An artist in his capacity to seize essentials . . .
Impenetrable.
And with a touch of irony that he uses as a rampart for his thoughts and to protect himself.

Uses irony as a means of keeping people at a distance.
Having by a prolonged effort saturated his character and his appear-
ance with a coldness that one day will give him prestige . . .
More grandeur than virtue.[17]

De Gaulle was unusual on the outbreak of war in 1939 in that years of
proximity to Pétain had inoculated him against the myth. Pétain had
been a useful patron but de Gaulle's career had moved on. Intellectually and psychologically liberated from his former mentor, he admired
the Pétain of the past while having no illusion about the Pétain of the
present. His famous verdict on Pétain in his *Memoirs* was that 'old
age is a shipwreck'.

De Gaulle and Pétain found themselves in proximity again as members of Paul Reynaud's government in the last days of the Battle of
France. De Gaulle, who opposed an armistice, was much too junior to
prevail against the prestige of Pétain, who supported one. On 11 June
they both attended a Supreme War Council meeting with Churchill at
Briare, in the Loire region. De Gaulle had recently been promoted:
'You're a general!' Pétain exclaimed. 'I won't congratulate you on it.
What good are ranks in defeat?' The last ever meeting took place on
14 June, after the government had retreated to Bordeaux. De Gaulle
was setting off for London to seek British aid to ship French men and
materiel to North Africa. Lunching at the Hotel Splendid before his
departure, he had spotted Pétain at a nearby table. He walked over to
greet him: 'He shook my hand, without saying a word. I was never to
see him again, ever.'[18]

When de Gaulle returned from London on the evening of 16 June
1940, it was to discover that, following Reynaud's resignation, Pétain
was now premier. The next morning de Gaulle flew back to London
and would not set foot in metropolitan France for four years. When
the terms of the armistice were announced on 22 June, de Gaulle
responded on the radio with an adieu to Pétain in which contempt
was tinged with melancholy:

Monsieur le Maréchal, over the airwaves, across the sea, this is a French
soldier who is speaking to you. Yesterday I heard your voice that I
know well, and not without emotion I heard what you said to the
French people to justify what you have done . . . Ah! To obtain and

accept this humiliation, we did not need you, Monsieur le Maréchal, we did not need the victor of Verdun; anyone would have sufficed.[19]

Despite his unrelenting attacks on Pétain, de Gaulle realized that the Marshal aroused fervour and devotion as much as hatred, and that a trial of the hero of Verdun threatened his hope of binding the nation's wounds. When asked in private, in the weeks after the Liberation, what he intended to do with Pétain, he batted the question away with a quip: 'And what do you want me to do with him? I will assign him a residence somewhere in the Midi and wait till death takes him.' 'Let him go and live on the Riviera and we can forget about him,' he said on another occasion.[20] De Gaulle knew perfectly well that this was not possible, but he had hoped, at least, for a trial in Pétain's absence. He wrote in his *Memoirs*:

> On 17 March 1945 the High Court decided that Marshal Pétain would be judged *in absentia*. This was a lamentable and inevitable outcome. But just as it was in my eyes necessary, in the eyes of the nation and of the world, that French justice render a solemn verdict, I also hoped that circumstances would keep away from French soil the aged defendant, this 89-year-old man, this leader once so covered with dignity, in whom, at the moment of the catastrophe, so many French had placed their confidence, and for whom, despite everything, many still felt respect or pity.[21]

De Gaulle's reaction on hearing that Pétain hoped to return to France was: 'What a nuisance! ... He's going to go on causing us headaches right until the end.'[22] He joked to a friend that it would have been so much easier if someone had slipped him a cup of poisoned coffee.[23] De Gaulle informally let the Swiss authorities know that, although the French would obviously be obliged to ask for Pétain's extradition, they would not pursue the matter if the request were denied.[24] In the end, he was lumbered with the trial he had hoped to avoid.

In the weeks leading up to the trial, Claude Mauriac, son of the novelist, who was working in de Gaulle's secretariat dealing with correspondence, was surprised that de Gaulle, while paying no attention to the many letters calling for Pétain's execution, took more trouble over those favourable to him:

He commented: 'It takes courage to have signed them' (I had not shown him the anonymous ones). 'It is a fact that there are men and women who still believe in him' and then he said what I have heard him say before: 'I don't think he expected to go so far ... He was a great man who was destroyed by ambition ... I saw that great man die in 1925 ... And it is also true that he did not take power in 1940 with very commendable intentions.'[25]

To his future son-in-law, Alain de Boissieu, de Gaulle put the matter in more lapidary terms a few weeks later: 'Pétain is a great figure, very intelligent, very stubborn. Without character; died in 1924.'[26]

PÉTAIN AND THE FRENCH

Pétain's defenders presented his return to France as a gesture of noble heroism by a man ready to assume responsibility for his actions. But Pétain was not a natural martyr. He probably believed that he was still protected by the magic of his legend. For four years he had lived in the bubble of his regime's propaganda, adulated by cheering crowds on choreographed provincial tours. The hagiographical effusions of the Pétain cult are beyond parody. This saccharine extract from one of three books on Pétain by the writer René Benjamin gives a flavour:

> After several moving and happy meetings [with Pétain] I had one which I believe was more extraordinary than all the others. I found myself one day alone in front of his overcoat. Yes, his overcoat, which was lying just like that on the armchair in his study. It was a magnificent moment. I was overcome. Then all of a sudden I became as motionless as the coat when I noticed that the seven stars were gleaming like the seven stars of wisdom of which the ancients tell us.[27]

The 'seven stars' worn by Marshals of France were a favourite theme of hagiographers, as were Pétain's blue eyes and his moustache 'white with the impeccable white of virtue'.

Some of the truth about the growing unpopularity of the Vichy regime did penetrate the corridors of the Hotel du Parc. In August

1941, Pétain recognized this in a speech lamenting an 'ill wind' of discontent blowing through France. But he was partly spared from the unpopularity of his regime as if people desperately needed to hold on to the idea that Pétain was their saviour. Instead they blamed his advisers, first Laval, then his successor Admiral Darlan, and then Laval again. Even some resisters clung at first to the idea that there had been some kind of secret pact between Pétain and de Gaulle. It was only after April 1942, when the Occupation started to affect every citizen, and Laval returned to power, that Pétain's popularity began to suffer. Rather extraordinarily, it then recovered slightly in the last grim year of the Occupation.[28]

In 1940, Pétain had posed as a father figure shielding the French from the ravages of the war; in 1944 he recreated this role by touring cities in the Occupied Zone that had suffered from Allied bombing. The most famous visit was to Paris in April 1944, when crowds turned out to cheer him. Cynics later commented that it was statistically certain that many of the same people must have been cheering de Gaulle four months later. But Pétain's visit was the only time since the defeat when the citizens of Paris had seen the French flag and heard the *Marseillaise*. Applauding Pétain in these circumstances might seem like an act of patriotism.

In his last weeks on French soil, Pétain could take comfort from signs that he remained popular. When he was 'kidnapped' by the Germans in August 1944, a large crowd assembled in Belfort to cheer him. When he arrived at the château of Morvillars, the mayor welcomed him warmly, seeming more pleased than embarrassed to have Pétain in his village.[29] On his journey across Switzerland in April 1945, he was greeted by cheers. When his party stopped to picnic on his final drive, onlookers approached with bottles of wine and bouquets were presented to his wife – although General Debeney had the good sense to recommend that these be left behind before crossing into France. Thus, during his last days in France, during his walks around Sigmaringen, and during his last hours as a free man in Switzerland, Pétain might have continued to believe that he was viewed more as hero than traitor. These were the last cheers he would hear.

When the train taking him from the Swiss frontier back to Paris stopped at the station of Pontarlier to change locomotives, a crowd of about 1,500 people gathered, shouting 'death to the traitor' and 'Pétain to the scaffold'. Stones were thrown at the windows. His alarmed wife asked the guards: 'Are we going to be assassinated here?'[30] This hostile reception was a rude awakening. Perhaps Pétain's feelings on the train home were similar to those of Louis XVI as he was forcibly taken back to Paris after his abortive flight to Varennes in 1791. Perhaps the thought crossed the Marshal's mind that he might have been wiser to stay in Switzerland.

The demonstration at Pontarlier had been organized by the Communist Party. Over the next weeks, it plastered posters and organized demonstrations all over France calling for Pétain's execution. 'Pétain-Bazaine to the scaffold!', read one; 'Louis XVI betrayed and he paid, Pétain has betrayed and he must pay', promised another. In Toulon on 31 May the population was invited to attend a mock trial of Pétain in the Grand Theatre. In Clermont-Ferrand, a mock guillotine for Pétain was set up on 14 July, the anniversary of the Revolution.[31]

Although the Communist Party was especially vociferous in its denunciations, polls confirm that public opinion had moved decisively against Pétain since the Liberation. Over the course of seven months, respondents were asked what his fate should be:[32]

	no penalty	death	penalty but not death
September 1944	64 per cent	3 per cent	32 per cent
January 1945	39 per cent	21 per cent	40 per cent
April 1945	24 per cent	31 per cent	45 per cent
May 1945	16 per cent	44 per cent	40 per cent

Another poll, in June 1945, asked: 'If you were a juror in the trial of Marshal Pétain and the prosecution asked for the death penalty what would be your verdict?' The answers were striking: 44 per cent of respondents answered a straight 'Yes' and 32 per cent 'Yes with mitigating circumstances'. Only 18 per cent said 'No'.

Of those wanting the death penalty, the pollsters reported, the 'tone of these responses is generally very violent and expressed with a

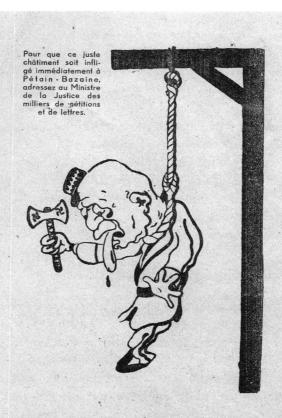

Pour que ce juste châtiment soit infligé immédiatement à Pétain - Bazaine, adressez au Ministre de la Justice des milliers de pétitions et de lettres.

Mort aux traîtres !

Vive l'Armée Française Victorieuse !

Vive les Officiers et Sous-Officiers F. F. I. !

Vive l'Union de la Jeunesse Républicaine de France!

4. Communist flyer, May 1945. The top text reads: 'So that this just punishment be meted out immediately to Pétain-Bazaine, send thousands of petitions and letters to the Ministry of Justice.' The hanged figure of Pétain is carrying a *francisque*, a double-headed axe that was a Vichy symbol and a Vichy decoration. Below Pétain are the words 'Death to traitors!'

mixture of hatred and contempt'. 'He will only get what he deserves,' one respondent offered. Others commented: 'He killed so many French'; 'He shook the hand of the Führer'; 'He went to take refuge with his friend Hitler'; 'Let him be hanged in the place where my son was hanged'; 'If he is not guilty, no one is'; 'The *épuration* should have started with his trial'; 'He made the gift of his person ... to Hitler.' Some respondents proposed their own punishments: 'Take him around France in a cage' or 'Force him to swallow a VI rocket.'

Those who believed there were mitigating circumstances gave a variety of reasons: his age (40 per cent), his glorious past (20 per cent), that he was a victim of his advisers (20 per cent), that he had made mistakes but was not a traitor (10 per cent). Other comments: 'He will soon die anyway'; 'Before 1942 his policy was defensible'; 'All the crimes were committed in his name. But did he know? Were they ordered by him? Could he stop them?'

Among comments offered by those proposing acquittal: 'Pétain believed in 1940 that Germany would emerge victorious' and 'He saved lives in asking for the armistice.'[33]

This hardening of views since the Liberation is partly explained by the fact that French men and women were no longer getting their news from the Vichy-inspired press. Another factor was that Pétain's return coincided with the return of deportees to France after the liberation of the Nazi concentration camps. On 16 April, Albert Camus wrote: 'Each step which brings victory closer at the same time increases the hopes and anguish of all the French. That is why the days of victory do not find France as happy as they might.'[34]

The state in which many of these deportees arrived, more dead than alive, was a shocking revelation of a horror that people had not previously imagined. Some 300 women survivors from the camp of Ravensbruck reached the Gare de Lyon on 15 April. Those chosen for the journey had seemed fittest to travel. Even so, eleven died in transit. A crowd bearing bouquets was waiting to greet the survivors. Janet Flanner, who observed the scene, wrote:

> All the women looked alike: their faces were grey-green, with reddish brown circles around their eyes, which seem to see but not to take in. They were dressed in what had been given to them at the camps, clothes

taken from the dead of all nationalities. As the lilacs fell from inert hands, the flowers made a purple carpet on the platform and the perfume of trampled flowers mixed with the stench of illness and death.[35]

The arrival of these living skeletons became almost a routine event over the next three months. Reception centres were set up inside the biggest Paris cinemas and at the Gare d'Orsay railway station. At the Gaumont cinema, still displaying posters for Chaplin's *Great Dictator*, a huge crowd turned out to greet the arrival of returning prisoners of war. Each was given a packet of cigarettes, a coffee and a sandwich.[36] The most important reception centre was the luxury Hotel Lutetia, which had been the headquarters of the German intelligence services (Abwehr). Relatives haunted the Lutetia for news of missing family members. One long corridor was lined with panels containing tens of thousands of photographs each with the name of the missing person and the day of their disappearance. This desperate search for missing relatives became such a part of daily life that newspapers started carrying a regular rubric headed 'Recherches' which developed its own sinister shorthand:[37]

Dep = Deporté [deportee]
Wag = Wagon [carriage]
Fam = Famille [family]
Rap = Rapatrié [repatriated]
Ss nou = Sans nouvelles [no news]

Two typical advertisements read:

Searching for Martin du Putison Jean. Number 77.777 or 77.774, 27 yrs, *dep.* Buchenwald from 17–8 to 3–9, Dora from 3 to 6 September. Odette Elina, *rap.* Birkenau, 32, Rue d'Empare, Castres, seeks info. on her parents and brother Jean-Max, *dep.* 29/10/43, direction Auschwitz.[38]

At the traditional May Day parade in 1945, the marchers were accompanied by former deportees dressed in their pyjamas. There were shouts of 'Death to Pétain'. Two cardboard effigies of Pétain were carried. In one he was dressed in a German uniform with his tongue hanging out. The other showed him in his uniform of the last war with 'Bazaine' written across his stomach.[39] Bazaine, that Marshal tried for treason in 1873, remained remarkably present in French memories in 1945.

The Communist press was full of stories comparing the treatment meted out to Pétain with the fate suffered by many victims of the Occupation. Why, it asked, had 'Pétain-Bazaine' been taken to Paris in a special train when deportees had gone to their camps in cattle trucks? A few days after Pétain's arrival in France the Communist newspaper *L'Humanité* carried the headline: 'Mussolini Shot; Pétain Pampered'.[40] As for the fort of Montrouge, where Pétain was incarcerated, headlines referred to it as 'Montrouge Palace' as if Pétain was being held in a luxury hotel.

Montrouge was no luxury hotel. It was one of a ring of forts constructed around Paris in the nineteenth century. Pétain shared with his wife a small cell with two beds. They were allowed a walk in the courtyard each day. At the time of the Liberation, Montrouge was the place where convicted collaborators had been shot, including Robert Brasillach, whose fate had recently divided French intellectuals. The courtyard where the executions had taken place could be seen from Pétain's window. During his incarceration, to spare him this chilling reminder of the fate that might await him, executions were carried out instead in the nearby fort of Chatillon.

It was at Montrouge, on the afternoon of 30 April, that Pétain met his judges for the first time.

5

Preparing the Trial

In the French legal system, preparations for any trial begin with the *Instruction*, the gathering of evidence and the interrogation of the defendant and the witnesses. At the end of this process, a decision is made as to whether the case should go forward. If the answer is yes, an indictment (*Acte d'accusation*) is drawn up. The *Instruction* had already been completed for Pétain before his return, but now a supplementary investigation (*Supplément d'instruction*) was needed. In this first meeting with Pétain, the magistrate chairing the *Instruction* commission, Pierre Bouchardon, was present just to read out the accusation:

> According to the *arrêt* issued on 23 April by the Commission d'Instruction of the High Court, you are accused of attacking the internal security of the State and of collusion with the enemy. Do you have today any comment to make about the actions with which you are accused?

'All of this is completely false from my point of view,' Pétain replied. 'I don't understand anything in this double accusation. During the course of the interrogations, I will reply in detail.'[1]

Before the interrogations could begin, Pétain needed to secure a lawyer. The only two he could name turned out to be dead. The head of the Paris Bar, Jacques Charpentier, was asked to propose other candidates. He offered up two names: Chresteil, the lawyer who had so vigorously defended Esteva, and Vincent de Moro-Giafferi. Pétain was keen on Chresteil but Chresteil demurred, saying that as he had defended Esteva by arguing that it was not his client who should be tried but the man whose orders he was obeying, it would be difficult now to defend that man.

As for Moro-Giafferi, he was a legend at a time when French law-yers could be national celebrities. People would attend court just to witness his performances. Firmly associated with the left, he had sup-ported anti-fascist refugees staging a symbolic counter-trial in Paris to that taking place in Berlin of Communists accused of burning the Reichstag in 1933. 'Göring, you are the arsonist,' he proclaimed. When his name was floated as a possible defender of Pétain, the left-wing journalist Madeleine Jacob huffed that he could not possibly take the case. Moro-Giafferi replied that he would have no qualms. 'Why not?' reflected a colleague, 'After all he defended Landru.'[2] The trial of the notorious serial killer Henri Landru in 1921 had been a judicial *cause célèbre* in the interwar years. It was allegedly for Moro-Giafferi's association with the Landru case that Pétain refused him. How could a Marshal of France be represented by the man who had defended a serial killer? But Pétain may simply have wondered if a lawyer so identified with the left could have pleaded his case with conviction. This was probably wrong. One of Pétain's circle thought that Moro-Giafferi, although a bit of a 'turkey cock', would have been a good choice.[3] He would certainly have done the job professionally – but not with the emotional investment of Jacques Isorni, the lawyer who was ultimately chosen. Pétain's instinct in this matter was sound.

When Bouchardon arrived on VE Day for the first proper interro-gation, Pétain still had no lawyer. He nonetheless agreed to proceed. During the questioning, the sound of bells ringing and crowds cele-brating Germany's defeat and the end of the war in Europe, victory could be heard outside the fort. The interrogation was a fiasco. Until his return, Pétain had always had advisers at hand. Now, except for his wife, he was completely alone. He had copies of the notes Méné-trel had drafted in Sigmaringen but these only covered a few specific issues. He was now confronted with questions that leapt randomly from subject to subject which anyone at the height of their mental powers would have struggled to answer. His responses were a mixture of evasion, blame-shifting, amnesia and perplexity. A few examples:

> On the vote to abolish the Republic on 10 July 1940: 'The main organ-izer was Laval ... I thought I was rendering a great service to the

country . . . I totally lack experience, I was encouraged by the parliamentarians themselves, and not for a second did I think I was participating in an illegal situation.'

On the armistice: 'What else could I have done? If I had not asked for the armistice France would have suffered the fate of Poland.'

On his message of 6 November 1941 to a leader of the ultracollaborationist Legion of French Volunteers against Bolshevism (LVF), that it embodied 'part of our military honour': 'I never played a role in the recruitment of the anti-bolshevik legion . . . I saw the message, but it was not written by me and someone must have got my signature on some pretext or even forged it.'

On a telegram to General Dentz dated 15 May 1941 supporting Franco-German negotiations in Syria as a sign of our 'desire to collaborate in the new order': 'I don't understand; I am flabbergasted; I have no memory of this telegram.'

On his decision to remain on French soil after November 1942: 'I was always hypnotized by this gift of my person that I had made to France which linked me to French soil.'[4]

These answers did not promise a revealing trial.

When Bouchardon returned on 11 May for a second session, Pétain refused to speak to him without a lawyer present. He must have realized how disastrous the previous session had been. In fact, he had now found a lawyer, Fernand Payen, but he was waiting for him to start.[5] Payen, in the meantime, secured the assistance of a younger colleague, Jacques Isorni, to help on the case. The main actors of the drama were now assembled.

THE PROSECUTORS

Pierre Bouchardon had a long experience of treason trials.[6] Recruited in 1917 to serve as *juge d'instruction* on a special military tribunal dealing with treason cases, he had rapidly acquired a fearsome reputation. This was a moment in the war marked by a feverish obsession with spies. He had prepared the case against the 'exotic' dancer Mata Hari, who was found guilty of spying and shot in October 1917.

Another one of his wartime cases, a shady adventurer known as Bolo Pacha, also ended in execution. One person who came up against Bouchardon in the war remembered how during interrogations his 'two eyes never quite looked directly at you and shined with a kind of sinister glint'; another described him as the 'sadist' of the *instruction* procedure.[7] This was also the view of Maurice Garçon in 1918, himself just starting his own legal career: 'In the last six months, skulking in his office, he carried out his interrogations with ferocity. Torture is not available to him but apart from that his methods make the blood run cold. He enjoys making people suffer.'[8] Certainly, there is an unseemly relish in Bouchardon's own later description of how he broke down the resistance of Mata Hari, circling menacingly around her during his interrogation as she cried out, 'You are pitiless in the way you torture a poor woman like me.'[9] Nonetheless these cases had turned Bouchardon into such a celebrity that at the end of the war he was featured on the cover of *L'Illustration*, along with Foch and Clemenceau, as one of 'Three Men who saved France'.

Bouchardon revelled in the human comedy of crime and retribution. He was dubbed the 'Balzac of the assizes' when, after 1920, he embarked on a parallel career writing racy popular books about murder trials: *Dumollard the Killer of Maids*, *Vacher the Ripper*, *The Assassination of the Archbishop*, *The Fateful Loves of Angelina*. There was a book on Lacenaire, that master criminal portrayed in *Les Enfants du Paradis*, and another on the execution of Marshal Ney in December 1815. A journalist who admired Bouchardon remembered standing with him on the balcony of the Senate as he pointed, in a kind of exalted trance, to the exact spot where Ney had been executed.[10] Was he imagining a similar fate for Pétain?

Bouchardon had not been the person initially selected to run the *instruction* process for the High Court. But the first choice for the post had been discreetly removed in January 1945 because of what a note to de Gaulle described coyly as some 'imprudent actions of his wife during the occupation'. Bouchardon had not wanted at first to take on the position because he was worried about the possibility of reprisals against his son, who had been deported to Germany for resistance activities.[11] One reason for his appointment was his long experience in matters of treason, but also the fact that, having retired in November 1940, he had never taken the oath of allegiance to Pétain. Still, his own conduct under the Occupation had its murky side. In June 1942, promoting his thirty-fourth crime book, he had given an interview to the collaborationist newspaper *Je Suis Partout*. The issue in which the interview appeared contained articles denouncing Freemasons and Jews, an article by Robert Brasillach celebrating Germany's struggle to save France from Bolshevism, and a cartoon depicting Roosevelt and Churchill as transvestites wearing the star of David and enfolded in the arms of Stalin. Appearing in such a publication was obviously compromising. Bouchardon told his interviewer that he was an 'assiduous reader' and took the opportunity to express his 'contempt for the *cartel des gauches* [France's left-wing government in 1924]' and the Jews ('I know these people, I have had them as clients').[12] Brasillach's lawyer had drawn attention to this article, pointing to it as emblematic of the compromises French magistrates had made during the Occupation.[13]

Jacques Isorni, hardly an impartial witness, offered a vivid description of Bouchardon during the preparation of the Pétain case:

> An old Balzacian, with the appearance and gestures of an eighty-year-old cleric. His impenetrable face emerged from a huge stiff collar. He hobbled as he walked, with a little stoop, holding his hands crossed in front of him over his stomach. He was astonishingly erudite, armed with endless anecdotes that he would recount with great brilliance, but . . . he felt an almost animal-like hatred for Marshal Pétain.[14]

He made a point of never shaking Pétain's hand at the end of the interrogation sessions.

Bouchardon had a long history of working with André Mornet, the public prosecutor (*procureur général*) for the High Court and thus the public face of the prosecution. Their association went back to 1917 when Mornet had been prosecutor in the Mata Hari and Bolo Pacha trials. From that moment the two men shared Bouchardon's obsession with rooting out treason.[15] Years later Mornet remarked of the Mata Hari case, seemingly without remorse, that there was 'absolutely nothing to it' (*pas de quoi fouetter un chat*). She was a sacrificial victim, killed to satisfy a bloodthirsty public. Maurice Garçon found Marnet even more antipathetic than Bouchardon:

He scents blood and charges like a wild boar. He just failed to get the death penalty for Esteva but got it for Dentz. These sentences are perhaps merited but one would like to see him demand them with less joy. He rubs his hands with glee. He is the person needed when it comes to killing. What a vile man.[16]

The private Mornet was a teetotalling vegetarian bachelor, fussy about every plant in his garden and vigilant that his housekeeper not displace a single object in his house. 'Living like an anchorite,' as Bouchardon recalled, 'his wasted body was eaten up by the flame that burned inside him.'[17] Isorni painted a more favourable picture of him than of Bouchardon:

He was helpful and did pass on to me the documents I needed to see. I often chatted to him. A strange old man. Bent double, hair sprouting everywhere, passionate. Not lacking in charm. He lived for courtroom *plaidoiries* and would have pleaded against his own brother. He had no illusions. Once he said to me: 'Treason? Hmm! All that is just a matter of regimes.'[18]

Once Mornet had prepared his case, he was impermeable to new evidence. Mata Hari's lawyer complained that he had not even bothered to ask his client any questions.[19]

Bouchardon and Mornet made an odd couple: one corpulent and dishevelled; the other ascetic and driven. They were vividly described by Garçon on the eve of Pétain's trial:

Mornet has not changed in all the time I have known him. Our first meetings go back to 1915. His hair was then red. Now his beard is white. He is a little stooped but he is still the sturdy fighter he has always been. Fighter? Perhaps one should say sanguinary brute. A friend of Bouchardon whose sadism no longer needs to be recalled, he complemented that necrophiliac monster at the *conseil de guerre*. Not a capital sentence was carried out without one of them accompanying the other. They loved to make people sweat during the *instruction* and the audience, then having obtained the condemnation, they loved seeing blood flow.

Then, once peace had come, they joined that great cemetery the Cour de Cassation [the highest French appeal court where Mornet had been appointed in 1922] ... Sometimes, in the early evening, I would see them, bent forward, leaving the Palais huddled in conversation, presumably recounting their sinister exploits.[20]

Everyone agreed that once in court Mornet was like a man possessed – perhaps all the more so in this instance because his own wartime record was not unblemished. In 1949 he published a book called *Four Years to Erase from our History*, a fantastical reconstituted diary he had allegedly kept under the Occupation. If anyone could have wanted to erase that period, it was Mornet himself.[21] Having reached retirement in 1940 he had not sworn the oath to Pétain, it is true – but this had not stopped him from volunteering to serve on the special court of Riom created by Vichy to try former politicians. Luckily for him, the offer was not accepted. He did, however, serve on the Denaturalization Commission set up in July 1940 to review all grants of French citizenship since the introduction of a generous naturalization law in 1927. This was part of Vichy's objective of weeding out 'aliens' – and most of those targeted were Jews. Mornet carried a lot of baggage.

He started distancing himself from Vichy in good time, and by a combination of happenstance and nifty opportunism ended up as one of the magistrates most associated with the Resistance. He was helped by a stroke of luck. In 1943 a group of resistance lawyers had set up a committee to prepare for the Liberation. When one member was arrested by the Germans, Mornet was brought in to replace him.[22] It was supposedly around this time that he remarked, 'I do not want to die until I have pleaded the case against Marshal Pétain.' In the end he was so successful at cleansing his own reputation that he was appointed to chair the purge commission of the magistrature. He was a powerful and busy man at the Liberation.

The High Court's *Commission d'instruction* started its work preparing the cases in December 1944. Chaired by Bouchardon, it was made up of five magistrates (Mornet among them) and six members of the Assemblée Consultative. The Commission had a massive task on its hands: there were 100 cases to examine with pressure to produce quick results. Mornet and Bouchardon had few scruples of conscience. At one early meeting Mornet reflected: 'One regrets that for Déat, Darnand, Doriot and others, one cannot, as in 1793, declare them outlaws and allow someone just to strike them down.'[23]

The senior lawyer Jacques Charpentier, concerned by the excesses of the *épuration*, warned that the danger of replicating 1793 was to invite the same reaction that had brought down Robespierre, and 'jeopardize the unity of the Liberation'.[24] Mornet was not impressed: 'We need to satisfy public opinion, which wants speedy results,' he told his colleagues. 'We are not historians. In the future it will be their role to carry out careful research, especially regarding the intentions that might have inspired the accused . . . Let us not go too deeply into the archives.'[25]

When Guy Raïssac, a lawyer working for the Commission, expressed his unhappiness about this line, he was slapped down. He felt that Mornet was turning into an 'intransigent Jacobin' with an 'idée fixe' about Pétain.[26] The member of the Commission assigned to deal with the Dentz case expressed similar qualms: 'I am going fast, very fast, as fast as possible. But we are dealing here with a grave matter where the accused risks his life . . . Justice must prevail over questions of opportunism or public opinion.'[27] Mornet slapped him down. 'In a business like this,' he said, 'we just need to get hold of one or two documents which provide the proof.'[28]

In most cases the problem was finding the necessary documentation. In Pétain's, it was the opposite. In addition to sixty crates of archives from Vichy, material flooded in from everywhere. One member of the Commission described boxes piled up to the ceiling and blocking access to desks: 'a Himalaya of official papers which soon made our corridors and offices look like wartime trenches'.[29] To prevent them from drowning under the weight of papers, a team of archivists and palaeographers was drafted from the National Archives.[30] It was said that only one person, an archivist who came to be christened Ariadne, could find their way around this labyrinth.[31]

The chaotic demise of the Vichy regime meant that documents kept surfacing haphazardly. There was the case of a former Vichy officer who presented himself to the authorities in September 1944 with three documents with which Ménétrel had entrusted him as he headed for Germany. The officer had sewn them into the lining of his wife's fur coat. One turned out to be the photograph of a note Pétain had written in August , explaining that he had been compelled to condemn de Gaulle to death in 1940 but had never intended that the sentence be carried out. This was presumably one of Ménétrel's building blocks for the trial he knew would come.[32]

Great excitement was precipitated a few weeks later by the discovery near Vichy of an old wooden trunk labelled 'Etat-Major du Maréchal Pétain'. Once again this could be traced back to Ménétrel. In the summer of 1944 he had confided the trunk to an officer at the Hotel du Parc. It had moved around different locations until finally it surfaced in the kitchen of a local château. On 14 October 1944 it was handed over to the new authorities. The next day, the policemen guarding the precious trunk returned from their lunchtime break to find it had been taken away by three men claiming to be members of the local Resistance. But it reappeared a few hours later, seemingly intact, presumably because the pseudo-resisters had only been looking for money. When the trunk finally made its way to Paris, there was a solemn opening at the Ministry of Justice. The press dubbed this 'Pétain's trunk' (la malle de Pétain) and claimed it held his 'secret archives'.

The idea that the trunk might hold some smoking gun was a fantasy, but its thirty boxes of files did contain interesting material. For example, there was a note from Admiral Darlan to Pétain in July 1941, affirming his desire to continue the policy of collaboration 'decided by you', with Pétain's marginal annotation, 'yes, but not armed collaboration nor handing over of naval and air bases that would not be accepted by public opinion'. Such a document could be read in different ways: to prove that Pétain had supported collaboration; that he had put limits on it; or that he was only prevented from going further by public opinion.[33] After an inventory of the trunk's contents had been made, they were distributed rather haphazardly by Mornet to lawyers working on the case – though some documents only surfaced many years later, in one of his drawers, after he had retired.[34]

The last big discovery, just before the opening of the trial, was of another sixty crates of Pétain-related material that surfaced in a village in Creuse. Later the local resistance committee, sniffing a possible cover-up, complained that their documents had not been used in the trial. On further inspection these turned out to be of no interest:

one box contained a luxury edition of Shakespeare, some children's books, an empty stamp album, and a reproduction of a Matisse painting.[35]

Given the immensity of the task, hard-pressed prosecutors relied heavily on journalistic anti-Pétain polemics published during the war by French exiles in New York, where many brilliant French personalities had gathered. Two articles by the French dramatist Henry Bernstein in *The New York Times* in 1941 caused a great stir; as did the book *The Pétain Affair* published in New York in 1944 by the journalist André Schwob.[36] These were the 'armchair' resisters who so excited the scorn of Simone Weil. Since they had left France immediately after the signing of the armistice and lacked personal experience of the Occupation, they tended to fixate on the 1930s. Their position was summed up by Schwob: 'Pétain was the head of a conspiracy whose aim was to overthrow the Third Republic and replace it with a dictatorship.'[37]

Anti-democratic ideas had certainly been rife in the 1930s among conservatives obsessed with Communism. In some cases this tipped over into active plotting against the Republic. A group of right-wing army officers had formed a network which was on standby to neutralize a Communist coup. Another group of conspirators calling itself the CSAR (Comité Secret d'Action révolutionnaire), founded by the industrialist Eugène Deloncle, carried out terrorist acts intended to destabilize the Republic. When the CSAR was unmasked in 1937, it came to be popularly known in the press as the Cagoule (the 'Hood'), a term that was soon used indiscriminately to describe all of these subversive activities. The author of another anti-Pétain polemic wrote 'Behind the Cagoule lurks Pétain.'

Lurid rumours also circulated about the 'Synarchy', an alleged network of bankers and industrialists plotting to establish a dictatorial regime. One report prepared for the *Instruction* of the Pétain case shows how elaborate these conspiracy theories could become:

> Even if Pétain was not the real Chef of the CSAR he was at least the Chef 'chosen' by the CSAR. The distinction might seem important. In practice it is not because Pétain allowed people to plot to bring him to power, his responsibility is as great as if he had himself conspired to 'take power'.

5. *Franc-Tireur*, 26 July 1945. The first cartoon shows the Marshal wearing the hood of the so-called Cagoulards; in the second he is the 'artisan of Hitler's victory', strangling the Republic while Pierre Laval, *left*, watches him.

The report then veered off into ever more fanciful speculations. Perhaps the Cagoule itself was manipulated by the 'Synarchic Committee of revolutionary action'. In that case neither Deloncle nor Pétain were pulling the strings: 'The members of the CSAR thought they were knowing conspirators; perhaps they were just their lackeys. In that case who are the real leaders??? Will they be unmasked one day???'[38]

The indictment that Mornet drafted for the Pétain trial certainly shows the influence of André Schwob's book. It contained an entire chapter on the pamphlet 'We need Pétain', published in 1935 by Gustave Hervé, a former leftist turned admirer of Mussolini. Schwob's chapter was called 'Gustave Hervé, Pétain's "manager"' – and Hervé's name found its way into Mornet's indictment.

The problem for the prosecution was that Pétain could hardly be held responsible for everything that had been written about him. The evidence linking him to these anti-Republican plotters was tenuously circumstantial. The fact that some *Cagoulards* had ended up in influential positions at Vichy did not prove that Pétain had plotted with them before 1940 to take power. There were in fact also others with de Gaulle in London.

One figure who excited the prosecution's interest was Raphaël

Alibert, a right-wing jurist connected to anti-Republican circles. Pétain had met Alibert in the mid-1930s and he had played an important role in the early days of the Vichy regime as Minister of Justice before he fell out of favour in January 1941. An actor in, and then a victim of, the many intrigues punctuating the history of the regime, Alibert was an unstable mythomaniac with many scores to settle. He emerged as the possible missing link connecting Pétain to plots against the Republic.

Bouchardon could not believe his luck when, just before Pétain's return, he was handed an explosive document by the former resister and now minister Alexandre Parodi. This was a note written by Parodi's friend Jean Rist, an engineer who had been in the Resistance, reporting some words of Alibert in 1942:

> We hoped, in joining the Cagoule, to do in France what Franco succeeded in doing in Spain. Marshal Pétain in his period [as ambassador] in Spain used Franco as an intermediary with Hitler who was favourable to our projects, sent us funds and promised military help . . . Those in the plot included Pétain, Darlan and others . . . When war broke out and the army was defeated we asked for an armistice on the terms that had been agreed with Hitler.

Rist had been told all this by a certain 'N', who had had a conversation with Alibert. Was this the smoking gun that proved Pétain had been involved in a pre-war plot? Since Rist had been killed in 1944, Bouchardon interviewed his father, a distinguished economist, who confirmed that his son had indeed written the note. In the indictment he prepared just before Pétain's return, Mornet brandished this 'decisive document' as irrefutable evidence of Pétain's complicity in a plot. On further investigation, things turned out to be more complicated.

Had the trial been conducted *in absentia*, this 'decisive' document would never have been scrutinized. But Pétain's defence lawyers immediately spotted the flaws and drafted a note protesting that such shaky evidence should be allowed to find its way into the indictment.[39] The mysterious 'N' appeared to have been Rist's boss, the industrialist Louis Vergnaud. He too was interviewed by Bouchardon and confirmed that he had reported these comments to Rist but only as rumours – not something he had heard from Alibert, whom he had not seen since 1936. Vergnaud wondered whether he was really the mysterious 'N' and added for good measure that Jean Rist was a 'hothead' (*'exalté'*). Since Rist junior was dead and Alibert had fled to Spain, the matter could not be pursued.[40] Mornet's *supplément* to the original indictment had to concede that it had not been possible to identify the person designated as 'N' but insisted that the 'honourable reputation of M. Jean Rist remained a guarantee of the authenticity of the remarks he had reported'. But that the *'exalté'* Rist had in good faith reported something he had heard did not make it true. Once Pétain had a defence team, the prosecution would need to be less slapdash.

THE DEFENCE

Fernand Payen, the most senior member of Pétain's defence team, was a well-known civil lawyer with little penal experience. He had been the *batônnier*, or head of the Bar, in 1929 and was president of the professional association of *avocats* (ANA) under the Occupation. In this capacity he had met Pétain in 1941, after which he wrote enthusiastically in the Bulletin of the ANA about his 'admirable physical form and mental agility'. On another occasion he had written how 'parliamentarianism, economic liberalism, the rights of man, the sovereignty of the individual' were at the 'origins of our decadence'.[41] So Payen was certainly not among those lawyers involved in the Resistance. But at the Liberation he had tried to straddle both sides by publishing a pamphlet calling for national reconciliation.[42]

Even in the fusty world of the Paris Bar, Payen was a throwback to another era – fussy, pernickety, and dressed with a formality that would not have been out of place a century earlier. His main obsession was to be elected to the Académie Française, which usually had one seat for a celebrity lawyer. Maurice Garçon, on a similar quest, recounts several comical episodes when, lobbying for his own candidature, he would stumble across Payen on the same mission. Each was assured of the unwavering support of the academician they were visiting. (As the first task of a newly elected academician was to give a eulogy to the previous incumbent of the chair to which they had been elected, this would have caused problems since the vacant chair was that of Louis Bertrand, who had in 1936 written an admiring biography of Hitler and had even once raised his arm in a Heil Hitler salute at a meeting of the Académie.)[43] Payen hoped the celebrity he would acquire in defending Pétain might reinforce his candidature to this augustly conservative body. This ambition also influenced his approach to the case. He planned to avoid an outright defence of Vichy and instead to emphasize the Marshal's age and diminished faculties. Appealing for pity for a fallen hero was the most consensual line to take.

Payen's cautious tactics brought him into conflict with his impetuous young colleague. Over the years, Jacques Isorni became so identified with his thirty-year crusade to rehabilitate Pétain's reputation that it is difficult to disentangle fantasy from fact in his many tellings of his story. In the earliest version, the request to join Pétain's defence team had been a (welcome) surprise. In a later version, we are told that the moment he heard Pétain was to be tried, he had had a presentiment that it would be his destiny to defend him.[44] Whatever the truth, among these weary old men approaching the end of their careers – Mornet, Bouchardon, Payen – the talented thirty-four-year-old Isorni stood out as young and ambitious, energetic and eager.[45]

Isorni's lifelong identification with Pétain marked him out as a figure of the extreme right. To counter this image, when writing his memoirs in the 1980s, he dwelt on features of his background that marked him out as a non-conformist outsider. His mother, from a Parisian Catholic bourgeois background, had shocked her family by becoming an ardent Republican. Family legend had it that she had broken with her fiancé after seeing his signature on an anti-Dreyfus petition. Sacrificing love for justice, she married instead an immigrant of Italian origin, a commercial artist specializing in supplying fashion drawings to department stores. Isorni remembered being teased at school, where he was called 'macaroni' because of his Italian origins. In his telling, Isorni was thus the son of an immigrant and of an ardent Republican. But his father was extremely conservative, an admirer of the monarchist polemicist Charles Maurras, the leader of the ultra-right Action Française movement. The son followed in the same tradition. As a schoolboy, he joined Action Française, and by the time he graduated from university he was writing regular columns for right-wing student papers.

When he qualified for the Bar in 1931, Isorni was the youngest lawyer in France. He entered the competition for young lawyers at the Paris Bar – an exercise in oratory that conferred the winner with the title *'Secrétaire de la Conférence du Stage'* – and won on his second attempt. The prestige of this success remained with him forever. When choosing the twelve lecturers the following year, he and his colleagues selected five Jews – an act of provocation when anti-semitism was rife at the Paris Bar, and an early sign of his contrarian personality. The advent of the Vichy regime might have terminated his career since a law passed in September 1940 excluded those of foreign parentage from practising law, but Isorni managed to secure an exemption. He seemingly bore no grudge against a regime that made such discriminations. He boasts in his memoirs of defending Communist resisters in the Vichy courts and it is true that he had a non-conformist streak and a romantic sympathy with persecuted underdogs. In his book, *Je suis avocat*, written in 1951, he outlined his conception of the lawyer's role:

> To remain a free man who neither asks nor owes anything to any person . . . Independence, too! Never hoping for anything from power, not even a decoration. Attack power if it deserves it, speak to it from on high, whether or not it lends an ear, and, once back under one's tent, know that power regrets having let us speak.[46]

What made the moment of the Liberation perfect for Isorni was that his sympathy for the persecuted coincided with his politics: he now shared the beliefs of the underdogs. He first gained notoriety as Robert Brasillach's defence lawyer. Brasillach was almost certainly a lost cause, but the case appealed to Isorni's taste for the grand gesture. During many conversations with Brasillach, he came to identify emotionally with the young writer, who was only two years his senior. Tactically, the most effective defence of Brasillach might have been to argue that, however regrettable his writings, they had had no impact on the world. But this approach did not satisfy Isorni's sense of drama. Instead, he argued that Brasillach was a great writer who would be a loss to French letters. In *Je suis avocat* he wrote:

If the man exists who is ready to sacrifice his ideas in the hopes of saving himself, there also exists the man who refuses to betray his ideas, who persists in seeing in these ideas the justification for his actions. The task of defence is simpler in the first case, although it lacks grandeur.[47]

According to one commentator, Isorni wanted a 'beautiful trial'.[48]

The Brasillach trial crystallized Isorni's sympathy with the values of the Vichy regime into something more passionately personal; he later joked that he had become a collaborator retrospectively in 1945. From this moment Isorni also developed a violent hatred for de Gaulle. For years afterwards, he would dwell on the visit he had paid to de Gaulle on 3 February 1945 to deliver the clemency petition for Brasillach:

> He picked up the cigar that he had started to smoke and blew the smoke towards me. I asked myself if this was really the moment to be smoking cigars. There was perhaps a metre between us – perhaps a bit more. His eyes set closely together seemed to be fixed on something in the distance – and I never succeeded in catching his gaze . . . In a meeting between two men where the life of someone is at stake, it takes a great strength of will to continue when one only meets silence.[49]

No pardon was forthcoming. Three days later, Isorni accompanied the thirty-five-year-old Brasillach in the prison van that took him to Montrouge, and stayed to witness his execution by firing squad. Isorni wrote later: 'from that moment his death has governed my life'.

It is not clear why Payen asked Isorni to assist him on the case, but he soon regretted it.[50] His junior partner had no intention of being confined to an accessory role. On 16 May the two men arrived at Montrouge for Pétain's second interrogation. Isorni had not been at Montrouge since Brasillach's execution; it was his first ever meeting with Pétain. This second interrogation was as disastrous as the first. To most of Bouchardon's questions, Pétain either answered that he could not remember or he blamed Laval. In one, he confused a meeting with Hermann Göring in Belgrade in 1934 with another in December 1941. The session ended with Pétain replying to a question about the scuttling of the French fleet in 1942: 'I would ask if I can delay my response; I am feeling very tired.'[51] Whenever Pétain gave a particularly unconvincing answer, Payen would kick Isorni under the table or wink with a mixture of pity and satisfaction. This was Pétain as he needed him for the case he was preparing. Afterwards he told Isorni that Pétain was 'completely gaga'.[52]

Early the next morning, without consulting Payen, Isorni cycled across Paris to Montrouge to see Pétain alone. He had no car and taxis, still in short supply, were only authorized for patients, doctors and midwives.[53] He was disconcerted that Pétain seemed more interested in talking about the garden of his villa near Antibes than his impending trial.[54] Isorni tried to instil a sense of purpose in his elderly client while also appealing to his vanity:

> What must you do? Remain who you are! You must remember that you are a Marshal of France, Head of State. That is what you must become, you must accept no infringements of your dignity. Have you forgotten the importance of the trial of Joan of Arc? The captivity of the Emperor at St Helena? The trial of Louis XVI? Millions of French are thinking of you. For them you are a symbol and an idea . . . Your attitude must be in accordance with the faith you inspired. Do not behave like a gardener accused of having stolen some vegetables.[55]

As Isorni took his leave, he looked Pétain in the eye and declared solemnly, 'I make you the gift of my person.' He reflected later, 'I had the feeling that I had given him back the grandeur of his role and of his person.'[56]

All this was probably true, but the relationship between the two men was complicated. Isorni was genuinely awed by Pétain, but he was also a seductive and manipulative personality who intuitively sensed Pétain's vulnerability. Each was up to a point making use of the other. Isorni had a great romantic cause – on the day he heard he was to defend Pétain he remarked, 'I have defended André Chénier [a poet executed during the revolution in 1794] and now I am going to defend Louis XVI.'[57]

For his part, Pétain grasped that he had encountered someone committed to his defence with every fibre of his being. About Payen's strategy of pleading senility, Isorni commented: 'It was perhaps juridically more effective. But there is a conflict between juridical opportunism and historical truth.' Isorni was thinking of History – Pétain's place in it, but also his own.[58]

A pattern now emerged. While the two lawyers attended the inter-rogations together, Isorni and Pétain formed a bond behind Payen's back. Isorni regularly visited Montrouge on his own, telling Pétain he felt a bit like a lover visiting his mistress behind her husband's back. On one occasion he even acted as a go-between, passing on a letter from one of Pétain's former lovers, an old lady dressed in black who had presented herself at his office. This was Jacqueline de Castex, known as 'Mella', yet another woman to whom Pétain had apparently proposed marriage in 1920. When Isorni told Pétain he had seen 'Mella', the Marshal flushed 'like a sixteen-year-old' and asked, 'Does she think I am a traitor?' The Maréchale firmly put an end to the con-veying of any more messages.

On one occasion, when Payen arrived unexpectedly to find them together, Isorni hastily concocted an explanation which Pétain quick-wittedly backed up. Payen was not taken in. The tensions were obvious to Pétain's guard, Joseph Simon, who noted in his diary that the two lawyers visibly 'mistrusted each other'. Isorni told Simon on one occasion: 'Payen is old and doddery (*gateux*), jealous, even more doddery than the Marshal, and he understands nothing about polit-ics.' In turn, Simon told Isorni that Pétain had told him, 'Payen appals me, he understands nothing', and that he had described Isorni as his 'saviour' (*messie*).[59]

On 11 June a third lawyer joined the defence team. Payen and Isorni each hoped to find an ally in the new arrival. Isorni's candidate had been rejected by Payen who imposed his own, Jean Lemaire. At forty-one, Lemaire lay in age between his two colleagues. Living in a grand *hôtel* in the Marais, he was a jovial *bon vivant*, closer in tem-perament to Isorni than to Payen. The two men struck up an immediate rapport. Since Lemaire was also the owner of a car, Isorni no longer had to make the long bicycle journey to Montrouge for his meetings with Pétain. Now the interrogations could begin in earnest.

6

Interrogating the Prisoner

The defence lawyers' first task was to erase any record of the disastrous interrogation on 8 May. They drafted a note in Pétain's name to say that he had been emotionally disturbed by the sound of sirens celebrating victory outside his prison. Eight more interrogations took place over the next month, the last on 19 June. Sometimes Bouchardon was joined by another magistrate, Pierre Béteille, who was less unfriendly to Pétain, even shaking his hand. On two occasions all fourteen members of the Commission de l'Instruction arrived together. Those two hearings were especially confusing for Pétain, who was flanked by his two lawyers and subjected to a barrage of questions from all sides.

To avoid his tying himself up in knots or giving inappropriate answers, Pétain's lawyers encouraged him, when in difficulty, to reply that he would respond with a written note. In the end eleven such notes, usually drafted by Isorni, were presented.[1] Where Pétain did answer himself, his responses, as in the first interrogation, were characterized by a mixture of evasiveness or forgetfulness, self-delusion, blame-shifting or mendacity, and self-pity, as in the following examples.

Evasiveness or forgetfulness:

Did I write to Maurras? It is possible but I have no memory of it.

Self-delusion:

I always resisted the Germans. So I could not but be favourable to the Resistance. The Resistance is the sign of the vitality of a people. But as Head of State I could not approve it publicly in the presence of the Occupier. I always made a distinction between those resisting the Germans and those who used this as pretext for crimes.

Blame-shifting or mendacity: when asked about Laval's notorious speech of 22 June 1942, expressing his wish for a German victory, Pétain replied:

> I was not in agreement with him ... It is clear I should have made an opposite declaration. But I could only have done that by resigning. But at the head of a nation under enemy occupation, I had to give apparent satisfaction to the Germans while the Allies prepared victory. M. Laval having been imposed on me by the Germans, I used him to appease them, which allowed me to hide the real orientation of my policy.

The most striking feature of the interrogations was the questioners' obsession with Pétain's alleged role in a 'Cagoulard' plot against the Republic before 1940. Half of the questions focused on this issue, which genuinely perplexed Pétain. On 22 May he was asked about his relations with individuals alleged to have been associated with the Cagoule:

> Dr Martin?

> The Head of State does not get involved in details of this kind. I do not know this Dr Martin ... The link that you are making between all these people and me is an insult and this accusation is satanic.

> Méténier?

> I have never heard the name.

> Gabriel Jeantet?

> I don't know M. G. Jeantet ... I have already told you that I knew nothing about the Cagoule.

> Alibert?

> Very unstable and I regret that I made him a Minister.

On 1 June the interrogators came back to this issue yet again:

> QUESTION: 'You claim to know nothing about the Cagoule and the Synarchy. So how is it that, as soon as you came to power, you appointed men from the Synarchy and the Cagoule to key positions?'

PÉTAIN: 'If someone can tell me exactly what the Synarchy is, I would be grateful . . . And the Cagoule? What exactly was it, I have no idea. That name was usually mentioned ironically.'[2]

In a similar vein, there were many questions about Pétain's period as ambassador in Spain between January 1939 and May 1940. According to the conspiracy theory, this was the moment when he started plotting from the sidelines. The magistrates were especially intrigued by a letter from Pétain to General Alphonse Georges in this period: 'My dear Georges, I have just spent three days in Paris incognito.' Was this 'incognito' visit the smoking gun that proved a plot? Pétain replied: 'I do remember coming to France, but I cannot remember the precise dates. I should add that during my period in Spain I never came incognito to France and that my stays were of short duration.'[3]

In fact, he had used the term 'incognito', but there was probably nothing sinister about it – just the desire not to cause offence if Georges came to hear about the visit.[4] It is hardly surprising that Pétain could not recall such minute details. Perhaps he preferred his interrogators not to know that one destination during his Paris visits was the famous brothel One-Two-Two.[5]

Since Pétain would remain mostly silent during his actual trial, these interrogations, however frustrating, offer our only glimpse into his real views. On occasion there flickers a momentary recognition that he was not entirely blameless:

I am of course the person who picked my advisers. But no one ever spoke to me of matters that I might find disagreeable. That is a fault for one should have people around one who have the right to say anything.[6]

What emerges overall is Pétain's personalized, even petulant, conception of politics. Isorni witnessed this on his first meeting, and later recalled how Pétain had launched into a diatribe against de Gaulle: 'If he was a prisoner, he said, it came from de Gaulle's jealousy towards him since he was first a young officer at Arras under his command. He underlined also the important role he had played in the writing of de Gaulle's books.'[7]

Quite apart from the distorted memory of their quarrel, this reduced the tragic history of France over the previous four years to its most trivial elements. Bouchardon, not the most objective witness, commented to another lawyer: 'Pétain is brutally dismissive when it comes to blaming his collaborators ... The old man has no heart.'[8] He certainly had a black sense of humour. When Isorni announced the death from cancer of Joseph Barthélemy, who had been his Minister of Justice, Pétain joked: 'Well, well ... We could make him a scapegoat. He is already dead, after all.'[9]

In the notes they drafted for him, Pétain's lawyers, especially Isorni, sketched out their case. This was not easy because Isorni, like most of the French, knew little of the true history of his country between 1940 and 1944, and Pétain offered little assistance in the crafting of a plausible narrative. On one occasion, Isorni asked Pétain about his declaration – unhelpful for the defence – that French workers drafted to German factories were working in the interests of France. As Isorni tells the story, 'the text, determined by overriding political considerations, appeared to him, two years later, inexplicable'. All he could say was: 'You will have to rack your brains [tirebouchonner].'[10]

Pétain was in remarkable physical shape for a man of eighty-nine, but his mental state was difficult to judge. Jacques Charpentier, who had visited him in Montrouge to discuss the choice of lawyers, told Isorni: 'I have the impression of a magnificent façade with nothing behind it.'[11] At Vichy it was often said that Pétain was only capable of concentrating for two hours a day. In the Montrouge prison a doctor monitored his health and provided updates for the government. On 23 May he reported:

> On some days I find the Marshal buried in his papers, reading them endlessly again and again, and I am unable to get a single word out of him. On other occasions he mixes up dates, does not remember recent events, but can summon to mind others without difficulty.
>
> After the visit of his lawyers or after the interrogation he is prostrate with exhaustion. Having been instructed to bring the Marshal to his trial in good physical and moral shape, I think that his wife's presence at his side is indispensable. She helps him order his papers, remember dates, boosts his morale, and without her I fear that he would not be in a fit state to get through the interrogations and support the pressure of

the trial . . . Her absence would definitely have considerable and irreparable consequences on his fragile psychological equilibrium which does, however, remain satisfactory for his age.[12]

Isorni contested any suggestion that the Marshal was senile, insisting that 'this cunning peasant of the Nord had the suppleness of an Italian diplomat'.[13] But his notes on their meetings tell a different story. On 24 May he wrote: 'Pétain is very tired. I have some difficulties in making him understand my arguments. Today he has serious memory lapses, and I need to repeat the same thing several times.' When a week later Isorni told Pétain that those testifying against him would include former Third Republic politicians like Léon Blum and Paul Reynaud, his reaction was: 'But what have they got against me? What did I ever do to them?' When Isorni reminded him that he had thrown them into prison, 'he seemed surprised and had no memory of it'.

Pétain took refuge in memories that were not much use to his defence. He was especially proud of his 'Messages' to the French people during the Occupation. Often, at the end of the day, he would read one of these to his lawyers, not noticing, as Isorni comments, that 'in the muggy heat of summer it would end by sending us to sleep'. They were often treated to a speech of March 1941 presenting his ideas on labour reform. When he had finished Pétain would purr smugly: 'Not a word too many.'[14]

In constructing his defence, Isorni was left to his own devices to invent the Marshal he needed for history. Later he said: 'I made him in his prison, or rather I remade him.'[15] He received some help from Guy Raïssac, a lawyer on Mornet's team who was unhappy about the prosecution's conduct of the trial. Raïssac passed some documents on to the defence. Isorni also gathered the Pétainist faithful, some of whom had known Pétain since the Great War. They would meet every Sunday at the house of a lawyer in the Rue Gay-Lussac to discuss the case. As Isorni puts it, these meetings 'allowed us to relive, with those who had been present, events we only knew through texts, and minutes and reports'.[16] Isorni also consulted some Vichy insiders who could not attend the Sunday gatherings because they were in prison awaiting their own trials.

One surprising absence among these names was Ménétrel, who had almost never left Pétain's side until being forcibly separated from him at Sigmaringen. Repatriated to France from Germany a few weeks after Pétain, he had immediately been sent to the prison of Fresnes. Ménétrel, who had no illusions about Pétain's ruthless capacity for ingratitude, worried in prison that he might be made into a scapegoat. The prison bush telegraph was effective, and when it became clear that this was not going to happen, he offered his services to the defence despite his lawyer warning that this might jeopardize his own case. But Isorni did not take up the offer. The rivalries among former Vichy courtiers still burned intensely, and Isorni may have been warned off Ménétrel by others who had resented his influence over Pétain. Perhaps he was worried that Ménétrel might not necessarily be a helpful witness given the document he had written at Sigmaringen saying that 'the policy of the Marshal is not easy to defend' – although Ménétrel had only been trying to save the Marshal from himself.[17]

THE MYSTERIOUS PROFESSOR ROUGIER

A promising line of defence was suggested by rumours that there had been contacts, even a secret 'agreement', between the British and Vichy – Pétain's alleged 'double jeu [double game]'. Unfortunately, Isorni reported, Pétain 'had on this particular point a memory lapse which meant that he could be of no help to me'.[18]

The main source of the rumours was Louis Rougier, a professor of philosophy at the University of Besançon. One of Rougier's areas of interest was liberalism, and like many liberals in the interwar years he worried about the consequences of mass democracy. In 1938 he had organized in Paris a colloquium on liberalism which furnished him with good contacts in Britain and America. After the armistice Rougier became obsessed with the consequences of the economic blockade which the British had imposed on Vichy France. He believed that even if Germany lost the war, the French people might never recover from the privations imposed on them. In the autumn of 1940 he proposed himself to the Vichy government as an interlocutor with the British thanks to his academic contacts. This self-important and meddling provincial academic saw a chance to make History.

Rougier was received in person by Pétain, who authorized him to go to London. He arrived on 22 October 1940 and met Lord Halifax, the Foreign Secretary. By an extraordinary stroke of fate, Rougier was still in London on 24 October, the day Pétain met Hitler at Montoire. The Montoire meeting caused alarm in Whitehall. Was Vichy moving towards a military alliance with Germany? Was there a risk that the Germans might get access to French bases in North Africa? To seek reassurances Churchill agreed to meet Rougier on 25 October. Rougier, as startled by the events of Montoire as everyone else, insisted that Laval's support for collaboration was not widely shared – though in truth he had no inside knowledge of any kind.

After returning to France to report on his conversations, Rougier made his way to New York at the end of the year. No more might have been heard of his lightning London visit except that, alienated by the anti-Pétainism of many French exiles in New York, he started making increasingly wild claims about the importance of his 'mission'. The American press reported his claims in 1943 but never produced any evidence; the British Embassy in Washington, describing Rougier as a 'thoroughly mischievous' character, would have nothing to do with him. All this increased Rougier's bitterness.[19] His story resurfaced in January 1945 during the *instruction* interrogations for the trial of Pierre-Etienne Flandin, who had served briefly as prime minister at Vichy. Then in March 1945 Rougier published a book with the grandiloquent title *The Pétain–Churchill Agreements: History of a Secret Mission*, which contained photographs of documents allegedly proving his case.[20]

All this was enough for Isorni to draft a short but bold note for Pétain on 8 June: 'It is correct that I had a treaty negotiated, which had to remain secret, with Monsieur Winston Churchill. This treaty [the word 'treaty' went further than Rougier himself had dared], on which negotiations started the same day as Montoire – this rapprochement reveals the real meaning of Montoire and inspired my policy even when the English seemed to be moving away from it.' When asked by his interrogators to comment further, Pétain replied mysteriously that he could not say more unless authorized by the

British government. This was an ingenious line, suggested by Isorni, which claimed the moral high ground while side-stepping the truth that Pétain had no recollection of Rougier.[21]

When the Foreign Office advised that it was no longer possible to ignore Rougier's claims, Churchill, who had no more recollection of Rougier than Pétain did, took a more robust line. 'We need not get excited about it,' he said. 'Naturally it was our policy to get whatever we could out of Vichy.'[22] British silence became increasingly unsustainable as Rougier's allegations got front-page headlines in *The New York Times*. It was also embarrassing to the British for it to be suggested that there had been secret contacts with Vichy behind de Gaulle's back. Rougier claimed that during his London visit the British had forbidden

6. Pétain's handwritten note claiming to have negotiated a 'secret treaty' with Churchill in October 1940.

him from seeing de Gaulle. He also wrote personally to de Gaulle in March 1945 enclosing documents to show that while Laval might have been a collaborator, Pétain was not.[23] De Gaulle's advisers did some detective work and reported that there was nothing to worry about, but the French Embassy in London was keen that the British reply to Rougier.[24] The British Embassy, which had so far not sent any observers to the purge trials, reported to London that it would do so for Pétain: 'The trial will clearly be an historical event of great importance of which you ought to have an eyewitness account.'[25] The Foreign Office set about drafting an official response to Rougier in time for the trial.

SMOKING GUNS?

The last interrogation on 19 June 1945 was short. Pétain was quizzed about two recently discovered documents which the prosecution hoped might nail the claim of treason ('collusion with the enemy'). Both would play a key role in the trial. The first was a letter from Pétain to Ribbentrop on 18 December 1943 stating that 'modifications of laws will be submitted before publication to the occupation authorities'. The context of this letter was that abortive attempt by Pétain's advisers to reassert his power at the end of 1943. Ribbentrop had responded with a furious missive to Pétain containing a whole series of demands and grievances. Pétain had capitulated to them in the letter with which he was now confronted.

His response to his interrogators, fuller than many other answers, was that he was not sure if the letter had been sent but that, if it had been, it was a 'purely formal concession' since he would never have submitted legislation for German approval. This was an absurd claim since no French law could be published without prior submission to the Germans – as Pétain himself partially admitted in the next sentence stating that he was sometimes 'forced under their pressure to take certain legislative measures'.[26]

The second document related to an unsuccessful Anglo-Canadian landing at Dieppe on 18 August 1942 – a trial run for D-Day – easily repulsed by the Germans. Two days later the press of the Occupied Zone published a communiqué signed by Pétain and Laval congratulating the

Germans for their success in defending France's borders. In a previous interrogation, Pétain had blamed this on Laval, as usual when confronted by a tricky piece of evidence. But even more incriminating than this communiqué, which could be explained away as an empty gesture – embarrassing but hardly treasonous – was a new document that had surfaced a few days earlier in papers seized from Brinon. This was a telegram to Hitler on the same date:

> In light of the recent British aggression on our soil, I propose to envisage the participation of France in her own defence. I am ready to examine the details if you accept the principle. Please consider this intervention as the sincere expression of my desire that France should contribute to the protection [*sauvegarde*] of Europe.[27]

If this meant the French were offering to fight with Germans to defend French soil, it was a clear and dangerous step towards military collaboration. The document was preceded by the words: 'please pass to M. de Grosville, attaché of M. Benoist-Méchin'. Benoist-Méchin was a Vichy representative in Paris, committed to extreme collaboration but distrusted by Pétain.

There were several oddities about this document. Why was Pétain not communicating with the German Embassy through the usual channels? Why use an obscure press attaché – Grosville – and the controversial Benoist-Méchin? Had the document ever been communicated to the Germans? Did it even come from Pétain, since it was signed not as 'Philippe Pétain', as was usually the case, but just ended with the words 'signed Pétain'?

So obsessed were the investigators with this document that police were dispatched to interview the two postal functionaries responsible for sending telegrams from Vichy to Paris. They confirmed that the original of the telegram had been on Pétain's official notepaper but, unfamiliar with his writing, they could not be sure whether he had signed it. The investigators also interviewed Brinon's *chef de cabinet*, his secretary (and mistress) Simone Mitre, and a typist in his office. Finally, they even tracked down the mysterious Grosville who, under a new name, was driving trucks for the Americans in Marseilles. Grosville told them he had never heard of the telegram, and that having never had contacts with the Germans he would not have known whom to pass it on to. Since he was currently being investigated for dealings with the Germans during the Occupation these protestations were unconvincing. But a search of his apartment uncovered nothing. This excursion into a murky collaborationist world redolent of the novels of Patrick Modiano had produced no answers. Would Pétain be able to throw light on the matter?[28]

Presented with the document, Pétain said that he had never ordered the sending of such a telegram, and that the views expressed were diametrically opposed to his own. This did not conclude the matter. More time would be devoted in the trial to this single document than to the fact that in the month it was sent – or not sent – over 11,000 Jewish men, women and children were arrested by French police in the Unoccupied Zone of France for deportation to Auschwitz.

The revised *Acte d'accusation* was ready on 11 July 1945. It opened with Pétain's responsibility for the signing of the armistice on 22 June and for the first three Constitutional Acts promulgated on 11 July 1940, which went 'markedly beyond, even against' the full powers he had been granted on the previous day: 'They were the culmination of a plot prepared a long time before against the Republic, a plot which succeeded thanks to the defeat but whose definitive success was only guaranteed if the defeat was not called into question.' There followed a description of the 'plot': Hervé's propaganda; the Synarchy; the Cagoule; the relations between Pétain and Franco, his 'intermediary with Hitler'. All this was 'incontestable' proof of Pétain's 'collusion with Hitler' before 1940.

The second, shorter section of the *Acte d'accusation* traced Pétain's 'treason' after July 1940: 'not only a humiliating collaboration but the subjection of France to Germany'. The evidence included: contribution to the German war machine; allowing Germans to use French airfields in Syria in 1941; firing on Allied troops in North Africa in November 1942. The third section refuted any attempt to separate Pétain from his government and insisted that he was fully behind the 'abominable racial laws', the 'monstrous creation of the Special Sections'. In consequence, Pétain was accused of:

1. 'Attacking the internal security of the State'.
2. 'Collusion with the enemy in order to favour his own ambition which correlated with those of the enemy'.[29]

These crimes fell respectively under articles 87 and 75 of the Penal Code.

The 'supplement' to the *Instruction*, dated 11 July 1945, contained eleven clauses presenting new pieces of evidence, as well as a partial corrective to the Rist testimony. The prosecution's obsessions had not changed: seven of these new clauses concerned the period before 1940. Of newly discovered documents concerning the period after 1940, the last one mentioned was the infamous Dieppe telegram. The ten weeks since Pétain's return had not radically changed the shape of the indictment that Mornet had already prepared.

While Mornet and Bouchardon were finalizing their case, de Gaulle's Minister of Justice, the jurist and former resister Pierre-Henri Teitgen, told American and British Embassy officials that the prosecution would devote 'comparatively little attention' to the period before November 1942, when the defence might be able to make a case, and more to the period after it, when Pétain's failure to leave the country was impossible to defend.[30] This approach to the trial would certainly have made sense, but it was not the one taken by Mornet. Since de Gaulle firmly believed that Pétain's original sin was the signing of the armistice, it may be that Mornet felt obliged to take account of his view. Whatever the reason, Mornet's task would have been easier if he had adopted Teitgen's approach.

Mornet fell ill at the end of June, which delayed the opening of the trial. One final matter remained to be resolved: where was it to be held? There was a widespread feeling that it required a grander setting than a normal courtroom, and one able to accommodate a larger audience. Bazaine had been tried in the sumptuous surroundings of the Palais de Luxembourg, seat of the French Senate, and Louis XVI in the National Convention. The problem was that the Assemblée Consultative was currently housed in the Palais de Luxembourg. This would have meant deferring the trial until the summer recess. Another possibility was Versailles, but it was judged to be too far from Paris. The government, which wanted to avoid accusations of mounting a political trial, opted instead for the courtroom that had been used already for the trials of Esteva and Dentz: the Première Chambre de la Cour d'Appel de Paris, situated at the heart of Paris in the Palais de Justice. This venue seemed to guarantee juridical seriousness. It was also rumoured to be Mornet's preference because he was worried that his voice would not carry in a larger space.

Most of the press opposed the decision. So did members of the Commission d'Instruction, who wrote to de Gaulle formally on 11 July proposing the trial take place in the Palais de Luxembourg:

> One of the most important trials in our history, an occasion when twenty years of French history is to be discussed, is going to take place in front of 200 people, in a room packed with journalists and police where not only will there be no room for the world's press, but where members of the diplomatic corps, parliamentarians, representatives of workers and employers organizations, prisoners, and deportees will be excluded . . . We deplore your choice.[31]

Just before the trial was due to open, speakers in the Assemblée Consultative took the same line. One proclaimed:

> This is about establishing in the eyes of the world that Pétain does not incarnate either France or France's traditions. If Pétain is judged to be France, we would be reduced humbly to solicit the forgiveness of humanity in the name of the French people . . . But we do not have to demand forgiveness from anyone for we know well that Pétain was not France. On the contrary he is the man who, for the sake of our enemy, crucified the people of France.[32]

Although the government ignored these pleas, it did accept another demand emanating from the Assemblée to publish a full stenographic record of the trial proceedings in the *Journal officiel* (the French *Hansard* or Congressional Record). Few members of the general public were able to attend the trial, and places for journalists were restricted by space constraints, but everyone wishing to do so would have a chance to read every word of the debates.

PART TWO

In the Courtroom

PETAIN-BAZAINE

U NE salle étroite, mesquine, si resserrée que les témoins accusent Pétain à moins d'un mètre du vieux traître impassible. Un public de trublions, d'avocats fascistes, de jolies femmes aux chapeaux extravagants, de journalistes, de policiers.

Ceux qui témoignent, ce sont les naufrageurs des dernières heures de la troisième République : Reynaud, Daladier, Lebrun.

Ceux qui accusent, ce sont des hommes au passé trouble, aux mains salies du sang des fils du peuple français.

Quand passera-t-il dans cette atmosphère lourde un souffle d'air pur ?
Quand entendra-t-on les véritables accusateurs, les véritables victimes ?

Quand verra-t-on les femmes, les enfants des fusillés, des déportés, venir témoigner du martyre des disparus ? Quand le vrai peuple français pourra-t-il venir retracer son terrible calvaire et dénombrer les blessures saignantes qu'il doit au vieux bandit ?

D'après les statistiques officielles, 94 % des déportés politiques, 99 % des déportés « raciaux » ne reviendront pas. N'est-ce pas là un beau résultat de la politique de collaboration ?

L'homme qui se prélasse encore dans son uniforme de maréchal de France est un des plus grands assassins que l'Histoire ait connus.

Une caricature, ces jours-ci, montrait la République, en bonnet phrygien, se présentant à la porte du Palais de Justice ; la garde, dédaigneux, lui disait : « Vous avez votre carte ? »

Oui, au procès Pétain, il ne manque qu'un seul témoin : la France.

Le président Mongibeaux.

Le procureur général Mornet

Le *Figaro* du 24-7-45 : Jean Schlumberger écrit : « Puisque la mort n'a pas accordé à l'homme qui va être jugé la grâce de disparaître dans la débâcle du régime qu'il a dirigé, puisque chaque jour on fusille, on envoie au bagne des coupables qui n'ont fait qu'obéir à ses ordres ou mettre à profit ses capitulations, la nation ne pouvait plus longtemps accepter l'offensant dilogisme qu'il y a à la frapper les exécutants sans chercher la faute chez celui qui les a couverts de son autorité. »

Le 26-7-45, François Mauriac insiste sur le fait que : « le double jeu ici n'excuse rien, car il n'existe pas de marchandage sans complicité. »

Franc-Tireur du 20-7-45 : Albert Bayet a trouvé la juste formule : « *Pétain premier traître de France.* »

Le 26-7-45, parlant de Reynaud, Daladier et Lebrun, Georges Altman écrit : « Ils n'ont pas su vouloir, et l'Histoire ne leur pardonne pas. »

Combat, du 24-7-45 : « Si la France commence à tolérer l'intolérance, à refaire constamment la part du feu, c'est qu'elle n'est pas victorieuse, mais qu'elle en demeure battue et qu'elle a toutes les mines, toute la veulerie du chien qui vient de l'être.

«...ce procès dépasse la personne de Pétain, le faire sérieusement, c'est le faire jusqu'au bout. »

La Voix de Paris, 25-7-45, de Pierre Favreau : « Le sang de nos morts plane sur ce procès. D'abord le sang des F. F. I. et des morts de la Résistance et aussi celui de tous les pauvres gosses de France tombés par milliers sous les balles françaises et alliées en Syrie, en 1941 à Oran, à Casablanca en 1942, parce qu'ils ont cru au Maréchal félon. Le Maréchal qui a failli tuer la France. »

Le Monde, 25-7-45 : Rémy Roure souligne que : « les avocats qui ont provoqué le tumulte lors de la première séance du procès gardaient un silence complet quand les Cours spéciales et le tribunal d'État condamnaient les patriotes ».

---

7. The Communist magazine *Regards*, 1 August 1945, juxtaposed images of the trial with bodies from the recently liberated concentration camps. On the top left is the judge, Mongibeaux, and below him the prosecutor, Mornet.

DOIT PAYER !...

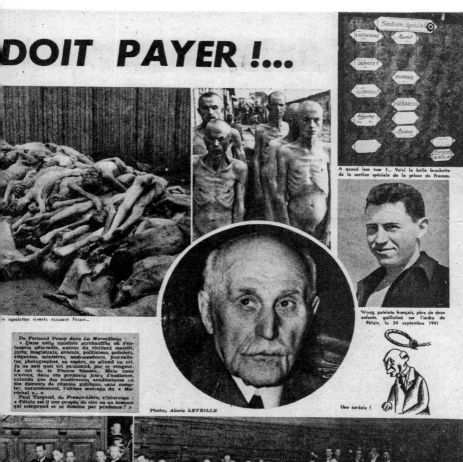

A quand leur tour ?... Voici la belle brochette de la section spéciale de la prison de Fresnes.

s squelettes vivants accusent Pétain...

Woog, patriote français, père de deux enfants, guillotiné sur l'ordre de Pétain, le 24 septembre 1941

De Fernand Pouey dans *La Marseillaise* :
« Dans cette enceinte surchauffée où s'entassent pêle-mêle, autour du vieillard maudit, jurés, magistrats, avocats, policiers, élégantes, ministres, ambassadeurs, journalistes, photographes, on espère, on attend un cri. Je ne sais quel cri passionné, par et vengeur. Le cri de la France blessée... Mais nous n'avons, dans ces premiers jours d'audience, entendu que des conférences académiques ou des discours de réunion publique, sans compter, naturellement, l'ultime message du « Maréchal »... »
Paul Turpaud, de *France-Libre*, s'interroge : « Pétain est-il une poupée de cire ou un homme qui comprend et se domine par prudence ? »

Photo, Alexis LEVEILLE

Une auréole !

7

France Waits

The Palais de Justice in Paris is a building intimately linked to the history of France. Located in the heart of the capital, on the île de la Cité, that island in the Seine where the Romans planted their settlement, it is a stone's throw away from the Cathedral of Notre Dame. The île also harboured the first residence of the kings of France, which incorporated from the thirteenth century the Sainte-Chapelle, one of the glories of French Gothic architecture, constructed to house a fragment of the True Cross. When King Charles V moved his main residence across the river to the Louvre palace at the end of the fourteenth century, the royal law tribunals remained behind on the île de la Cité. The law courts have stood here ever since. Behind the classical facade of the Palais, erected in the nineteenth century, much of the medieval structure remains.[1]

The Palais is a sprawling complex of buildings with the Sainte-Chapelle still embedded inside it. On its north side, overlooking the River Seine, are the medieval towers of the Conciergerie, which for centuries was a prison. This was where Marie-Antoinette, and many aristocrats and disgraced revolutionary leaders, were incarcerated during the Revolution. Their trials took place at the Revolutionary Tribunal in another part of the Palais. The exception was Louis XVI, who was tried across the river in the Convention. The Conciergerie had not served as a prison since 1934, but the Palais still housed a warren of insalubrious cells (the *dépôt*) where prisoners were kept in temporary police custody. The actress Arletty spent a few days there in October 1944. These cells were in close proximity to the headquarters of the *Police judiciaire*, the French equivalent of London's Scotland

Yard, situated at 36 Quai des Orfèvres, an address familiar to readers of the detective novels of Georges Simenon.

It was through the gates of 36 Quai des Orfèvres that Pétain was driven around midday on Sunday 22 July. He had been transported from Montrouge in a *panier à salade*, the French slang term for a prison van, a nod to the wire-netting covering the windows. His lawyers claimed to be shocked that a Marshal of France should be transported like a common criminal, but this had probably been done less to humiliate Pétain than to avoid drawing attention to his arrival.[2] The government wanted to avoid demonstrations, whether negative or positive. Pétain was taken not to the *dépôt* but to rooms in the Palais, a few steps from the courtroom, which had been hastily prepared for him and where he lived for the duration of the trial. This temporary prison had been carved out of the office of a court clerk (*greffier*) and the cloakrooms of the magistrates. Pétain had a small room with two beds for him and his wife, and a washroom next door. The windows overlooking the courtyard had been bricked up for security reasons. Neighbouring offices were converted to accommodate his two nurses, his doctor and Joseph Simon, his jailor.

CHOOSING THE JURY

On the afternoon before Pétain's arrival, the jury was sworn in. The High Court was composed of three judges and twenty-four jurors – twelve resisters and twelve parliamentarians – drawn by lot from a pool of fifty in each category. The pool of resisters was selected by the Assemblée Consultative from its members, and that of the parliamentarians from among those pre-war senators and *députés* who had not voted full powers to Pétain on 10 July 1940.

In April 1944, when de Gaulle's provisional government had granted women suffrage, it had also conferred on them the right to act as jurors for the first time in French history. These measures, 'rewarding' women for their courage in the Resistance (while others were having their heads shaved for 'horizontal collaboration'), had been opposed only by old anti-clerical *députés* who feared that women would vote as their priests directed. Women had first exercised their right to vote in the municipal elections in April 1945. This novelty was reported with condescending sexism by one resistance newspaper:

> I explained to my wife the way that the operation proceeded; I even took the precaution of giving her the voting paper and folding it care-fully into its envelope ... It seems to me that women for the moment lack confidence and discretion. My neighbour declared to an electri-cian: 'I am voting for an honest man.' Men were giving advice to these inexperienced *citoyennes* ... One woman caught her coat in the curtain of the booth and pulled it over ... I noticed a very pretty *citoyenne*, very blond, who carefully pulled the curtains of the booth as if she was going to undress and perhaps take shower.[3]

In the end, no women sat on the Pétain jury. Both of the potential female jurors whose names had emerged from the drawing of lots – Lucie Aubrac, a famous resister close to the Communist Party, and Germaine Picard-Moch, a journalist and wife of a leading Socialist politician, Jules Moch – were rejected by the defence.

The defence also rejected Robert Pimienta, a well-known journal-ist. Although he was not identified with the left, his reaction to his exclusion, widely reported in the press, suggests that the defence had acted prudently: 'I thank the defence for the honour it has bestowed on me. It will not prevent Pétain from receiving five bullets in his car-cass. And I would be the first to volunteer to join the firing squad.'

From among the parliamentary jurors, the defence also rejected the names of two known Communists. It had the right to contest six names, but no objection was made to Louis Prot, another Communist parliamentary juror, seemingly because he was so obscure that no one knew much about him. All the other parliamentary jurors were Social-ists (six) or members of the centrist Radical Party (five). They were mostly unremarkable figures, only there because they had not voted for Pétain in 1940 – either because they were among the eighty who had voted against him or because they had been unable to attend the vote. Two of them, Tony-Révillon and Léandre Dupré, had been con-sidered suspect enough by the Vichy regime to be kept under close surveillance; another, Marcel Bender, had refused to take down the bust of the Republican symbol, 'Marianne', in the village where he was mayor. Still another, Georges Lévy-Alphandery, had been persecuted by the regime both as a Jew and a Freemason. The resistance jurors are less easy to pigeonhole politically. Four were officially members of the Front National, a Communist organization which cast its net so widely that members were not necessarily Communist.[4]

The most striking difference between the two categories of jurors was their age: the oldest juror was the eighty-three-year-old parliamentarian Alphandery-Lévy; the youngest was the twenty-six-year-old resister Roger Lescuyer. The average age of the parliamentary jurors was sixty-one, and that of the resistance jurors forty. One of the curiosities of the High Court was that four reserve jurors (*suppléants*) in each category were also allowed to sit in the Court and participate fully – but not pronounce a sentence at the end. One of the resistance *suppléants*, Jean Worms, who sported the resonant resistance pseudonym of Germinal, had been rejected as too partisan by the defence in the Esteva trial. He would be one of the most active members of the Pétain jury in asking questions. It was rightly noted by critics of the *Épuration* that this was not an 'objective' jury, but it would have been impossible to find jurors without personal experiences of the events they were judging. Germinal and Marcel Levêque were both fathers of children who had been deported to Germany and never returned.

Isorni was contemptuous of the intellectual quality of the jurors: 'Decent enough chaps, mostly honest … simple and simplistic … united only in their hatred of the Marshal'.[5] Such derision was predictable coming from this source, but the view was shared by many journalists. Many of the jurors were unknown figures, so obscure in the case of the resistance juror Yves Porc'her, who had run an escape network for allied airmen from the Parisian hospital in which he worked, that newspapers were reduced to describing him indiscriminately as 'Dr Porcher' or 'Dr Poricher'. Certainly, some jurors were out of their depth. To be fair, it was hard for anyone to concentrate during long afternoons in a stiflingly hot courtroom. But many jurors were individuals of stature: the resistance juror Pierre Meunier, who had been a key aide of the famous resistance leader Jean Moulin; the parliamentary juror Jean Pierre-Bloch, a promising young Socialist *député* who had joined de Gaulle in London in 1942. Meunier did not speak once during the trial whereas Bloch was very vocal – but neither could be accused of not being intellectually up to the task.

The jurors were sworn to secrecy, as was customary, and only three broke their silence years later with a few details of their final deliberations. We are fortunate, however, to have the diary of one resistance juror, Jacques Lecompte-Boinet, son-in-law of the famous First World War general Charles Mangin. In 1940, Lecompte-Boinet had been a local government official in Paris, and he became a founding member of a major resistance network in the Occupied Zone (Ceux de la Résistance, CDLR). When Jean Moulin, de Gaulle's representative to the Resistance, set up the National Council of the Resistance (CNR) to unite resistance leaders and former politicians in a single body, Lecompte-Boinet represented the CDLR. In 1943 he managed to get to London and then Algiers where he met de Gaulle.

Unsurprisingly Lecompte-Boinet shared the ordinary prejudices of the Resistance: contempt for politicians who had let France down in 1940, admiration for de Gaulle mixed with resentment at his high-handed treatment of many resistance leaders. But as a bourgeois conservative, he had no sympathy with the radical politics of the Resistance. Hostile to Pétain, he was equally repelled by the sanguinary rhetoric of the Communist Party. He took his responsibilities as a juror seriously and saw the trial as an opportunity to understand the history he had lived through over the last four years. This makes his reactions more interesting than if he had lacked doubts or scruples. He perfectly exemplified the ambivalence many ordinary French citizens felt about the events of the last four years – and about Pétain.

Lecompte-Boinet had already served as a juror in the first trial of the Haute Cour, that of Admiral Esteva. He felt the sentence was justified but it left him uneasy because Esteva was so 'manifestly unintelligent' that he had been guided only by the idea of obedience. 'The person really responsible is the person who appointed him,' he reflected. He was annoyed by an article in the conservative *Le Figaro* accusing the jurors at the Esteva trial of being too tough:

> That is ridiculous and if we can be reproached with anything it is with not being tough enough . . . The charity that is defended by Mauriac [in *Le Figaro*] against the Vichy bastards (*salopards*) would be more useful in the [Socialist] *Le Populaire* or the [Communist] *L'Humanité* to try to convince their readers of the need to seek justice than in *Le*

Figaro where it just gives arguments to bourgeois readers who certainly don't need them.[6]

Lecompte-Boinet's reaction to Pétain's return to France was typical: 'Hitler has sent us back Pétain who now has new work to do in France to divide us. His return really sets me against the old boy.'[7]

Lecompte-Boinet realized that his presence on the jury could have negative consequences if he were to embark on a political career. He was bitter that some of his colleagues had not made themselves available for jury service for that reason. The left-wing juror Pierre-Bloch told him: 'If we condemn him, I will be attacked by some; and if we do not, I will be accused of being soft. Either way I lose votes in the elections.'[8] As a conscientious citizen, Lecompte-Boinet was ready to put these considerations aside, but he was shocked by the atmosphere around the jury selection. After the defence had successfully rejected five names, he heard a juror remark, 'With a jury like this Pétain will not be condemned' – which proved to him that 'this is going to be much more a political trial than one about treason'. He wrote:

> I would have liked to make the following declaration: 'Pétain was named head of State by the National Assembly composed of men properly elected by the Nation. The fact of choosing the Jurors among the Resisters and among the 80 parliamentarians who voted against Pétain in 1940 while 800 voted for, will taint the judgement that is made. I am happy to participate in the judgement, I do not want to participate in an assassination.'[9]

He kept these views to himself – but we shall return to his thoughts as the trial unfolded.

FRANCE WAITS

During these weekend preparations, events in the streets of Paris reminded people of why the trial was taking place. On Saturday 21 July crowds gathered at the Parc des Princes sports stadium to commemorate one the most horrific events of the Occupation. On 16 July 1942 over 13,000 Jews had been rounded up in Paris, dumped in the

Vel d'Hiver sports stadium in atrocious conditions, and sent on to an internment camp at Drancy outside Paris before being deported to Auschwitz. One survivor told the meeting that mothers like herself had been falsely assured they would be reunited with their children. Another proclaimed: 'Pétain must be confronted with the thousands of Jewish corpses. We have the right to say that he was their killer.'[10]

The following day (22 July) another ceremony was organized by the Communist Party to commemorate the shooting of fifteen resisters including the seventeen-year-old Guy Moquet. The crowd assembled at the Place de la République to follow the coffins to the cemetery of Père Lachaise was so huge that *L'Humanité* reported it had taken seven hours to make the short journey: 'a solemn procession in a deathly silence, a silence which cries out for vengeance. Despite the crushing heat, a huge crowd, tense faces, their eyes burning with anger.' Readers who were fed daily denunciations of the traitor 'Bazaine-Pétain' knew whom that anger should be directed against.[11] Newspapers were still carrying their familiar lists of poignant appeals from families seeking news of relatives who had been deported and not yet returned. *Le Figaro* carried five, for example: 'Odette Elina, rep. from Birkenau, 32, rue d'Empare, Castres, seeks info. on her parents and brother Jean-Max, dep. 29 Oct. 1943 to Auschwitz.'

Otherwise this was a normal weekend in post-liberation Paris. Broadsheets reported the bars and restaurants that had been closed down for illegal black-market activities and provided updates on food rations. Over thirty films were showing, including still *Les Enfants du Paradis*. But the city's cultural life was already shutting down for the holidays. Paris is notoriously dead in the high summer. The Opéra had closed, its doors open only one night for a Franco-American gala evening that included a short film on the fighting in the Pacific – a reminder that, outside Europe, the war was not yet over.

As for theatres, the main auditorium of the Comédie Française had closed for the summer but its other theatre, Le Vieux Colombier, was showing a much-lauded production of T.S. Eliot's *Murder in the Cathedral* by the up-and-coming director Jean Vilar. The play, which dramatized, in the words of one reviewer, 'the choice between the social and economic wellbeing of peoples and the laws of human conscience', prefigured themes that would soon be debated at Pétain's trial. The Paris literary 'season' had climaxed with the ceremony for the prestigious Prix Goncourt, awarded for the first time to a woman, Elsa Triolet. She and her husband, Louis Aragon, were the Communist intellectuals of the moment, and her success was more evidence of the cultural dominance of the Communist Party.

On Sunday, newspapers across France announced the death of Paul Valéry, widely viewed as France's greatest poet. His State Funeral two days later was attended by de Gaulle in person. No one chose on that occasion to recall the famous speech Valéry had made in January 1931, welcoming Pétain to the Académie Française.

Galleries and museums remained open for the summer to cater to the tourists flocking to the Louvre to view treasures on display for the first time in four years. Most important among these was the *Mona Lisa*, which had been moved to no fewer than four different secret French locations over the course of the war before returning to Paris in June 1945. There was no urgency about seeing the *Mona Lisa* but only one more week for anyone eager to visit the big exhibition at the Grand Palais devoted to 'Hitler's Crimes'. Admission was prohibited to those under sixteen, but the aim of the exhibition, according to the catalogue, was 'not to spread horror' so much as to define what was meant by 'war crimes'. The shadow of war was omnipresent.

Over the weekend de Gaulle was visiting Brittany. At Rennes, on Saturday, he delivered a speech outlining his thoughts on France's constitutional future. Since the Liberation, France had been living in a constitutional limbo under de Gaulle's provisional government. Until the official end of the war in May 1945, no one challenged this situation as too many Frenchmen were still languishing in German prison camps for proper elections to be held. Now that the prisoners were back decisions about the future had to be made. De Gaulle had always promised that he would consult the French on their future, without disguising his view that the regime existing in 1940 had let France down and should be reformed.

Now, he presented his ideas for the first time. He proposed that elections be accompanied by a referendum asking whether the new parliament should be designated as a 'Constituent Assembly' and given the task of drafting a new constitution. If the answer were 'yes' (as he hoped), the Third Republic was superseded; if the answer were 'no', France would resume where she had left off in July 1940. The referendum would also pose a second question: if parliament was to be designated as a constituent assembly, would it be fully sovereign (as had been the case in 1793 and 1848) or would the constitution have to be ratified by another referendum (as de Gaulle preferred)?

The debate on these proposals in the Assemblée Consultative would begin on Friday 27 July, four days into the trial. Behind these seemingly arcane issues hovered ghosts of French history. To French politicians with long memories, referenda recalled the plebiscites on which Napoleon III had based his power. These were distant echoes, but there were also more recent ones. A speaker in the debate asked whether the disaster of 1940 was 'due to institutions [as de Gaulle believed] or to individuals?' After all, those institutions had not served France so badly in 1914–18, he reflected. Perhaps the problem in June 1940 lay in the role of 'that eternal advocate of Defeatism, Philippe Pétain?' Those debating France's future always had Pétain in their minds, just as those deliberating Pétain's fate in the courtroom always had an eye on France's future.

De Gaulle's speech was the main story carried by newspapers on the eve of the trial. Paper restrictions did not allow much room for other news apart from brief speculation about the conference in Potsdam (17 July–2 August), where Churchill, Truman and Stalin were meeting to discuss the post-war order. Since these talks were shrouded in secrecy there was little to report. The fact that France was not participating in the conference, just as she had not participated in the Yalta conference (4–11 February 1945), was a reminder of her diminished status in the world despite de Gaulle's efforts to persuade the Allies that the 'real' France had been with him in London and not with Pétain in Vichy.

Anticipating a moment of national reckoning, newspaper editors prepared their readers for the weeks ahead. The tone was sombre. Albert Camus, who had emerged as the conscience of the Resistance through his editorship of the newspaper *Combat*, warned:

> Whatever the sentence, it will leave in its wake a muddy scum of partisan controversies and tenacious prejudices which will, one fine day, lead to calls for the revision of the trial. People will say that I am excessively pessimistic. But the moral health of France is fragile . . . There is

also the fact that among the accusers of Pétain, magistrates but above all witnesses, there are men whose previous actions or relations with the accused do not exactly predispose them to give lessons to others ... None of this must let us forget the fact that facing them all there is a corpse: that of France in 1940 ... When Mornet tells us he plans to examine how Pétain used the defeat to come to power he is dangerously isolating one issue ... For the Pétain case is first and foremost an abuse of confidence pushed to its most extreme consequences ... That duplicity is at the heart of his treason.[12]

An editorial in *Franc-Tireur*, another resistance publication, was hardly less pessimistic:

This old traitor no longer interests us as an individual. He ought already to be dead. He deserves to die a hundred times over ... The wound of Pétainism is still suppurating ... Our hope has been that the trial will lance it with a red-hot iron. That is what we still hope. We hope that in judging the man, it is a regime that we will expose, the sickness of shame, of self-interest, of cowardice.[13]

Another former resister expressed equally grandiose expectations for the trial:

I will recall the arguments of Camille Desmoulins and St Just at the trial of Louis XVI demonstrating that the criminal had to be judged not as a citizen but as an enemy, for the salvation of the French people was at stake.[14]

Finally, in the more moderate *L'Époque*, Maurice Clavel sounded a different note:

The trial is a sad affair. There can be no pity for a felon. We need to condemn Marshal Pétain by our verdict but not by our squawkings. Just as the execution of traitors in France is not accompanied by a dance of the scalp, so it would not be desirable for the sentence to be accompanied by shrieks of glee ... We know that the world, witness over four years of our 'national indignity', will be watching out for the slightest indignity in the liquidation of this affair ... The condemnation of a Marshal of France is something whose majestic sadness means that inappropriate language would be a fault of honour.[15]

8

First Day in Court

Bystanders began to gather early on Monday morning, 23 July 1945, outside the gates protecting the courtyard of the Palais de Justice. There were not many, as it was known that few places would be available for the public. The building was protected by 600 policemen, one of whom tried to satisfy disappointed punters by dangling the consolation prize of the trial of the 'Georgian Gestapo', a band of foreigners who had perpetrated gruesome acts of atrocity during the Occupation. Seats were available.[1]

That morning, police were even stationed on the roof of the Sainte-Chapelle. The previous night seven prisoners – collaborators awaiting trial according to some reports, common criminals according to others – had escaped from their cells in the *dépôt*, climbed through a central-heating pipe, clambered on to the roof of the Palais and jumped down to the *quai* below. No one believed that the Marshal, however sprightly, would be capable of a similar feat, but this incident had been an embarrassment.

Around midday journalists started to trickle into the courtroom. Among the first was the legendary Reuters correspondent Harold King, who wanted to secure a good seat. Most French journalists were familiar with the solemn and gloomy surroundings: the faded *fleur de lys* wallpaper, the sombre panelling and dark wooden benches, the heavily coffered ceiling with its allegorical painting of 'Truth protecting Innocence from Lies and Calumny', the Gobelins tapestries recounting the story of Esther. Six rows of wooden benches had been installed in the middle of the courtroom to accommodate extra journalists – their light colour jarring with the muted tones of the rest of the court, the smell of new wood still detectable. Three rows of benches were reserved for French press and three for the foreign press, which faced each other across the courtroom.

Behind the journalists were the benches for the twenty-four jurors: the resisters on the left, behind the French press, and the parliamentarians on the right, behind the foreign press. Representatives of the diplomatic corps sat behind the judges' bench. Most embassies sent only junior officials, but the Czech ambassador was there in person almost every day, perhaps hoping to glean information about the betrayal of his country by the French at Munich in 1938. Crouched on the floor below the judges' bench were stenographers, portraitists and photographers.

In the narrow alley between the rows of press benches stood an armchair for the defendant, with a policeman stationed just behind. In front of it was a small table. The 'witness stand' consisted of another chair placed a few feet further forward. Since witnesses spoke facing the magistrates, they had their back to Pétain a few feet behind them. Photographs of the trial show him often cupping his ear to hear what was being said. His deafness was partly tactical but given the spatial arrangement of the court it is understandable that he found it hard to hear the witnesses. Pétain's lawyers sat just behind him, and the prosecutor, Mornet, in a little box to his left, behind the foreign press. Behind the defence lawyers were the benches where witnesses could sit and watch the trial. Squashed next to each other on these benches on the first day were some of the most famous figures of the defunct Third Republic: one president and three prime ministers. Slightly incongruously at the end of this row of dignitaries, nearest to Pétain, sat the nun who acted as his nurse. Pétain's wife sat out the sessions in their room just outside the courtroom.

The entrance was by a small door between the defence benches and the witness bench, the passage between them so tight you had to squeeze sideways in order not to brush against the knees of the seated witnesses. Further behind was a little standing room for members of the Paris Bar and some members of the public. Above the court, on the right, was a balcony where extra benches had been installed to accommodate more members of the public.[2] Film footage of the trial shows people leaning dangerously forward for a closer view of the chaotic proceedings below them. One journalist wrote: 'all that is missing are the Phrygian bonnets of the Revolutionary tribunals'.[3]

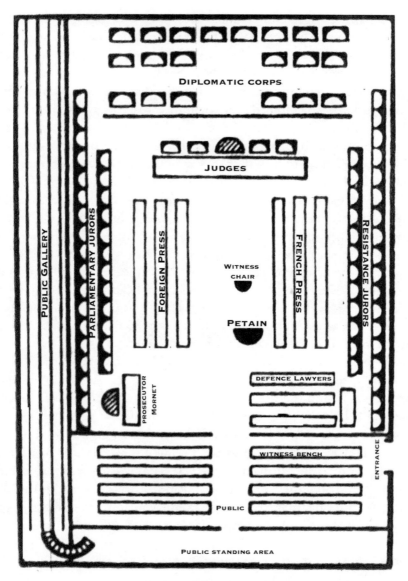

8. A plan of the courtroom.

The upper windows of the court were open for the first time in decades – possibly for the first time since the nineteenth century – but this hardly alleviated the stifling heat. Paris summer heat is often oppressive but in this stuffy courtroom it was unbearable. In the upper galleries, spectators fanned themselves with newspapers. Every day there were cases of heat-induced somnolence, even occasionally affecting the judges. Through the open windows splendid views of the golden spire of the Sainte-Chapelle imparted a note of historic grandeur that was otherwise missing from the bustling and noisy courtroom. The court was so cramped that when the prosecutor and judges filed in, Pétain had to pull back the small table in front of him to allow them to squeeze by. The journalists sitting in the front row on each side were so close to him that they could hear his every grunt, sigh, snigger and snore.

Many famous names covered the trial. The two most celebrated were Albert Camus, writing in *Combat*, and François Mauriac, writing in the conservative *Le Figaro*. Neither attended the court in person – Camus was rehearsing his new play *Caligula* – and they wrote their articles after reading the reports. Another occasional commentator was Georges Bernanos, a celebrated Catholic novelist, who had spent the war in exile in Brazil as a fervent supporter of the Free French. His articles, appearing in *Combat*, read like jeremiads hurled down to earth by some Old Testament prophet.

The best-selling *France-Soir* had secured the services of the globe-trotting Joseph Kessel, who during the interwar years had reported on Sinn Fein and the rise of the Nazis in Germany. In 1940, Kessel had made his way to London where he enrolled in de Gaulle's Free French air force. In a London pub he and his son-in-law Maurice Druon had written the words of the famous *Chant des Partisans*, which became the 'anthem' of the Resistance. In 1943 he wrote *Army of the Shadows*, one of the greatest novels about the Resistance. Another distinguished writer, Léon Werth, was commissioned to cover the trial for the newspaper *Résistance*. Werth had spent the entire Occupation in a small village in the Jura where he kept a journal which was published after the war.[4] Unlike those who harboured some illusions about Pétain in the early days of the Occupation, Werth had been implacable about Vichy from the start, yet both he and Kessel, in their sketches of the trial, were sensitive also to its pathos. Like every other Frenchman they had lived with Pétain's presence for over two decades. Kessel's first-ever newspaper report had described the victory parade down the Champs-Élysées on 14

July 1918 with Pétain at its head, 'proud and simple like a Roman in triumph'.[5]

In addition to publishing Mauriac's occasional articles, *Le Figaro* hired Jean Schlumberger, novelist, poet and friend of André Gide. Schlumberger was a member of the writers' committee which compiled in September 1944 a blacklist of writers to be censured for their role under the Occupation, though he later signed the petition seeking clemency for Brasillach. He was one of the few commentators with no regrets that the trial was taking place in this banal courtroom. On the contrary: 'In this musty, but properly judicial, opulence where the words "Jus and Lex" are repeated ten times on the walls and coffers of the ceiling, the trial will avoid taking on the appearance of a bullfight in an arena as it would have done in the Senate.'[6]

In addition to these celebrity journalists, others would become well known in years to come. In the centrist newspaper *L'Époque* there were daily articles by the twenty-five-year-old Maurice Clavel, who would later achieve fame as a journalist and novelist. In 1940, Clavel had been an ardent Pétainist, working in Vichy's Ministry of Education, before joining the Resistance in 1942. In August 1944, as a member of the Resistance he welcomed de Gaulle into the city of Chartres and remained a mystical admirer of de Gaulle for the rest of his life, but his brush with Pétainism distinguished his articles from the more Manichean contributions of other commentators. Clavel's trajectory was not unusual.

Some journalists were familiar figures in the corridors of the Palais de Justice, like the tiny hunchback Géo London (the pseudonym of Georges Samuel), who had covered trials all over the world, including that of Al Capone. He lived for the drama of the courtroom and covered the *épuration* for two publications, the moderate *Carrefour* and the Communist *Ce Soir*. In the former he was indulgent towards the defendants and in the latter ferocious against them. When taxed about this inconsistency he was unabashed: 'Oh, you know, I am not sectarian!'[7]

In this very masculine space, where all of the jurors and the lawyers, and all but one of the sixty-seven witnesses, were men, the only female presence was found on the press benches: Janet Flanner for *The New Yorker*, Germaine Picard-Moch (rejected as juror) for

9. The courtroom on day two. *Franc-Tireur*, 25 July 1945.

Cité-Soir, Francine Bonitzer for *L'Aurore*. Bonitzer, a lawyer as well as a journalist, was one of the most photographed figures of the trial because, seated at the end of the French press bench, she was closest to Pétain. 'For once when I am not in court to plead a case,' she told a fellow reporter, 'I find myself being photographed.'[8] The most famous female journalist was Madeleine Jacob, writing for the former resistance paper *Franc-Tireur*. Famously implacable, Jacob was a familiar presence in the corridors of the Palais de Justice. On the day the courts started their work she had written in *Franc-Tireur*: 'What the French people expect from you is what they have been promised, a justice that is rapid, clear, inexorable . . . Some will deserve the death that you are going to inflict on them. Death? The execution squad perhaps, but why not the guillotine?'[9] For Isorni she was a 'hyena', for Céline, the 'muse of the charnel house', and for others the 'Passionara' of the High Court. No one doubted that her reports of the Pétain trial were among the most vivid. In photographs of the trial, she stands out in the front row of the French press bench, a few seats down from Bonitzer, just in front of Kessel, scribbling notes, scrutinizing Pétain or whispering to her neighbour, her expression by turns startled, quizzical, incredulous, absorbed, bored and contemptuous. We can almost read the trial through her face.

ENTER PÉTAIN

As the courtroom filled, Joseph Kessel described the scene:

In the corridor leading up to the judges' bench stands an old worn leather armchair. In front of it a little table. That is where the defendant, Marshal Pétain, will take his place.

While we wait, the assembled journalists chat with each other; photographers and film operators prepare their cameras.

Then the characters in the drama file in to take their places: a nun who is there to watch over Pétain's health, politicians of the defunct Third Republic, who sit next to each other like a row of schoolboys.

Suddenly the court falls silent. By a little door at the side, between the packed benches, the accused is led in by two guards. He is in uniform. The only decoration he is wearing is the Médaille Militaire. He walks erectly, looking at no one. He goes to the old armchair, puts his *képi* with its laurel decoration on the little table, and sits down.

The silence goes on. But the atmosphere of tense expectation is palpable. What is the nature of this emotion? Pity? Indignation? Sympathy? Hatred? No, I think it is none of these things. It is a sense of unease, a malaise, a sort of abstract pain which is not directed to the old man

10. The journalist Madeleine Jacob looks into the distance as the first witness, Paul Reynaud, take the oath on 23 July.

who has just sat down. It goes beyond his person; it is about the glory, the destiny, of the *patrie*; it is about those great symbols of which that old man, sitting in that old armchair, bore the weight on his shoulders. But the man himself does not seem to excite any real emotion – because he does not seem to be experiencing any real emotion himself.

The silence, of which he is the source and the still centre, drags on. Surely he must find it unbearable. But he seems not to notice. His hands play with a large scroll of rolled-up paper. They seem to be independent of him; with a life of their own. They never stop moving. But Marshal Pétain seems not to be aware, nor to be aware of this, or of his tired eyes continuously blinking. He is immobile, impassive, impenetrable.[10]

What Kessel does not say is that as Pétain entered, followed by his three lawyers, Isorni looking extraordinarily young next to his two colleagues, a wave suddenly rippled across the courtroom as everyone rose to their feet. Was this an automatic reflex of deference or was it – as some claimed – simply because once some observers had risen to their feet, others had to imitate them in order to see over the heads of those in front. Was it irrepressible curiosity or involuntary respect? Probably both.

For four years everyone in that courtroom had lived in the shadow of this old man whom few had seen in person. Since that day on 17 June 1940 when Pétain had announced he was making the 'gift of my person' to the French people, everyone had come to recognize his plaintive, quavering, occasionally hectoring, voice. In cinemas, spectators had to sit through images of Pétain's provincial tours: Pétain adulated by crowds, Pétain patting children on the head like the grandfather of the nation, Pétain greeted on the steps of cathedrals by prelates, Pétain handed bouquets by curtseying women in regional costumes. Pétain's image had been on posters, stamps, handkerchiefs, napkins, plates, cups, ashtrays, children's colouring books, board-games, tapestries, paperweights, penknives, even barometers. He could be purchased in Aubusson tapestry, Baccarat crystal, Sèvres porcelain.[11] Now he was there in person.

Léon Werth, who hated him, wrote that he looked amazingly like his portraits: 'His face is animated by a few nervous tics. There is a certain absence that one sometimes sees with some old people. His face is smooth, symmetrical . . . A sort of King Lear.'[12] Jean Schlumberger was relieved to see 'not a cornered victim but a man who seems twenty years younger than his age who, if he is going to crumple, will not do it under the weight of senility but of irrefutable arguments'.[13]

The defence team had discussed how Pétain should be dressed for the trial. He wanted to appear as a civilian so as not to sully the prestige of the Marshal's uniform. Isorni persuaded him to overcome this objection, but he refused the suggestion that he carry the Marshal's baton.[14] He was dressed in the khaki field uniform of a Marshal with the seven stars on his sleeve, and wearing only the yellow and gold ribbon of the *médaille militaire* – an honour which could be awarded to the most humble soldier as well as the most famous.

The silence greeting Pétain's entry into court was followed by a hubbub of whispering, the fluttering of fans in the public gallery, the clicking of cameras and the bustling of film crews. Cameras were not usually allowed in French courtrooms but in this trial photographers and film crews were permitted to attend for a few minutes at the start of each day. Extracts (without sound) were shown in cinema newsreels. Pétain became increasingly restive at the photographers crouched at his feet to get a good angle. He turned to his defence lawyers and muttered: 'What is going on?' 'How much longer is this going to last?'[15] Some people shouted out 'Enough'. Pétain clearly had supporters in court.

After fifteen minutes, an usher instructed the court to rise as the three judges made their entrance, followed by the prosecutor. The chief judge (*président*), Pierre Mongibeaux, had sworn the oath of loyalty to Pétain but he had not otherwise distinguished himself in any way, negatively or positively, during the Occupation – though he had raised eyebrows when he suddenly appeared from nowhere at the Palais de Justice at the Liberation with a tricolour resistance (FFI) armband on his sleeve.[16]

Official files on magistrates tend to be unrevealing unless they have blotted their copybook. In Mongibeaux's case the blandness becomes almost an art form. The words that recur most often in his file are 'calm' and 'prudent'. His wife had died young, leaving him responsible for the education of their four children, and in 1938 he had been appointed to the Cour de Cassation, France's highest appeal court. This was the reason why he ended up on the High Court in 1945. The post of *président* (Chief Judge) of the High Court went automatically to the *premier président* of the Cour de Cassation. Charles Frémicourt, *premier président* since 1937, had been purged for having briefly served in Pétain's government. The pool of alternatives to replace him was small as it had to be someone already serving on the Cour de Cassation before 1940 and not appointed under Vichy.

One eligible candidate would have been the jurist Léon Lyon-Caen, who had been sacked from the Cour de Cassation under Vichy legislation excluding Jews. Later, he had narrowly escaped arrest by the Gestapo, one of his sons had died at Auschwitz, and two others in the Resistance. Lyon-Caen was readmitted to the Cour de Cassation in 1945, but he refused to be considered for the role of *premier président* on the grounds that he could not be impartial.[17] The trial might have been very different if he had presided over it. It was said that the post of *premier président* was offered to seven people before Mongibeaux. Most did not want the responsibility of sentencing a Marshal of France. Mongibeaux, on the other hand, may have been attracted by the idea of ending his drably respectable career in such style. And there were material benefits: immediately after his appointment he set about securing an apartment of sufficient standing in Paris and an official car.[18]

Looking considerably older than his sixty-six years, Mongibeaux, with his neat little beard and his air of genial benevolence, reminded one observer of a portrait by the French seventeenth-century painter Philippe de Champaigne. Only a ruff was lacking to complete the illusion.[19] During the trial, Mongibeaux would often be challenged for his open partiality, perhaps explained by his desire to efface the memory of the oath he had sworn to Pétain. Overall he seemed out of his depth, and his successor as head of the High Court commented that 'without diminishing his merits one cannot deny that he had little inclination for hard work'.[20] Mongibeaux's silent fellow judges were Henri Picard, about whom we know little, and Charles Donat-Guigne, who was known to be a friend of the Pétain family. He may have accepted the role in the hope of acting as a moderating influence. Isorni commented: 'I have rarely seen a man whose face so clearly registered how much he wished he were not there.'[21]

In the procession into court, the three judges were followed by the prosecutor, Mornet, propelled by an intense suppressed energy that belied his age. Janet Flanner caught his intensity in a memorable snapshot: 'He rushed into court to his private little pulpit – a torso bent almost horizontal with age, eagerness, and speed, his pointed greasy beard and peaked nose leading his blood-coloured robe trailing behind him like a sanguine silhouette from a sketchbook of Goya.'[22] Another observer imagined him like 'a hunchbacked devil turned white that one could imagine flying off through the high windows towards the Sainte-Chapelle, on his broomstick, with his red robes floating in the wind'.[23] Once ensconced in his box, Mornet was largely hidden in the mass of journalists, photographers, ushers, stenographers and lawyers, though he occasionally popped up like an angry jack-in-the-box to protest against some slur on his reputation.

Mongibeaux opened the proceedings with a short statement appealing for decorum:

> The trial that is about to open is one of the greatest in history. It must take place in an atmosphere of serenity and dignity . . . The accused who appears today has aroused for many years the most contradictory feelings, an enthusiasm that you will recall, a sort of love. And also feelings of hatred and extremely violent hostility . . . History will one day judge the judges, and will also certainly judge the atmosphere in which his trial has been conducted.[24]

An usher called out: 'Accusé, levez-vous!' Pétain remained seated. He seemed not to have heard; or to have forgotten momentarily that *he* was the accused. Payen tapped him gently on the shoulder and Pétain rose to his feet. Asked to give his name, age and profession, he replied: 'Pétain, Philippe' – and, after the tiniest hesitation, 'Marshal of France'.

Payen leapt to his feet to contest the authority of the court. His argument was that a French Head of State, according to the constitution of 1875, could only be judged by the Senate. The parliamentary vote of 10 July 1940 had granted full powers to 'the government of the Republic under the authority and signature of Marshal Pétain'. This meant that although Pétain had styled himself 'Head of the French State', not 'President of the Republic', the Republic had never been abolished. So Pétain could only be judged by the Senate – just as Louis XVI had been judged by the Convention and Charles I of England by parliament. Payen then added a predictable swipe at the judges who had only three years earlier sworn an oath to the man on whom they were now sitting in judgement.

Mornet sprung up to refute both points. The first, he claimed, was specious because Pétain had used the powers granted by parliament to suppress the Republic. As for the second, he smugly reminded the court that, having retired in 1940, he had never sworn the oath to

Pétain. But, he added, he would have had no compunction in doing so: an oath to a government in thrall to a foreign power was 'a parody of an oath and a parody of justice'. Mornet's remarks were greeted with what the stenographic record described euphemistically as 'Movements'. Shouts came from the section of the court reserved for members of the Bar who thought he was insulting them. Mornet, losing his temper, screamed that members of the 'fifth column' should keep quiet. This caused even more uproar and Mongibeaux threatened to clear the court. Pétain turned to a journalist sitting only a few feet away and asked for the second time: 'What is going on?'

These legal skirmishes were just for form's sake. During a short recess to discuss the points raised by Payen, a man dressed in military uniform – a certain Captain Paulin, wounded in the French armies a few months earlier – approached Pétain, saluted and shook his hand 'because of the admiration I have for you'.[25] Once the judges had predictably rejected Payen's arguments, the trial could begin.

First came the reading of the indictment, which lasted some fifteen minutes. One newspaper reported:

> It was read out badly in a dull voice by the clerk (*greffier*) in black and red robes wearing his military medals and obviously rather overcome ... While Pétain continued to twist his papers in his hands, the judge examined his nails, the journalists mopped their brows and the defence lawyers scrutinized the faces of the prosecution witnesses.[26]

Pétain's thoughts seemed elsewhere. He stroked the arms of his chair, sniffed audibly, and occasionally shrugged his shoulders. Probably he was not listening to what was being said so much as concentrating on the intervention he was about to make.

PÉTAIN'S DECLARATION

Normally the reading of the indictment would have been followed by the interrogation of the defendant. But Payen now announced that his client wished to make a declaration. This was the signal for Pétain to unroll the large scroll he had been nervously twisting in his heavily veined hands – as if it were a substitute for a Marshal's baton – and read out a text printed in huge letters over several pages. This declaration had been written by Isorni, after, he later said, a long day and lots of champagne 'in the state of exaltation and lucidity that one gets from cold wine'.[27] Pétain had made corrections to the first draft which went through four more versions. Some of his changes were merely stylistic: he liked prose to be simple and direct. But he also corrected Isorni's suggestion that he had no future role to play. Where Isorni had written that he was addressing France 'for the last time', Pétain had corrected this to 'yet another time'.

Apart from this declaration, Pétain remained almost silent throughout his trial. For this reason, his intervention deserves to be quoted in its entirety (the passages marked in bold were added by Pétain personally):

> It was the French people of France who, through their representatives, meeting as a National Assembly on 10 July 1940 conferred power on me. It is to the people that I have returned to explain myself.
>
> The High Court, as it is constituted, does not represent the French people; and it is the people alone that the Marshal of France and Head of State will address.
>
> I will make no other declaration. I will reply to no questions. But I have entrusted to my counsel the task of replying to the accusations **which seek to besmirch me but which in fact only besmirch those who proffer them** [*a little provocation Isorni might have preferred to avoid*].
>
> I have spent my life in the service of France. Today, at the age of almost 90, thrown into prison, I wish to continue to serve her, by addressing her one more time. Let France remember! I led her armies to victory in 1918. Then, having earned the right to rest, I have never ceased to devote myself to her.
>
> I have answered all her calls despite my age and my fatigue. On the most tragic day of her History, it was once again to me that the country turned. I neither asked for nor desired anything. I was begged to come and I came.
>
> I found I had inherited a catastrophic situation not of my making. Those who were really responsible hid behind me to deflect the people's anger from themselves.
>
> When I sought an armistice, in agreement with France's military leaders, I carried out a necessary act of salvation. Yes, the armistice

saved France and contributed to the victory of the Allies by keeping the Mediterranean free and preserving the integrity of our Empire.

Power was conferred upon me legitimately and was **recognized by all the countries in the world, from the Holy See to the Soviet Union** [*Pétain at the last moment wisely deleted the next sentence of the text that he had added: 'I still represent the legitimate power'.*][28] I used that power as a shield to protect the French people. For the people I sacrificed my prestige. I remained at the head of a country under occupation.

Do people understand the difficulty of governing in such conditions? Every day, with a sword at my throat, I fought against the demands of the enemy. History will reveal all that I spared you while my adversaries only think of blaming me for what was unavoidable.

The occupation required me to humour the enemy, but I did this only to spare you worse until our country was liberated. The occupation also required me, against my will and my feelings, to accomplish certain acts which caused me greater suffering than they did you but in the face of the enemy's demands I gave up nothing that was essential to the existence of our fatherland.

On the contrary, through my actions over the course of four years I maintained France, I ensured the livelihood of the French, I obtained for our prisoners the support of the nation.

Let those who accuse me and claim to judge me scrutinize their conscience and ask what would have happened to them without me. While General de Gaulle, outside our frontiers, pursued the struggle, I prepared the path to liberation in preserving a France that was suffering but alive. What would have been gained in liberating a France in ruins, a France of cemeteries?

It was the enemy alone who by his presence on our soil attacked our liberties and put obstacles in the way of our desire for renewal. [*Isorni had proposed to Pétain either the more Republican sounding 'Liberty' or the more ancien régime sounding 'liberties'; Pétain chose the second.*]

Yet I prepared new institutions: the constitution that I had received a mandate to set up was ready but I was not able to promulgate it. Despite immense difficulties, **no government did more than mine to honour the family and, in order to prevent the class struggle, sought to guarantee the condition of workers in our factories and on our soil.** [*Pétain*

still lived in some illusion about the impact of the reforms of his
National Revolution. Isorni was probably correct that these would not
carry much weight.]

Liberated France might change words and name. She builds but she
can only build usefully on the foundation laid by me. These are the
examples which demonstrate, despite all partisan hatreds, the continuity of the Fatherland. No one has the right to breach it.

For my part, I have only thought about the union and reconciliation
of the French, as I said on the day when the Germans carried me off as
a prisoner because they blamed me for having never ceased to fight
against them and for having undermined their efforts.

I know that, **although the fact I am no longer exercising power
means some people have forgotten what they said and wrote,** millions
of French are thinking of me and have given me their confidence and
loyalty, not to my person but because for them, as for many others
throughout the world, I represent a tradition of French and Christian
civilization, in the face of the excesses of all tyrannies.

By condemning me, you will also be condemning the faith and hopes
of millions of other men. Thus you will increase or prolong the discord
of a France which so needs to find herself and to love herself again in
order to resume the place that she used to hold among the nations of
the world.

My life matters little. I made to France the gift of my person. It is at
this supreme moment that my sacrifice must no longer be put in doubt.

If you condemn me, let my condemnation be the last, and let no
other Frenchman ever be condemned for having obeyed the orders of
their lawful chief. But I say it before all the world: you would be sentencing an innocent man though you would believe you spoke in the
name of justice and it is an innocent man who would carry the burden –
for a Marshal of France asks for mercy from no one.

Your judgement will be answered by that of God and of posterity.
They will suffice for my conscience and for my memory. I put myself in
the hands of France.[29]

Pétain read this out, without glasses, in a surprisingly firm voice for
those used to his quavering over the radio during the last four years.
There was something eerie about hearing again the phrase he had

used in his first speech on 17 June 1940: 'the gift of my person'. Time was suspended. Everyone present could remember where they had been on that day and the emotions they had felt.

Overall, the declaration was a compilation of dubious assertions and half-truths, approximations and provocations. The phrase that some acts 'caused me greater suffering than they did you' would surely have been better omitted given that many in the court had suffered unimaginable personal losses. He was saying this in the presence of Jean-Richard Bloch, editor of the Communist newspaper *Ce Soir*, whose daughter had been shot in Hamburg in February 1943, whose mother had died in Auschwitz aged eighty-six and whose son had been killed by the Milice in June 1944. The idea that Pétain had always sought reconciliation hardly squared with the reality of a regime that had started by attacking many categories of French citizens (Jews, Freemasons, Communists) and imprisoning former political leaders (many of whom were now in court). The language of reconciliation had only appeared at the end: Vichy reached out to its enemies only when it no longer had friends.

Even so, Pétain's declaration, received in complete silence, was skilfully composed. The reminder of his glorious past; the fact that Vichy had been legally recognized by most countries; the implicit homage to de Gaulle (only inserted in the final draft) – none of these would have changed the minds of those convinced of his guilt but they offered arguments to those seeking reasons to excuse him. Madeleine Jacob warned her readers not to be deceived: 'That abominable voice of disaster, that of our humiliations, the voice which injected poison and dissension among us, went beyond all that one could have expected to hear in terms of hypocrisy and cynicism.'[30]

Normally the next stage of the trial would have been the interrogation of the accused by the judge, a process that could last several days. Since Pétain had taken a vow of silence, Mongibeaux had no choice but to proceed to hearing the witnesses. But there was another delay. Isorni and Lemaire followed Payen's example by raising some procedural points. Isorni merely noted, for the record, various irregularities in the conduct of the *Instruction*, but Lemaire weighed in much more aggressively – to the surprise of his fellow lawyers.

Before the trial, Lemaire had acted as a conciliator between Isorni and Payen; in the courtroom he was consistently the most aggressive of the three. His particular *bête noire* was Mornet; he once told Isorni, 'he revolts me'. In this first intervention Lemaire read out a comment by Mornet reported in a newspaper in April, saying that Pétain deserved the death penalty. When Mornet jumped up again to say that he had been misquoted, jeers exploded in the court. Mornet lost his temper again, shouting 'there are too many Germans in this room'. Isorni told him to withdraw this insulting remark. Mornet shouted back that he had only said there 'were too many people in the room who were playing the game of the Germans' – which was not true as the stenographic record shows. The court erupted again. *The New York Times* reported: 'Spectators rose from their seats and 25 minutes of bedlam ensued as lawyers and indignant spectators plunged into the melee. Pétain was hustled from the dock as newspaper men, witnesses and court attendants climbed on desks.'[31] The evacuation of the court was so chaotic that the correspondent of one British newspaper found himself 'unwittingly contesting the right of way of Marshal Pétain who, guarded by only one man, was trying to make his way to the same exit'.[32]

The head of the Paris Bar, Jacques Charpentier, was called in by Mongibeaux to mediate. Once Mornet provided assurances that his comments were not intended as a slur on the Bar, Charpentier promised there would be no more incidents. The explosion had less to do with Pétain than resentment against Mornet, an indication of the scars that the *épuration* had inflicted on the French legal profession.[33]

The trial had not opened well. The main sentiment in the press was a sense of shame at what the chaos of the opening day had conveyed to the world. Throughout the turmoil, the man supposedly at the centre of events, Philippe Pétain, had sat quietly in his chair – as if none of this had anything to do with him. For Joseph Kessel, the abiding memory of the day was not the uproar in court but 'a voice that belongs to radio recordings more than to a man . . . A *képi* girded by laurels on a little old table . . . An old man on an old armchair.'[34]

9

Republican Ghosts

The first week of the trial was devoted to hearing witnesses for the prosecution. Their statements, often lasting several hours, were followed by questions from the defence lawyers, punctuated by interventions from Mongibeaux and Mornet. These sessions were often confused because jurors were permitted to interrupt with questions however off the point. One juror, for example, interrupted to ask a question about the notorious Dieppe telegram that Pétain had allegedly sent to Hitler. But since the witness to whom he posed the question had been in prison at the time, he was the last person in a position to throw any light on the matter. Mongibeaux was not good at keeping his courtroom in order.

The prosecution witnesses were mostly leading politicians of the defunct Third Republic. That regime, set up in the wake of France's defeat in 1870, had lasted longer than any other since the French Revolution. It had been originally a compromise between those who wanted a constitution that embodied the principles of the French Revolution in their purest form – a single-house parliament to represent the will of the people, with no checks and balances of any kind – and conservatives who wanted some restraints on untrammelled popular sovereignty. As a concession to the conservatives, there was a parliament with two houses, a lower one (the Chamber) elected by universal suffrage and an indirectly elected upper house (Senate); and, at the apex of the system, a president elected by the parliament for seven years. But due to the suspicion of pure Republicans about anything smacking of 'Bonapartism', about too much power in the hands of one man, the president's role had become increasingly ceremonial. The cynical Georges Clemenceau had a repertoire of quips on the subject: the president existed merely to open flower shows, only the prostate gland was more useless than the president, and so on. This did not stop Clemenceau himself standing for the position in 1920, but precisely because he was such a forceful personality, parliament instead elected an innocuous candidate, Paul Deschanel, who promptly went mad and had to be removed from office.

Presidents played a part in guiding the choice of the *président du conseil* (as the premier or prime minister was called), but they had to choose someone who could command a majority in the Chamber, the source of real power. This was not always easy because France's fragmented party system meant that no party ever secured an overall majority at elections; governments were cobbled together from unstable coalitions which never lasted long. The chronic instability was not as bad as it seemed because the same faces would reappear in a seemingly endless political merry-go-round.

Despite its deficiencies, this system had survived numerous political crises and successfully steered France through the Great War. But in the 1930s it seemed to be entering a terminal crisis. The economic depression of the 1930s had sharply polarized French politics. Between 1932 and 1934 nine governments had grappled unsuccessfully with the consequences of the economic crisis, a rapid turnover even by French standards. In February 1934 anti-parliamentary sentiment exploded into violent riots fomented by so-called anti-parliamentary Leagues. The parties of the left, fearing democracy was in danger, formed an anti-fascist coalition called the Popular Front. It won the elections of 1936 and for the first time France had a Socialist prime minister, Léon Blum. These elections also marked a breakthrough for the French Communist Party, which further alienated conservatives from the system. The defeat of 1940 swept the whole system away.

The witnesses who paraded in front of the court over this first week were the ghosts of that past. So many tragedies and atrocities had occurred since 1940 that there was something surreal about reliving this old history – like being taken back to events before the flood.[1] But there was also a thirst to understand exactly what had happened in 1940 when France had been defeated and French democracy had been swept away. This first week of the trial was a kind of history lesson, since, as one newspaper wrote, 'the disastrous events of the year '40 are still not fully known except by a small number of initiates'. In one extraordinary moment, it even emerged in the interrogation of the first witness, Paul Reynaud, that the text of the armistice had never been published. As Janet Flanner recounted: 'charming, smiling judge Mongibeaux leaned down from his bench, rather like an elegant host catering to his guest's whims, to ask if perchance there was a copy of the armistice in the house':[2]

> MONGIBEAUX: There is a page of the history of France about which the jurors would be interested to have some light thrown: the armistice. One can assume that this page of history was far from honourable for – I do not say that it was hidden – but I do not think it has ever been published. In any case, the jurors do not know it . . .
> ISORNI: Marshal Pétain is reproached with signing the armistice and no one knows what it contained![3]

Over the course of the first week the court would hear the testimonies of four former premiers, a former President of the Republic, the two men who had presided over France's Chamber and Senate in 1940, and other leading politicians. All had been victims of the Vichy regime; some had been imprisoned; three had only just returned to France from deportation. This did not necessarily win them sympathy at the Liberation. The Resistance in France and the Free French in London often disagreed but both believed that France had been let down by her politicians in 1940 and would have no future place for these discredited survivors of a shameful past. Throughout the first week of Pétain's trial, the Assemblée Consultative, just across the river, was debating France's constitutional future – and de Gaulle, for one, hoped it would be different from her constitutional past. This was not lost on Paul Reynaud, France's premier in 1940 at the moment of defeat:

> Pétain's first thought was to overthrow the Republic. For it seems, *Messieurs*, that the Republic was to blame for the defeat. There is lots of talk today of Constitutions. And there were certainly reasons preceding the defeat to modify the Constitution of 1875 . . . But one must be careful! There is something much more difficult than having texts that are all new, shiny and fresh: it is having the right men. That is

what was missing . . . If we were beaten it is because the parliamentary regime was not operating as it was supposed to operate, for if it had done so it would not have let its leaders and parliamentarians trust in those military heroes and have such a blind confidence in their glorious incompetence.[4]

This endorsement of the former Republic was double-edged. If the problem in 1940 was that the Republic lacked the 'right men', was this not an indictment of those individuals now giving evidence? These witnesses were walking a tightrope: in court to convict Pétain they also sought to rehabilitate themselves and the defunct Republic.

Of no one was this truer than Reynaud, the man who had made Pétain possible. Reynaud had brought Pétain into his government to bolster morale after the first military reverses; when Reynaud resigned on 16 June 1940, he knew that Pétain would succeed him. Reynaud had lived with the consequences of that moment for the last four years; now was his chance to explain himself to the French people. Like every witness, Reynaud was asked to give his name, age, profession and address; to raise his right arm; and to swear he would tell the truth:

Name: Paul Reynaud
Age: 66
Profession: Avocat at the Cour d'Appel de Paris
Address: 5 Place du Palais Bourbon, Paris

REYNAUD'S REVENGE

De Gaulle was not someone who easily bestowed compliments. The letter he wrote to Paul Reynaud in May 1937 is a reminder of the esteem in which that tarnished politician was once held by his contemporaries: 'You are today the only Statesman of first rank who has the requisite courage, the intelligence and sense of the national interest to tackle the military problems on which France's destiny depends.'[5] But just as Anthony Eden's once-stellar reputation is forever linked to the Suez crisis of 1956, Reynaud's is forever overshadowed by the six fateful weeks in June 1940 that led to

France's defeat. Once considered the most brilliant conservative politician of his generation, he was fated, like Eden, to be forever a man with a great future behind him.[6]

Reynaud had always been a maverick and a loner. In 1932 he had taken up the unpopular (but correct) position that France needed to devalue her currency in order to remain competitive on world markets and have any chance of overcoming the Great Depression. Since the defence of the currency was viewed by France's political elite as a test of patriotic virtue – a moral issue more than an economic one – this turned Reynaud into a kind of political pariah for several years. He was entirely unconcerned. Convinced he could persuade others by the logic of his arguments, he never disguised his sense of intellectual superiority. A brilliant parliamentary debater, he shunned the camaraderie of French parliamentary life. Too pleased with himself to win friends, Reynaud was like an annoyingly eager schoolboy always first with his hand up to remind everyone he was the cleverest. He was neat and dapper, vain about his personal appearance; in a period when bibulous banquets and gargantuan menus were central to French politics, he was unusual in frequenting a gym. His diminutive stature delighted cartoonists.

In the second half of the 1930s the devaluation debate was over, but Reynaud had then adopted another brave stance which alienated him from his own conservative colleagues. This time the issue was foreign policy. Traditionally, conservatives, suspicious of Germany, had sought alliances in eastern Europe – even if necessary with the Soviet Union – to contain Germany. But as French politics became more polarized, they became so alarmed by the internal threat from the left that Nazi Germany seemed a bulwark against Communism. This idea was encapsulated in the phrase circulating in some circles: 'rather Hitler than Blum'. Appeasement of Germany culminated in the Munich conference of September 1938, which averted war by sacrificing to Hitler territory belonging to France's ally Czechoslovakia. But unlike most other conservative politicians Reynaud opposed appeasement of Germany and advocated a military alliance with the Soviet Union. His opposition to appeasement was shared by the relatively unknown Charles de Gaulle, author of a controversial book in 1934 on the modernization of the French Army. Reynaud was the only important politician to support de Gaulle's ideas – another maverick cause. The two men became close at a time when de Gaulle needed a new patron after Pétain.

After the outbreak of war in September 1939, Reynaud's moment seemed to have arrived. He pitched himself as the man who would prosecute the war more vigorously than the premier, Édouard Daladier, who had signed the Munich agreement. Reynaud would be a French Churchill to Daladier's Chamberlain. When Daladier fell in March 1940, Reynaud succeeded him as premier. Two months later the Germans attacked. Reynaud was not responsible for the ensuing military disaster but his response dismayed his admirers. Rather than forming a united war cabinet, he gave posts to former appeasers lukewarm about the war. Much ink was later spilled to explain why Reynaud so disappointed those who had believed in him. One common explanation was that he had been under the sway of his lover Helène de Portes, who was in the camp of those lukewarm about the war. Portes is a ubiquitous presence in all accounts of the Fall of France but since she died in a car crash in July 1940 (Reynaud was at the wheel), she never lived to tell her story. During the Pétain trial, Reynaud's friends were worried that her name would surface but she was never mentioned – although it was surely in everyone's mind.[7] But Reynaud's main problem in 1940 was that France's political divisions made it impossible to form a government of national unity. For de Gaulle, the explanation for Reynaud's failure was that he remained a prisoner of the political system that had created him; that he lacked the spark of self-belief necessary for leadership; that, in short, he was not de Gaulle.

Reynaud's two most fateful decisions, both taken on 28 May, were to replace the commander-in-chief, General Maurice Gamelin, with General Maxime Weygand and to bring Pétain into the government. Gamelin had made many miscalculations in the conduct of the war, but he was a loyal servant of the Republic. Weygand took over at a moment when it was too late to reverse the military disaster but unlike Gamelin he despised the Republic. Weygand might have been more suited to command at the outset; Gamelin was more suited to confront the political consequences of defeat. As for Pétain, Reynaud had hoped that his name would bolster morale. He did not predict that

Pétain would quickly conclude the war was lost. In a final reshuffle on 6 June, Reynaud brought de Gaulle into government as Under Secretary for National Defence. But this junior post gave Reynaud little power to combat those prominent figures arguing for an armistice. In the end, Reynaud lacked the authority, conviction or force of personality to impose his opposition to an armistice.

In September 1940, Reynaud was interned by the Vichy government, a measure of pure vindictiveness against a politician who had committed no crime but was seen as a former 'warmonger'. For this reason he was also a *bête noire* of the Germans. When Hitler sent troops into the Free Zone in November 1942, Reynaud was extracted from his French prison and deported to Germany. He ended the war interned in a castle in Austria with other high-profile politicians.

Reynaud's prison diary is revealing of his flawed personality. Perceptive comments on the war are marred by his insistence always to be in the right. His diary entry for 22 June 1941, recording the German attack on the Soviet Union, reduced this world historical event (whose importance he grasped) to himself: 'What a revenge for the person who was only just re-elected by 27 votes in 1936 because I was calling for a Franco-Russian alliance.'[8] Rare flashes of self-criticism – 'every day I ask forgiveness for France' – are outweighed by self-justificatory evasions: 'when one tries to analyse the responsibility of a human being who has committed an error, it dissolves as one goes back to the deepest causes'.[9] Reynaud raked compulsively over the events of June 1940, justifying his actions to himself and to posterity. His obsession was heightened because he found himself attacked not only by Vichy, for having taken France into the war, but by opponents of Vichy for having lost the war. This was the line of an influential polemic published in New York by the French journalist André Géraud with the title *The Gravediggers of France*. The 'gravediggers' included obvious suspects like Pétain and Weygand – but also Reynaud. In reaction to such attacks, Reynaud began in prison to write his memoir of 1940 with the characteristically boastful title: 'France Saved Europe'.

Reynaud was freed from his German prison and returned to France in early May 1945. A few weeks later de Gaulle invited him to dinner. To Reynaud's chagrin, de Gaulle's conversation was genially evasive

with no questions about Reynaud's future plans. Reynaud had griev-
ously disappointed him in June 1940; he clearly did not think he had
a future in 1945. Reynaud did not agree. Desperate to be back in the
limelight, two days after his return he told an English newspaper that
he would be 'one of the principal witnesses' at Pétain's trial. Asked
whether Pétain or Laval was the more guilty he replied: 'Pétain of
course.' One British Foreign Office official commented: 'The interview does not make a very pleasant impression. Reynaud protests his
innocence too much.'[10]

When he entered the courtroom, Reynaud had been rehearsing this
moment for years. This was his opportunity to vindicate himself,
rehabilitate his reputation, and relaunch his political career. So much
had happened since 1940 that few people in the court had given Reynaud much thought over the last four years. His reappearance revived
semi-buried memories of bombastic speeches in 1940 which seemed
hollow in retrospect. But if everyone else had moved on, for Reynaud
the clock had stopped on that afternoon of 16 June 1940 when he
resigned the French premiership. To add to the eerie sense that time
had frozen, Reynaud hardly appeared to have aged. While in prison
he had used a skipping rope to keep fit. *L'Humanité*, hating him as the
embodiment of bourgeois politics, commented waspishly that he
looked healthily bronzed by the Tyrolean sun – as if he had returned
from holiday rather than prison. Another newspaper noted that he
was so spruce in his neat British pin-striped suit that he seemed to
have come to court straight from the hairdresser.

Reynaud opened with the nearest he would ever offer to a *mea
culpa*: 'Messieurs, one needs a great effort of imagination today to
imagine what Marshal Pétain represented in May 1940, for, in this
affair, we are all guilty, we all worked to turn him into a God.'[11] Having established that the fault was collective not personal, Reynaud
embarked on an almost minute-by-minute narrative of the chaotic
events following his government's evacuation of Paris on 10 June
1940. Between 11 and 13 June ministers had been dispersed around
châteaux in the Loire region; on 14 June, as the Germans approached
the Loire river, those ministers were on the move again, heading south
along roads clogged with refugees; finally, on 15 and 16 June, three
desperate cabinet meetings took place in Bordeaux, culminating in

Reynaud's resignation. The chaos and disruption continued for several weeks. No less a personality than Jules Jeanneney, President of the Senate, told the court two days later that when at the end of June the government moved from Bordeaux to Vichy, he got lost en route. He only arrived four days late, having lost contact with the administrative services of the Senate, which landed up in an entirely different location: 'for four days I found myself completely isolated'.[12]

Reynaud's narrative took his listeners to places many had hardly heard of: the Château du Muguet near Briare for a meeting with Churchill on 11 June; the Château de Cangé for a cabinet meeting on 12 June; the Prefecture of Tours for another meeting with Churchill on 13 June. Briare, Cangé, Tours, Bordeaux: these place names would recur repeatedly during the first week of the trial, like the stations of the cross of France's defeat, as one witness put it. What increased the chaos was the remarkable fact that most of the châteaux where ministers were housed lacked telephones. It was impossible for members of the government to communicate with each other, let alone with the outside world. In the Château de Cangé, where Albert Lebrun, the President of the Republic, was housed, the one intermittently functioning telephone blocked access to the lavatory. General Spears, Churchill's envoy to the French government, enjoyed prolonging his phone conversations when he saw that General Weygand, whom he hated, was bursting to relieve himself.

It was at Cangé on 12 June that Weygand formally communicated his view that an armistice was inevitable. In Reynaud's story, Weygand was as much a villain as Pétain, shifting the blame for defeat on to the politicians. Reynaud claimed that Weygand was desperate to preserve the reputation of the army in case defeat led to revolution – as the Commune of 1871 had followed the defeat of 1870. Thus Weygand had advocated an armistice for political not military reasons: 'I answered that honour should prevail over order ... That is what I still believe. If one wanted to carve on the wall of St Cyr the words "Order comes before Honour", signed Weygand, and "Honour comes before Order", signed Paul Reynaud, I would be happy.'

Reynaud had told his ministers that it was an illusion to believe in the possibility of a deal with Hitler: 'Do you take him to be an old "Gentleman" like the Kaiser Wilhelm II who took two provinces from us – and then life went on as before? You are wrong. Hitler is Genghis Khan.'

What was the alternative to an armistice? Reynaud's solution was that the French government should relocate to French North Africa. This was a tricky moment in his testimony. After all, he had been in charge: what prevented his ordering such a decision if that was what he wanted? His answer was to blame Pétain and Weygand:

> How would the French people have reacted if these two men – two men who were believed to incarnate military honour and military knowledge – had remained on French soil and denounced as *fuyards* those who had abandoned the French people to the violence of the enemy?

Over the next few days, Reynaud's ministers started wavering in their opposition to an armistice, climaxing in a showdown between pro- and anti-armistice factions on 16 June. Early that afternoon de Gaulle, in London discussing the transportation of French troops to North Africa, phoned through an extraordinary proposal from Churchill that the two allies merge into one nation by signing a Franco-British Union. When Reynaud's government met later that day in Bordeaux to discuss this desperate bid to keep the French faithful to their alliance, one minister commented that it would be like France tying herself to a corpse; Weygand scoffed that Britain would soon have her neck wrung like a chicken. Impotent to stop the drift towards an armistice, Reynaud handed his resignation to Albert Lebrun, President of the Republic.

Reynaud ended his testimony with a defence of his former ministers:

> It is not my intention to condemn them, *Messieurs*. You need to put yourself back in the atmosphere of the period. These men saw the force of the Germans which seemed irresistible, and then the crowds of unfortunate refugees pouring south with mattresses on their car roofs, towards the Pyrenees ...
>
> But I will be much more severe about those who told them, because they had the authority to say such things ... that in three weeks England would have her throat cut like a chicken. I am more severe about

those who weighed in the decision of these ministers, those who corrupted them – Pétain and Weygand.

Reynaud had spoken for three hours without notes and without interruptions: the performance of a brilliant barrister who had prepared his brief for four years. When he delivered a particularly neat (and obviously prepared) line – 'What point is there in playing a double game if one of those games is shameful' – a little smile of self-satisfaction would play over his features. One journalist wrote: 'indefatigable, his tone by turns ironic, trenchant and emotional . . . It was sometimes a speech for his own defence (*plaidoyer*), sometimes a speech for the prosecution (*réquisitoire*), sometimes a political speech.'[13] The juror Lecompte-Boinet commented in his diary: 'Reynaud's tone is clipped [*sec*] and antipathetic. And yet he is right.'[14] If Reynaud – 'the sly, little mouse-faced politician' as one observer described him – sensed he had not made an entirely favourable impression, he did not show it – or did not care.[15] Most other witnesses did not reappear in court after giving their testimony, but Reynaud was present almost every day, ready to jump out of his seat every time he detected a slur on his reputation. As he had written in his prison diary: 'My reason for living is not to end my life on the failure represented by the armistice.'[16]

IO

Debating the Armistice

Reynaud's version of the events leading to the armistice was broadly confirmed two days later by Albert Lebrun, who had been President of the Republic in 1940. The self-effacing Lebrun, elected president in 1932, had been ideally suited to that curious position. He was an honest, decent former engineer, with a strong sense of duty and the appearance of a provincial bank manager – 'the epitome,' wrote Léon Werth, 'of the solid provincial bourgeoisie, with furniture and with principles'.[1]

In recognition of his former office, Lebrun was treated with special ceremony when he entered the court. The chair that had served for the previous witnesses was replaced by an armchair. Like most witnesses, he did not sit down but leant on the back of the chair when giving his evidence, his voice often breaking as he spoke.

Lebrun recalled, almost as if it had been the day before, the cabinet meeting in Cangé on 12 June when Pétain had risen to his feet and read out a declaration supporting an armistice and rejecting the pursuit of the war from abroad:

> One does not abandon a country suffering as France is suffering . . . one rests at her side; one defends her – her body, her soul, her spirit. Can one hope for a recovery in an indefinite future thanks to the Allies . . . No we must accept that France and the children of France must bear her suffering. That is the principle of her renewal.[2]

This declaration encapsulated the entire ideology underpinning the future Vichy regime: that France was definitively beaten; that to leave the country was desertion; that suffering would engender renewal. But what especially shocked the punctilious Lebrun was an issue of decorum: 'it was the first time in twenty years that I was present at a *Conseil des Ministres* when a minister read a paper out. Ministers were supposed to speak not to read.'

After Reynaud's resignation, Lebrun's duty as president was to select the next premier. This normally involved prolonged negotiations with politicians to find someone able to command a parliamentary majority. Since none of this was possible in the chaos of Bordeaux, Lebrun found himself invested with unexpected power for which his timorous personality had not prepared him. Having concluded that most of his ministers supported an armistice, Reynaud suggested to Lebrun that Pétain was the logical person to succeed him. Lebrun, himself opposed to an armistice, was not required to accept this advice. He recalled his dilemma:

> Who was at Bordeaux among the possible personalities? We did not know. And among those who were at Bordeaux – I am sure many of you in this room today were there, and you will remember the chaotic atmosphere – where could one find them? What were their addresses? I would never have been able to reach them . . . It was perhaps 11 p.m. and my preoccupation was to give France a government by the next day for all these lost souls that I saw everywhere around me . . .
>
> So I summoned Marshal Pétain and told him: 'So go on, form a government.'
>
> At that moment, the Marshal, with a gesture that was very familiar, opened his wallet, took out a list and said: 'Here is my government.'
>
> I had to admit that in the terrible sadness of that moment I did feel a little moment of relief. I remembered the difficulty in forming governments during my eight years as President; that could last, you will remember, three or four days. While I had had this one in a minute.[3]

What came as a relief for Lebrun was of course sinister for those who believed in a plot.

Only one other direct witness of the debates in Reynaud's government over the armistice gave his testimony. This was the conservative politician Louis Marin. Embarrassingly for the prosecution his recollections slightly contradicted Reynaud's.[4]

Marin had been a fixture of Third Republic politics since almost the turn of the century. Representing the city of Nancy in that part of Lorraine which had remained French after France's defeat by Prussia in 1871, he was an intransigent French patriot. With his huge white moustache making him resemble a nineteenth-century depiction of a Gaulish warrior, and always wearing his trademark loosely knotted polka-dot necktie, Marin looked like a politician of the 1890s. Quivering with rage from the moment he started to speak, Marin studiously avoided ever using the words 'Marshal Pétain', whom he referred to pointedly as 'the accused', on one occasion having to correct himself: 'When the Marshal -- I mean the accused --':

> Norway did not sign an armistice.
>
> Belgium did not sign an armistice.
>
> Holland did not sign an armistice.
>
> Luxemburg did not sign an armistice.
>
> Greece did not sign an armistice after she was attacked in 1941.
>
> Yugoslavia did not sign an armistice after she extricated herself from the pact that her regent had signed with Hitler in 1941 and was then attacked.
>
> Only France signed an armistice.

Marin took the court back over the armistice debate. He offered a telling example of Weygand's threats to intimidate the government into accepting an armistice when at one meeting at Cangé he conveyed the alarming news that the Communists had seized power in Paris and set up a revolutionary government. One phone call to Paris from the Minister of the Interior, Georges Mandel, demonstrated that this was false.

Where others were inclined to excuse the armistice as a kind of collective cowardice, Marin would have none of it:

> When people say, *Messieurs*, that the French people had supported the armistice, certainly it is true that the people did not live through these great calamities without fear and terrible grief. Of course, people were not brimming with hope. But the truth is that they felt stunned by the news of the armistice. Even in the streets of Bordeaux ... where as if by a magic wand ... all the defeatists of France had gathered, I saw, on the very evening the armistice was signed – and many of you will

have seen the same – churches filled with women on their knees, weeping, their bodies twisted and shaken by sobs. I saw men in the street, crying, their faces ravaged.

The unconvincing claim that the armistice had not been greeted with relief by most people led Marin into territory unhelpful to the prosecution. Revisiting Reynaud's resignation, he contested the claim that most ministers had been won over to an armistice. Since it was not normal procedure to hold a vote in cabinet, Reynaud had not called one even in these exceptional circumstances – but Marin's calculations suggested there would have been a majority against (14–10). His implication was that 'mon ami M. Reynaud' should have called a vote.

At this point Reynaud, who had been scribbling feverishly in the witness bench, jumped up. After a politely inconclusive exchange with his 'ami' Marin, he backtracked by claiming that the real question was not whether there had been a majority for an armistice, but whether he could have stayed in power with a divided government. But if that really was the question, what had stopped him asking Lebrun to allow him to form a new government in the image he wanted?

Mornet did not like the drift of the discussion:

MORNET: To me it is a matter of indifference to know whether there were in the government two votes in favour of the armistice or two against . . .

MARIN: The scepticism of the *procureur général* on this question of the majority does rather surprise me because he has said that what matters to him is to discover who was guilty of the armistice. *Messieurs*, the guilty men included some ministers who helped the accused. That is surely not a matter of indifference to this court.

MORNET: I am not going so far in my search for the guilty. There are people who were deceived and committed errors, who were subjected to the influence of others; and there are those responsible for the influence they exerted on those who did make mistakes.[5]

Mornet's message was clear: focus on Pétain.

THE NORTH AFRICAN OPTION

Reynaud's resignation had not necessarily sealed the victory of the pro-armistice camp. Pétain became premier on the evening of 16 June; the armistice was signed on 22 June. Those five days presented an opportunity for opponents of an armistice. One of these was Jules Jeanneney, President of the Senate. In terms of protocol, he was the third most important figure of the Republic and, in the absence of a functioning parliament in June 1940, he alone represented the Senate.

A member of parliament since 1902, Jeanneney was a Republican sage. He had been close to Clemenceau in the previous war and had known Pétain longer than anyone else in the courtroom. 'Just a youngster,' muttered Pétain as Jeanneney gave his age when being sworn in. He was the first witness to give his testimony seated – on the armchair supplied for Lebrun and which the court had forgotten to replace. Stiff and formal, with a little goatee beard and bow tie, Jeanneney delivered his testimony with slow deliberation, eschewing the rhetorical effects of Marin or Reynaud.[6]

Recounting the 'sinister day' when Reynaud resigned, Jeanneney told the court of his concern that, with the Germans drawing closer, the government in Bordeaux would not be able to deliberate freely on any armistice proposals. He proposed to Pétain that the government, or at least the President of the Republic, be moved to safety:

> He answered immediately: 'I will not leave France.' And this phrase recurred like clockwork in response to whatever I said to him. 'But you do recognize that the President of the Republic should not find himself a prisoner.' 'Of course.' 'But you must also recognize that the President alone can do nothing, that his acts need to be countersigned by a minister. It is indispensable he has the government around him.' 'That is true. But I will not leave France.'

Since Pétain would not budge, Jeanneney came up with the idea of transporting some senior politicians, including members of Pétain's government, out of German reach. On the morning of 20 June, as French negotiators were setting off to meet their German counterparts, Pétain's government grudgingly accepted Jeanneney's plan. It agreed that some politicians would leave for Perpignan on France's south coast, conveniently close to Port Vendres, the port nearest to North Africa, if it proved necessary to leave French metropolitan soil. Jeanneney was among those who set off on the afternoon of 20 June. But once he reached Toulouse, only about 320 kilometres from Bordeaux, he received the order to return:

> This was completely incomprehensible to me. I could get no explanation but had to obey ... I have tried to work out exactly what had happened. I could not find out at the time. And even today, after carefully reading everything that has been written on the subject I still do not know exactly.

President Lebrun, another of those who had hoped to go to Perpignan, offered the court a possible explanation for what had happened:

> We were to leave at 14.30. But at 14.00 there was another cabinet meeting – which I must say surprised me – and after a new discussion, it was decided to adjourn the departure ... I have since read that M. Alibert claimed to have sent a letter in the name of Marshal Pétain but we did not really know ... In short I have no idea what happened, I do not know what happened because no one communicated anything about all that to me, for, Messieurs, the situation of a President of the Republic is a bit special ... things are done that he knows nothing about; telegrams are exchanged that people forget to communicate to him.[7]

This was almost the only mention of the infamous Raphaël Alibert in the entire trial. Perhaps his reputation for mythmaking had made the prosecution wary of bringing up his name. In this case, however, Alibert's intervention had been genuinely important, and it is odd that no more was made of it. Fearing that the operation to move senior politicians from Bordeaux might prove an effective rearguard action by the anti-armistice camp, Alibert had taken two steps. First, he had assured Lebrun mendaciously that there was no urgency about leaving Bordeaux since German troops had not yet crossed the Loire. Secondly, he had written a letter in Pétain's name on the afternoon of 20 June ordering ministers to remain in Bordeaux until at least the next morning. He later claimed that by this action he had 'made Pétain by a lie and a forgery'.[8] Another piece of self-aggrandizement – but with a kernel of truth.

In theory, the decision to leave for Perpignan had only been delayed. There was nothing to prevent Lebrun going the next day. But having introduced one villain in the shape of Alibert, Lebrun introduced a second in the shape of Pierre Laval:

> I had an unexpected visit from M. Laval whom I had not seen for a very long time, accompanied by about 20 MPs ... They arrived gesticulating, all speaking at the same time, and I would say, almost having lost any control of themselves.
>
> Laval addressed me in a loud voice and said to me: 'How can you think of leaving France! The battle is lost and you know that perfectly well. We have lost; and we have to pay; we have to be loyal. If you go abroad it will be called treason.'

Lebrun replied that the presidents of both parliamentary assemblies – the Chamber and the Senate – supported the idea of going abroad:

> M. Laval – in a very strange voice – stared insulting the President of the Senate [Jeanneney] in language I don't want to reproduce. It was such that the Secretary General of the Presidency who was just outside the door asked himself: 'What are they doing to the President?' ...
>
> Other members of the delegation started to speak in the same vein. One of them said to me: 'You want to leave the country! But as soon as you have left a government will be formed here; and over there you will no longer count for anything.'[9]

When testifying during the *instruction* interrogations Lebrun's recollections had been even more precise. He remembered Laval screaming about the President of the Senate, Jeanneney: 'I hate him, I hate him, I hate him.'[10] Under this barrage, Lebrun crumpled and abandoned any idea of leaving.

But another group of politicians did succeed in getting to North Africa on the cruise-liner *Massilia*. The *Massilia* operation was conceived at the same time as the move to Perpignan. The ship was commandeered by the government to transport politicians directly to French Morocco from Bordeaux. Originally it had been due to leave on 20 June but members of the crew, hostile to what they perceived as politicians scuttling to safety, initially refused to lift anchor. In the end, the ship set off the next day. Although the Perpignan plan was cancelled, the departure of the *Massilia* went ahead on 21 June. The story was told in detail by another important witness, Édouard Daladier.

Daladier, who had preceded Reynaud as France's premier, had also been Minister of Defence in all governments between 1936 and 1940. Like Reynaud, Daladier had been a pillar of Third Republic politics but otherwise the two men could not have been more different: Reynaud was a political loner, Daladier one of the leading personalities of the centrist Radical Party, backbone of French politics. Reynaud was a forensic parliamentary debater, Daladier a stirring orator but more at ease addressing the party faithful; Reynaud a Parisian bourgeois, Daladier a baker's son from Provence – a scholarship boy who perfectly embodied the way in which the Republic's secular education system enabled children from modest backgrounds to succeed.

Unlike Reynaud, who seemed eternally young, Daladier had aged visibly during his four years of imprisonment. He entered the court looking tired and wary. But as he warmed up, Daladier rediscovered his rhetorical bravura. By the end he seemed to be addressing not so much a court as a party conference. At one point he lifted his chair and banged it on the ground. His was a 'gesticulating, chest-thumping and chair-bashing speech' in the words of one reporter.[11]

Daladier told the court a lot about his efforts to rearm France in the 1930s, but the most relevant part of his testimony to the Pétain case concerned the *Massilia*: 'We left on 21 June; while at sea we heard the conditions of the armistice and we decided, unanimously, to organize in North Africa . . . the resistance of French patriots.' By the time the *Massilia* reached Casablanca on 24 June, their trip no longer had any point; the armistice had been signed two days before. Daladier and others, like the conservative politician Georges Mandel, one of the most vociferous opponents of the armistice in Reynaud's government, hoped the French military authorities in North Africa might be willing to continue resistance. They were not. Mandel and Daladier tried to make contact with two envoys sent by Churchill, but they were forbidden to meet them:

Our plan had failed. The *Massilia* was stranded off the coast like a sort of floating prison. M. Mandel himself was arrested, and later assassinated but – I ask you – was our position really one of fugitives? Were we cowards? And yet day after day the leaders of Vichy never ceased to heap insults and lies on us, portraying us to the French people as men who were afraid and had taken flight.[12]

Daladier offered no opinion as to whether or not the Pétain government had deliberately set up the *Massilia* operation to remove and discredit opponents of the armistice, or whether it had merely seized an opportunity that presented itself. He did not mention Alibert. But his reminder of this episode will certainly have echoed with the jurors, five of whom had been on the ship. One of them, Tony-Révillon, even published his diary of his experience.[13] Two *députés* on the ship, Pierre Mendès France and Jean Zay, both serving in the army, were put on trial for desertion after being repatriated to France. They were both imprisoned. Mendès France managed to escape and join de Gaulle; Zay was assassinated by the Milice in 1944.

When the *Massilia* parliamentarians, stranded in North Africa, heard that Pétain's government had summoned a meeting of the French parliament to Vichy to revise the constitution, they urgently asked to be transported back to France so that they could participate in the vote. The government dragged its heels and when they finally returned the vote had taken place. Had the *Massilia* parliamentarians been present, Pétain's majority would have been smaller, but there were not enough of them to have reversed the course of events.

SUICIDE OR MURDER OF A REPUBLIC?

According to the Constitution of 1875, any revision of the Constitution was a two-stage operation. First, the Chamber and the Senate had to meet separately to decide on the principle of a revision; then a joint session of both houses, designated Assemblée Nationale, had to decide what form revision would take. Lebrun was the first witness to testify about this key moment in the birth of the Vichy regime. As a non-parliamentarian, Lebrun did not have a vote but as President he was consulted about the preparations:

> I had the impression that Marshal Pétain was covering many things that he had not initiated ... One evening Laval and Marshal Pétain came to see me. It was the first time M. Laval had spoken to me about his projects, the future law, the constitution, etc ...
>
> The Marshal was at his side. Not a word, not an explanation. Nothing.
>
> A few days later ... I said to the Marshal: 'I would like to have from your mouth information of what is being planned.' The Marshal answered: 'I am not really fully briefed (*au courant*); get M. Laval to come, he will give you all necessary explanations.'[14]

The first stage occurred on 9 July. Almost unanimously each house agreed on the need for a revision of the constitution. The more important vote occurred the next day when meeting together as an Assemblée Nationale in the Casino of Vichy, the parliamentarians voted on the form that constitutional revision would take. They were presented with a bill to delegate their authority to revise the constitution to Pétain, who would be accorded 'full powers' to do the job. Jules Jeanneney was central to the process because, as President of the Senate, he chaired *ex officio* the Assemblée Nationale. In his testimony Jeanneney did not linger on details except to emphasize that he had tried to insist that regular parliamentary procedures were observed. They were not; the bill was rammed through with little opportunity for debate; of the 649 parliamentarians voting, only eighty voted against: 'between 17.15 and 19.00 [on 10 July 1940]', Jeanneney told the court, 'full powers were given for France to acquire a new constitution. There can be no doubt today for anyone that this vote was extorted. I hope I will be permitted to repeat how on that very evening I characterized what had happened: "sharp practice [*entôlage*]" – and I still think that this remains true.'

Lebrun described what happened next:

> On the next day [11 July], Marshal Pétain came to see me. I can still see him entering my office: 'Monsieur le Président,' he said to me, 'the painful moment has come. You have always served the country well; the

vote of the National Assembly has created a new situation. I am not your successor; a new regime is beginning.' And I replied to him: 'Monsieur le Maréchal do not worry about me; all my political life I have served the law even if I have not morally approved it. So today I take note that the National Assembly has given its judgement. That is enough for me.'[15]

Thus Lebrun had not so much resigned as faded away. The coup d'état of 10 July 1940, if coup d'état it was, could hardly have been a politer affair. As de Gaulle later wrote scathingly of Lebrun in his Memoirs: 'As Head of State he lacked two things: that he was a Head; and that there was a State.'[16]

The most vivid recollection of what happened on 10 July in the Casino theatre of Vichy was offered by the Socialist Léon Blum, one of the eighty who had voted 'no'.

Socialist, Jew, intellectual, aesthete: in the interwar years Léon Blum represented everything loathed by the extreme right. The Action Française polemicist Charles Maurras once wrote of Blum that he was a man who should be shot – but in the back. Conservatives hated his Jewishness; they hated his beliefs; they hated his physical appearance. Starting out as a literary critic, Blum all his life resembled an effete *fin de siècle* man of letters. The Dreyfus Affair propelled him from literature to politics and in 1920 he became leader of the Socialist Party. The hatred of Blum was not only verbal. In 1936 he was set upon by right-wing thugs in the centre of Paris and hospitalized for several days. After the election, Blum became France's first ever Socialist premier. When he appeared before parliament after his victory, the right-wing *député* Xavier Vallat, later Vichy's Commissioner for Jewish Affairs, lamented the fact that 'this old Gallo-Roman country will be governed by a Jew', a '"subtle Talmudist"', rather than someone rooted in the entrails of our soil'.[17]

In the face of Nazism, Blum had rethought his commitment to pacifism. Contrary to what would be alleged at the Vichy-organized trial in Riom, it was his government that launched French rearmament. But the Socialists themselves were divided on foreign policy in the 1930s, many of them refusing to abandon pacifism. This was true of the party's deputy leader, Paul Faure, who was on the list of

ministers that Pétain produced as if by magic when Lebrun asked him
to form a government. According to Reynaud's testimony in the trial,
when Lebrun expressed surprise at the inclusion of such a notorious
pacifist, Pétain had allegedly replied: 'Oh, I was told it would annoy
Léon Blum!'

Blum was in an odd position in 1939–40. He fully supported the
war and was hugely esteemed by Reynaud, but Reynaud judged that
the Socialist was too controversial a figure to be included in his government. Thus Blum was reduced to being a close observer of the
events leading up to the armistice but not a participant in them. Obviously a primary target for the Vichy regime, he was interned in
September 1940 and put on trial at Riom. The brilliance of his defence
was one reason why the trial was suspended – and why he was sent
back to prison. When the Germans occupied the Free Zone in November 1942, Blum was deported to Germany with another prominent
politician, Georges Mandel. They were imprisoned near the camp of
Buchenwald, but apart from strange smells which wafted over they
had no idea of the horrors taking place there. Blum's conditions of
internment were not too arduous, since he and Mandel were considered as possible negotiating pawns by Germany in the last stages of
the war – but each knew they might be shot at any moment.

Blum's defence at Riom, published as a pamphlet by the British
Labour Party, turned him into an international hero of the left. His
appearance at Pétain's trial was eagerly awaited. Although thinner and
his reedy voice weaker – he had only been in court a few minutes when
a juror interrupted to ask him to speak louder – Blum seemed physically unchanged by his ordeal. Dressed elegantly as always, he was
wearing mourning for his brother who had been killed in Auschwitz.

Blum opened with his memory of hearing on 9 June 1940 that the
government was to evacuate Paris: 'I had lived with the conviction –
the illusion – that Paris would be defended, would be defended with
boldness, with energy, and I wanted to stay there during the fighting.'
Persuaded by friends that it would be dangerous to stay, Blum left
Paris that night to join his daughter:

> But on Tuesday 11 June I came back to Paris; I was desperate for news,
> I wanted to remain in contact with people who were perhaps still

there . . . I found a Paris already empty, deserted, in the process of being evacuated. I realized that any idea of resistance had been given up . . . I tried everywhere to find someone to speak to, and I ended up going to the Invalides, to the military governor . . . I asked with emotion and anguish: 'So Paris is to be abandoned?'

He replied: 'What do you want me to say? We know nothing, we have no instructions, we have no orders. Yesterday we had a telephone call from General Weygand, we are waiting for another one, we know nothing' . . .

I said to him: 'But Paris is surely not just the capital of France, the city that symbolizes France, incarnates France, it is the centre of all communications, it has the crossing of the Seine . . . So all that is to be given up? . . .' He simply replied: 'We are waiting for a telephone call, it could come at any moment.' I left in despair.

When the government headed south, Blum followed. In Bordeaux, he kept in constant touch with a group of *députés* meeting at the Prefecture to organize opposition to an armistice. Then came the news of Reynaud's resignation. Blum was one of those who now pinned his hopes on leaving for North Africa. At one moment he was told this would happen; the next he heard the opposite. He told the story, already recounted by Jeanneney and Lebrun, of setting off for Perpignan on the morning of 20 June, arriving at Toulouse in the afternoon, then being ordered to return. Back in Bordeaux, Blum was told that the police could not guarantee his safety. So he returned to Toulouse where he read in a newspaper the news of the armistice. Blum's voice broke as he remembered that moment:

I could not believe my eyes. I saw that France was betraying her allies . . . I saw France occupied and divided into two parts. I could clearly see all the future dismemberments that were to follow. I saw that abominable clause, without precedent, I think, in our history, by which France committed herself to handing over to Germany those 'outlaws', exiles who had found refuge on our soil.

Finally, Blum moved to the vote at Vichy on 9–10 July. By universal consent, his account of this event was one of the most gripping moments in the entire trial:

It was a spectacle that still chills me if I think back to it. In those two days I saw men transformed and corrupted in front my eyes, as if they had been dipped into some kind of toxic bath. What made them change was fear: fear of the fascist bands of Jacques Doriot prowling the streets, fear of the military, fear of the Germans who were at the town of Moulins only a few kilometres away. The group called the 'Marsh' (*marais*) in the French revolutionary assembly had known the same kind of fear on 31 May 1793 [when the *sans culottes* invaded the Assembly] or the night of 9 Thermidor [when Robespierre was arrested]. Now I properly understood why they were called the Marsh. This really was like some kind of human swamp in which, I repeat, the nobility and courage of men that one had known corroded and dissolved in front of one's eyes . . .

I left Vichy not so much discouraged as desolate. When I saw [the Radical politician] Camille Chautemps for the last time in a corridor I said to him: 'So then, that is the end of the Republic.' He replied: 'Yes I fear so!'

I left Vichy for my house in the country. It was there that I was arrested on 15 September.[18]

Blum's testimony had been the high point of the trial so far. The impact derived from his avoidance of declamatory rhetoric or point scoring. Every sentence was phrased with intellectual fastidiousness – but also artistry. Even Isorni, whose account of the trial is sprinkled with barbs against all prosecution witnesses, admitted that Blum spoke like 'a *grand seigneur* . . . with a fluency and precision that was a sign of great art, and despite his thin and feeble voice, an authority no other witness had shown before him. He also had that force which came from the absence – at least in appearance – of passion.' Isorni could not resist lacing this praise with an anti-semitic barb: 'the numerous Israelites who occupied the press benches were in a state of ecstasy. The Prophet was speaking!'[19]

Before his appearance, the court had lived through the events of Cangé, Tours and Bordeaux; it had heard about the *Massilia*; it had revisited the vote of full powers to Pétain. But these events seemed to have taken place in another century. As Léon Werth wrote, the court had heard only 'dead history . . . schoolbook history . . . witnesses

11. Louis Marin.

12. Albert Lebrun.

13. Léon Blum

14. Jules Jeanneney.

expounding dead facts which are already forming their deposits at the bottom of our memories'.[20] When Blum spoke the past came alive. Madeleine Jacob wrote: 'Blum's quavering voice suddenly transplanted us back into the moment which remains for us a wound that has not healed. One had to witness Blum's tears to feel so vividly all that we have suffered.'[21]

11

The Defence Fights Back

After each witness took the stand to tell their story, the defence law-yers moved in with their questions. This was a delicate exercise with a jury half composed of former resisters, hyper-sensitive to any slights on the reputation of the Resistance. At one point in the defence cross-examination of Reynaud, one juror shouted out: 'I would like to know if we are conducting here the trial of Paul Reynaud or Pétain . . . If we go on like this, we could be here for two months.'

In the first week of the trial Janet Flanner had been distinctly unim-pressed by Pétain's lawyers:

> Pétain's trio of defenders seems peculiarly, unnecessarily poor, lacking tact, teamwork, grace, and with one exception, brains. His chief defender, *batônnier* Payen, has a scattered jerky mind, and an unfortu-nate tic which makes his mouth pop open and shut like a bullfrog's. Pétain's second man, *maître* Lemaire, raises unimportant legal points in the loud declamatory voice of the Comédie française. The youngest Pétain defender, *maître* Isorni, has brains but they don't seem their best at the bar where his habit of continually interrupting everybody seems to distress even his client.[1]

Of the three lawyers, Lemaire was the most aggressive, repeatedly displaying 'an unerring instinct for making gaffes'.[2] Cross-examining Reynaud, he picked up on the latter's claim that Vichy had done noth-ing to protect him when the Germans took over the Unoccupied Zone in November 1942. Lemaire countered this accusation by reading out Pétain's letter of protest following Reynauld's seizure by the Ger-mans. This was a tiny point for the defence – even if it was only a protest after the event – but Lemaire spoiled the effect through his tendentious presentation of the letter: 'I ask you, M. le President, if there are many people, who call themselves resisters, who could find in their resistance dossier a letter of protest as solemn as that of Marshal Pétain.' The jurors exploded at this extraordinarily tactless comment. As Lemaire seemed unable to resist such provocations, he left most of the questioning to his colleagues.[3]

Isorni and Payen remained wary of each other. Whether intimidated by Reynaud's self-assurance or because, as a civil lawyer, he was not used to aggressive questioning, Payen had not planned any questions after Reynaud's long testimony. When Isorni looked as if he was about to rise to his feet, Payen whispered furiously: 'I forbid you to ask any questions.' Since Isorni would not be deflected, Payen jumped up himself to launch into a convoluted question about a speech Reynaud had made in May 1940. Reynaud batted this away easily by showing that Payen had misquoted him. Payen slumped back on to the bench, muttering that this was what happened if one asked questions – to which Isorni hissed, 'when one asks bad ones'.[4]

After this false start, Payen's main tactic was to try to lure witnesses into blaming Laval. Since Laval was in exile there was no danger of his answering back. Most witnesses avoided Payen's trap, but he had sowed a seed of doubt and brought Laval's name into the proceedings:

DALADIER: What took place between the two of them? I am simply unable to tell you for the simple reason that I do not know ... but I have to say that in my opinion there is a leader and that the leader is responsible not his collaborators.[5]

JEANNENEY: I had known Pierre Laval for a long time in parliament ... I always felt a particular aversion towards him ... What I do know is that Laval carried out vigorous and effective action to precipitate an armistice for reasons that might have been personal, but which were at root in accordance with his naturally underhand (*basse*) and cowardly nature. What influence did he have on the Marshal? I cannot say.[6]

BLUM: It is true that in the operation of 9–10 July at Vichy, we were faced with Laval. He was the one who masterminded the affair. When asked an embarrassing question, he would say: 'I will ask the Marshal; I will refer it to the Marshal.'

I feel I do not have the knowledge to decide between the responsibilities of the Marshal and Laval . . . But there is a hypothesis that cannot
be discounted: that they were each as guilty as the other . . . I did know
Laval but I did not really know the Marshal. There is in him a mystery
that I cannot penetrate. I cannot explain to myself satisfactorily the real
motives of his acts.[7]

Isorni was more inventive in his questioning, pursuing his quarry with
unexpected lines of attack. He had studied the preliminary evidence
carefully. Questioning Lebrun, he picked up on something the former
president had said which he had asked to remain confidential so as
not to upset the British government.[8] This concerned the agreement
with the British on 28 March 1940, that neither government would
sign a separate peace while the other was still at war. A lot of ink had
been spilt over the arcane question of whether by signing the armistice France had breached the agreement, as Reynaud and Marin had
argued. Isorni read out what Lebrun had previously said when ques-
tioned in preparation for the trial:

From the moment when one of the signatories of a convention like that
of 28 March holds back part of her forces to defend her territory
instead of throwing all into the common struggle, as was the case of
Britain, it can always brandish a piece of paper recalling the obligations
written on it, but it no longer has the moral authority to say: 'I cannot
free you from your obligations.'[9]

To secure such an admission from a former President of the Republic
was a neat point for the defence.

Isorni was also deft at exposing hypocrisies in the wartime trajectories of Pétain's accusers. One accusation against the Vichy regime was
that it had persecuted Communists, but Isorni took the opportunity
to remind the court that in September 1939, after the signing of the
German–Soviet Pact, Daladier's government had outlawed the Communist Party because it opposed the war. Thus when Vichy started
persecuting Communists it dusted off legislation introduced under the
Republic. But there was more. Daladier's clamp-down on the Communists had made him so hated by them that one Communist leader,
François Billoux, had offered to testify against him at the Riom trial

organized by Vichy to try those responsible for the defeat – a fact embarrassing to the Communists once they had reinvented themselves as heroes of the Resistance. This same Billoux was now in de Gaulle's government, giving Isorni a perfect opening:

ISORNI: Do you know that a current minister accused you of being one of those who had been responsible for the war: Billoux? . . .

A JUROR: You are pursuing an anti-Communist trial not the Pétain trial.

ISORNI: Pétain is accused of having tried to make a court pronounce on the culpability of France in the war. Billoux asked to testify against you! . . . There is something paradoxical that Pétain is in prison for doing what was proposed by a minister now in power. We could put three names on the same sheet of paper: you, Monsieur Daladier, you put Monsieur Billoux in prison; the Marshal put you in prison; Billoux is today in power, and the government of which he is a member, has put Marshal Pétain in prison. Does all that not make you somewhat sceptical about justice in political matters? [Laughter, shouts, protests].[10]

Isorni made some inroads in his cross-examination of Daladier, but it was paradoxically Léon Blum who offered him his best chance of unmasking the hypocrisies of Pétain's accusers.

Before the Riom court had convened, Pétain had in August 1941 issued another of his Constitutional Acts granting himself the right to judge those responsible for France's defeat. Using this authority, he had found Daladier and Blum guilty a few months later. So why proceed with a trial whose defendants had already been convicted? The Riom judges contemplated resigning, but decided to go ahead regardless. At the opening session, however, the presiding judge declared that the court would proceed as if all decisions taken so far regarding the defendants 'did not exist'. But was it conceivable that the court could contradict a sentence pronounced by Pétain to whom they had recently sworn an oath?[11] In the end, because the Riom court was suspended the judges were let off the hook, making it impossible to know what verdict they might have reached.

In his testimony to the Pétain trial, Daladier had given the Riom judges the benefit of the doubt, congratulating them for asserting their independence at the start of the proceedings. Blum would have none of this and he explicitly disassociated himself from Daladier's comment. For Blum the magistrates were guilty even for agreeing to participate in the charade. This judgement unsettled Mornet. While reminding the court that he had not sworn the oath to Pétain, he repeated his view that an oath sworn under duress was worthless. Were the judges not right to have remained in their posts to ensure that justice was served rather than risk being replaced by more subservient figures? Blum refused to excuse the judiciary:

> What would have occurred if there had been a general resignation to prevent justice from functioning? I ask the Court's pardon but persist in my belief: it would have been better for France that the court be interrupted than to see it, as was the case, subservient to the enemy.[12]

Mornet did not push the point any further, but the presiding judge of the Riom court, Pierre Caous, appeared in court the next day at his own request to refute Blum. 'A Vichy pill macerated in vinegar' was Madeleine Jacob's description of this dessicated figure who entered the court on a suicide mission to defend the honour of the French judiciary. Caous reminded the court that the Riom judges had *not* sworn the oath for the simple reason that they had been appointed before it was imposed. The only exception was Caous himself who had taken up his position later. But oath or no oath, he refuted Blum's claim that the magistrates would have confirmed a guilty verdict:

> What does he know? Who knows? I do not know, I did not know the views of any of my colleagues . . . During the suspension and between the sessions we never talked among ourselves about the trial . . . I refuse to give anyone the right to say that we would have condemned the defendants.

This offered Isorni an opening to lob a seemingly innocent question whose answer he knew perfectly well: was it true that Mornet himself had volunteered to sit on the Riom court? Mornet's scandalized response showed that he had hit his target: 'That is an infamy!' he screamed, 'his voice roaring and his ermine robes shaking like a vulture suddenly caught in a gust of wind'.[13] Caous's rectification of the facts hardly let Mornet off the hook. He pointed out that although Mornet had not actually volunteered his services, he had been invited to join – and had agreed. The fact that he had not in the end been called upon to serve 'had nothing to do with him or with me'. Mornet was forced to squirm:

> I did indeed receive such a letter ... At that moment I knew there was the question of setting up a Supreme Court of Justice ... and I said to myself: 'If the court is going to act against those who were responsible for an inexplicable disaster, those responsible for what can only be explained as treason, then, why not, I will help out.'
>
> But when, a few days later ... I heard what was expected of the Riom magistrates ... then I can tell you that I regretted the letter I had written ...
>
> Perhaps I might have attended the court; but the next day I would have been in a concentration camp; and possibly the day after in Germany, because I can be a bit forthright.

Caous closed the matter with a double-edged compliment: 'I am sure ... that in this matter you would have done neither better nor worse than we did.' For once Mornet remained prudently silent.[14]

Isorni's tactic of chipping away at the reputation of the witnesses for the prosecution was especially effective in his interrogation of Édouard Herriot, the last big beast of Republican politics to testify. Herriot's appearance was much anticipated. He was a celebrated orator, and those who managed to squeeze into the public galleries were expecting a star turn. Herriot, with his younger rival Daladier, had been the pre-eminent figure of the Radical Party in the interwar years. Like Daladier, he was a brilliant scholarship boy – another exemplar of the meritocratic virtues of the Republic's secular education system. From 1905 until France's defeat in 1940 he had served as mayor of Lyon. His enormous girth reflected his complete identification with the French city most identified with gastronomic excess: Herriot was the provincial Republic made flesh. What made his testimony so important was that in 1940 he had been President of the Chamber, the counterpart to Jeanneney in the Senate.

Thinner now, and wearing a huge sock on one foot as he was suffering from gout, Herriot was a diminished figure compared to his glory days. His ailments had delayed his appearance in court, and by the time he took the stand most of the ground he covered was familiar: the debate over the armistice, the *Massilia*, the vote of powers to

Pétain. He did, however, offer a different view of that vote than his colleague Jeanneney, who, although believing that the vote had been 'extorted', had expressed the view that Pétain's next step was 'exorbitant but not contrary to the letter of the constitutional law'. Herriot now asserted that Pétain's next step – his first Constitutional Act on 11 July – had changed everything: 'Between the text voted by the Assembly and the first constitutional act, there was a coup d'état; it is there that the coup occurred.' Herriot ended with an uplifting peroration, recalling how one day he had thrown away his Légion d'Honneur after hearing that Vichy had awarded the same honour to French officers who had fought with the Germans.[15]

Two lines of questioning dented Herriot's account of his unbending patriotism. The first related to that strange episode just before the Liberation of Paris when Laval conceived the scheme of reconvening the parliament of the Third Republic. He had driven over 30 kilometres east to the city of Nancy, where Herriot was under house arrest, and brought him back to Paris. The outline of the story was already known. Now, Herriot was asked to give his version:

> On 12 August 1944 M. Laval in person appeared in the room where I was locked up. You will believe me if I tell you that I had neither asked for this nor desired it. He had come to announce that I was free . . . He even took me in his arms.[16]

The two men set off for Paris. Herriot told Laval that parliament could not be convened unless the President of the Senate, Jeanneney, also agreed. Meanwhile Herriot was confined to the Hotel de Ville; it was clear that he had not really been 'freed': 'M. Laval came to see me again. I had a conversation with him which did not go as far as some have suggested. He was sounding me out.'

Since Jeanneney would have nothing to do with the scheme, it would have failed even if the Germans had not turned against it. After four days in Paris, Herriot was arrested again and taken back to Nancy. It is not clear what game he had been playing. Perhaps he briefly envisaged a role for himself as the man who would restore the Third Republic. But even if he had not compromised himself badly, the image of being hugged by Laval on the eve of Liberation was hardly glorious.

Isorni had another surprising question up his sleeve. He recalled that Herriot had declared Lyon an open city in June 1940: did this not prove that, like Pétain, he believed further resistance was futile? Herriot's answer provided the court with a vivid picture of the conditions prevailing in Bordeaux at the moment of defeat. On 17–18 June the Prefect of Lyon had telephoned to say that the Germans were approaching. Since Lyon was defenceless, what should he do? Herriot went to the building where the Ministry of War was lodged in Bordeaux:

> On that night of 17–18 June, while France was on the rack (*claie*), there was not a soul at work, not an office open; not even a single light on! So, I went to the Présidence du Conseil in the adjoining building. On that same night, in the midst of our national drama, there was not an office open, no one at work. I repeat: not a light on.
>
> There were just two republican guards, two soldiers, one of whom I happened to know . . . and two officers, one asleep on a sofa . . . and at the moment there was a bombing raid, and I was pushed into a cellar . . .
>
> My *directeur de cabinet* manged to get hold of the address of Marshal Pétain . . . We rushed over there in the night. At 2 a.m. the Marshal was woken up. And it was at his bedside that I asked him if, in these conditions, we should let Lyon be bombarded, while the military governor of the city was crying out for help and saying: 'I have nothing to defend the city.'
>
> In this affair who was, if not the guilty party, at least the one who should be considered responsible? The person or persons who had not armed that great city or the poor Mayor [i.e Herriot!] who, at the moment when his city was about to be burnt down . . . begged that there should not be a pointless massacre.[17]

By the end of the interrogation, Herriot seemed a somewhat less glorious figure than when he had entered the court.

'WAS MARSHAL PÉTAIN A TRAITOR?'

Once the defence had exposed the sinuous trajectories of these old Third Republic warhorses, it became harder for them to declare unequivocally that Pétain had been a traitor. 'Do you think Marshal Pétain betrayed his country?' Payen asked Daladier. The reply was evasive:

DALADIER: In all conscience I will reply that in my view Marshal Pétain betrayed the duties of his office.
PAYEN: That is not the same thing.
DALADIER: My answer is that the word 'treason' has numerous different meanings. There are men who betray their country for money, there are men who betray through simple incompetence, as was the case, I think, of Marshal Bazaine. Of Marshal Pétain I would say, frankly, and it is painful for me to say it, that he betrayed his duty as a Frenchman.[18]

The same question – was Pétain a traitor? – was put to Reynaud, after he was asked to explain a warm letter he had written to Pétain on 8 July 1940 expressing fond memories of their work together?

REYNAUD: It was only when I was in prison that I realized the truth about Marshal Pétain.
Isorni: But the armistice came before you were in prison.
REYNAUD: Just as when one develops a photograph the image gradually emerges, so it was in prison that I gradually came to understand. Before then, I still believed in the patriotism of Marshal Pétain ...
ISORNI: Would you please reply succinctly? The armistice was signed on 25 June. You considered that it was a treason?
REYNAUD: I never said it was treason but that it was contrary to the honour and interest of France.[19]

As for Jeanneney, he was confronted by some flattering remarks he had made about Pétain on the Senate floor on 9 July 1940:

My relations with Marshal Pétain go back to 1917. I was then a member of the Clemenceau government's War Committee ... General Pétain appeared on various occasions before this committee. I was impressed by the sobriety and lucidity of his exposés ...

But one fact overshadowed all others: the memory I had of that morning in December 1918, when on the esplanade of Metz, Poincaré and Clemenceau jointly awarded Pétain his Marshal's baton ...

In reality, was there much of a choice in 1940? It is undeniable that, at this moment, all eyes were turned towards Marshal Pétain. He was even a kind of life raft towards which all hands were stretched.

So did Jeanneney consider Pétain a criminal?

If I had held Marshal Pétain to be a criminal, I would not have pronounced to the Assembly the words that I used about him. The armistice was an unpardonable mistake, and unfortunately one that was largely irreparable.

Finally, Lebrun was confronted by a letter of good wishes he had written to Pétain in January 1941: 'That proves at least that you did not consider him to be a dishonest man?' Lebrun squirmed in his reply: 'The word "dishonest" has not been used by me'. He concluded lamely that his letter had been a pure formality from a president to his successor, containing no words of approbation for his policy. Payen neatly reminded the court that it had been sent in January 1941 – 'that is to say after Montoire'.[20]

Only Léon Blum refused to let Pétain off the hook:

'Betray' means to hand something over, deliver it up. I would say, despite everything, that the armistice did offer the French people a certain number of guarantees and protections. It was the duty of the government that had signed it to ensure that these were respected by the enemy. But these conditions were given up point by point, like everything else.

I would also say that, in the most favourable hypothesis, Marshal Pétain had only received a mandate to reform Republican institutions. The fact that he destroyed them, and left nothing of them, creating for himself and the band of ambitious arrivistes and cowards around him a government that was almost farcical by the sheer enormity of its power, surpassing that of any eastern potentate . . . represents a treason towards the Republic and a betrayal of it.

Yet phrases like 'betraying the interests of France', 'betraying the duties of his office', 'betraying the Republic' are to my mind still somewhat mealy-mouthed . . .

In June 1940, I could see with my own eyes – all of you could see – a country, which, after the shock of a brutal, vast, and incomprehensible defeat found itself in that dazed state in which a bombardment can leave certain sensitive natures ... There was a population stunned, paralysed, knocked senseless to the ground by stupor and despair. And this is what this population was told: 'No, no, the armistice that we are proposing to you, that degrades you, that hands you over, is not dishonourable; it is natural; it is in conformity with the interests of the *patrie*.'

And this population who did not know its terms, who had not read it, who did not understand it, who only saw its implications as events unfolded, believed what it had been told because the man who had uttered these words spoke with the authority of his great military past, in the name of glory and victory, in the name of the army, in the name of honour.

So that for me is the key issue: the massive and atrocious abuse of moral confidence. Yes, I think that can be called treason.[21]

12

Last Witnesses for the Prosecution

One of the obsessions of the prosecution had been to try and prove that Pétain's arrival in power was the 'culmination of a plot against the Republic hatched a long time beforehand'. The *Acte d'accusation* insisted that Pétain enjoyed close relations 'with the principal members of the association known as the Cagoule'. The debates of the first week threw little light on the matter. When Jeanneney was directly asked by the defence if he thought there had been a plot to take power, he replied: 'I never heard of a plot.'[1]

After the parade of Republican grandees, the prosecution had produced two insignificant journalists to provide some scraps of unsubstantiated information about Pétainist plots. The first, Paul Winckler, reported some gossip from an unnamed Spaniard he had met in 1939. This informant had attended an 'intimate' dinner with the Spanish fascist leader Primo de Rivera where Pétain was allegedly present. But Winckler's flimsy testimony was tarnished when he had to return to court the next day to refute an accusation (probably false) that before 1940 he had run a press agency in receipt of German funds.

The other journalist, Denise Petit, only in court for a few minutes, attracted disproportionate press attention because she was the only woman called to testify during the entire trial. Before the war she had worked for an Italian newspaper in Paris. She reported that her employer was told by Laval in January 1939 of a plan – supported by a 'high military personage' – to establish a military dictatorship in France. Her credibility was undermined when she admitted that during the Occupation she had worked in Paris for a German newspaper, as a cover for resistance activity. Isorni countered neatly: 'If the

Germans had won the war, you would presumably have told them that it was the newspaper *Pariser Zeitung* that had asked you to work for the Resistance!'[2] Isorni later caused amusement in the corridors of the Palais de Justice by recalling that he had previously encountered Denise Petit as a singer in an operetta he had written as a young man.

It was Pétain's fourteen months as ambassador in Spain that most obsessed the conspiracy theorists. He had been appointed in March 1939 at the end of the Spanish Civil War when France was desperately seeking to improve relations with the Franco regime. There could have been no more symbolic gesture of goodwill than sending this revered military hero. The fact that he was often scuttling back to France to meet politicians suggested he might be harbouring political ambitions. Daladier offered two pieces of information about this period. He recalled that when war was declared in September 1939, Pétain had refused to join his government. This was a blow to Daladier's efforts to harness Pétain's prestige behind the war effort. Did it have a more sinister implication? Was Pétain holding out for the day when he could take over? This idea was given a certain plausibility by another piece of information which had surfaced in the diary of Anatole de Monzie, one of Daladier's ministers. According to de Monzie, Pétain had remarked at the start of March 1940, 'They will need me in the second half of May.' Was it not suspicious that he could have known already in March that a catastrophe would occur in May? Did it not prove that he was planning a future political role for himself?[3] All of this was enough for one newspaper to carry the headline 'Daladier Demonstrates Pétain Plot'.[4]

The prosecution also called two officials who had served in the French Embassy in Spain under Pétain. They were only in court for a few minutes each. The only possibly incriminating piece of evidence reported by the first, Armand Gazel, was that Pétain had twice read out to him a list of names – the famous list! – for a government he one day intended to form. But Gazel added that Pétain 'never gave me the impression of plotting'. The second witness, Albert Lamarle, repeatedly folding and unfolding an enormous handkerchief with which he nervously wiped his spectacles, had one nugget of information. In September 1939, Pétain had mistakenly handed him a letter believing it to be about some routine issues. It turned out to be from Georges

Loustaunau-Lacau, a right-wing army officer involved in various anti-Republican plots, and it contained the words: 'I have seen Pierre Laval. He proposes to form a government that will rid you of all and sundry.'[5]

There was an understandable frisson in the courtroom when the author of that incriminating letter, Colonel Georges Loustaunau-Lacau, was called to testify. He was the nearest the court would come to hearing a flesh-and-blood 'Cagoulard'. If Pétain had conspired to overthrow the Republic, Loustaunau-Lacau was the man to know about it. No witness left a more unsettling impression than this ravaged figure who hobbled painfully into the court supporting himself on a stick, having been released only two weeks earlier from the concentration camp of Mauthausen. Like other witnesses the court had already heard, he was a ghost – in his instance a ghost not of the Republic but of the anti-Republic, of that penumbra of right-wing conspirators who had turned against democracy in the 1930s.

In the 1920s, Loustaunau-Lacau was considered one of the most brilliant young officers of the French Army. A contemporary of de Gaulle at the École Militaire in 1924, he had been one of his closest friends. Both went on to serve on Pétain's staff: de Gaulle in the 1920s, Loustaunau-Lacau in the 1930s. But in the 1930s the trajectories of these two conservatives diverged. Loustaunau's fear of Communism had brought him into the orbit of conspirators plotting against the Republic. After the armistice, he had stayed in France since he supported the political values of the Vichy regime while assuming it would not prevent him working against the Germans. Reaching out to de Gaulle in London at the end of 1940 in the name of their previous association with Pétain, he received a firm reply: 'What Philippe was in the past changes nothing regarding the way we judge what Philippe is in the present.'[6]

Soon Loustaunau-Lacau discovered that his anti-German activities were incompatible with his support for 'Philippe'. Arrested in 1941, he was deported to Germany after being interrogated by the Gestapo. He described his profession to the court as 'political deportee'. 'Professional conspirator' would have been more accurate. Since he had been close to Pétain before the war, he seemed a possible missing link to prove the prosecution's claim of a Pétainist plot.

When asked about the Cagoule in the pre-trial interrogations, Pétain had replied: 'You can go on and on about the "Cagoule". I can tell you nothing, I know nothing. I knew only one cagoulard; that was Loustaunau-Lacau and when I discovered this, he was gone in 24 hours.'[7] Pétain's claim to have severed relations with Loustaunau-Lacau in 1938 was an outright lie. Not only had he seen him in the early days of the Vichy regime but he had remained in touch with him after 1938. This was demonstrated by the long letter Loustaunau-Lacau had written to him on 22 September 1939, reporting on the situation in Paris. At Pétain's request he had met Laval, who expressed his view that the days of the Daladier government were numbered – after which Pétain could replace him and make Laval Foreign Minister.[8]

On his return from Mauthausen, Loustaunau-Lacau was interviewed by the lawyers preparing the case against Pétain. He also visited Isorni, who could not figure out what to make of him. On one hand, he seemed possessed by a rage against Pétain for having done nothing to protect him from the Germans; on the other, he hated the left-wing atmosphere of Liberation France. Because he seemed so unpredictable and unstable, neither the defence nor the prosecution wanted to risk calling him as a witness. It was Judge Mongibeaux who exercised his prerogative to summon him. Isorni was on tenterhooks, concerned that Loustaunau-Lacau might any moment utter some 'some enormity'.[9]

Loustaunau-Lacau delivered his testimony seated, speaking in a toneless voice, gazing fixedly into the distance as if discerning conspiracies visible to no one else. He opened:

> I owe nothing to Marshal Pétain, but that does not prevent me from being disgusted by the spectacle of all those people, in this very room, trying to shift all their own errors on to the shoulders of an old man almost a hundred years old . . . I also affirm, under oath, that Marshal Pétain was never part of the Cagoule in any form whatever, for if he had been, I would have known.

A good start for the defence.

Now Loustaunau-Lacau proceeded, for those insufficiently acquainted with the labyrinth of pre-war conspiracies, to describe the network he had set up in the army to counter Communist infiltration:

> What did Marshal Pétain know about all this? Nothing. Why would I have kept him abreast of the clandestine activity we were carrying out in barracks? Lack of trust in him? No. Rather it was fear that he might mix up his files, or that his forgetfulness, which was sometimes total, might lead him to make some massive blunder.

Not flattering for Pétain, but another point for the defence.

Loustaunau-Lacau now moved on to the relations between Pétain and Laval. He recalled a reception at the Quai d'Orsay in 1934 when Premier Gaston Doumergue had taken Pétain into a corner and remarked to him, 'the Republic is done for and there is no one left except him over there' – pointing to Laval:

> The Marshal repeated this phrase to me often during our meetings and discussions with the obstinacy shown by certain old men to repeat endlessly the same thing almost like a reflex . . .
>
> There is no doubt M. Laval wanted one day to use this glorious *képi* to cover his political schemes. There is no doubt also that Marshal Pétain saw this extraordinary manipulator of humanity, with his feline intelligence, as someone to offer counsel at certain moments. It never went further than that.

Finally, Loustaunau-Lacau came to his meeting with Laval, which he had reported in the infamous letter of September 1939. He told Laval that Pétain wished to have his view of the situation:

> 'The situation,' answered M. Laval, 'is quite simple. Daladier must be got rid of' . . .
>
> 'You can tell the Marshal,' Laval said to me, 'that Daladier is a dung-heap, a bastard.'[10]

Since Loustaunau-Lacau lived in his own paranoid world, the reliability of his testimony was uncertain. But even if, as seemed plausible, this conversation was true, it hardly represented a plot to bring down the Republic. He hobbled out of the court – and, in the words of Isorni, 'returned to his mystery'.[11] The defence lawyers could breathe more easily.

The failure to demonstrate the existence of a plot led Mornet to make a startling announcement on the next day: 'It is time for the Pétain trial to begin . . . It is not the trial of the armistice. Nor is it the trial of the vote of 10 July 1940.' The defence jumped in to ask whether the court was now also dropping the accusation that Pétain had plotted to take power. Mornet was evasive:

> What I am not abandoning is that an attack on the Republic was committed on 11 July, and it matters little whether this was preceded by a plot for which, I admit, that I lack the necessary elements to establish precisely the role of the individuals who played a part.

This was an extraordinary admission, implying as it did that most of the first week had been wasted. Mongibeaux had seemingly come to a similar conclusion:

> Since the start of this trial, we have been trying to find out the conditions in which the armistice was sought and accepted; the civil and military witnesses have been shifting on to each other the responsibility for this act. I believe that we are fully enlightened about this issue and that we need now to move on to another part of the trial: what did the Marshal do *after* 10 July with the powers that were granted to him?[12]

There was widespread relief that at last the trial might move on from being an obsessive raking over the events of June and July 1940.

A DIPLOMAT AND A GENERAL

Although the prosecution had centred its case on the plot and the armistice, it did have two witnesses who could testify about the Vichy regime. These two figures, a general and a diplomat, were not well known, but each had served the Vichy regime in its early days: General Paul-André Doyen, who represented France on the Armistice Commission at Wiesbaden until July 1941, and François Charles-Roux, former head of the French Foreign Ministry, the Quai d'Orsay.

General Doyen described his early encounters with his German counterparts on the Armistice Commission, the body responsible for overseeing the daily implementation of the armistice. At a meeting on 15

September 1940 he was confronted with a German demand for control of copper mines situated in Yugoslavia but belonging to France. When Doyen replied that this went beyond any requirements of the armistice, he was told: 'You don't seem to understand yet that France has been beaten, and that if she does not do everything that Germans ask her to do, she will be punished.' Doyen fared no better when trying to protest against another even more flagrant violation of the armistice: the annexation of Alsace-Lorraine and the appointment of two German administrators, Gauleiters, who embarked on a rapid policy of Germanization. When Doyen tried to protest on behalf of the French government, the general commanding the German occupation forces slapped him down with no diplomatic courtesies: 'Furious he rose to his feet and said: "Seven generations of Stülpnagels have waged war against France. Mine must be the last."' What most alarmed Doyen was Vichy's reaction:

> I quickly realized that there were two policies confronting each other: the policy that we were leading at Wiesbaden, one of resistance to Germany in all domains, and the policy being conducted by the Vichy government, which was entirely different, and which consisted in going to Paris to demolish all we were doing in Wiesbaden – the policy of Laval.

When Doyen warned Pétain that Laval was taking him down a dangerous path, he was told: 'Laval is a dung-heap [*fumier*].' To Doyen's relief, on 13 December 1940 the 'dung-heap' was sacked. But then he was asked to transmit a letter from Pétain to Hitler assuring him that 'the removal of M. Laval does not signify the end of the policy of collaboration'. When Laval's successor, Admiral François Darlan, went to meet Hitler at Berchtesgaden, Doyen sought another interview with Pétain: 'I did not this time,' he reported, 'meet the same reaction as when I had talked to him about Laval.'

The next few months witnessed 'all the major acts of treason', the most serious of which was to allow the Germans to use French airfields in Syria. Finally, in July 1941, Doyen was told that his services were no longer required. He wrote a long report for the government warning that there was nothing to be hoped for from Germany: 'When I went to take my leave of the Marshal, he said to me: "I have read your note with much attention and I share your views."'

In the space of seven months, Doyen had seemingly encountered three different Pétains: which was the true one?[13]

The next witness, Charles-Roux, was a caricature of the professional diplomat. Listeners had to decipher his meaning through the muffled courtesies of diplomatic understatement. Every protagonist from 'Chancellor Hitler' downwards was given their title; dramatic events were concealed in a labyrinth of parentheses, conditionals and sub-clauses. French uncertainty as to whether Spain would join the war was rendered in Roux-speak as 'the information one received justified what I would describe as a certain perplexity'.

Charles-Roux opened with the day he heard, after Reynaud's resignation, that Laval, who had been promised a portfolio in Pétain's government, was holding out for the Foreign Ministry:

> There were rumours circulating that he was advocating a reversal of our alliances ... And his name was so unpopular in England that it might add a coefficient of Anglophobia to any initiatives that the new government might take' [Diplomatic speak for: 'I was worried that until an armistice had been signed, it was necessary not to burn bridges with London.']

Charles-Roux told Weygand that he would resign if Laval became Foreign Minister. Weygand conveyed the message to Pétain and returned with the reassuring news that Laval would not be offered the post: 'Indeed after a few minutes the door opened, M. Pierre Laval crossed the room muttering and slammed the door after him' – a casebook example of how easily Pétain could be influenced by the last person he talked to.

Next, Charles-Roux gave a vivid account of the course of the armistice negotiations. Humiliatingly the German conditions had been presented to the French at Compiègne, in the very railway carriage where the armistice of 1918 had been signed. On 21 June, General Weygand in Bordeaux received a telephone call from General Huntziger, head of the French delegation: 'I am in the carriage.' 'My poor friend,' replied Weygand. General Huntziger continued: 'I will telephone you the conditions. They are tough but nothing dishonourable.' Charles-Roux told the court:

For the rest of the day I knew no more.

That evening at 10.00 I was summoned to Weygand's Headquarters . . .

The conditions of the armistice had arrived. They were being typed up and the pages were being brought over as they were ready.

I arrived a little late and the first two pages had already begun to circulate.

When I entered, the first place name I heard was Saint-Jean-Pied-de-Port. I could not believe my ears.

For me, Saint-Jean-Pied-de-Port recalled the Basque region. I looked at the map on which the demarcation line was being gradually traced in blue pencil. And indeed I saw that the entire Atlantic coast and the Channel were in the Occupied Zone . . . I shouted out that if those were the conditions it was better to go to Africa.

The Marshal, very gently, made it clear to me that the issue was closed.

For a few more months, Charles-Roux remained in his post, ostensibly working for the Foreign Minister, Paul Baudouin, but increasingly aware that Pierre Laval was taking control of foreign policy through his personal contacts with the German ambassador in Paris, Otto Abetz. It was via the circuitous route of the Brazilian ambassador to Vichy that Charles-Roux heard on 23 October about Laval's meeting with Hitler at Montoire – the prelude to the meeting with Pétain:

And here is the only detail, rather picturesque, that I heard of the account Laval gave to the Conseil des Ministres, of his interview with Hitler at Montoire. He claimed that he had left Vichy thinking he was going to meet only M. von Ribbentrop. Then, once in Paris, having indeed met M. von Ribbentrop, he got into a car with him, and they set off from Paris. M. von Ribbentrop said to him:

'Do you know whom you are going to meet?'

M. Laval replied: 'Non.'

And Ribbentrop answered: 'You are going to meet Chancellor Hitler.'

To which Laval replied: 'You must be joking [*sans blague*].' [This 'picturesque' detail was as risqué as Charles-Roux allowed himself to be; others report Laval saying '*Merde alors!*']\[14]

Charles-Roux resigned two days later.

THE SILENT MARSHAL

On leaving the court, Charles-Roux paused to shake Pétain's hand – a gesture that shocked many observers. *L'Humanité* raged, 'Roux ostentatiously shook the hand of the old traitor. A fact without precedent in the history of a trial for treason.'[15] This was the reflex of the diplomat. Charles-Roux would have shaken the hand of Hitler. Beneath the velvety understatements, his testimony had been devastating. Most witnesses simply ignored Pétain's presence, although they all had to squeeze past him when entering and leaving the tiny court. Pétain would move his table slightly to make way for them. When the aged Jeanneney, who had known Pétain longer than anyone else in the court, was leaving the court, Pétain half raised himself to give a bow – the first time he had done so for any witness. Jeanneney responded with the slightest of bows while looking straight ahead.

Witnesses spoke with their back to Pétain and often they seemed unaware of the old man sitting only a few feet behind. There was one exception. While Blum, answering Payen's question whether Pétain had been a traitor, made his comment about the Pétain 'mystery', his voice fell so low that Mongibeaux asked him to turn round and address the courtroom. As he did so, Blum moved forward slightly, until he found himself just in front of Pétain, separated only by a small table. Joseph Kessel wrote: 'The eyes of the two men locked. Pétain raised his hand slightly. His pale lips remained tightly closed. Not a muscle in his face moved. But with his heavy old hands, twice he made a gesture that seemed to say: "No".'[16]

This was a rare moment. Most of the time, Pétain, slumped in his chair, seemed indifferent, impassive, in another world, as if unaware of what was going on around him – except for the rapid blinking of his eyes. He seemed to have been sitting in the armchair all his life, playing with his gloves, stroking his *képi*, massaging the arms of his chair, clasping and unclasping his freckled hands, his chin occasionally falling on his chest as he struggled to keep awake in the stifling heat of the courtroom.

One day, when the photographers crouched at his feet for their usual ritual before the start of the proceedings, instead of ignoring them as he normally did, Pétain showed a flash of irritation, flapping his gloves as if to shoo them away like flies. One journalist captured the moment: 'His face became alive, his demeanour imperious. The man who had seemed absent suddenly showed a flash of military authority.' But quicky he slumped back into his normal torpor, his demeanour as inscrutable as ever. Madeleine Jacob warned her readers against feeling respect or pity: 'People talk of his "marmoreal" countenance. No. It is a wooden face, the face of a cunning old peasant, the face of a "false witness", a face without nobility . . . The face of a traitor . . . Mendacity and ruse in every feature, in each blinking of his eyes. The man looks locked into himself, egoistically. He feigns absence.'[17] One journalist, trying at the end of the first week to penetrate the mystery of this 'indecipherable man', wrote: 'Is he a man like other men? Or is he just a legend from which the gilding is cracking and peeling off . . . a sort of collective illusion suddenly emptied of the lies which kept it alive?'[18]

Some observers wondered if he could even hear what was being said. He certainly could. One day he told his guard, Joseph Simon, 'it is difficult to remain impassive. I do all I can to keep calm but it will be very hard.'[19] Three times, to the alarm of his lawyers, Pétain's seeming impassivity came close to cracking. The first time was during Daladier's testimony, after a question from a juror about a matter that Daladier was in no position to know anything about since he had been in prison at the time. The question related to the notorious

15. Pétain waves his glove angrily at an importunate cameraman.

telegram from Pétain to Hitler after the Allied raid on Dieppe in August 1942. Isorni, Lemaire, Payen and Mongibeaux launched into an abstruse discussion to determine whether this telegram had even been sent. Meanwhile Pétain was becoming visibly agitated. His face turned red; he looked as if he were about to rise to his feet; his lawyers leant over to stop him. Payen whispered audibly, 'Don't say anything; don't reply.' Since it was obvious to everyone that Pétain had clearly heard something, another juror (Perney) intervened:

PERNEY: Marshal Pétain, who it seems to me has heard, is not answering the questions asked. His honour is at stake. He is the person who could give us the definitive explanation and interpretation of the telegram . . .
PAYEN: He gave it during the *instruction*.

There were shouts and boos, but Pétain had recovered his calm. When Payen repeated the question, he replied: 'How to give explanations? I am hard of hearing. I did not hear anything and I do not know what all this is about.'[20]

This incident proved one thing: Pétain could hear when he wanted. There was a similar incident later that day when the court was told about Pétain producing his list of ministers. The juror Jean Pierre-Bloch saw an opening: 'We are at the very heart of the debate, of the accusation of a plot against the Republic . . . The accused must be asked again how long in advance his ministerial list was prepared.' Mongibeaux instructed the 'accused' to rise. When Pétain seemed not to have heard, the policeman at Pétain's side was instructed to make him stand:

PÉTAIN: I cannot answer since I did not hear.
MONGIBEAUX: I will repeat the question. How long in advance had you prepared the list of ministers that you proposed to President Lebrun?
PÉTAIN: What was the question?

Payen repeated it again:

PÉTAIN: I did first ponder some names but the list I proposed was not the same . . . I mean that the list I had in my pocket was not the one that was put in place. I have answered.

PIERRE-BLOCH: I do not think that is an answer to the question I asked.
MONGIBEAUX: That is all I can do.[21]

Nothing in the first week seemed to affect Pétain more than the short testimony of Michel Clemenceau, who was neither a politician, soldier or diplomat, and had played no role in the events being debated in court.[22] He was the son of Georges Clemenceau, the leader of France in the Great War. Michel was not in court because he looked uncannily like his father, but in order to summon up the memory of the conservative politician and resistance leader Georges Mandel, Clemenceau's closest parliamentary aide in the Great War, who had been executed by the Milice in the last weeks of the Vichy regime, on 7 July 1944. Because Mandel was a Jew, the extreme right accused him of dragging France into the war for personal reasons. In Reynaud's government no one had more implacably opposed the armistice. Mandel, who had been on the *Massilia*, was arrested on his return to France. When the Germans moved into the Occupied Zone he was deported to Germany where he shared a prison with Blum. In their enforced confinement, these two dissimilar Jewish politicians, the subtle and generous Socialist intellectual and the intransigent and cynical conservative patriot, developed a close bond. After the assassination of the ultra-collaborator Philippe Henriot by resisters in June 1944, Mandel was extracted from prison, brought back to France, and assassinated by the Milice, Vichy's paramilitary police organization.

Michel Clemenceau had visited the fortress of Portalet where Mandel was interned. Describing his efforts to intervene with Pétain on Mandel's behalf, he told the court that, before admitting him into the Marshal's presence, Pétain's aide-de-camp had made a disconcerting request: 'Since you are going to see the Marshal to tell him what is going on outside, do also tell him what is going on here ... The Marshal has no confidence in the people around him, he does not believe them. He stays for hours at his table, probably pondering grave questions of war, diplomacy and politics, but he does not seem interested in what is going on around him.' Pétain received Michel Clemenceau amiably and invited him to stay for dinner. Clemenceau refused:

'I have just spent two days with those two unfortunates that you illegally interned at Portalet; if I shared their provisions for two days, it was not then to sit down at the dinner table with you.' 'A pity, we could have had lots of interesting things to discuss.'

As the silence dragged on, I said: 'So why not say them now.'

Pétain launched into a defence of his policy. The conversation between the two men became more heated; Clemenceau left and did not see Pétain again.

Payen fought back by reminding the court that Pétain had protested against Mandel's deportation. Clemenceau countered that Pétain's letter was only written after he himself had written imploring him to remove Mandel to safety before the Germans arrived. Clemenceau had clearly demonstrated that Pétain was indirectly responsible for Mandel's death and had barely lifted a finger to save him. While this discussion was going on in court, Pétain turned red in the face and started waving his hands. 'His whole person,' one reporter wrote, 'cried out "no".' Perhaps this had stirred Pétain's memories of Clemenceau senior and the glory days of the Great War; perhaps he felt guilt about the death of Mandel. Pétain's agitation was so visible that when Michel Clemenceau finished a juror asked whether Pétain wished to comment. The moment had passed; he refused to respond. 'Suddenly, as if released from a nightmare,' one journalist reported, he relaxed once more. 'His face became impassive again, he laid down his hands and returned to his silence.'[23]

'THE PÉTAIN TRIAL IS MAKING ME PHYSICALLY SICK'

'Sunday 29 July. At last, a day without having to see Pétain!' The juror Jacques Lecompte-Boinet was probably not the only person to feel a sense of relief on the first Sunday of the trial. In his case, however, a day without Pétain was not a day off. As a parliamentary juror, he was free instead to attend the last day of the debate on the new constitution. De Gaulle was due to appear in person to defend his proposal. Lecompte-Boinet, who wanted to talk to him about another matter, buttonholed de Gaulle in a corridor:

He took me by the arm and said: 'Don't you need to take a leak? I'm bursting', and so it was that my chat with de Gaulle took place in the urinals, which was uncomfortable from an intellectual standpoint. At the best of times he is like ice, and standing there with him in front of the marble is even more refrigerating.[24]

Lecompte-Boinet managed to raise his point even in these unpropitious conditions. We do not know if they discussed the trial but we do know that Lecompte-Boinet was increasingly unhappy with the partisanship of many fellow jurors. He felt strongly enough to approach Payen in a moment of the court's recess:

'I came here with the firm desire to form a judgement and not give a verdict decided in advance. And I am unhappy that there is so little in this trial about Pétain for in my view the question is as follows: on one side of the scales, the facts we know (the dishonour inflicted on France, the fateful armistice, the recruitment of the LVF, the Milice . . .); on the other side, services that Pétain did genuinely render' . . . Payen replied to me: 'I am happy to know that there is a juror like you, at least one, and when I speak, I will know that at least one juror is listening to me.'

According to the reports received by the government, most people, having so eagerly anticipated the trial, were now feeling 'general lassitude' and hoped the proceedings would be over as fast as possible. There was a sense that the trial was presenting a bad image of France to the world outside. Susan Mary Jay, who later married the journalist Joe Alsop and became a noted Washington hostess, was working in the US Embassy at that time. She wrote to a friend back home:

The Pétain trial is making me physically sick. You will have read it all in the papers, but it is remarkably unpleasant to be in that little courtroom day after day; yet one wouldn't miss it – it's morbidly fascinating. Of course I shouldn't be there; each embassy has one bitterly fought-for ticket, but an official gave me his own because he didn't want to see it . . . He does not wish to relive the decay of French democracy in a hot courtroom . . . I listen to former members of the government getting up day after day to exonerate themselves from any guilt and bringing tears to the eyes of everyone . . . with moving descriptions of how the country was plunged into a bath of poison by the nefarious treason of

Marshal Pétain. Sometimes they get so far off the point that the Marshal doesn't come into it at all. The witness is never stopped in his monologue, and there is almost no cross examination. The Marshal sits there looking extremely spry and somehow dominates the proceedings by remaining silent.[25]

Much of the resistance press shared a similar view about the witnesses: 'curious to see all these old men complaining how they had been duped like little children by this nonagenarian,' wrote *Franc-Tireur*.[26] 'One is not going to disarm those who remain faithful to Pétain by confronting them with representatives of a regime that had itself capitulated,' commented another newspaper.[27] Jean Schlumberger ventured the heretical thought that people did not much care about the final moments of the Third Republic: 'Let us be honest, if France had found in the Vichy regime a fortress that defended her interests inch by inch . . . she would probably overlook irregularities in the way Pétain took power.'[28] As was often the case, it was François Mauriac who put his finger on why many people felt uneasy. Collaboration, he pointed out, might have been the logical consequence of the armistice, but the armistice was the logical consequence of Munich. And few people had not supported Munich:

> We would be hypocrites if, before joining the chorus of voices of all those who accuse him, each of us did not ask: what did I think at the moment of Munich? What were my real feelings on hearing of the armistice? . . . Let us not hide from ourselves the thought that each of us was perhaps complicit, at certain moments, with this old man now struck down.[29]

In the atmosphere of the Liberation, with concentration-camp deportees still arriving back in France, this was as far as any newspaper could go in offering any positive opinion on Pétain. But reports on public opinion which the government received regularly from Prefects suggested that Pétain still enjoyed support among the peasantry, elements of the middle and upper classes, and in Catholic circles. In some *départements* it was necessary to prevent over-zealous prelates from organizing masses for Pétain. One report from Rouen commented that Pétain's sympathizers 'only express their views around the family dinner table . . . But in no public place or in the street do they venture to express their feelings.'[30]

The many hostile letters received by the conservative politician Louis Marin after his appearance in court offer a window into this hidden world of Pétainist resentment and nostalgia. Some, threatening and abusive, were written in angry capital letters:

'THE PEOPLE WILL NOT BE CHEATED AND HAVE ALREADY SINGLED OUT A GALLOWS FOR YOU. LONG LIVE DE GAULLE. LONG LIVE PÉTAIN.'

'HITLER MUST BE LAUGHING IN HIS GRAVE. POOR IDIOTS LIKE YOU WHO PREPARE THE VICTORY OF COMMUNISM.'

'WHAT A GAFFE YOU COMMITTED IN TESTIFYING AGAINST MARSHAL PÉTAIN OR IS IT AN ACT OF INFAMY ON YOUR PART?'[31]

There were many more in this vein insulting Marin as a freemason and a traitor. Other letters were written more in sorrow than rage by former members of his party offering their resignation after decades of membership. One wrote:

Do you not think that in France there are more men who were mistaken in believing that collaboration was possible with the Germans – especially before they revealed to us the refinements of their cruelty – than men who really intended to betray? And do you not think also that with regard to the outside world it would be better for our reputation to show indeed that these men were mistaken instead of parading them as a procession of traitors from every class of society . . . I hope with all my heart that people in France will now demand the trial of those in charge of France in June 1940 who did not hesitate to shift their responsibility on to a man more than eighty years old![32]

Occasionally these views would emerge in court. Among the small number of people in the public galleries, many of them women, there was clearly sympathy for the Marshal and hostility to the prosecution witnesses. When on leaving the court Blum shook the hand of Reynaud and Daladier, who were sitting on the witness bench to listen to him, someone shouted from the gallery, 'the bastards'.[33] Otherwise, since the explosions of the first day, and occasional eruptions by jurors, the trial had been calm. The journalist Géo London, an habitué of courts and parliaments, remarked that between sessions the atmosphere resembled the corridors of the Chamber of Deputies before the war: 'groups form; people discuss the latest events as if after a parliamentary debate with a splash of colour added by the gold of the military kepis and the purple robes of the lawyers.'[34] Lawyers and witnesses who had been screaming at each other in court could be seen chatting amicably a few minutes later. After their angry clash during the appearance of the Riom judge, Pierre Caous, Mornet gave Isorni a friendly clap on the shoulder, muttering 'dear old Isorni'. Even Reynaud, after having been grilled by Isorni, came up to congratulate him as a 'loyal adversary'. The two men knew each other well since Reynaud's daughter, a friend of Isorni, was married to a lawyer friend of his.[35] All trials have a degree of simulated outrage. In the trial of Brasillach, Isorni, his defence lawyer, had been a friend of the prosecutor Marcel Reboul. They lived in the same building and even sometimes travelled to court on the same bus.[36] The protagonists in this High Court drama all came from the same elite milieu: this round of France's civil war was a polite affair.

What had the first week of the trial revealed? None of the witnesses for the prosecution, other than Blum, had been willing to say outright that Pétain was a traitor or that the armistice was itself treasonable, as de Gaulle believed it to be. A number of facts had been clearly established: that Pétain had undermined Reynaud's efforts to avoid an armistice; that Pétain had reneged on his promise to allow ministers to leave Bordeaux; that the *Massilia* had turned into a trap; that the vote of full powers to Pétain had been 'extorted' while not being technically illegal. Little had so far been said about the post-armistice period. Most witnesses had sidestepped Payen's attempts to get them to blame Laval – but no one had ventured a firm view as to the nature of the relations between the two men. It had still not been established whether Pétain had been duplicitous, easily swayed or deceived. At one meeting General Doyen had got the impression that Pétain had opposed the concessions to Germany; at another, the opposite seemed to be true. Would the next week bring greater clarity?

Curieux ce Procès !

On entend

PAUL REYNAUD (le rat pesteux) : il parle de lui...
DALADIER : il parle de lui...

Il est vrai qu'en 1940 ils ont fait assez triste figure et sentent qu'ils ont pas mal de choses à « expliquer »...

Mais les Français oublient si vite ! **Après quatre ans, on peut venir leur raconter ce qu'on veut et ils le croient :**

- que la France avait des chars et des avions à ne savoir qu'en faire,
- que la République avait bien préparé la guerre,
- qu'il n'y a pas eu d'exode,
- que Daladier et d'autres n'ont rien signé à Munich ni à Paris avec le boche,
- que Thorez est parti le premier au front en 1939,
- que Pétain a perdu la bataille de Verdun...

ALBERT LEBRUN vient déposer qu'aux conseils des ministres qui ont précédé l'armistice, il y avait des partisans de la continuation de la lutte (des résistants) et il y avait des gens qui, comme le Maréchal PÉTAIN, voulaient demander l'armistice. Alors un membre de la Cour de Haute-Comédie lui demande : **« Pourquoi, pour remplacer Reynaud, n'avez-vous pas fait appel à un résistant plutôt qu'au Maréchal Pétain ? ».**

En somme, pourquoi ?...

16. 'A curious trial!' A tract denouncing the Republican politicians who testified against Pétain in the first week. It opens: 'Paul Reynaud, the pestiferous rat, talks about himself; Daladier talks about himself. It is true that they made a pitiful impression in 1940 and have a lot of things to explain away.'

13

'You Will Not Make Me Say That
the Marshal is a Traitor'

The court had already heard quite a bit from Paul Reynaud about the
first witness for the defence, General Weygand, who had been the
French Commander-in-Chief in the last weeks of the Battle of France.
On the morning of Tuesday 21 July, when Weygand was due to testify,
Reynaud was present in court again, notebook at the ready, poised to
defend any slur on his reputation. This was not the first time the two
men had crossed paths since June 1940. They had both ended up in
the same German internment camp in Austria. The Germans could
hardly have invented a more exquisite psychological torture for these
two individuals whose reciprocal hatred was undimmed by their new
shared status as victims of the same enemy. In the camp, Reynaud had
refused to address a word to Weygand, or even to shake his hand.
Reynaud's group had eaten their meals separately from Weygand's.
On one occasion when Reynaud passed by Weygand without acknowledging him, Weygand had audibly muttered 'hooligan' (*voyou*).[1] This
time, Reynaud did not intend to keep silent.

Weygand had come directly from his sickbed in the Val-de-Grâce
military hospital in Paris, where he was awaiting his own trial. Tiny,
wizened, his yellow skin stretched over his face like parchment, he
entered the court leaning heavily on a stick. The old general paused,
clicked his heels, and bowed as he passed in front of Pétain, who,
somewhat taken aback, responded with a nod. Invited to sit because
of his age, Weygand remained standing throughout his testimony. In
his civilian suit he resembled a lawyer more than a soldier. As he
warmed to his theme, it became apparent that, however ancient he
looked, Weygand's mind was as sharp as ever, and his temper as
violent.

Weygand was a simple man. A certain mystery surrounded his parentage – born in Brussels, he was rumoured to be the illegitimate son of the Belgian empress of Mexico – which meant that the army was the only real family he had ever had. He had fully internalized its values, its prejudices and its codes. In the First World War, working on the staff of Marshal Foch, he had acquired a reputation as a brilliant staff officer. Like Foch he was known for his reactionary political views, which surfaced in an exchange with Reynaud in June 1940. At one point when Reynaud suggested that there was nothing shameful in following the solution adopted by the Dutch – whose army had surrendered in the field while the queen had taken her government to London – Weygand countered that no Third Republic politician could command the legitimacy of a historic monarchy. Weygand's contempt for politicians was bottomless. When Isorni warned him before his appearance in court that Reynaud would be lying in wait to catch him out, Weygand told him he relished the prospect: 'Don't worry,' he said, 'I will pulverize [*écrabouiller*] him.'[2]

Although Weygand's responsibility in signing the armistice was incontestable, his role at Vichy was complicated. He had supported the regime's conservative political agenda, deplored de Gaulle's opposition to the armistice and viewed him as a traitor for defying France's legal government, but he also opposed the pro-German policies of Laval. In September 1940, Weygand was put in command of Vichy's army in North Africa, a position which bestowed considerable influence. Although the armistice had limited the size of the French Army, it was in Germany's interest that French forces in North Africa be strong enough to keep the Allies out – despite the risk that those forces might be used one day against her. The Allies continually nursed the hope that Weygand might break with Vichy's neutrality and rally to them. Weygand never made this leap, but this did not allay German suspicions of him, and Pétain was final forced, under German pressure, to remove him from his post in November 1941.

The first part of Weygand's testimony was more an attack on Reynaud than a defence of Pétain. He reminded the court that Reynaud had placed him in command of the army at a moment of military catastrophe – on the same day that panicked officials of the French Foreign Ministry were burning documents in the interior court of the

Quai d'Orsay. Could anyone accepting the command of the armies at such a tragic juncture be accused of harbouring personal ambitions? This was the signal for Weygand to offer a detailed account of his attempts to reverse the military disaster: 'One might think, reading certain accounts in newspapers, that there was no battle, just a Marshal and a General hatching their plots in the night while no fighting took place.' He took great pains to show the court that this was hardly the case. It was only after the Germans had breached the new defensive line he had set up behind the rivers Somme and Aisne that Weygand informed Reynaud on 12 June that an armistice was inevitable. He emphatically refuted Reynaud's claim that he had put 'order' before 'honour'. Where was the 'honour' in Reynaud's instruction on 15 June to order the capitulation of the armies?

> I refused and I told Paul Reynaud that I would refuse always, whatever happened, to cover our flags in that shame . . . No force in the world would make me sign the capitulation of an army that had fought as our army had fought.

Then Weygand effectively turned the tables on his accuser:

> M. Reynaud said in his statement that, having called on Marshal Pétain and myself to serve . . . he regretted it; nonetheless he did call on us.
>
> He said that finding me too pusillanimous . . . he several times thought of replacing me. He may have thought about it; he did not do it.
>
> He said that as I refused to capitulate, he had thought of sacking me; he did not do it.
>
> Then at the end of the day on 16 June he resigned. He asked the President of the Republic to ask Marshal Pétain to take over the government when he knew that the government which took over was going to ask for an armistice . . .
>
> I admit, Messieurs, that I no longer understand . . .
>
> I see only terrible weakness . . . And, Messieurs, on the other side, the military side, I see a certain firmness in holding to a certain line of conduct.[3]

The second part of Weygand's testimony offered the first sustained defence of the armistice that the court had heard to date. In his view, a capitulation of the army, without a simultaneous agreement between governments to end hostilities (i.e. an armistice) would have delivered France over to the enemy: France would have been subjected to the fate of Poland or Holland ('in everyone's opinion the invaded country which suffered the most'). But would the suffering of the French under direct German administration have been justified if a French government had continued to operate from North Africa? For Weygand such an idea was a fantasy: North Africa lacked anti-aircraft defences and heavy artillery; there was no time to transport significant numbers of troops from the mainland; Germany would have moved into North Africa through Spain with Italian support from Libya. 'Could one say,' Weygand asked the court, 'that after losing our honour and losing French territory by a capitulation . . . we could have kept Africa? No: we would have lost honour, lost French territory and lost Africa.'[4]

Weygand argued also that one important side-effect of the armistice was to keep the Germans out of North Africa. 'When the Allies arrived in North Africa,' he said, 'they found an Africa that was free, and they found the core of the army that fought later with them in Sicily and Italy.' So the armistice had not only protected France; it had helped the Allies win the war. This argument was repeated next day by General Alphonse Georges, second in command of the French armies in 1940. He told the court that Churchill had said to him in 1944: 'In June 1940, after the battle of France, England had no arms . . . So the armistice had rendered us a service. Hitler made a mistake in granting it. He ought to have gone into North Africa to allow him to move on to Egypt. We would in that case have had a difficult task.'[5]

Did Churchill really say this? It is certainly not what he later wrote in his memoirs. Probably, if Churchill did utter these words, they were just a passing outburst caused by one of his regular bouts of irritation with de Gaulle. But the argument that the armistice helped the Allies win the war would become a staple of Pétainist apologetics over the years. Recruiting Churchill to that cause was not an opportunity to be missed.

Once Weygand had finished, he faced a barrage of questions from Mongibeaux and the jurors. Had Weygand not underestimated the possibilities of British resistance as revealed by his notorious remark that England would have her neck wrung like a chicken?

I formally deny uttering such words . . . But to say that . . . I asserted, as others claim to have done in June 1940, that English victory was certain. Ah no! That I did not assert. I am not enough of a prophet for that. At that moment, England was alone in the war. Russia was allied to Germany. America was not in the war.

The obvious riposte was that 'others' had not just 'claimed' to have made this prediction in 1940: it was exactly what de Gaulle had said on 18 June 1940. Weygand's relationship with de Gaulle was behind a seemingly innocent question from the juror Pierre-Bloch, asking if Weygand had received any letters from London in 1940:

WEYGAND: I would be grateful, since you want me to speak openly, if you would speak openly yourself . . . I do not understand your question . . . It is a trap.
PIERRE-BLOCH: The leaders of the Free French in London sent you letters in Algiers.
WEYGAND: But who are you referring to, Monsieur? [He knew the answer perfectly well] . . .
PIERRE-BLOCH: Did you receive a letter from General de Gaulle?
WEYGAND: Yes.
PIERRE-BLOCH: What did you do about it?
WEYGAND: I kept it. The letter ended with these words: 'I send you my respects if your answer is yes.' That is not how one writes to me.[6]

Uttering these words, the famously irascible Weygand smashed his stick on the floor. The letter in question had frostily invited Weygand to join de Gaulle's Free French, which de Gaulle knew perfectly well he had no intention of doing.

Another juror (Levêque) broached what he called the 'heart of the trial':

You said earlier: an armistice is not peace. So we were still technically at war? What, then, do you think about the terrible treason of your leader, Marshal Pétain, who created legions to fight against the Allies who were still our allies. And who gave orders to fight against the Allies in North Africa in November 1942? . . . That is what this trial is about!
Weygand: No, M *le juré*, that is not what the trial is about. The trial is about: armistice or capitulation.

LEVEQUE: No [shouts in the court] . . . The question is treason.

WEYGAND: . . . Never will you make me utter such a word in relation to Marshal Pétain; my conscience would not allow it . . . I spoke earlier about the Legion of Volunteers against Bolshevism [LVF]. I said that I did not approve, and that soldiers wearing German uniform were in my opinion soldiers who had dishonoured themselves.

LEVEQUE: And the Marshal who was their leader?

WEYGAND: I am not speaking of the Marshal. I am speaking about your question. You can draw the conclusion you wish. You will not make me say that the Marshal is a traitor.[7]

PÉTAIN SPEAKS

At this moment, to the alarm of his lawyers who were desperately trying to keep him silent, Pétain suddenly jumped up to speak:

> Never have I more regretted that I am so hard of hearing. I sometimes hear my name being pronounced, I hear scraps of answers, but I cannot follow every detail of the conversation. So I cannot take part in it. But in what I have followed of what General Weygand has said, because I am sitting closest to him, it seems to me that he was completely following my doctrine.

Mongibeaux, delighted at the breach in the wall of silence, seized the opportunity:

> MONGIBEAUX: Weygand has said that those who served in German uniform dishonoured themselves . . . and that the leader who had associated himself with them had an attitude which could be considered reprehensible. Can you give any explanations on this matter?
>
> WEYGAND: Me?
>
> MONGIBEAUX: No, the Marshal, since the Marshal has replied . . .
>
> PÉTAIN: I did not hear what was said.[8]

The moment had passed.

Now Reynaud, who had been scribbling furiously throughout Weygand's testimony, was granted the right to respond. He went back over Weygand's arguments: why had he not sacked Weygand? Because, having sacked General Gamelin only days earlier, it would have been too severe a blow to morale to sack another general so soon. Had he ignored the sufferings of the French Army? On the contrary: his solution for an immediate ceasefire was a 'more humanitarian solution' since it would have stopped the fighting at once.

Weygand jumped up again:

WEYGAND: I see a new manoeuvre on the part of M. Reynaud: it is no longer about capitulation but a ceasefire.

REYNAUD: It is the same thing to my mind.

WEYGAND: Call things by their proper name: capitulating is to capitulate without conditions . . . It is not the same thing. For a ceasefire [He was here seeing the terms ceasefire and armistice as equivalent] there need to be two, one who stops fighting and the other who goes on.

REYNAUD: It is the same if one capitulates . . . The key point is this: the armistice had a double effect: it took the French fleet, the second fleet in the world, out of the Allied camp . . . and it was contrary to the word we had given to our Allies.[9]

As the two men re-enacted the arguments they had engaged in five years earlier, it was almost with irritation that they were distracted by a second interruption from Pétain.

When Reynaud returned to the idea that the armistice was a breach of honour in regard to Britain, Pétain jumped up to ask whether or not it was true that Churchill had said in 1940 that he would 'not reproach the French if they asked for an armistice'? In a spirit of exactitude, Weygand had to correct Pétain on this point. The Marshal then slumped back into his usual torpor. It was clear why his lawyers preferred him to remain silent.

Reynaud and Weygand resumed their interminable quarrel. Paradoxically, although the two men hated each other, they both shared the conviction that the armistice was the key to everything. As Reynaud launched into another demolition of Weygand's conduct in 1940, Weygand snorted derisively – recorded by the court stenographer as 'Pfft!!' – and spat out: 'Have you finished now?'[10]

'One could physically feel the hatred swirling between the two men,' Joseph Kessel wrote in *France-Soir*. When Reynaud had finished, Mongibeaux allowed Weygand a last word – but insisted that it must be final otherwise 'this could go on for another three weeks'. Weygand's last words were devastating, and not without some truth:

> Our exchange of views – if that is the word – has gone to the limits of violence tempered by the manners of a good education. This is explained, Messieurs, by the fact, that in a moment of calamity, M. Paul Reynaud, when his shoulders were too weak to support the burden he had so avidly taken on, was only too happy to call upon Marshal Pétain and myself . . . In this affair M. Reynaud demonstrated the worst crime that a leader can commit: he lacked firmness and was not up to the example of great leaders of the past . . . And after all that, he accuses us – men like us – of treason![11]

There were shouts in court. Mongibeaux brought the discussion to a close. Weygand returned to the military hospital to wait for his own trial, at which Reynaud certainly intended to continue his vendetta against him.

LETTER FROM AMERICA

The next day, Wednesday 1 August, started with the reading of a letter from the former American ambassador to Vichy, Admiral William Leahy. No foreign country followed the Pétain trial more avidly than the United States; no aspect of American policy during the war had been more controversial than its conduct towards France.[12] Roosevelt's plan had been to normalize relations with Vichy and woo it away from Germany. For that reason among others, he was wary of de Gaulle's Free French. When, in December 1941, the French islands of St Pierre and Miquelon, off the Newfoundland coast, were seized by Free French forces on behalf of de Gaulle, the United States Secretary of State, Cordell Hull, condemned this action by the 'so-called Free French'. That description of de Gaulle's movement sparked outrage at home. Newspapers mocked the 'so-called' Secretary of State. The popular support for de Gaulle in America was exemplified by the film *Casablanca*, released in November 1942. At the end of the film, Humphrey Bogart leaves Vichy-controlled Morocco to join de Gaulle's forces in the Congo. He is accompanied by the local French police chief, played by Claude Rains, who, having broken with his Vichy superiors, throws a bottle of Vichy water into the wastepaper basket as the film ends.

Roosevelt's courting of Vichy had led him to send his friend Leahy as ambassador to Vichy in December 1940. Leahy's posting lasted eighteen months until Laval's return to power in April 1942. Even after he was recalled to Washington, the United States left two chargés d'affaires in his place. All this caused friction with the British, who had backed de Gaulle since 1940 despite Churchill's occasional bouts of Gaullophobia. When, in the weeks leading up to the Pétain trial, the American press gave extensive coverage to Professor Rougier's claims that he had visited London on Pétain's behalf, Churchill told the worried Foreign Office that the Americans were in no position to throw stones: 'Leahy was sitting in Marshal Pétain's pocket at Vichy ... I have the draft of Roosevelt's proposed broadcast on the eve of *Torch* [the American landing in North Africa] which addressed Marshal Pétain as "My dear friend, and the great and trusted hero of Verdun"' or words to that effect. With some difficulty I persuaded him to withdraw this as it would have been spat at in France.'[13]

Roosevelt's policy had left a legacy of French suspicion towards the United States after the Liberation. President Truman had inherited Roosevelt's distrust of de Gaulle – 'I don't like the son of a bitch,' he commented on one occasion – but now that de Gaulle was France's leader he had to live with him.[14] The Pétain trial threatened to rake up an embarrassing past.

From his prison cell in the Palais de Justice, Pétain wrote directly to Admiral Leahy on 25 May, asking him to testify at his trial:

Victory has finally crowned the efforts of the Allies ... The joy that I feel about this great event is overshadowed by a cloud that gets bigger every day ... I am in the situation of an accused who betrayed his country whereas I did all I could to defend it.[15]

In his memoirs Leahy wrote, 'It was a difficult letter to answer.'[16] As he was now chairing the American Joint Chiefs of Staff it was inconceivable that he would testify in person. Although his memoirs drip with contempt for most Vichy leaders – Laval was described as 'black Peter', Admiral Darlan as 'Popeye' – and for the 'self-appointed French leader', de Gaulle, Leahy is markedly warmer in his treatment of Pétain, whom he refers to as 'my good friend of the Vichy days'. Had Pétain seen Leahy's confidential reports to Roosevelt, however, he might have been warier about soliciting his aid. Soon after his arrival in Vichy, Leahy described Pétain as a 'feeble, frightened old man surrounded by self-serving conspirators'. He lambasted the 'jellyfish reactions' of Vichy leaders.[17] Nonetheless Leahy clearly saw Pétain as more of a victim than a traitor. He did his best for him in his tortuously convoluted reply to Pétain's letter:[18]

My dear Marshal Pétain,

Your note of 10 June was delivered to me today by a mutual acquaintance. I learn from it the sad predicament in which you find yourself as a result of developments in Europe, whose positive aspect has allowed the liberation of France and destruction of Nazi barbarism. You will understand that it is impossible for me, as Chief of General Staff, to become involved in any degree in any internal French controversy in France in which you may find yourself enmeshed. I have no information regarding the specific charges that you are required to answer. My knowledge of your personal and official attitude towards the Allies and the Axis powers is strictly limited to the period January 1941 to April 1942 when I had the honour to be ambassador to France.

During this period, I held your personal friendship and devotion to the well-being of the French people in the highest regard. You often expressed to me your fervent hope to see the Nazi invaders annihilated.

During this period on various occasions and at my request, you acted against the desires of the Axis and favourably to the Allied cause. In every instance where you failed to accept my recommendation to oppose the Axis powers you stated that the reason was that by such positive action you would bring additional oppression on your people through the invaders. Your principal concern was the welfare and protection of the helpless people of France. It is impossible for me to believe that you had any other concerns.

However, in all honesty, I must repeat my personal opinion, expressed to you at the time, that positive refusal to make concessions to the Axis demands, while it might have brought immediate hardship on the people of France, would, in the long view, have been advantageous for France.[19]

After the letter was read out, Mongibeaux alerted the court to one key point: 'it would have been better to refuse Axis demands'. Payen riposted that there were 'ten phrases which say that Marshal Pétain always acted for the good of France'. 'Ten' was a rather optimistic count. This was probably a draw. Leahy had appeased his conscience; he had not much helped Pétain.

MARKING TIME

The Leahy letter did not detain the court for long. It had defused a potentially embarrassing situation and therefore excited little interest. But nothing that was happening in court could compete with the dramatic news exploding outside it: Pierre Laval would very soon be back in France. Little had been heard of Laval since the end of the Sigmaringen adventure. Indeed little had been heard of Laval during the Sigmaringen adventure. A lonely figure, keeping his distance from both Pétain and Brinon, he had spent his days chain-smoking, ruminating on human ingratitude, and working on his defence. Céline, treating his ulcer, was the recipient of interminable self-justificatory monologues. Since Laval's brooding presence in the castle was undermining the morale of Brinon's pseudo-government, the Germans eventually moved him to another residence a few kilometres away. As the end approached, Laval planned his escape. Refused entry to Switzerland, he managed to get to Spain on a German plane.

Laval's presence in Spain was an embarrassment to Franco and he was offered the chance to move to Ireland, whose government had agreed to take him. Laval refused, saying he did not want to be handed around like a soiled package. He was housed at the Fort of Montjuic in Barcelona while Spanish and French diplomats worked on a solution. The French wanted him back but no extradition treaty existed with Spain. Finally, it was agreed that Laval would be flown to the American zone of occupation in Austria where he could be handed over to the French. He landed near Innsbruck on Wednesday 1 August and was back in France the next day.

Pétain's defence lawyers argued it would be improper to call Laval without a full preliminary investigation by an examining magistrate. Their rearguard action was purely for the record. It was inconceivable that the judges would forgo the chance to hear Laval; he was called to appear the day after he landed on French soil, on Friday 3 August. Meanwhile, for two sweltering and muggy days, the court had to sweat through a procession of six relatively minor witnesses, including three generals and a diplomat, when all anyone could think of was Laval. The final witness of the six, Charles Trochu, a right-wing politician who had served on the Paris municipal council, had light to throw on a particularly dramatic day in Vichy's history.

In the summer of 1941, following Hitler's offensive against the Soviet Union, Communist resisters had launched a campaign of direct attacks on German officers. On 20 October the German military chief in Nantes was assassinated. Hitler insisted on immediate reprisals. In the next two days the Germans executed ninety-eight French hostages. They announced that another hundred executions would be carried out – a terrible blow to Pétain's claim to be France's shield against the occupiers. In response Pétain's advisers concocted a theatrical plan. Pétain would make a radio speech announcing his intention to hand himself over to the Germans as a hostage and he would then present himself as a prisoner at the demarcation line between the two zones. Pétain enthusiastically embraced the idea. Some members of his entourage, seized by an impulse of sacrificial zeal, offered to join him. So too did Trochu and another conservative politician. They waylaid Pétain as he was leaving for lunch:

> I asked him: 'Would you allow us to join you in your train this afternoon to present ourselves also to the Germans?' The Marshal answered: 'Agreed. Go and pack your bags.' I can't say that we were overjoyed but we went and packed our bags. We waited all day at the Hotel du Parc.

That evening Trochu heard that Pétain had been talked out of the plan, although news of his intentions had filtered out. So Pétain achieved the feat of demonstrating his compassion for the French without taking any personal risks himself. Hostages continued to be shot.

This was one of several anecdotes dredged up by Trochu to depict Pétain as someone animated by good intentions, but surrounded by advisers who either sapped his will or exploited his political inexperience:

> Whatever his youthful appearance, one does not confide the political destinies of a great country like France to a political novice of 85 ... In the kingdom of Vichy things were like those African kingdoms where it is not really the big chief who governs, especially, when the Great Chief is very old, but it is the Grand Sorcerer. And the Grand Sorcerer was called Pierre Laval ... who at least had the physique that suited the part.[20]

Trochu was a good raconteur; he even made a weary court laugh. But by the time he had finished, Pétain and at least three jurors were asleep. Everyone was waiting for the appearance of the 'Grand Sorcerer' the next day.

14

The Pierre Laval Show

For ten days Philippe Pétain, while physically present, had often seemed absent from his own trial. And for those same ten days Pierre Laval, while physically absent, had often seemed present. Payen never missed an opportunity to coax witnesses into making Laval the scapegoat. The court had heard him described variously as a 'dungheap', Pétain's 'evil genius', Vichy's 'grand sorcerer'. Weygand caused amusement when he remarked: 'Laval who was – I am searching for a respectable expression . . . '; and Mongibeaux won an easy laugh in return: 'we are accustomed, when talking about M. Laval, to hearing expressions that are not respectable'.

As they crowded into court on Friday 3 August, journalists were not disappointed. In the flesh, Pierre Laval perfectly matched the part he was scripted to play. Watching him in court, Kessel could not resist a comparison with the noble features of the Marshal sitting just behind him:

> What a strange creature . . . His ugliness is almost fascinating. This ugliness – with his enormous ears, his thick pendulous lower lip, his reptilian eyes, his arms that remain stuck to his side and his abnormal hands, hands that are too weak and too small – makes one think of some animal without nobility.[1]

Another journalist summed him up more pithily: 'white tie, black teeth'.[2]

Ever since childhood Pierre Laval's ugliness had been a source of wonder. It had marked him as an outsider, and whetted his appetite to succeed. As a boy he had been nicknamed the 'Jamaican' because of his dark skin, thick lips and hooded eyes. It was rumoured that his mother must have had foreign blood to explain the appearance of this ugly changeling in that most quintessentially 'French' region of France, the granitic Auvergne, where the Gauls had held out against the Romans. Laval's origins as a man of the people rooted in the peasantry of the Auvergne were part of his myth.

In fact, his origins were not as modest as he liked to suggest: his father, an innkeeper in the town of Châteldon, near Vichy, was comfortably well off, but socially and culturally the family was a world away from the bourgeoisie. Although his parents had been prosperous enough to provide him with a *lycée* education, Laval had financed the rest of his studies by working as a *surveillant*, a supervisor responsible for keeping discipline among the *lycée* pupils of rich parents. Thus, unlike Herriot and Daladier, he was not a brilliant scholarship boy who owed his success to Republican meritocracy. He was a self-made man who owed nothing to anyone. Laval had risen through the ranks thanks to hard work, native intelligence, guile and determination.

Having trained as a lawyer, Laval started practising at the Paris Bar in 1909. He specialized in the defence of strikers and trade unionists at a time when the left was strongly anti-militarist. For him this was less about a commitment to the cause than an emotional identification with ordinary people. His pacifism was instinctive and not ideological: people without power were those who suffered most in war. In 1914, Laval was elected to parliament as a Socialist for a working-class constituency north of Paris. While anchoring himself in left-wing politics, he also started moving up the social ladder. In 1909 he had married the daughter of Châteldon's doctor, who was also a local politician. This was a sign that he was seen as a young man with a future. It was also a marriage of love. Laval and his wife were devoted to one other, and her faith in him was blind. Until the moment they descended the steps of the plane returning them to Paris in 1945, they had hardly been apart for more than a few days.

In parliament after 1914, Laval was identified with the most anti-militarist wing of the Socialist Party, but he distanced himself from outright defeatism. When the Socialists had to take a position towards the Bolshevik Revolution, Laval was one of those who opposed it, a step on his journey from the extreme left to the right. As his most recent biographer remarks: 'he ceased to be internationalist when revolution was coming from abroad'.[3] Like many Socialists, Laval lost his seat in the conservative backlash of the post-war elections. When he was elected mayor of the working-class suburb of Aubervilliers outside Paris in 1923, Laval described himself as an 'independent Socialist'. From now on he was always an 'independent' and never again belonged to any party. Aubervilliers remained his electoral base even as he shifted to the right. This was no problem as Laval was a supreme practitioner of parish pump politics, always ready to shake a hand, never too busy to receive a constituent in search of a favour.

In the 1920s, Laval became immensely rich. No one knew exactly where the money came from – certainly not from his legal practice alone. Venality was built into the fabric of Third Republic politics, but Laval practised it with artistry. He moved into a smart villa in Paris's bourgeois 16th arrondissement and purchased the château of Châteldon as well as two local springs producing bottled water. He also became a media baron, acquiring a radio station and two newspapers in the Auvergne. For a while he also owned an estate in Normandy, playing the role of gentleman farmer, watching over his cattle. His only moments of enjoyment at Sigmaringen were his walks in the countryside sizing up the herds and observing farming techniques.

Despite his bourgeois lifestyle, his attempts at sartorial elegance and trademark silk white ties, Laval never seemed so different from what he had always been. His suits never seemed to fit, his fingernails never seemed clean. He preferred eating modestly at home with his wife to cutting a figure in the *beau monde*. The social gloss that evaded him was provided by his daughter Josée, to whom he was devoted. Josée was dressed by the best couturiers, gambled on the Côte d'Azur, sailed at Biarritz, skied in the Alps, and attended exhibition openings and theatrical first nights in Paris. In 1935 she married the aristocratic René de Chambrun, familiarly known as 'Bunny'. Descended from the Marquis de Lafayette on his father's side, de Chambrun had Franco-American citizenship. His father, a general, had been close to Pétain, who was Bunny's godfather; Pétain treated Bunny almost like a son. Such connections were gold dust for Laval.

Laval's progression from the extreme left to the right was so snail-like that when he became premier for the first time in 1931, in a centre-right government, no one quite knew whether he was there as leftist camouflage for the right or as a Trojan horse of the left. It was often remarked that his name was a palindrome. Apart from his versatility, Laval's political ascension is hard to explain. He had no talent as an orator or writer; he read no books; his ignorance of history, geography and literature was legendary. The civil servant Pierre Tissier, who worked closely with Laval in the 1930s, offered two explanations for his success. Since Tissier was one of the first people to join de Gaulle in London, his memoir *I Worked with Laval*, published in 1942, was not the work of a man well-disposed towards his subject. This makes his account of Laval's qualities all the more convincing. Tissier wrote: 'it may seem paradoxical to speak of his charm. Yet it was a very real thing. Personally, although I knew him well enough and knew just what his convictions were worth, I could never help succumbing to it.'[4]

So although Laval was not at his best when trying to win over a large audience by his rhetoric or his arguments, he was in his element when seeing people individually. Tissier's other observation related to his quick-wittedness: 'His very keen intelligence allows him to understand the most complicated question very rapidly. Often, when I used to accompany him to the Senate or the Chamber ... it was quite enough for me to whisper a few words to him about a problem of which he was completely ignorant; immediately he could expatiate at length on the subject without making any mistakes.'[5] Laval liked to make a virtue of his ignorance. 'I know less about Germany than Daladier because that is his job,' he once remarked, 'he is a professor of history. But ... I know about men. Believe me, they are always the same.'[6]

By the time he became premier for the second time in 1935, Laval was firmly anchored on the right while remaining faithful to his early pacifism. It was the only conviction he had ever held. In that year of intensive diplomacy, his obsession was to safeguard peace. He set about courting the leaders of the Nazi regime but also, as an insurance policy, tried to isolate Germany by reaching out to fascist Italy. He offered Mussolini a free hand to pursue his imperial ambitions in Africa. With less conviction Laval also signed a pact with the Soviet Union. To have met in the same year Göring, Mussolini and Stalin (in Stalin's case, the first French premier to have done so) made this an *annus mirabilis* for the innkeeper's son from Châteldon. It convinced Laval that he had a golden touch as a negotiator. But one key element of his policy – winning over Mussolini – unravelled when the British government and French left-wing anti-fascists forced him to reverse his support for Mussolini's invasion of Ethiopia. When the leftist Popular Front coalition won the elections of 1936, Laval was convinced that his policies had been sabotaged by the British – whom he never forgave – and by French anti-fascist idealists who put ideological conviction above the interests of France. For Laval no cause, however noble, could justify a war.

All this made Laval increasingly bitter about the political establishment of the Third Republic. This did not mean that he was won over to anti-democratic ideologies – Laval was impervious to ideologies – but he picked up moods. After France's defeat in a war he had never supported, he saw an opportunity for revenge over the politicians who had not listened to him. Seeing his policy of collaboration with Germany as consistent with his lifelong opposition to war, he was convinced that the same qualities that had allowed him to rise to the top in French politics would allow him to outwit Hitler. 'When one has spent years with the peasants of the Auvergne,' he once said, 'one does not need to know other people. Hitler is a child by comparison.'[7]

By the end of the war Laval certainly had no illusions about his unpopularity with the French people. In 1942, after his controversial speech declaring that he 'wished for a German victory', Weygand had said to Laval 'you have 95 per cent of France against you'. Laval replied: 'You are joking! It is 98 per cent but I am doing what is best for them despite them.'[8] This makes it odd that he turned down the possibility of taking refuge in Ireland when it was offered. But quite apart from his pride, Laval's indestructible self-confidence convinced him that he had a chance. Innately cynical about humanity, he believed in his own lucky star. During the last months at Vichy he had spent more time with his astrologer than his ministers, and the predictions were encouraging. Even so, he always carried a phial of cyanide in the pocket of the fur coat that he had been offered by Stalin and from which he was never parted. He had spent months in Sigmaringen honing his defence. The Pétain trial offered him an opportunity to test the waters before his own case came to trial.

As someone who responded to situations intuitively, Laval was handicapped by having been cut off from the French people for the last few months. On his return to France, he was not at first allowed to see his daughter Josée, who might have filled him in. By chance, at the prison of Fresnes he found himself in a cell next to Pétain's former doctor and close adviser Bernard Ménétrel, and they managed to snatch some conversation. The two men had detested each other at Vichy, but now, two survivors of a shipwreck clinging to the same life raft, they avidly exchanged their impressions. Laval was desperate to glean any information about the trial, Ménétrel to find out what Laval was planning to say about Pétain.[9]

On the night before his appearance in court, Laval was transferred from Fresnes to the Palais de Justice, where he spent two nights in the cells of the *depôt*. Pétain's jailor, Joseph Simon, was appointed to look after him. Laval, addicted to nicotine, was desperate for cigarettes and newspapers. The former request was granted, the latter refused. Simon found Laval by turns obsequious, apprehensive and threatening, alternating between bluster and self-pity: 'I am curious to know the mood of the court because I have no idea what has been said in court so far. What about the old boy [*le vieux*]? Has he said bad things about me? If so I will go for him . . . You must not forget that it was *he* who gave the orders for the *maquisards* to be arrested and hung outside doors and windows.'[10]

LAVAL STARTS HIS DEFENCE

On the day of Laval's appearance, the courtroom was like opening night at the theatre – with Laval as the star. One journalist described it as resembling a 'special press conference for the benefit of Laval'.[11] Even Albert Camus put in his only personal appearance at the trial.[12] Pétain, compulsively fiddling with the buckle of his belt and the ribbon of his *médaille militaire*, seemed more agitated than on any day so far. This impression was correct. Simon observed the night before that Pétain was 'devastated' (*catastrophé*) by Laval's return. Isorni comments: 'one felt that he was frightened of Laval. He simultaneously detested, admired and feared him.' Newspapers had printed some threatening comments allegedly made just before Laval's departure from Spain: 'Pétain knew perfectly well when the Germans arrested Léon Blum, Daladier and Reynaud that it was to have them shot . . . and it is I, and I alone, who ensured that they were not shot. I have had enough with always being the person blamed.'[13]

What no one knew was whether Laval's appearance would work in Pétain's interest or against it. The Communist press warned against allowing Laval's crimes to deflect blame from the 'old traitor' Pétain: 'there are two of them, that makes 24 bullets'.[14] Pétain's defence lawyers were also worried. Before the trial started Isorni had seen Josée and assured her that he was not planning to make her father a scapegoat. But apart from the fact that Josée had not had a chance to communicate this information to her father, Payen was clearly not following the same line. What the defence did not know was whether Laval saw himself as a witness for the defence or the prosecution. Was he going to distance himself from Pétain? Or was he going to hide behind him and risk bringing the two of them down together? Perhaps Laval himself had not yet decided.

Laval entered the court accompanied by five policemen, clutching a little briefcase to his chest, his white tie loosely knotted and grubby, his suit crumpled as if he had been sleeping in it all night. The briefcase turned out to carry a few papers which he consulted occasionally, but perhaps it also provided reassurance, a memento of happier times. Stamped in gold were the words 'Pierre Laval, Président du Conseil, January 1931' – the year he had been premier for the first time and figured on the cover of *Time* magazine as 'man of the year'. Passing by Pétain without looking at him, and blinded by the flashlights of the photographers, Laval looked round nervously, anxiously searching for comfort in faces he knew. Lecompte-Boinet wrote that he resembled a 'hunted beast entering an arena or like a prisoner who has not seen the light for a long time . . . plunged into a France that hates him, into the heart of the France that he had called the enemy, among the "terrorists" of the Resistance'.[15] One journalist wrote: 'His dark beady, watchful, frightened eyes moved around the court to fathom the temper.'[16] Everyone was startled by how terribly he had aged. Janet Flanner wrote:

> Carrying his gray hat and his worn brown briefcase in his hand, in confusion and in a low voice, he asked where the witness stand was, and

when he saw that it was only a carved, cane-seated parlour chair, he deposited his hat and briefcase on the seat and stood erect. He was at first unrecogizable. The fat of his face is now gone. His oily moorish hair is now dry and gray and his moustache is the colour of tobacco juice. His crooked stained teeth make a dark cavernous background for his large lips. Until he spoke, he was some other man who had been announced as the infamous Pierre Laval . . . Above his habitual white string tie, his low white collar was ruffled round the thin neck, which was hung with loose wattle like those of a brunette turkey cock.[17]

17. An emaciated Laval testifies on 4 August.

Mongibeaux's first question could not have been more simple: when had Laval's political relations with Pétain begun? He asked the witness Laval to be brief but fifteen minutes later Laval had not even begun to address the question. He was plunged into a detailed account of his efforts to avoid a European war by winning over Mussolini in the 1930s, a policy he believed had been sabotaged by British liberals and French anti-fascists. As he got into his stride, reliving his glory days, he lost his haunted look and perhaps started to believe that his wheedling persuasiveness would work its magic again.

All Mongibeaux's efforts to get him back on track were unsuccessful. As he grew in confidence, Laval started showing flashes of aggressiveness:

> MONGIBEAUX: I am going to interrupt you yet again . . . It is the Pétain trial that we are we meant to be judging at the moment . . .
>
> LAVAL [shouting]: I am sorry for being so long. If what I am saying is not interesting to the public I am sorry . . .
>
> MONGIBEAUX: I am sure it does interest the public but . . .
>
> LAVAL: In any case it does interest the people of France [boos] . . .

This was a tactical mistake; Laval immediately corrected himself:

> I am not saying that this does not include you here. I am saying that it interests other French people. It is not a habit of mine to insult people . . .
>
> My view was that governments who worry about the internal regimes of other countries threaten peace, and I thought that the Marshal who had a great authority, great prestige, could perhaps carry out the recovery of our situation in the world . . . That is how I came to the idea of Marshal Pétain in power.[17]

Finally, he got around to the question. He did not deny that he had hoped one day Pétain might come to power but said he only saw him infrequently:

> LAVAL: I cannot invent some fiction just to please those who wanted to hear one because I would have to manufacture it entirely.
>
> MONGIBEAUX: I am not asking for some fiction: I am asking precisely if your relations were regular. I am not asking you for the number of conversations and meetings but whether they were frequent.

LAVAL: They were very irregular. I would sometimes go to see him to chat. But I cannot say when or on what date.[18]

Increasingly flustered as Laval sidestepped his questions, Mongibeaux made an error relating to Pétain's official responsibilities in the inter-war years. Laval watched with satisfaction as the judge tied himself up in knots. In court was a young lawyer, Albert Naud, who would later find himself given the task of defending Laval at his trial. Nothing predisposed Naud in favour of Laval, but he was seduced by the performance: 'by turns *pathétique*, funny, moving, subtle, aided by a voice that is not without beauty, and using his hands effectively to assert, refute, blame, convince'.[19]

Laval requested a short pause to catch his breath. He asked for a glass of water and a bottle was brought over. (One eagle-eyed journalist noticed that it was neither Vichy nor Châteldon!) During the break Laval started chatting to some journalists he recognized who were seated close to him. 'What paper are you working for?' he asked Madeleine Jacob? 'And you?' he asked her neighbour. 'I don't know any of these newspapers. It is such a long time since I was last in Paris.'[20] This was quintessential Laval, seeking reassurance in familiar faces, trying to charm – but also discovering how much the world had changed. Léon Werth commented: 'For a moment one could imagine oneself in a small village café, at one of those political meetings . . . where everyone knows each other and where the *notaire* and his *fermier* listen, open-mouthed, to a local candidate from the *pays*.'[21]

So far there had been nothing to worry the defence lawyers – but as Laval reached his first period in government under Pétain, he was entering more dangerous territory. He was asked about Pétain's capacities as leader:

LAVAL: My conviction is that . . . he was the only one capable, that in France at that moment there was no other personality who could fulfil that mission . . .

MONGIBEAUX: What mission? A façade or a real one?

LAVAL: A real one . . . I thought that the Marshal of France would have been a leader of great quality and enjoying great prestige in France and abroad . . .

MONGIBEAUX: But not governing? . . .

LAVAL: I thought he would let the Government govern under his supervision . . .

Mongibeaux pushed him further on Pétain's responsibility for Vichy's policies:

LAVAL: People would go to see the Marshal, and he would say 'All right'.
MONGIBEAUX: So knowing him, you discovered that, in general, either through weakness, ignorance or political inexperience, he would easily agree, even on very serious matters.
LAVAL: M. le Président, you can go off on a monologue; so could I but I am not in a position to reply to a question like that . . . I think I am already prolix, and I will only answer on issues I know about . . .
MONGIBEAUX: When you explained something important to him did you have the impression he was able to discuss it?
LAVAL: He expressed reservations, I explained the difficulties, and we finished by finding an agreement . . .
MONGIBEAUX: His will and his lucidity were intact.
LAVAL: Absolutely.[22]

In the course of this exchange, Laval distanced himself from the regime's early measures of repression against Freemasons and Jews. This was self-serving but not untrue: Laval had played a key role in the operation to give Pétain total power, but he was uninterested in using that power to implement a conservative counter-revolution. His interest was collaboration with Germany.

MONTOIRE

Collaboration brought Laval on to the infamous handshake at Montoire:

I was not the man who asked to go to Montoire. I was told by the German Embassy that I should appear the next day, at 10.00 a.m. at the Rue de Lille, with a suitcase, and that I had no need of a car. I understood, since I was told to bring a suitcase, that the interview would not occur in Paris, that it would last at least a day, and that I would have to spend the night away from the Hotel Matignon.

I arrived at the embassy. I had never seen so many uniforms, cars, a whole commotion that suggested a very important move.

I got into the ambassador's car and said: 'Where are we going?' He replied: 'I have no idea, I am just the pilot. There is a car ahead that is leading us.'

When we reached Rambouillet it was about 11.30, and I said 'So it is not the Château of Rambouillet.' He replied: 'No! Much further.' 'But where are we going to have lunch?' He said: 'At Tours . . .' We arrived at Tours. We lunched. I said: 'Where is M. de Ribbentrop?' The ambassador replied: 'He is not there. But we are going to set off at 5.00 for another destination; I don't know where, but the car in front is guiding us.'

At 6.00 we were back in our cars. The car was taking me in a direction I did not know. I do not know this region very well. But after a while time I started to notice soldiers behind trees, more and more of them.

When we crossed the Loire, M. Abetz said to me: 'I must warn you – I was not authorized to let you know before – it is not only M. von Ribbentrop you are going to meet but also Chancellor Hitler.'

During their conversation Laval was told that Hitler wished to meet Pétain after his return from Franco. Laval had no intention of letting Pétain off the hook:

MONGIBEAUX: Did the Marshal go there of his full accord?
LAVAL: Yes, of his full accord, I did not take him by force.
MONGIBEAUX: But while not taking him by force, he might have shown some reticence, made objections? . . .
LAVAL: I see your position, which is not mine. You want me to say things you want to know. But I can only tell you what I know. What I know is that when I informed the Marshal of Hitler's desire for an interview, he accepted this request without difficulty.

Was Montoire the prelude to a reversal of alliances?

LAVAL: How can you speak of a reversal of alliances in October 1940? . . . In October 1940 where was England? America was not in the war. The Russians were on the side of the Germans . . . Do you think that in 1940 anybody of good sense could imagine anything else

but a German victory? [shouts and protests] . . . I am sorry if I am saying something that wounds people, I was speaking about the facts of
that time . . .

MONGIBEAUX: You are a jurist. You know that an armistice is a suspension of hostilities not a peace . . .

LAVAL: I know. The armistice was signed. I know that what I say might
wound or shock but I would like people to judge according to the
impressions of the time – not the month of August 1945 – but the
month of October 1940. France's interest at that time was obviously to
reach with Germany a formula which allowed us to escape the consequences of the defeat.[23]

Now Laval moved on to his sacking on 13 December 1940, which
still rankled as if it had taken place yesterday. He remained convinced
that it had changed the course of history – that he had been on the
verge of a breakthrough in his relations with Germany. The background to his dismissal was Hitler's quixotic offer to return the ashes
of Napoleon's son, who had died in Austrian exile, to France for
reburial next to his father. The date chosen was 15 December 1940,
one hundred years to the day since the repatriated ashes of Napoleon
had been buried in the Invalides. Laval was in Paris when he heard
Hitler's offer:

> Given Hitler's character, I thought that this was one of those sentimen-
> tal gestures which were characteristic of him alongside other less
> sentimental initiatives.
>
> I said to myself: 'The Marshal must be present' . . . It was in two
> days' time. The temperature was unbelievably cold, one of the worst
> winters we have ever had. The Marshal was old. I said to the German
> Ambassador Abetz: 'You are giving me a very disagreeable mission. I
> do not know if he will come.' He answered: 'If he does not come, Chan-
> cellor Hitler will take it as a personal insult.'

Laval rushed to Vichy to persuade Pétain of the importance of the
gesture. Pétain's initial reaction was negative; then he agreed. The
next step was to work out where Pétain would stay in Paris and to
arrange a meeting. It was decided that he would stay at the Hotel
Matignon, the only residence that could be sufficiently heated. This

was where Laval stayed when he was in Paris: 'I said to the Marshal: "I will move out before you; I will remove everything in my apartment that is mine so that you can be more comfortable." ' The two men compiled a list of those to be invited to the lunch after the ceremony: 'the conversation could not have been more courteous. I had no reason to think that the Marshal was preparing my arrest on the same day. To tell the truth I don't think he was thinking about it himself.' Unexpectedly a cabinet meeting was called for the evening:

> I saw that some of the ministers present had a strange look on their faces. The Marshal himself, next to M. Baudouin, was very pale. He said: 'I am asking all of you, Messieurs, to sign a resignation letter for me.' I had a moment's hesitation, and I thought I could not really sign because constitutionally I was his successor . . . But I signed anyway. I did not think it had anything to do with me.

A few minutes later Pétain returned to announce that two names had been accepted. One was Laval's:

> I tried to go and see the Marshal and speak to him. I was told he could not be seen. General Laure blocked the Marshal's door and I was not going to force it. I went to my office; I began to collect up my papers. I am accustomed, M le Président, to leaving ministries and coming back to them; I know one has to pack one's papers.[24]

This was no ordinary change of ministry. A few hours later, Laval was placed under house arrest. In the end the Germans intervened to have him released and he spent the next eighteen months nursing his grievances in Paris.

This palace coup was one of the most dramatic events in Vichy's history. But the key point Laval needed for his defence – the point least helpful to Pétain's defenders – was that his arrest was caused by internal politics, by the jealousies he had excited, by incompatibilities between himself and Pétain: 'I was not arrested for reasons of foreign policy.' In other words, the arrest was not a disavowal of collaboration. Even if Laval believed he would have pursued collaboration more effectively than his successors, he needed the world to know that Pétain was fully implicated in the policy.

'I WISH FOR THE VICTORY OF GERMANY'

The questioning moved on to the period after April 1942 when Laval returned to government at German insistence. Two months later, in a radio speech on 22 June, he uttered the most shocking sentence of his entire political career: 'I wish for the victory of Germany because without it tomorrow Communism will install itself everywhere in Europe.'

Laval did not deny what he had said or his awareness of its enormity: 'I drafted the text knowing that it would wound the French,' he admitted, 'that it would be like a drop of sulphuric acid on the skin of people who were suffering.' No one in the courtroom would have forgotten where they were when they heard the speech. Léon Werth, sitting on the press benches, had heard it in a village in the Jura. On the evening of 22 June 1942 he wrote in his journal:

> I decided this evening to go and hear Laval at the farm . . . He makes an effort not to be too solemn, nor too declamatory, to be simple. He rolls his Rs. He holds in his vulgarity as one holds in one's belly . . . He says: 'I wish the victory of Germany because otherwise Bolshevism will install itself everywhere.' The 'why' – perhaps even for those who fear the Bolshevik spectre – is too feeble to compensate for the 'I wish'. That 'I wish' demolishes all arguments, creates shock. One stops listening. One can take no more in. One knew that Laval wanted Germany's victory. But one could never have believed he would say it so brutally.[25]

The question for the trial was what Pétain had thought of the speech. Laval gave a long answer:

> That day, pressed by all kinds of things, and wanting to pronounce my speech the same day, I did not do what I usually do, which is to reflect for one or two nights; for I have always thought that one corrects a document when one reads it again after 24 or 48 hours. This time I did not do that . . . [This was not true but the court had no way of knowing it.]
>
> I read my text to M. Rochat, *secrétaire général* of the Foreign Ministry. He had once been my *chef de cabinet*; he was in the next office to

mine, I saw him often. He is an honest, level-headed man, a civil servant of the highest quality . . .

When I got to the phrase, he said to me: 'M. le Président, in your place I would not pronounce the phrase.' 'Why?' 'You are not obliged to pronounce it because France is a country that has signed an armistice.'

I replied: 'You are certainly right but I am pronouncing this phrase for political reasons . . . It is a matter of making a gesture, an *éclat*.'

Laval's rationale was that this 'gesture' was the price to pay to win credit with Germany for future negotiations:

But I said to Rochat: 'Since this is your view . . . let us go up together to see the Marshal and seek his arbitration.' So I went to see the Marshal with M. Rochat and submitted my draft to him.

The Marshal said to me: 'You are not a military man, you do not have the right to say "I believe". You know nothing about the matter . . . In your place I would remove: "I believe in the victory of Germany."' So I removed 'I believe' and I left 'I wish for'.[26]

Laval, who had been speaking for over four hours with only a short break, was now tiring. On several occasions he had referred to Mongibeaux as 'Monsieur le Maréchal' instead of 'M. le Président'. There was also a revealing slip when he referred to D-Day as 'the aggression in Normandy'. The court exploded with laughter and he corrected himself: 'I am sorry, I have been speaking for a long time, and please note that I did not mean the aggression but the *débarquement* in Normandy . . .' It was time to stop.

Despite these lapses, Laval's performance had been skilful. He had avoided direct criticism of Pétain, distanced himself from some of his measures, and shown that Pétain was no less implicated in the policy of collaboration than he was.

After Laval had left the court, Pétain was asked as usual if he had any comment to make. For once he did:

I had a very violent reaction when I heard in the speech that phrase of M. Laval: 'I wish for the victory of Germany'.

He said just now that he came to find me with M. Rochat . . . to show me the phrase. Well, never would M. Rochat have accepted keeping such a phrase, and I was in agreement with him.

So when I heard the phrase on the radio – I thought the matter had been arranged, settled – I jumped up in amazement.

I had not realized. I thought it had been cut out, and I was devastated that it was still there.

Pétain, his deafness miraculously disappearing, had deftly stabbed Laval in the back the minute after he left the courtroom. Who was telling the truth?[27]

Laval was locked in the *dépôt* for a second night. Simon found him pleased with his own performance:

I was not too muddled was I? . . . You should have seen the parliamentary jurors, my former colleagues of the Senate and the Chamber, how they were with me. I am sure that if I had been free they would have said to me: 'Come on Pierrot, let's go and have a snack together?'

He reminisced about his youth, his love of his country; he was certain 'history will vindicate me'. Laval was allowed for the first time to see his daughter Josée, who told him that it was not Isorni's plan to turn him into a scapegoat. Meanwhile, the Maréchale told Simon that Laval was 'a dreadful wog [*bicot*]' who should have been a carpet seller in Morocco.[28]

The court was less packed for Laval's reappearance on the next day. The novelty had worn off. When Laval entered the room he displayed none of his previous wary hesitation. At one point he protested angrily at a photographer crouched at his feet while he was speaking. Since the previous day had ended with Laval 'wishing for' German victory, he opened by insisting that he had always opposed *military* collaboration with Germany. This took the court neatly to the Dieppe telegram, which the prosecution viewed as a possible smoking gun to convict Pétain.

The complication was that there were two telegrams: one whose existence no one contested, congratulating the Germans on repelling the Allied attack; and another in which the French government proposed to join Germany in defence of French soil. About the first telegram Laval was happy to admit that since the Germans had congratulated Dieppe's population for its exemplary conduct – from the German point of view! – he had hoped to negotiate some favours in return. But he claimed to know nothing about the second telegram, and insisted that it was contrary to his opposition to any *military* collaboration. The court could only take Laval at his word, but this did not stop the lawyers from meandering into interminable wrangling over the telegram. Madeleine Jacob commented sardonically that the trial was degenerating into a discussion of the technicalities of the postal service. In the end, the mystery remained: had the second telegram been communicated to the Germans? Had Pétain really signed it?[29]

Once the court abandoned its discussions about the two telegrams, Laval needed to prove that his controversial speech of June 1942 had won him credit in his negotiations to protect the French population. Since he was moving on to the most painful period of the Occupation, the case was difficult to make. In that period, Laval had been subjected to ever more pressing demands for French manpower to work in German factories. He had tried at first to institute a voluntary scheme by which one prisoner of war would be released for every three volunteers. When this did not produce the requisite numbers, he was forced to introduce a compulsory conscription scheme (Service du Travail Obligatoire – STO). Laval told the court that he had warned the German Gauleiter Fritz Sauckel that the STO was the most effective possible recruiter for the Resistance – but all he could do was to negotiate a reduction in the size of the quotas demanded. His main defence was that the proportion of workers deported from France to Germany was lower than that deported from Belgium or Holland. Since the court had no way of verifying whether this was in fact true, it was difficult to challenge him. But everyone had vivid memories of the increasingly violent repression imposed by the Vichy regime from 1943: the creation of the sinister Milice in January 1943, Darnand's appointment as Interior Minister in January 1944, the creation of courts martial to circumvent the courts in June, the murder of Mandel in July. Laval could only plead that this was a 'tragic period when the authority of the government hardly existed any longer':

> We were not free, the Marshal was not free . . . The Marshal was sometimes obliged to deliver a message; they would ask once, twice, ten times, twenty times. The German minister would knock on his door

and say: 'Deliver a message' ... We resisted but finally he was obliged to give in.[30]

Mongibeaux interrupted with the pertinent point that when the armistice was signed, Pétain had told the French that the 'government remains free; France will be administered only by Frenchmen'. Laval had also undermined his own argument that his notorious speech of June 1942 had won him any German goodwill.

Throughout this section of his testimony, Laval never lost an opportunity to remind the court that Pétain had been fully implicated in all decisions:

> MONGIBEAUX: What were the Marshal's reactions when he heard about the terrible things that were happening in so many villages of France?
> LAVAL: When M. Darnand was appointed, the Marshal did not seem especially unhappy.[31]

When Laval was told there were no more questions, he turned to leave, briefcase and hat in hand. Suddenly he stopped in his tracks, returned to his chair, and requested that the court call him back if his name were to come up again. He seemed regretful that the session was over. Perhaps he had enjoyed his two days back in the limelight; perhaps he preferred the cut and thrust of the court to being thrust back into his cell with nothing to think about but his own impending trial. Laval's last words to the court were: 'the Marshal was kept abreast [*au courant*] of everything important that I did, I had regular contacts with him every morning, I briefed him fully, as far as I could, I took account of his opinions ... Of course the Marshal was *au courant*.'

Throughout the second day of Laval's defence Pétain sat motionless as always. Once when Laval turned, with an obsequious smile, to say something favourable about him, Pétain lifted his hand in an almost imperceptible half-contemptuous gesture of acknowledgement. As he brushed past Pétain, leaving the court, Laval turned, bared his black teeth, bent over and muttered in his thick Auvergnat accent, rolling the rs: '*Au revoir messieu le Maréchal*'. Pétain looked away, pretending not to see him.[32] Even Isorni was disturbed by this cold contempt: 'As Laval bent forward, in that rapid moment, I detected compassion, a fugitive but genuine feeling of solidarity and mutual help which seemed to me to deserve a better response.'[33]

Laval's line that Pétain had always been *au courant* was so obviously self-interested that listeners had no easy way of knowing if it were true. Again and again, the trial came up against the problem of establishing the extent of Pétain's personal implication in the actions of the Vichy regime. Had he taken political initiatives of his own? How much did he know? Had others acted behind his back? How much of a free agent had he been? What did he really believe?

Immediately after Laval left the court there occurred a curious episode, obviously stage-managed by the prosecution to offer its answer to these questions. A juror asked for the court to hear the draft of a message by Pétain which had been mentioned in the *Acte d'accusation*. Mornet feigned not to understand: 'Which document are you talking about? I have a lot. Is it the one written in the Marshal's own hand?' The juror confirmed that it was, and Mornet started to read it out with relish:

> News coming from outside has drawn my attention to an evil which is spreading in our overseas possessions and acting on people like a subtle poison which makes them lose their sense of reality and turns them away from their duties to the motherland. This evil is called Gaullism from the name of the ex-French General, de Gaulle.

This text went on in the same vein for a few pages and then suddenly stopped in mid-sentence. 'What is this?' asked Payen. 'A message from the Marshal?'

MORNET: A draft written in the Marshal's hand.
PAYEN: What happened to it?
MORNET: I have no idea . . .
ISORNI: Is there not something on the envelope where it was found?
MORNET: Only this: 'Document belonging to Dr Ménétrel. Project for a message against Gaullism, April 1942, not delivered.'
ISORNI: Ah! Not delivered!
MORNET: But meditated and written in the Marshal's own hand.
PAYEN: Temptation has never been a crime . . . One can have a temptation but if one does not succumb . . .

MORNET: I consider that such writings are equivalent to acts.
ISORNI: The act would have been to read it.[34]

At one point during this exchange, the once again not so deaf Pétain burst into laughter. Having been asked by the defence to discount speeches that Pétain had delivered on the grounds that he had been forced to deliver them, or to exculpate him from speeches that had been delivered by others like Laval, the court was now presented with an opposite example: a message that Pétain had clearly written himself but was not delivered.

Whatever view those in court took about this exchange, newspaper headlines over the weekend showed Laval had got his message across:

> L'Humanité: Laval declared that he pursued his policies with the approval of Pétain-Bazaine.
> Combat: Laval declared that Pétain approved what he said in 1942.
> Franc-Tireur: The Marshal went of his own accord to Montoire.
> Ce Soir: The two accomplices blame each other for the crime.
> L'Aurore: Pétain always approved my policy of collaboration.

Francine Bonitzer in L'Aurore drew the moral for her readers that Laval's guilt only increased Pétain's:

> Laval never won people's confidence. Everyone knew his craftiness, his venality, his cowardice, his spinelessness . . . Not a single Frenchman, ever, would have followed Laval alone. But people believed in the other one . . . It was the man believed to be the purest, the most noble, who entered into collaboration, put his hand in that of Hitler.[35]

The juror Jacques Lecompte-Boinet was still wrestling with his conscience:

> Laval once again dragged the Marshal to his side, sticking close to him as at Vichy: either they will both get away with it or they will go down together. The defence will no longer be able to invoke the evil genius who dragged the Marshal down the path of Wrong; their only defence will have to be that that was not Wrong.

But then his thoughts veered off in another direction:

Why not admit that this evening I understand better the realistic position of Laval than the violent and sentimental one of the jurors around me. Did these two accomplices, Laval and Pétain, really betray France? Did they really do France harm?

In their defence, the scale is certainly weighed down with all those French people who were saved from deportation by them ... by all the lives that their policy saved and I think back to what I was asked at the Foreign Office in London at the start of 1944: 'Why are you anti-Pétainist? Compare the material situation of France and that of Holland for example.'

But on the other side of the scale there are the material benefits that we lost by this policy – in the first place French unity, a unity more spiritual than territorial, a unity so damaged that it is still threatened today, precisely because of this trial. And apart from this rather blurred idea of French honour, there is also the way France's interest was jeopardized: if the Allies were going to win the war, it would have been better to have a French government, a legal government to represent France among the Allies, above all if one thinks of the difficulties experienced by de Gaulle to get France respected, because people said to him: 'But there is Pétain.'[36]

Lecompte-Boinet would in a few days be voting on Pétain's fate. He had not yet made up his mind.

15
Generals and Bureaucrats

After the excitement of Laval's appearance, the last week of the trial was an anticlimax. Lawyers and journalists gossiped in the corridors of the Palais de Justice about when it would end. The August holidays beckoned; there were empty seats in the court. The trial was displaced from the headlines for the first time by international events. The Potsdam conference had finally ended. The French were granted a zone of occupation in Germany, but this only partially effaced the humiliation of having not been consulted. One resistance newspaper wrote:

> The Three Great Powers have decided the future organization of the world in Potsdam without the presence of France ... At the same moment as, on the banks of the Seine, in the very heart of our city, we were witnessing debates which, however necessary they might be, are nonetheless painful ... We are listening to ghosts dragging their chains behind them, but where is France in all this?[1]

Potsdam was overshadowed on Monday 6 August by the dropping of the atomic bomb on Hiroshima. Writers of editorials turned their minds from the trial to the implications of this event for the future of humanity. Even Pétain was momentarily distracted from his own fate. He told Joseph Simon that he might write something on the implications of the atom bomb for the future of warfare.

Originally the prosecution had planned for twelve sessions, but the trial was now entering its thirteenth day – and there were many more defence witnesses to hear. Public interest was also flagging as the remaining witnesses were not well-known personalities. 'The trial,' wrote one reporter, 'was like one of those summer seasons at the theatre which are packed for the star performers but which thin out once the understudies take on the main roles.'[2] Many of the Vichy top brass were not available to testify: Admiral Auphan, Vichy's Naval Minister, was in hiding as was the notorious Alibert. The former head of the Foreign Ministry, Charles Rochat, whose name had come up in relation to Laval's speech wishing for a German victory, was in exile in Switzerland. Another notable absence was Admiral Darlan – assassinated in December 1942 – the most important Vichy personality after Laval and Pétain. This meant that the court heard surprisingly little about the moment when Vichy came closest to military collaboration with Germany after offering airbases in Syria to the Germans in May 1941.[3]

Many witnesses, awaiting their own trial, were plucked from the prison of Fresnes, just outside Paris, to give their testimony.[4] During the Occupation, Fresnes had housed resisters and common criminals. At the time of the Liberation, the resisters were replaced by collaborators but the common criminals remained. As one former collaborator wrote of his Fresnes experience: 'mixed up together were prefects, governors, ministers, ambassadors, admirals, writers, journalists, singers, prelates, industrialists, bankers; magistrates, doctors and surgeons; judo champions, boxers, policemen, actors, film-stars, gangsters and traffickers of various kinds'.[5] The wardens and ordinary criminals took the opportunity to collect celebrity autographs.[6]

In this flotsam and jetsam washed up by the tide of collaboration, those awaiting trial in the High Court constituted a prison aristocracy. Housed in the same section of the prison, they formed an intense little community. Laval, as we have seen, was able to communicate easily with Ménétrel from his first night in prison, but he was so unstoppably garrulous that Ménétrel asked to be moved. The Fresnes bush telegraph was effective. The prisoners feverishly followed the Pétain trial and clutched at every encouraging rumour because they knew their fate was linked to Pétain's. Xavier Vallat, Vichy's first Commissioner for Jewish Affairs, reported to his fellow inmates that in cinema newsreels showing extracts from the trial Daladier and Reynaud were apparently being booed whereas Pétain was cheered – something that police reports do not confirm.[7] Meanwhile the Fresnes prisoners polished their arguments, assembled statistics, collated documents and scrutinized newspapers to judge the mood of the court.

18. François Charles-Roux.

19. Marcel Peyrouton.

20. Fernand de Brinon.

21. Pierre Mongibeaux (*top*) and André Mornet (*bottom*).

The Republican ghosts of the first week had excited mixed feelings but they were trained to hold an audience's attention. These Vichy ghosts, however, had lived entirely in the shadow of the Marshal. Isorni wrote: 'After an especially dull session listening to witnesses whose goodwill did not compensate for their lack of oratorical skills, Pétain grabbed me by the sleeve and muttered in my ear: "Bad programme today! I hope you have something better for tomorrow."' Lemaire, enervated by the heat, sighed under his breath one day, 'Isorni. I am bored.' He could not prevent himself from occasionally nodding off.[8] The defence did its best to liven things up. 'We have got to keep our programme varied,' Isorni told a journalist, 'civilians and Generals'.[9] He even produced a Bourbon Prince, François-Xavier de Bourbon Parme, the pretender to the Spanish throne who had settled in France after his expulsion from Spain in 1938. Active in the French Resistance, he had been arrested by the Germans in 1944 and condemned to death. Thanks apparently to an intervention by Pétain, the sentence was not carried out.

Apart from this flash of aristocratic exoticism, the court was treated to a parade of soporific generals and boring bureaucrats who had served Vichy at various levels. Some, like Jean Berthelot, Vichy's Minister of Communications, oozed the sleek self-satisfaction of professional *fonctionnaires* who were self-righteously convinced they had nothing to apologize for. Others were visibly ill at ease, like the ailing General Bergeret, Vichy Air Minister, who was extracted from a prison hospital. Racked by coughing, he squirmed and twisted in his seat during his interrogation. Other witnesses were truculently aggressive, like Marcel Peyrouton, who had been Vichy Minister of the Interior. Thickset, with a drawlingly lazy voice, arms crossed defiantly, Peyrouton defiantly gave his address as 'the prison of Fresnes'. He had what Madeleine Jacob described as 'a gangster's elegance' and was 'probably quite a brute when he gets angry'.[10] For a man used to giving orders without qualms of conscience, Peyrouton was visibly irritated by the questions of the jurors, many of whom would have found themselves in prison two years earlier. 'Is this my trial or Pétain's?' he burst out at one point.

All these witnesses presented themselves as apolitical, animated by patriotic duty, working within the terms of the armistice to defend

French interests. When asked how he could justify Vichy's measures against Jews and freemasons, Peyrouton, who had been a high-ranking colonial administrator under the Republic, told the court: 'I did not ask myself this kind of question. I have told you, and I repeat: I am not a Republican; I am not an anti-Republican. I am an agent of the French government.'[11]

Berthelot presented himself as a pure technician only interested in protecting France's railway network from the Germans. He offered the court an exhaustive statistical balance sheet of every bridge rebuilt and every locomotive brought back into service. Listeners were jolted out of somnolence when he suddenly shouted out, 'the Germans capitulated'. But it turned out that 'capitulation' merely consisted of withdrawing a rather technical instruction relating to railway traffic. Eventually Mongibeaux could take no more: 'Do you need to list every railway line, every wagon, every bridge?' Mornet backed him up: 'The prosecution accepts that in the issue of transport ... there was an effort to put a brake on German demands ... But from the point of view of "intelligence with the enemy" I am trying to look at the matter from a more elevated point of view.' The 'elevated point of view' was precisely what these witnesses wished to avoid.[12]

None of them had any sympathy with Germany, but their apolitical posture disguised a penchant for authority and an impatience with the compromises of democracy – and a deeper sympathy with the values of the Vichy regime. Efficient bureaucrats can be more deadly than disorganized fanatics. These people had not welcomed France's defeat but they had seen it as offering political opportunities. And all were animated by a reverence for Pétain. There was much clicking of heels, saluting and bowing in court. As Léon Werth commented: 'So many nuances in a bow! Weygand had also bowed but with a haughty diplomatic reserve.'[13] These bows were more like prostration before a religious icon. Even Pétain seemed to find the adulation too much. At one point he interrupted irritably: 'Enough. Go away'; on another occasion when a general was expatiating on military tactics in the 1930s, Pétain was heard to mutter under his breath, 'That is quite enough of tactics.'[14]

General Campet, the recipient of this rebuke, had spent three years at the head of Pétain's military *cabinet*. A caricature of Pétainist devotion, he painted an idealized portrait of a Marshal with a bottomless generosity of spirit who had never believed in a German victory. Campet became nostalgically misty-eyed when recalling the eloquent nobility of Pétain's speeches, but he gave the game away in his closing comments: 'The Marshal was not swayed by sentiment, only reason mattered to him. The issue is not whether or not he wanted the victory of the Allies or the Germans, but to know which would prevail in the war so as to attach himself to the winner and profit from his victory.'[15]

The same arguments were recycled again and again. They would form the staple of the Pétainist defence for the next fifty years. The fatuously self-important General Lafargue presented Pétain as a twentieth-century Vercingetorix who had pursued a tactic of cunning duplicity at odds with the French cult of bravura: 'If Montoire and collaboration had not existed,' he told the court, 'I would even say that it would have been necessary to invent them to cover us.'[16] Many witnesses recalled that the Germans had called Pétain 'the old fox' and claimed that he had cunningly outwitted the Germans while allowing his subordinates to pursue a secret resistance. One former Vichy Prefect, Louis François-Martin, told the court he had accepted his post to protect the French population from the Germans, in what he called 'defensive resistance'. He was sure that he was interpreting Pétain's real wishes even if he conceded that these were difficult to decipher:

> His thoughts were often hidden under the veil of the complexity of appearances and contradictions, but it was precisely for us, the executants, to extract from them, if I can use such an expression, the means of action. We had the duty to interpret this in the direction of resistance.[17]

Finally, many witnesses deployed the argument of sacrifice. 'We needed someone,' General Lafargue told the court, 'capable of swallowing a bitter medicine, gall and wormwood, and wearing a crown of thorns.'[18] To explain why Pétain had not taken the opportunity to join the Allies in North Africa after November 1942, General Serrigny told the court that he had implored him to leave France at that moment. Pétain refused because he felt it was his mission to stay with his people. Serrigny then added:

I failed in my mission ... But I do recognize that there was something grandiose and moving in this gesture of a man who stayed to keep his oath and prevent his people from suffering. To the crown of glory that that I offered him – and that it would have been so easy for him to seize – he preferred a crown of thorns. That was a noble sacrifice.[19]

These testimonies had some impact. Jean Schlumberger wrote in *Le Figaro* that the court was being presented with events 'in three dimensions with their inextricable mixture of good and bad'; if Vichy did contain a 'swarm of sinister characters', there were also others working to save France from the 'yoke of an absolute and total shame'. Similarly, according to Maurice Clavel:

These witnesses were not important personalities ... But whether they intended to or not they did ... shine a tragic light on the clash of eternal ideas, all doubtless true, which confront each other in this trial ... Antinomies as eternal as those of Antigone ... For if every one of us knows that it is better to bury one's brother than obey the prohibition of the state, we do not yet know if it was better to leave France or to remain in France, to choose honour or charity.

Passion enters into the debate: to leave is seen as flight, to remain is seen as abject ... if those who chose honour were right to do so, what about those who sacrificed their honour for the attenuation of the misfortunes of their compatriots?

If they had the right to do so, did they have the right, at the same time as losing their honour, to lose the honour of France herself? ... The trial of Marshal Pétain is not 'historical' but 'metaphysical'; that is the source of the anguish that grips us and divides us all.[20]

No metaphysics, however, for Madeleine Jacob: 'It would seem that the road to hell is paved with good intentions. When a criminal kills someone and argues that his intentions were pure, he is executed. Pétain killed France while sighing. One does not judge a person by his sighs but by his acts.'[21] Nor was Léon Werth convinced by the way these witnesses had depicted a sort of 'anti-Pétain Pétain': 'we are plunged into a world of illusions. One wonders if History will deny that this old man in his Kepi ever existed, and was not just an imaginary being created by the fantasy of chroniclers.'[22]

DOUBLE GAMES AND SECRET
MESSAGES

Apart from these general defences of Pétain as a sacrificial martyr, the court also heard about two specific issues that would figure for years to come in Vichy apologetics: the alleged *double jeu* (double game) by which Pétain had secret contacts with the British and the 'secret messages' he had supposedly sent supporting the Allied landings in North Africa in November 1942.

Those who believed in the *double jeu* eagerly awaited revelations about Rougier's visit to London in October 1940 to negotiate a secret agreement with Churchill. The Foreign Office had been hard at work for weeks to refute Rougier's claims. This required archival detective work since Rougier had left little trace in London. It was established that Rougier *had* visited London; and that he *had* met Churchill on the day after Montoire, but his claim to have negotiated a 'secret agreement' turned out to be a wildly exaggerated version of what transpired during his short London stay. The key piece of evidence Rougier presented in his book was, according to Sir Alexander Cadogan, the head of the Foreign Office, 'a barefaced forgery of a British document'.[23] Handwritten annotations which Rougier claimed to be by Churchill were really by the British official William Strang. Once all of this had been laboriously established, the British published a 4,000-word refutation of Rougier's claims on the eve of the trial.[24]

Whether he was a mythomaniac or just a liar, Rougier was still buzzing around like an angry fly in New York peddling his assertions to whomever would listen. Embarrassingly for the British, his story received widespread press coverage, perhaps because it deflected attention from America's own relations with Vichy. On 21 July, *The New York Times* carried the headline, 'Rougier Reiterates he Carried on Secret Vichy-British Negotiations, Challenging FO Statement', and on 7 August, 'Rougier Accuses Britain of Forgery'.

Since Rougier was not in France, it fell to Pétain's adviser, Admiral Fernet, to give his version of events. Fernet confirmed that Pétain had received Rougier before and after the visit to London; and that Pétain had given 'full approval' to what had been agreed. But when pressed on the substance of that 'agreement', Fernet had no light to throw: 'At the distance that we are now from this interview, and given that I was only the Marshal's collaborator for the organization of his interviews, I did not scrutinize at that moment exactly all the terms of the Rougier documents.'[25]

In the end, what the court heard about the Rougier mission was as underwhelming as the mission itself. But the defence had another professor up its sleeve to tell the court about a further 'secret mission'. This was Jacques Chevalier, a professor of philosophy, conservative and Catholic, who had briefly served as Vichy's Education Minister. Chevalier had been summoned to speak not about education but about Vichy's relations with Britain. He was proud to boast an 'intimate' friendship with the former British Foreign Minister, Lord Halifax, whom he had known since their Oxford days together in 1904.

This was the narrative that can be pieced together from Chevalier's story:

4 December 1940: At 10.45 a.m. Chevalier was visited by the Canadian diplomat Pierre Dupuy with a personal message from Lord Halifax saying that although the armistice had imposed a 'state of artificial tension' between the two countries, the British government wished to renew contact.

5 December: At 3.00 p.m. Chevalier took the proposal to Pétain, who was supportive, commenting only that the term 'artificial tension' be replaced by 'artificial *froideur*'. That evening Chevalier and Dupuy drew up a 'projet d'accord': if Vichy guaranteed that Germany would not be given access to Vichy-held colonies, the British would ease their economic blockade of France.

6 December: Chevalier and Dupuy saw Pétain together; the 'project' was agreed.

7 December: Dupuy left for London.

9 December: A message was received from London saying '*tout va bien* [all is going well]', meaning that the agreement had been approved.[26]

The court had no way of knowing how much of this was true. By providing such precise details of his meetings, Chevalier gave an air of verisimilitude to his recollections. It is hard to challenge someone who provides not just the date but the exact minute that an event takes place.

Two conclusions could be drawn that were hardly helpful for the defence. First, if Chevalier had been approached by the British, the implication was that there was no Rougier agreement. Why negotiate another one to achieve the same ends? Second, even if the message '*tout va bien*' really existed, it could not have signified a formal ratification of a deal. It was inconceivable that any proposal would have been conveyed, deciphered, discussed and agreed in two days.

That London and Vichy both wanted to avoid open conflict and reach a minimal modus vivendi was different from a *double jeu* whereby Pétain was secretly working against Germany. But if Chevalier's 'revelations' amounted to little, in the black-and-white world of 1945 the existence of any contacts between Vichy and London was a surprise. When the trial was over a British Foreign Office official remarked with relief: 'I think we are lucky that no more was made during the trial about Franco-British relations.'[27]

Might the alleged 'secret messages' to Algeria turn out to be more useful to the defence than the rather nebulous double game? The task of telling this story fell to a young naval captain, Édouard Archambaud, whom nobody had ever heard of before. He was in court only because his superior, Vichy's Naval Minister Admiral Auphan, was in hiding. Archambaud had been at Auphan's side during *the* key moment of choice in the history of the Vichy regime when the Americans landed in North Africa. This was the moment when Pétain might have chosen to rally to the Allied cause but chose not to do so. The disappointment at Vichy's response had been recalled in a powerful rhetorical flourish at the end of Daladier's testimony in the first week: 'When, behind the bars of my prison cell, I heard on 8 November that the Americans and English had landed in North Africa, I turned in the direction of Vichy, hoping that across the airwaves I might hear a cry which announced at last the renaissance of the soul of France . . . But there was nothing! Not a gesture! Nothing!'[28] Even Pétain's most ardent defenders struggled to explain his silence.

The operation had not gone as smoothly as the Allies had hoped. In the weeks leading up to the landings, the Americans had been secretly in contact with a group of personalities ('the Five') primed to neutralize opposition when the landings occurred. They also planned to use the French General Henri Giraud. Taken prisoner by the Germans during the battle of France in 1940, Giraud had become a hero after escaping in April 1942. As a man of unimpeachable patriotism and unimpeachable conservatism, he was likely to be more acceptable to French army officers in North Africa than the 'traitor' de Gaulle. But the plot of the Five fizzled out because of poor coordination; and Giraud was stuck in Gibraltar trying to persuade the Americans to give him a bigger role. Everything therefore depended on whether Vichy would seize the opportunity to rally to the Allies and order its military leaders in North Africa not to fire on the Americans. This risked provoking German retaliation in metropolitan France. Whichever choice was made, Vichy's lopsided neutrality was now unsustainable. Pétain was pulled between those, like Laval, who wanted to preserve German goodwill, and those who wanted to join the Allies.

In the end, Vichy lost on both counts. Its forces in North Africa were ordered to resist the Allies but this was not enough to reassure Hitler that France could be trusted. On 11 November he moved German troops into the Free Zone to protect the Mediterranean seaboard. Pétain issued a message of protest which was broadcast at regular intervals. In the meantime, Admiral Darlan, one of the most senior figures of the Vichy regime, who happened to be in North Africa visiting his sick son, concluded that resisting the Americans was futile. After dithering for two days, he switched sides and signed a ceasefire, claiming that this was justified because, with the occupation of the Free Zone, Pétain was no longer a free agent and indeed secretly approved what he had done. The confusion in these days led Churchill to quip: 'If Admiral Darlan had to shoot Marshal Pétain, he would no doubt do it in Marshal Pétain's name.'

By the end of the week, Vichy had lost its Empire in North Africa and its Free Zone in France. A few days later it also lost its fleet, which scuttled itself on 28 November rather than fall into German hands. Many of Pétain's advisers urged him to leave for North

Africa. De Gaulle himself later commented: 'I shall never understand why the Marshal did not go to Algiers in November 1942. The French in Algeria would have cheered him, the Americans would have embraced him, the English would have followed him . . . The Marshal would have made a triumphant return to Paris on his white charger.'[29]

Before Archambaud's appearance, the court had heard from two witnesses that Pétain had secretly approved Darlan's actions, but they had given no evidence.[30] Archambaud was in court to provide the details. This is the narrative that could be pieced together from his convoluted testimony:[31]

8 November: News of the landings in North Africa reached Vichy in the early hours. The government decided to let Darlan handle the position on the ground as best he could.

Most members of the government were unhappy about a request from the Germans to fly over French airspace and use airbases in Tunisia, but permission was granted in a telegram by Laval.

'I think,' said Archambaud, 'that it was decided in the night at Châteldon [Laval's residence near Vichy] without the Marshal knowing about it.'

9 November: Since French forces in North Africa were being overwhelmed by the Americans, Darlan asked Vichy how he should respond to the American request for a ceasefire. The reply was that Darlan should *not* respond. This was at the insistence of Laval who was travelling to Munich to see Hitler. If Hitler believed the French could not be trusted in North Africa, Laval would have no bargaining position to prevent German retaliation against mainland France.

10 November: In the morning Darlan sent Vichy the ceasefire terms that the Americans were offering. Auphan and Weygand wanted Pétain to accept, but after an angry telephone call from Laval in Germany, Pétain reiterated his order to Darlan: 'I gave the order to defend North Africa. I reaffirm that order.' At the same time, Pétain ordered Auphan to send his first secret coded message to Darlan: 'Understand that this order [to resist] was necessary for the negotiations that are going on [Laval's negotiations with the Germans].'

11 November: After receiving the telegram telling him to resist (and before the corrective secret message) Darlan had given himself up as a prisoner to the Americans.

Pétain appointed General Noguès to replace him. On the same day, despite Laval's efforts to reassure Hitler that the French could be trusted to defend North Africa, German troops were sent into the Free Zone.

12 November: A day of total confusion in North Africa: it was no longer clear who on the French side was in charge (if anyone).

13 November: Darlan informed Vichy that he had reached an agreement with the Americans to terminate the fighting, ending his message with the words 'Long live the Marshal'. On the same day, Archambaud was instructed to send a second secret telegram: 'Intimate agreement (*intime accord*) of the Marshal and President [Laval] but before replying we are consulting the occupying authorities.'

16 November: Pétain publicly repudiated Darlan for his agreement with the Americans.

At a meeting of the Council of Ministers, Laval declared he was still committed to collaboration. Admiral Auphan resigned from his position as Naval Minister. Laval took full control of the government.

Probably no one in the courtroom managed to grasp all of the complexities of this labyrinthine story. But its main point was clear: Laval (as usual) had been the evil genius; the 'real Pétain' was to be found in the 'secret' messages of 10 and 13 November; and after that point the 'real Pétain' was no longer a free agent. As Archambaud summed up the situation: 'Those who had been faithful to Pétain in 1941 and 1942 now took the view he was a prisoner and we had to follow his real thoughts not his official speeches.'

The 'secret telegrams' were a staple of the Pétainist defence for years to come. Historians long doubted whether they really existed; or, if they did, what they meant. In 1989 a photocopy of the 13 November telegram was eventually published in a biography of Darlan.[32] This proved it had existed – but not how it should be interpreted. Events were changing minute by minute, and so many telegrams were speeding back and forth between Algiers and Paris that it is not certain what Pétain thought he was secretly agreeing to.

Since no one in the courtroom was willing to accuse Archambaud of lying, Mongibeaux took a different tack: 'So it was necessary to follow the thoughts Pétain did not express and not those expressed in his messages?'

> ARCHAMBAUD: Yes, but this thought was expressed by the telegrams that I coded.
> PAYEN: His thoughts were expressed in his secret messages.
> MONGIBEAUX: Secret messages are no longer messages it seems to me.[33]

Mongibeaux's riposte was weak – a message is surely still a message even if it is secret – but the court had no opportunity to go into more detail. The *instruction* files on the events of November 1942 ran to thousands of pages. It would have taken weeks of analysis to establish exactly what had happened. To complicate matters, while the trial was underway, more documents had surfaced in the form of notes kept by Ménétrel during that chaotic week. These were added to the High Court archives but arrived too late to be used in the trial. They would probably not have helped much. In one note, on 11 November, Ménétrel reports how Pétain glossed for Abetz his protest against the sending of German troops to the Unoccupied Zone:

> I will perhaps protest again ... My prestige is necessary for you ... Otherwise Germany will find only a void. All could have been sorted out if there had been from the start a proper decision for us to come to an understanding. Things can still be repaired. You will need to accept my little manoeuvres, my protests.[34]

Was this a pitch for collaboration from a man who still believed Germany would win? Was it his way of covering himself against German reprisals? What represented his real view: the public protest or the private reassurance to Abetz? Double games and secret messages slotted inside each other like Russian dolls. In truth, Pétain's reactions were probably explained more by confusion and exhaustion than by calculation and ruse. The old man, buffeted by contradictory advice, subjected to a rhythm of meetings that would have been punishing for a man half his age, fluctuated about the best course to follow – but somewhere he clung, amid the wreckage of his policies, to his original 'gift' of himself to the French. He had nothing else to cling to.

Rather than offering an exegesis of telegrams no one had ever seen, the prosecution tried a different tack. Mornet read out the minutes of a meeting of the Council of Ministers on 8 November 1942, showing that the decision to allow the Germans to fly over French territory and use Tunisian airbases was not Laval's solitary initiative (as Archambaud claimed): it had been approved by Pétain.[35] An even more crucial decision had followed on 10 November, authorizing German troops to disembark at Tunis – with the caveat that the Marshal accepted 'but under the reserve of an official protest . . . presented in the form of an injunction from the Germans'.[36] A telegram to Tunis on 11 November was unambiguous: 'The Marshal has decided to continue the struggle against Anglo-Saxon aggression within the limits of our possibilities.' Thus Vichy had permitted the Germans to instal themselves in Tunisia while the Americans were securing their position in Algeria and Morocco. It would take five months of fighting to liberate Tunisia.

Secret message or no secret message, Darlan was a cynical opportunist who would have switched sides anyway. But in Tunisia, the haplessly loyal Admiral Esteva could not bring himself to disobey. His fidelity to the Marshal was rewarded by a message of congratulation from Pétain saying that he was 'very happy' with his attitude.[37] A few weeks before Pétain's trial the High Court had sentenced Esteva to life imprisonment for this act of obedience to Pétain. No secret messages for him.

16

The Absent Jews

The fate of the Jews had been mentioned twice in the *Acte d'accusation*. One passage referred to a 'humiliating collaboration' that 'placed entire categories of French outside the law and organized their persecution as under the Hitlerian regime, then delivered up to the Reich the victims that it demanded'. Another passage asked: 'How to justify the fact that [Vichy] instead of invoking the impossibility of breaking with French laws and traditions, promulgated these abominable racial laws which it would have been a hundred times better to leave to the occupying authorities.' These two convoluted sentences linked Vichy's Jewish policies to collaboration, which was necessary as Pétain was being accused of 'collusion with the enemy'. But they blurred the degree to which Vichy's anti-semitic policies were home-grown and not opposed to all 'French traditions'.

Nor did the indictment identify what 'racial laws' were in question. Vichy had immediately imposed its own measures of discrimination against Jews, distinct from the measures promulgated by the Germans in the Occupied Zone. The most significant of these was the Statut des Juifs issued in October 1940, excluding Jews from the civil service and from some other professions. This was accompanied by an order authorizing the internment of foreign Jews in the Unoccupied Zone. When arrests of Jews began at Germany's behest in 1942, the French police carried them out.

One noticeable feature of Pétain's trial is that no Jewish witness was invited to testify.[1] Indeed the voices of the ordinary victims of the Occupation were hardly heard, although the court received numerous letters from associations of deportees asking to testify. These were mostly ignored.[2] Janet Flanner witnessed an old lady who presented herself to the security staff of Palais de Justice: 'Sweating in her heavy mourning in the afternoon heat,' Flanner reported, 'she told the Palais guard that one of her sons had been beaten to death by Vichy legionnaires, that the other had perished in the concentration camp of Nordhausen.' She was refused entry because she did not have a pass.[3]

Mornet, who disliked being deflected from his plan, did not think the testimony of the victims would add anything. For him the purpose of the trial was 'less to recall the horrors that we all know' than to explain how they had occurred. The voices of the victims could provide 'atmosphere', but he would at the end produce documents that 'will speak more tellingly than all the witnesses you might call'. Mongibeaux overruled him and the court heard brief testimonies from two former resisters, one of whom had been deported to Buchenwald and the other to Mauthausen. But neither was Jewish: no Holocaust survivor, no relative of a Holocaust victim, was heard in the court. In fact, no clear distinction was made at the time between 'deportees'. The term was used indiscriminately to cover both Jews and those deported to Germany as resisters. Most Jewish deportees had not returned from the camps to tell their story.

Historians have recently nuanced the view that in 1945 no one grasped the specificity of the Holocaust, or that Jews wanted only to fit back into France and not draw attention to themselves.[4] As Simone Veil, survivor of Auschwitz and future French politician, wrote many years later: 'We wanted to talk but no one wanted to listen.' One source of tension in the spring of 1945 came from attempts by Jews to reclaim apartments from which they had been expelled during the Occupation. Organizing themselves into associations to defend their interests, the new owners brazenly claimed to be patriots who had prevented these properties from falling into German hands. Ugly incidents exploded in Paris when demonstrators could be heard shouting 'Death to the Jews', 'France for the French'.[5]

In this poisonous atmosphere, Jewish representatives had to tread carefully. At the Liberation, most Jewish organizations in France – secular, religious, Zionist – had formed an umbrella organization, the Conseil représentatif des institutions juives de France – the Representative Council of Jewish Institutions of France or CRIF – to defend their interests. In May 1945 the CRIF was approached by the

Commission d'Instruction for the Pétain case to provide evidence regarding Vichy's role in anti-semitic persecution. The CRIF dele-gated one of its members to assemble the evidence. But two months later, shortly before the opening of the trial, the CRIF noted that there was still an absence of documentation 'demonstrating Pétain's respon-sibility'. The organization was divided as to whether it should put in a formal request to testify in the trial, and decided against it by a nar-row majority.[6] Given that the CRIF was in these months preoccupied with the anti-semitic incidents in Paris, the organization preferred to keep a low profile in the Pétain case.[7]

The Commission of Instruction preparing Pétain's trial did estab-lish a file on the 'Question Juive' – as part of a dossier treating the 'alignment of France with Germany in domestic policy'.[8] This file included some poignant testimonies. For example, the harrowing memories of the lawyer Jaqueline Lang on arrests of Jews in Mar-seilles in January 1943:

> We got into carriages as best we could under the mocking gaze and laughter of German officers who were taking photographs and some French who were also acting as police. It was 10 a.m. Then the car-riages were closed up and sealed; we lacked terribly for air because everything was closed up. We were 60 French and foreign Jews in my wagon. There was no water. There were no buckets ... Despite our requests during the journey and our saying that a woman was dying and needed something to drink, the doors were never opened ... When we arrived on the Tuesday morning after a night of delirium and hal-lucinations, there was one dead body among us and three women who had gone mad.

She ended: 'I do not know if Marshal Pétain knew about this and about all the arrests of Israelites.'[9]

Even more devastating – because it directly mentioned Pétain – would have been the testimony of the Abbé Glasberg about the camp of Venissieux, near Lyon, where 800 foreign Jews had been dumped in August 1942:

> Hearing the circumstances of women who were being separated from their children, the delegate of the Prefect of Lyon who was present for

the operation said to me: 'What an abominable thing we are doing!' I replied to him: 'And yet you are doing it.' And he replied to me: 'We have to obey the Marshal!'[10]

Although this material was not cited in court, the persecution of the Jews did receive some – limited – attention at the trial. In the pre-trial interrogations Pétain had said: 'I always vehemently defended the Jews; I had Jewish friends.' When in May 1942 the Germans had asked the Vichy government to impose the yellow star on all Jews living in the Unoccupied Zone, as the Germans were doing in the Occupied Zone, Pétain had refused; he also recalled telling the violently anti-semitic Commissioner for Jewish Affairs, Darquier de Pellepoix, 'you are a torturer' – though he might have meant that Darquier was torturing him with his relentless demands for ever greater measures against the Jews rather than bemoaning the fact that Darquier was torturing them.[11]

Jeanneney and Herriot told the court that they had refused to provide lists of Jewish parliamentarians when asked by Vichy. Anti-semitism had also come up for all of three minutes in Laval's deposition. On his second day in court, Laval recounted his reaction when in August 1943 the Germans demanded the denaturalization of all French Jews:

I realized all too well what they wanted: as soon as they had been deprived of their nationality, the Jews would be arrested and deported. I told the Germans, 'I refuse' . . . I need scarcely tell you that the Marshal agreed with me.[12]

Of course the truth was much more complicated, but no one was interested enough to explore further.

Only two witnesses were called specifically to discuss the fate of the Jews – and both of them for the defence. The first was Pasteur Marc Boegner, head of France's Protestant churches, which had more vigorously opposed anti-semitic persecution than the Catholic Church. Boegner had been called as a witness for the defence, not the prosecution. He had agonized over whether he should agree to testify but was reassured when he heard that Isorni had also approached a Catholic bishop and the Grand Rabbi had spoken on Pétain's behalf. In the end the Vatican would not allow any cleric to testify, and the Grand Rabbi also refused. Boegner agreed to appear nonetheless.

He described his six meetings with Pétain during the Vichy regime to protest against different Vichy policies: the imposition of the oath on magistrates, the persecution of the Jews, the delivery of refugees to the Germans. Boegner's description of each encounter followed almost exactly his account of his meeting with Pétain on 26 June 1942, just before the unleashing of the worst anti-semitic persecution:

> I read out to him a letter from the Conseil of the Protestant Federation . . . He received it with the courtesy with which he received all my interventions; he listened with the greatest attention; he reminded me of the interview we had had the previous January and, once again, I observed his deep emotion but, once again, I have to say, I had the impression that he was impotent to prevent these terrible evils that, privately, he condemned without reservation.[13]

Boegner was devastated when he saw that the press reported that he had hardly cast the man he was defending in a favourable light. He later revisited in his diary what he had said in court:

> Referring to racial deportations in my written statement I was sure I had said: 'Never was there a word suggesting that Marshal Pétain supported the policy. He always seemed to me to be in complete disagreement with his government.' I see now that I had omitted this phrase.[14]

That correction would surely have made no difference: ignorance is hardly more defensible than impotence.

The other witness was the civil servant Jean-Marie Roussel, who had chaired the Denaturalization Commission set up by Vichy in July 1940. Roussel was an unassuming figure, 'pallid, trembling in his tight little grey suit' as Isorni wrote. The Denaturalization Commission's brief was to review all naturalizations carried out in France since 1927, when a liberal naturalization law had regularized the citizenship status of immigrants who had arrived in France during the previous decade. Since many of these immigrants were Jews, the creation of the Commission was a barely disguised measure of anti-semitism. With the arrests of foreign Jews in 1942, its decisions might have fatal consequences.[15]

In Roussel's telling, the very existence of the Commission demonstrated that Vichy had rejected more extreme calls for the automatic denaturalization of everyone who had been given citizenship since 1927. Roussel told the court that he had only accepted the role after assurances that there would be no interference from either the government or the Germans. He had set up three sub-commissions. They had to process some 250,000 files concerning about 900,000 people. Thanks to the Commission's 'humane jurisprudence' which excluded 'racial or political preoccupations', they had 'only' denaturalized about 3 per cent of the total.

Roussel described his only two meetings with Pétain:

March 1941: He perfectly followed my exposé which lasted 20 minutes . . . and asked me to congratulate . . . the members of the Commission for the . . . humane way . . . in which they were acting.

28 August 1943: Worried by rumours that the Germans were pushing for blanket denaturalizations, Roussel asked to see Pétain again. In two minutes of private conversation, Pétain assured him that the Vichy government had rejected the German injunction. Roussel replied that the Commission would continue its work but that it would not denaturalize anyone whose address was known by the Germans. Pétain commented: 'You are right and I am very happy to hear that the Commission is going to act in this way.'[16]

Once Roussel had finished, Isorni made sure his listeners had imbibed two key messages: first, the Commission had saved Jewish lives by acting as a buffer against the Germans; second, Pétain explicitly approved of this.

While Roussel spoke, Mornet had been looking down, shuffling his papers, avoiding any eye contact with the witness. He asked no questions and seemed relieved to see him go. There was a good reason for this. Introducing his witness, Isorni remarked slyly that he had been called 'with no ulterior motives'. In truth, Roussel was in court primarily to embarrass Mornet, who had chaired one of the Denaturalization Commission's three sub-committees. This was an electric moment in the trial. On the floor of the court was a witness, who had been extracted from Fresnes prison awaiting trial for his role on the

Commission of Denaturalization; watching him from across the court was the Public Prosecutor who had worked with him on that same Commission. Roussel never needed to mention Mornet's name when giving his testimony. He knew that everyone knew why Isorni had summoned him to court; and everyone knew that he knew.

Mornet's participation on the Commission had already been raised by the defence in the Esteva trial. On that occasion he had offered a lame justification delivered with his usual feigned indignation:

> Yes I was part of it. When I was asked to take part, I said: 'I am willing to do so in order to remove French nationality from those who are its enemies, those who are unworthy of it or those with a criminal record – what the existing law did not allow. I am happy to do it if it is about targeting those who form themselves into some kind of separate community in the French nation ... But if it is to support anti-semites, I protest with indignation and vigour.'[17]

He even claimed to have accepted the position at the request of those 'unfortunate Jews who saw themselves being persecuted'.

Mornet had no questions and Roussel left the court. It was revealing that no one, either in the court or the press, thought to question the existence of the Commission or to ask what its creation revealed about the nature of Vichy. Whatever Roussel had said about the 'humanity' guiding its deliberations, or whatever had been meant by the 'superior interests of France', the Commission had denaturalized 15,000 individuals. This was the beginning of a steady stream of measures of persecution which progressively placed Jews outside the national community, excluding them from many professions and dispossessing them of assets. If the Commission's existence shocked no one, it was because the idea that a Jewish problem existed was widely shared during the 1930s – especially in the liberal professions. French lawyers in the 1930s had been vociferous in protesting against the Jews allegedly swamping their profession, and the Vichy policy was welcomed by many of them. This was true of the head of the Paris Bar, Jacques Charpentier, who later became a major figure in the Resistance but still believed that there were too many Jewish lawyers.[18]

Roussel's testimony was met with indifference. The only exception to this was to be found in the Jewish community press. On 1 August, before Roussel's appearance, one Jewish newspaper, *Le Réveil des Jeunes*, reminded its readers that Pétain had not only committed a treason against the nation, 'but also a treason against the most elementary principles of justice': 'It is difficult to believe that Pétain was ignorant about the fate of the Jews whom he handed over to the Germans.' *Le Réveil* regretted that this had not been mentioned in the trial, even if the 'other articles of accusation were certainly more important'.[19]

This qualification would not have been approved by the poet Henri Hertz, who penned a more forceful indictment of Vichy policy in the Paris-based Zionist publication *La Terre retrouvée*. His article, published on 25 August, was originally conceived as an intervention in the trial. But when it became clear that it would appear after the trial was over, the text was handed over formally to Mornet, Mongibeaux and the jurors on 10 August, the last day of the trial. An accompanying letter declared that this would become an 'historic date', ensuring that 'world Judaism is present, as a prosecution witness at this Trial'.[20] Hertz opened:

> At the moment of writing, no Jew, it seems, has been called to the witness stand. None had asked to be called. We do not know how much the accusation is going to make of the issue ... One must hope that this great purge trial will lift the secret which has descended on the Jewish problem since the Liberation ... In all the terrifying truths that make up the Pétain trial, there is a Jewish truth. It is distinct from any other.

He ended:

> We Jews of France ... bear witness that the accused, by his silence when he could have spoken out, by his impassiveness when he could have made a gesture, by his lies when today he says that he did not know, we bear witness that he accepted and presided over this torture, the logical culmination of the exclusionary legislation that he developed and concerted knowingly and deliberately, over five years.[21]

17

The Count, the Assassin and the Blind General

As the trial drew to a close, the debates shifted to the last days of the Vichy regime. Admiral Bléhaut and General Debeney were wheeled into court to tell the story of Sigmaringen. Debeney gave the court a vivid description of Pétain's final journey from Sigmaringen to Switzerland: the French party's installation in the castle of Zeil teeming with nuns, orphans and stray refugees; the stream of retreating German troops under constant attack from the air; the insistence of Pétain's German minder von Tangstein that he set off again; Pétain's refusal; the irruption of the German into Pétain's bedroom in the early morning with a proposal to take him to Switzerland; Pétain's insistence that he would not budge without a formal agreement from the Swiss government to let him into the country. Debeney described what happened next:

> The day passed slowly. We saw the continuous stream of German troops retreating.
> At 18.00h no answer from the Swiss.
> At 19h no answer.
> At 19.30 no answer.
> We sat down to eat, and then at 20.00 Tangstein and the Swiss *chargé d'affaires* arrived to say that the Swiss answer was favourable: the Marshal and his suite had an authorization to cross Switzerland.

The point of this testimony was to demonstrate that Pétain had been in Germany under duress; that he had played no role in the activities of the pseudo-government; and that he had done everything in his power to return to France and defend his honour. All this invited a tart comment from Mongibeaux: 'The Marshal wanted to return to

France to defend his honour. He is today in front of us, and he responds to all our questions with complete silence.' Despite this entirely pertinent observation, Sigmaringen was the period which overall posed the least problem for the defence.

It was more of a challenge to defend the nine months before Pétain had been taken to Germany. In that period, after his abortive attempt to free himself of Laval at the end of 1943, the Vichy regime had entered its most violent phase with the entry into government of ultra-collaborationists like Déat and Darnand. These were the months when the Milice went on a rampage against resisters and Jews; when Mandel and other politicians were assassinated; when the Germans perpetrated terrible atrocities of which the most notorious was the massacre of the entire population of the village of Oradour-sur-Glane. Pétain may have been effectively a prisoner whose every move was watched by his German minder Renthe-Fink, but his name continued to cover the actions of his government.

The defence lawyers were disconcerted when it was announced that Fernand de Brinon, head of the Sigmaringen 'government', and Joseph Darnand, head of the Milice, were going to be heard in court. Brinon had asked to testify. Mornet was no keener than the defence lawyers to invite them to speak since one was, in his words, a 'corrupt businessman' and the other an 'assassin', but Mongibeaux had overruled him. There was a frisson of anticipation at the prospect of seeing this sinister duo in the flesh on the final Thursday of the trial.

From an impoverished aristocratic family, the Comte de Brinon had in the interwar years been a journalist fervently committed to Franco-German reconciliation. Hitler's arrival to power did not change his views. In November 1933 he achieved a certain celebrity as the first French journalist granted an interview with the Führer. The meeting was set up by Hitler's Foreign Minister, Joachim von Ribbentrop, whom Brinon knew from the parties of a friend who owned Pommery champagne. That was his milieu. Five more meetings with Hitler followed. In 1937 Brinon had set up the Comité France-Allemand to foster friendship between the two countries. Idealism did not exclude venality: he was in receipt of generous German funds. These good German connections made him an obvious choice to represent Vichy in the Occupied Zone. The one oddity in Brinon's life was that he had married a Jewish woman, a convert to Catholicism, who shared his aristocratic snobbery and social prejudices. His wife's presence at dinner parties inhibited the usual anti-semitic banter of his circle.[1] When the government moved to Sigmaringen his wife was not allowed to lodge in the castle. De Brinon lived there instead with his secretary and mistress, Simone Mitre.

His appearance in court precipitated the same amazement as Laval's a week earlier. His wasted features seemed to bear no relation to those of the worldly socialite who had figured in the newsreels and glossy magazines of the Occupation, attending gala concerts or hosting grand parties where German officers rubbed shoulders with stars like Arletty in his sumptuous residence on the Avenue Foch (confiscated from its Jewish owners). Brinon's most striking feature was a prominent nose which, in his glory days, led commentators to refer to his 'Bourbon' profile. Now, on this visibly sick man who entered court leaning heavily on a stick, the famous nose only accentuated how ravaged he now looked. 'A villain of melodrama as imagined by Dickens,' wrote one journalist; a 'particularly repulsive personality,' wrote the Foreign Office observer. Even the author of the dry reports by the French police was moved to poetry: 'emaciated with the appearance of a startled vulture'.[2]

The central message of his short testimony was simple:

> The Marshal was partisan of an attempt at reconciliation with Germany, a settlement that was honourable and a renewal of France in liaison if possible ('liaison' is not exactly the right word . . . I am sorry, I am tired) with the German authorities . . . I never had with the Marshal any impression of a double game . . . In all the conversations I had with the Marshal, he always told me that it was his conviction that we must follow this policy.[3]

Although avoiding the tainted word 'collaboration', Brinon had immediately implicated Pétain in the actions of Vichy's last days. There were only two scraps in his evidence to comfort the defence. First, he confirmed that Pétain had refused to have anything to do with the pseudo-government in Sigmaringen. Second, he confirmed that, yes, the famous Dieppe telegram which so obsessed the court, was authentic, and, yes, it did contain the signature 'Philippe Pétain'.

But he could not rule out the possibility that Pétain had not actually seen it.

He told the court nothing about Montoire that it had not already heard, but his recollections of the events leading up to Laval's arrest on 13 December 1940 were unwittingly revealing of the byzantine amateurism of Vichy politics. Brinon had been closely involved in preparing Pétain's planned trip to Paris for the ceremony to receive the ashes of Napoleon's son. Once everything was ready, Brinon had left Paris for Vichy with Laval on the morning of 13 December. Seeing Pétain before lunch, he had handed over Hitler's letter of invitation to the ceremony; Pétain had called for a Michelin map to plan his itinerary almost as if it were a tourist outing; they discussed the guest list for the ceremony. Everything seemed to be in order. Pétain left for lunch and Brinon did not see him again that day. Then a cabinet meeting was suddenly called:

> Laval emerged ashen-faced announcing that he had been sacked . . .
>
> The atmosphere in Vichy was strange. The stairs of the Hotel du Parc were crawling with unofficial police called Groupes de Protection and M. Laval was very worried, wondering what would happen next. That evening I dined with him at the Chantecler restaurant. At a nearby table was M. Berthelot [the same who had been in court the previous day]. M. Laval asked him: 'What do you think about all this?'
>
> M. Berthelot replied: 'I have no idea what is going on.'

After dinner, Brinon was confined to his room. As he recalled:

> The next morning at 6 a.m. there was a knock at my door and I was told: 'M. l'Ambassadeur you are free.'
>
> I asked if I could have my toilet bag, still in M. Laval's car, which had been seized. I got dressed. I went up to see M. Dumoulin de Labarthète [the head of Pétain's *cabinet*] and asked him: 'What is going on?'
>
> He told me: 'It is the culmination of the difficulties I have often told you about and the bad atmosphere between M. Laval and the Marshal. I don't like the way this operation has been carried out.'

Before leaving for Paris, Brinon had a final meeting with Pétain. In recalling this conversation, he reiterated his key message which must have been music to the ears of the prosecution:

The Marshal told me that he simply could no longer bear working with M. Laval; that there was no difference between them regarding foreign policy, that the Germans should be told this, and that he had full confidence in me.[4]

The Count was immediately followed by the Assassin. It would be hard to imagine two more different personalities; nor two more different journeys to the last stand of ultra-collaborationism on the banks of the Danube. Joseph Darnand was from a modest background with little formal education. An undeniably brave soldier, he had been awarded the *médaille militaire* by Pétain in person in July 1918, forever sealing his reverence for the Marshal. While running a small transport company in the interwar years, Darnand had dabbled in extremist right-wing politics. Even so, there was nothing predetermined about Darnand's evolution to ultra-collaboration. Others of similar backgrounds gravitated into the Resistance and Darnand himself did have doubts. In 1943 he had explored the possibility of joining the Free French. But it was too late. De Gaulle reportedly remarked: 'And if Darquier de Pellepoix had himself circumcised I would have to accept him as well?'

Those expecting a pantomime villain when Darnand entered the room were disappointed. Dressed in a tight tweed jacket and plus fours, not the sinister uniform of the Milice, he looked unassuming, like a powerful labourer dressed in his Sunday best, as one observer put it, rather than the head of an organization that had unleashed a reign of terror. 'A man of considerable physical strength and obviously limited intelligence' was the view of the British Embassy. His voice was surprisingly high-pitched. While giving his evidence he stood erect, his arms stiffly at his side.[5] It was hard to believe this unimpressive figure had led an organization whose members swore an oath to eradicate 'democracy, Gaullist dissidence, Jewish leprosy'.

Darnand described the setting up of the Milice in 1943 'with the approval of the Marshal'. Mongibeaux cut to the chase:

MONGIBEAUX: Did the Marshal know that you had sworn an oath of loyalty to the Führer?
DARNAND: Not yet.

MONGIBEAUX: You mean you had not yet sworn it? But when you had done so what was his reaction?

DARNAND: The Marshal never mentioned that matter to me ... I do not think he can have been unaware of it. I did not only have friends in his *cabinet*.

Isorni's only intervention was to establish that Pétain had not approved the crimes of the Milice. Darnand would not play his game:

DARNAND: Until the moment we left France last year in August, I was received by the Marshal every time I asked ...

MONGIBEAUX: What did he say to you?

DARNAND: At his request I reported to him on the activities of the Milice.

MONGIBEAUX: He made no protests?

DARNAND: The Marshal always gave good advice and always asked me to be prudent ...

MONGIBEAUX [interrupting]: When you ignored this advice ... were you never criticized or blamed?

DARNAND: Only once, in a letter that the Marshal wrote to me on 6 August 1944 when the Americans had reached Rennes ...

Darnand refrained from quoting his reply to that letter:

For four years I have received your compliments, your congratulations. You have encouraged me. And today, because the Americans are at the doors of Paris, you begin to tell me that I am a stain on the history of France ... It might have been possible to discover this sooner.[6]

Darnand was only in court for ten minutes. No one seemed inclined to ask him questions, as if his very presence sullied the proceedings. When he left the court, swinging his arms at his side like a schoolboy, squeezing past Pétain as he left like every other witness, the two men hardly seemed to notice one another. His testimony was particularly devastating because no one doubted that, although Darnand was an assassin, he was at least an honest one.

The defence tried to remedy the negative impact of Darnand's testimony by calling a witness who had joined Pétain's *cabinet* in January 1944, the naval officer Jean Tracou. He had arrived at Pétain's side after that dramatic clash when Pétain's advisers had tried to mount an operation to free him from Laval. The Germans had responded with a ferocious letter from Ribbentrop presenting Pétain with an ultimatum to accept a whole series of new demands or to resign. Tracou read out extracts from the letter: 'For the last three years it is incontestable that the measures you have taken as Head of State have frequently had the result of working against collaboration.' There was also a sentence about Pétain's 'permanent resistance' to the German government. In case the court had not got the message, Tracou gave his gloss: the Germans themselves had accorded a 'certificate of Resistance' to Pétain.

Tracou avoided quoting Pétain's humiliating reply to Ribbentrop, the smoking-gun document with which Pétain had been confronted in the last pre-trial interrogation. But he had to find a way to explain away an extraordinary speech by Pétain on 28 April 1944, quoted in the *Acte d'accusation*. In this speech, less than two months before D-Day, Pétain had praised Germany's 'defence of the continent' against Bolshevism and warned against the 'so-called liberation' that the Allies were preparing. Tracou did his best:

> I can tell you, for having witnessed this on a daily basis, that this message was almost entirely written by Renthe-Finck. It was imposed by him from the first line to the last. There was a struggle of almost two months over this speech. Finally, one day he arrived with a telegram from Berlin – I was there – and he said: 'M. le Maréchal, enough procrastination, you need to choose: read the message or resign.'

Tracou's explanation was broadly accurate, but the fact remained that Pétain did deliver the speech: he did not resign. In mitigation, Tracou offered the usual repertoire of anecdotes about the 'old fox's' secret feelings about the Germans. He treated the court to a priceless story of a German officer showing Pétain a map of operations in Normandy after D-Day – the 'so-called' liberation:

> I saw him listening with a certain impatience, all the more so since he had just been subjected to an hour with Renthe-Fink.
>
> Then suddenly – this is a little detail – a fly landed on the map. The Marshal squashed it with his finger and said: 'Look, I have killed a Boche.' I can tell you that this incident which I alone witnessed caused a real chill in the atmosphere.[7]

THE LAST DAY

Friday 10 August.

The end was in sight. Just one more day to get through before the prosecution and defence put forward their case. Before the parade of final witnesses, a letter from General Alphonse Juin was read aloud in court. Juin was a national hero – one of only three soldiers to become a Marshal for his role in the defeat of the Axis. Under his command, three French divisions had been sent to Italy in 1944. His troops had helped liberate Rome in June. An exact contemporary of de Gaulle at Saint-Cyr, Juin was one of a tiny band who addressed de Gaulle as 'tu'. Serving Vichy as a top army commander in North Africa, he had worked to build up the French army in North Africa within the limits permitted by the Germans. In that cause he had even accompanied Brinon to Berlin in December 1941 to negotiate with Göring. Their talks had not come to anything as the Germans were never convinced that a stronger French army might not eventually be used against them.

General Juin had also been a key player, at Darlan's side, in the events of November 1942. Torn between loyalty to Pétain and hostility to Germany, he played a balancing act for a few days. Once the Germans had occupied the Free Zone on 11 November, Juin threw his hat in openly with the Americans.

When de Gaulle arrived in Algiers in May 1943 he immediately reached out to his old comrade Juin, appointing him commander of the French army in North Africa. His mission was to re-enter the war with the Americans and the British. This caused grumbling among resisters, unable to forgive Juin for his original loyalty to Vichy and his wavering in November 1942. If de Gaulle had chosen him it was not out of sentiment – that was not in de Gaulle's repertoire of qualities – but because he was the best person to overcome the reticence of army cadres in North Africa towards the Free French. Juin had served de Gaulle as a Pétainist alibi – and Pétain's defenders hoped now to use him as their Gaullist alibi.

To Isorni's delight Juin had agreed to testify for the defence and say that France owed more to the army of North Africa than 'those who monopolized the Resistance because they had fired a few shots or shaved some women's heads'.[8] Even if this was probably putting Isorni's words into Juin's mouth, for someone of his reputation to say anything in Pétain's defence was a scoop. But Juin, as a senior officer, needed de Gaulle's permission to testify. This seemed initially to have been granted, but at the last minute Juin was sent on a mission to Germany to avoid a potentially embarrassing situation – both for him and for de Gaulle. This was a blow to Isorni, but Juin at least agreed to answer some questions by letter. The letter was read out in court:

First question: What was the position of Vichy's army in North Africa before November 1942:

> This army did not hide its anti-German feelings . . . But overall it saw the victor of Verdun as a leader whose patriotism could not be called into question and it hoped that one day he would give the signal for the conflict to start again. Without approving all that happened in Vichy, about which it only heard vague rumours, it tended to separate the Marshal from the acts of his government.

Second question: Did he know about any secret telegrams to Darlan?

> I can confirm that Admiral Auphan's two telegrams were of a great help to us. They allowed us to set at rest the conscience of many who were tormented by their oath [of loyalty] to Pétain and were still hesitating as to what to do.[9]

Although this letter lacked the impact of a personal appearance in court, the defence could not have hoped for better. If Juin confirmed the existence of the 'secret' telegrams no one was going to deny them. And by avoiding an appearance in court, Juin had escaped embarrassing questions about his own past. If, as Talleyrand remarked, treason is a matter of dates, Juin had put himself on the right side of history – by a few hours. For Pétain's defenders this raised another problem: why had Pétain remained on the wrong side of history for another two years?

The last eight witnesses were small fry, mostly unknown to the public, although some of them had held important positions in Pétain's entourage. Their arguments were now tediously familiar: the double game; collaboration offering a cover for resistance; the cunning of the wily 'old fox'; the nefarious influence of Laval; Pétain's sacrifice of his person to protect the French from worse – and so on. Pétain, wisely asleep for most of the day, woke up for the last two witnesses, both of them generals.

When the retired General Eon had turned up offering to testify for the defence, Isorni could not believe his luck. Eon claimed to have been one of the first officers to rally to the Free French in London. To hear a historic Gaullist speaking in defence of Pétain was a perfect card to hold in reserve for the end of the trial. But Isorni had not done his homework. Eon had indeed rallied to de Gaulle in June 1940 but he had rapidly proved so eccentric that no one knew what to do with him. He spent hours in the lift at Carlton Gardens in London hoping to improve his English by chatting to the lift boy, and he emerged from the war speaking English with a cockney accent. Frustrated at being sidelined, he turned against de Gaulle and became notorious for barracking his speeches.

A tiny man who looked much older than his actual age of sixty-six, Eon bowed low to Pétain on entering the court. After several pirouettes to work out where the judges were sitting, he rambled incoherently for a few minutes until an alarmed Isorni tried to get him back on track by asking about de Gaulle. When Eon responded that de Gaulle's speech of 18 June had been 'very French' and 'very pretty', the whole courtroom doubled up in laughter. The general was discreetly ushered from the court, skipping out, one newspaper wrote, like one of Disney's seven dwarves.

General Lannurien, the last witness, had been a pupil of Pétain before 1914, and he had often visited him during the Occupation. Completely blind as a result of wounds received at Verdun in 1916, Lannurien entered the court tapping his white stick in front of him. His impeccable patriotic credentials and war wounds made him an excellent choice to win the jury's sympathy. Surely he would make a better impression than Eon.

The testimony started well but the court's mood changed as Lannurien embarked upon a celebration of the sublime nature of Pétain's sacrifice. There were shouts and boos; Mongibeaux's efforts to restore order were unsuccessful. Then Germinal, one of the reserve jurors, rose to his feet. Few jurors had participated more actively in the trial. On this occasion he had done his homework:

GERMINAL: With all the respect that I owe to the general for his injuries, I would ask him what he thinks of the maquis and the repression against it?

LANNURIEN: I know what the juror is referring to. It is a letter that I wrote to the Marshal.

He was correct. Germinal read out an extract from a letter that Lannurien had written to Pétain on 15 March 1944, commending Darnand for his suppression of 'terrorism'.[10] As Lannurien tried over the shouting and booing to justify himself, for the first time in the trial Pétain suddenly rose from his seat. Walking towards Lannnurien, who of course could not see him, he declared: 'I am for once speaking to say that I have nothing to do with the presence of General Lannurien here today. I did not even know he was going to come before the court.'[11]

Even Isorni was shocked by this intervention. He tried later to explain it away on the grounds that the modest Pétain had been embarrassed by Lannurien's praise of him. Since he had listened quietly until his name was linked to Darnand, it seems more plausible that Pétain, whose deafness was not in evidence on that day, grasped how unhelpful Lannurien's comments on Darnand were for his case. Pétain was never shy of ditching his most devoted followers if necessary. As Lannurien left court, he pressed his hand and muttered something to him. 'The double game,' noted Lecompte-Boinet acidly.

This had been a troubling end to the three weeks. The trial had opened with Pétain formally announcing he would not speak; it ended with him breaking that vow in order to repudiate the blind old man who had been the last witness in his defence.

18

Réquisitoire and *Plaidoiries*

PÉTAIN: 'How will Mornet be today?'
ISORNI: 'He will ask for your head with the greatest courtesy.'[1]

Mornet had not had a good trial. He was prickly and defensive, and flustered when he could not put his hands on the necessary documents. His hectoring style repelled most observers. Film footage of the trial shows him jabbing his finger and jerking his head up and down, the sleeves of his robes flapping like huge wings. Mornet's problem was that so much time had been lost debating a plot for which he eventually admitted he lacked the evidence. His witnesses had spent more time defending themselves than incriminating Pétain. Throughout the trial Mornet had urged the court to be patient, promising to prove his case through a logical presentation of the documents. Now was his chance.

As he rose to his feet to deliver his *réquisitoire*, documents piled up on the desk in front of him, Mornet knew he had still to prove himself. He opened:

> Messieurs, for four years, and still today, France has been victim of a deception, a deception that has thrown confusion into people's minds, that in which an illustrious personality has served as a cover for treason ... You will now see unfold, with an ineluctable logic, every step, from accommodation to accommodation, from treason to treason, from felony to felony, that led a government to live in collusion with the enemy.[2]

He would show that Pétain had committed treason. This had taken three forms: encouraging the French people to believe they had been definitively defeated and that they had no choice but to accept their place in a German-dominated Europe; humiliating the nation before the world, subordinating it to the conqueror by 'adopting its laws, its prejudices and its hatreds'; and, finally, helping Germany, under the cover of a 'hypocritical neutrality', in her war against France's former allies.

Convinced as he was that Pétain's treason was motivated by an 'old man's thirst for power', coupled with a hatred of the democratic Republic, he returned to his hobby horse: 'A Plot – I repeat the word here – against the internal security of the State.' Having again used the 'P' word, Mornet immediately backtracked, conceding 'I am not bringing proof of direct and personal implication on Pétain's part.' This did not stop him from taking the court back to the network of anti-Republican right-wing conspirators who had placed their hopes in Pétain in the 1930s. Two hours into his speech, Mornet was still mired in the plot he had supposedly abandoned. It is possible that this false start was part of an early draft he could not bring himself to jettison.

Having concluded his long-winded rehashing of the plot that was not a plot, Mornet dismissed the claim of a *double jeu*. This did not detain him for long. Where was the double game? It seemed only to consist of the nebulous Rougier and Chevalier negotiations, and occasional comments that Pétain had uttered in private. As for the secret telegrams of November 1942, even if they had existed, they were outweighed by the letter of approval to Admiral Esteva in Tunisia. 'That was not some secret instruction transmitted by Admiral Auphan to Admiral Darlan,' Mornet reminded the court, 'it was the personal wish, the personal policy of the Marshal.'

Over two hours into his remarks, there was a short recess. The *réquisitoire* had not started well. Mornet, usually so pugnacious, seemed unexpectedly subdued; his voice did not carry. As one journalist remarked, the echo in his name with 'morne' (dull) and 'mort' (death) seemed justified. Several jurors and one judge had fallen asleep.[3]

When he resumed, Mornet turned to the establishment of the Vichy regime, the acceptance of the annexation of Alsace-Lorraine, Montoire and the policy of collaboration, the decision to help Germany in

Syria and fight the Americans in North Africa, the scuppering of the fleet – and so on. As he listed concession after concession, capitulation after capitulation, declaration after declaration, message after message, his *réquisitoire* started to gain momentum. Among the evidence he marshalled were the following communications:

- A letter to Hitler on 24 October 1941, the anniversary of Montoire: 'This anniversary is a date for which I wish to note the meaning and the significance. Your gesture last year contained such grandeur that I feel the duty to underline the historic nature of our conversation.'
- The Dieppe telegram offering 'the participation of France in her own defence' (fighting alongside the Germans).
- Laval's speech of 22 June 1942 which Pétain had modified but approved.[4]
- Pétain's letter to Colonel Labonne, a leader of the LVF, assuring him that by 'participating in this crusade which Germany is leading . . . you embody part of our military honour'.
- The letter to Admiral Esteva on 18 November 1942 commending him for allowing German troops into Tunisia.
- The letter to Ribbentrop in December 1943 about which Mornet said 'it would be impossible to go further down the road of not just collaboration but subordination'.
- The message of 28 April 1944 denouncing the 'so-called Liberation'.

Mornet had spoken for five hours. Towards the end tiredness showed when he referred on two occasions to 'Marshal de Gaulle'. But the consensus was that he had redeemed himself with a performance that was all the more effective for being so low-key. Having abandoned his usual posture of simulated outrage, he seemed more like a company director reading out an annual report. Facts and quotations were allowed to speak for themselves. 'Patiently, stitch by stitch,' wrote one observer, 'he weaves the net which encircles, snares and then suffocates the accused.'[5] There was nothing the court had not heard before but this implacable litany of documents and messages was devastating, as noted by Jean Schlumberger and Maurice Clavel, whose reporting had been more dispassionate than most. Schlumberger wrote in *Le Figaro*:

I doubt that any of these texts he has cited is unknown: radio speeches of the Marshal, messages, official and private letters. The force of the argument comes from their juxtaposition and their quantity . . . But the accumulation is terrifying . . . Mornet's commentaries sometimes seem questionable but the texts he cites are there, multiple ones, terrible . . . One can take no more. It becomes too much. However willing one might be to explain these away by the cruel necessity to bow down to circumstances, there are words that no necessity could justify.[6]

Clavel made a similar point in *L'Époque*:

There *was* something new in this *réquisitoire*: less in the content than in the form of the Marshal's acts and words. If it is true that all these declarations were designed to avoid the worst, if it is true that they were pronounced reluctantly (*à contre coeur*), one could have expected that the laws of necessity, which might excuse them, might also have reduced them to the strict minimum . . . That is why we were stupefied by the sheer collaborationist gratuitousness, by the luxuriance and abundance of certain messages and telegrams read out by the prosecutor.[7]

Even Pétain seemed affected. He had said that morning to Joseph Simon that he found it 'hard to remain impassive. I will do everything I can to remain calm but it will not be easy. To say that I betrayed France is terrible; it is shameful.'[8] As Mornet pursued his implacable demonstration, Pétain showed his usual signs of nervous agitation – fiddling with his gloves, twisting the buttons on his uniform, rubbing the arms of his chair – but now there was a new gesture. He started compulsively twisting the *médaille militaire* pinned to his chest. 'Was he perhaps trying to detach it,' speculated Madeleine Jacob, 'or was he hanging on to it as the only intact symbol of his former glory?'[9]

As Mornet reached his peroration, Pétain swivelled around to look at him. Thus Mornet delivered his final words directly into his eyes:

Considering all the harm that has been done to France by this man with all the glory attached to his name, and speaking without passion, this is the most serious *réquisitoire* I have ever had to pronounce at the end of a long career, having myself reached the declining years of my life, and I do so now not without deep emotion but with the consciousness that

I am fulfilling a rigorous duty: it is the death penalty that I ask the High Court of Justice to pronounce against the person who was Marshal Pétain.[10]

SUNDAY 12 AUGUST

The three defence lawyers spent the next day working on their *plaidoiries*. Planning for this moment had sparked one of their most violent quarrels even before the trial opened. Payen, as senior lawyer, assumed that he would speak alone for the defence. Isorni would have none of it and threatened to withdraw from the trial entirely. As usual, Lemaire acted as broker. Payen conceded some ground while retaining the starring role. After all, this was his final pitch for the Académie Française. The three lawyers reached an unsatisfactory compromise. Payen would deliver his *plaidoirie* in three parts, opening and closing, and the other two would speak in-between. Once they had adopted this 'sandwich' solution, as Isorni called it, the three lawyers established a rough division of labour. But there was little consultation on details – so the combined seven hours of their speeches contained overlaps, repetitions, even contradictions.

As tensions mounted in the last week of the trial, jurors received threatening letters from both sides. They were escorted by the police between the court and their homes. A tract circulated widely giving the exact name and address of every juror – with a warning at the bottom: 'If these men commit an injustice, you will know who has committed it.'

Most of the jurors had in all likelihood made up their minds long ago – but not Jacques Lecompte-Boinet, who continued his careful sifting of the evidence of both sides and still felt a repulsion towards the 'abominable religion' of the Communist-sympathizing jurors:

> In all this I am a prisoner. I think it is my duty to remain here to try to preserve a semblance of intellectual honesty. I blame Pétain for having stayed in France while it was submerged by the *Boches*, when his authority was non-existent. I reproach him with having covered by his presence and his prestige what he could not prevent.

Les Jurés sont responsables

La France toute entière ne porte pas la responsabilité du juge-
ment que quelques hommes vont rendre à l'issue du procès du
Maréchal PÉTAIN.

Ceux qui prononcent la sentence engagent devant le peuple de
France leur propre responsabilité.

Il faut connaître leurs noms :

JURÉS PARLEMENTAIRES

Titulaires : *Bèche*, Député des Deux-Sèvres, 149, avenue de Li-
moges, à Niort.
Bender, Sénateur du Rhône, Audenas (Rhône).
P. Bloch, député de la Loire, 12, rue Labordère,
Neuilly-sur-Seine.
Delattre, député des Ardennes, 1, rue Bixio, Paris-7ᵉ.
Dupré, député du Nord, 113, rue Pierre-de-Roubaix,
Roubaix.
Lévy-Alphandéry, député de la Haute-Marne, Chau-
mont.
Mabru, député du Puy-de-Dôme, 2, rue du Port,
Clermont-Ferrand.
Prot, député de la Somme, Longeau (Somme).
René Renoult, sénateur du Var, 20 bis, rue La Boétie,
Paris-8ᵉ.
Tony Révillon, sénateur de l'Ain, 15, place Malesher-
bes, Paris.
Sion, député du Pas-de-Calais, 25, avenue Raoul
Briquet, Lens.

Suppléants: *Catalan*, à Cologne (Gers).
Chassaing, 15, rue Blaise Pascal, Ambert (P.-de-D.).
Rous Joseph, 17, rue de l'Horloge, Ax-les-Thermes
Ariège.
Jammy Schmidt, 22, rue de l'Abbé Groult, Paris-15ᵉ.

JURÉS NON PARLEMENTAIRES

Titulaires : *Marcel Bergeron*, U. N. I. T. F. 55, rue Pierre Char-
ron, Paris.
Gervolino, Hôtel Pereyre, 63, rue Madame, Paris-6ᵉ.
Maurice Guérin, 11 bis, rue Roquépine, Paris.
Jean Guy, 10, rue Saumères, Toulouse.
Jacques Lecompte Boynet, 6, rue Fréville le vingt,
Sèvres.
Roger Lescuyer, 83, bd. Gergovie, Clermont-Ferrand.
Loriguet, 14, rue La Fontaine, Paris-16ᵉ.
Meunier Pierre, 73, rue de Varenne, Paris-7ᵉ.
Perney, 31, rue des Batignolles, Paris-17ᵉ.
Docteur Poricher, 1, rue Cabanis, Paris-13ᵉ.
Seignon Henri, 8, av. Charles Floquet, Paris-7ᵉ.
Stibbe Pierre, 1, square Vermenouze, Paris-5ᵉ.

Suppléants: *Destouches*, 19, rue St-Georges, Paris.
Germinal, Périgueux (Dordogne), 4, rue St-Roch,
Paris.
Lévêque Marcel, 82, bd. de Picpus, Paris-12ᵉ.
Poupon Georges, 50, bd. Lamoureux, Vitry-sur-Seine.

Si ces hommes commettent une injustice, vous saurez qui l'a commise

22. 'The jurors are responsible'. A threatening tract giving the names and
addresses of the jurors so that 'If they commit an injustice, you
will know who is to blame.'

And like Pétain I remain here imagining that my presence will save something. I am allowing my name to cover what is happening. And I risk being sullied.

In his journal he weighed up the arguments yet again:

1. Pétain was ultimately responsible for all that happened 'under his regime'. Not to convict him would make a mockery of the previous sentences against Esteva and Dentz.
2. 'No double game can excuse the comment "I am beaten; we must repeat every day that we are beaten."'
3. How could he be forgiven for saying 'I go hand in hand with Pierre Laval' – the man who had 'wished' the victory of Germany – or for telling Colonel Labonne, who was fighting alongside the Germans, that he represented 'the honour of the French army'.
4. 'I accuse him of having breached French unity during the occupation and having . . . broken it again, out of vanity, by coming back for a trial that, whatever the verdict, will be a further element of discord among the French people.'

Just before the last day, he scribbled down some final thoughts:

Pétain did not intend to betray. He committed such errors and showed such weaknesses, that they are equivalent to treason.

But [with this juror there was always a 'but'] one must place oneself in the position of the ordinary Frenchman: Pétain rescued prisoners; it was Laval who ran things; Pétain rendered some services.[11]

Would the defence speeches bring clarity?

BETWEEN SOMNOLENCE AND PROVOCATION

Monday 13 August.

The first of Payen's three speeches covered the period before the armistice. This posed the least difficulties to the defence because the case against Pétain was flimsy. Payen opened his appeal by reminding the court of the portentous responsibility of sentencing to death a man of ninety years old, 'one of the most glorious of the sons of France'. He was not far into his speech when Pétain shouted, 'Leave me in peace' (*Foutez-moi la paix!*). People wondered momentarily if this was directed at his own lawyer. It turned out to be aimed at a photographer crouched at his feet. Newsreels show him angrily waving his gloves to shoo the intrusive photographer away. Mongibeaux asked the photographer to show more respect; Payen resumed.

He reminded the court that Mornet had not entirely dropped the claim of a plot: 'Today no one is speaking about a plot but it is replaced by ... what is the word that was used? – a preparation, a solitary preparation.' He rightly pointed out that this section of the indictment was couched almost entirely in the conditional tense: 'it would seem that ...'

Next he moved on to the armistice. He argued that it was justified by the terrible circumstances of the times and the impossibility of continuing the fight from North Africa. Not only had the armistice been inevitable, it helped France by sparing her the fate of Poland and the horrors of being governed by a Gauleiter. It had also helped the Allies by keeping North Africa out of German hands. Here, Payen cited no less an authority than de Gaulle, who in a speech in May 1945 had celebrated the 'importance of North Africa as a base of departure for the Liberation of Europe'.

Most telling was Payen's repeated reminder that if the armistice was a crime, it was a crime in which almost everyone was complicit. He quoted effectively from former President Lebrun:

> To weigh exactly the responsibility of an accused man, a judge must try to place himself in the atmosphere of the moment when his alleged crime was committed ... I am amazed at the ease with which certain people, comfortably installed in their chairs, four years after the facts, and when events have taken a different turn, cast blame or heap praise ... without taking account of the circumstances that caused the acts and remarks that are criticized.[12]

Finally, Payen ended with a long reminder of the mood of the population in June 1940:

> I cannot understand how M. Louis Marin could say here that the French soldiers did not want an armistice, that they wanted to go on

fighting . . . I am not sure what you think. You doubtless have your own views, but for me, speaking of what I saw and heard, the armistice was greeted with an immense sense of relief which was perhaps not heroic . . . It was welcomed because it ended the battle.[13]

In short: if Pétain was guilty so were the French – so was France.

Payen's first *plaidoirie* had been solidly constructed – but it was, Lecompte-Boinet noted, 'deadly boring' and delivered in a semi-inaudible monotone. *France-Soir* wrote: 'Under the weight of the heat and the droning of M. Payen . . . it was hard for anyone to stay awake. Those who managed to keep awake out of professional duty picked up the odd phrase here and there . . . buried in his monotonous monotone.'[14]

The problem for the defence, as one commentator wrote that morning, was that since the jurors were alternately 'implacable and somnolent', either one avoided provoking their implacability at the risk of encouraging their somnolence or one shook them out of somnolence at the risk of exciting their implacability.[15] Payen had opted for the first; Lemaire tried the second.

Where Payen had been underpowered and inaudible, Lemaire delivered his speech with bombastic declamatory rhetoric, hand-waving, grimaces and sneers – all the tricks, commented one newspaper, of a bad hammy actor (*gestes de mauvais cabotin*).[16] The speech opened not with a defence of Pétain but an attack on Mornet, who rose reliably to the bait. An angry shouting match with Lemaire was eventually closed down by Mongibeaux. Once Lemaire actually turned to the Pétain case, he focused on refuting that part of the indictment which had supposedly been abandoned by the prosecution: the long-laid plot to seize power. At another point, to counter the accusation that Pétain had appointed a number of individuals with extreme right-wing reputations in his first government, Lemaire scored a cheap point by reminding the court that many of the people Reynaud had appointed to his government in 1940 ended up supporting the armistice and were currently awaiting trial. Was Reynaud guilty of their crimes? Was political misjudgement a crime?

All of this gave Lemaire's speech an air of aggressive irrelevance. Both Isorni and Payen, for once united, were unhappy about his approach. Payen grabbed Lemaire's gown at one point to calm him down. Only Pétain was happy. During Lemaire's speech he was seen to smile and even laugh. Back in his room he told his wife that Lemaire had been 'Splendid! He really showed Mornet a thing or two.'[17] Yet no one else believed this had been a good day for the defence.

FINAL *PLAIDOIRIES*

The second part of Payen's *plaidoirie*, delivered on Tuesday 13 August, was constructed around three themes:

1. Pétain was not Laval

   'Laval's policy was entirely based around a catastrophic misjudgement: a definitive victory of Germany ... This does not concern the trial of the Marshal in any way – Laval's policy of abandonment ... of long-term union with Germany, was never that of Marshal Pétain.'[18]

2. Pétain as Metternich (a variant on Pétain the 'old fox')

   Pétain had manoeuvred as best he could. His policy was not, however, a 'double jeu', which meant playing two different cards. Pétain had only one card – the Allied one – but he could not always show it. Payen invoked the examples of General Scharnhorst in Prussia in 1806 after Napoleon's victory at Jena, and of Metternich in 1809 after Napoleon's victory at Wagram. In each case, these statesmen, later heroes in their own countries, had hidden their real intentions. Payen quoted Metternich as saying: 'Our principles are unshakeable but one cannot fight against necessity. We need to preserve our forces for better times ... Our system will be to manoeuvre to avoid any commitments and to flatter.'[19]

3. Pétain's age

   Since Pétain's concessions seemed to go beyond what might be strictly required by foxy 'Metternichianism', Payen reminded the court of Pétain's age. He quoted a Vichy insider saying that Pétain was only fully operational for three hours of the day: 'when he is tired, above all in the evening, one can make him sign anything'.[20]

Once again, Payen's speech was effectively constructed; once again, it was delivered in a semi-inaudible monotone. But when he broached the subject of his client's age, Pétain started waving his gloves in denial. 'This is going to be horrible,' Lemaire whispered to Isorni. When Payen returned to this theme later, he could no longer ignore the signs of Pétain's distress: 'I have made an allusion to the Marshal's age. The subject is extremely disagreeable to him. I fear an interruption but I must anyway say what I think.' When he had finished, Pétain remarked furiously to Isorni: 'He pleaded senility.'[21]

Now it was Isorni's turn to speak. He knew that the next hour would be the most important of his life. Expectations were high. By common consent he had been the revelation of the trial. On the previous day Madeleine Jacob of all people had offered him a 'medical stimulant' to keep up his strength. Whatever her views, Jacob was a connoisseur of courtroom performers and she wanted to see what Isorni could pull off. One advantage of the 'sandwich' format was that Isorni could easily shine after the soporific Payen. As he rose to his feet Isorni's nervousness was so visible that Jacob offered him a glass of water: 'I accepted it willingly: I was not poisoned.' One journalist described him as 'absolutely pale, with a pallor that seemed to inhabit his entire being'.[22]

Unlike Payen, Isorni did not read from a prepared text but extemporized from a few notes. In the division of labour between the three lawyers, he had willingly assumed the task of defending the seemingly most indefensible aspects of Vichy policy: the atrocities of the Milice, the STO, the LVF and the persecution of the Jews. From the beginning Isorni had wanted not to apologize for Vichy but to defend it with conviction; not to explain away Pétain's actions but to explain the principles underpinning them.

Isorni's argument was not that Pétain had played a 'double game' (he never mentioned the alleged contacts with the British), nor that he had believed in Franco-German reconciliation (he never uttered the word 'collaboration'), nor that Laval should be blamed (Laval was never mentioned):

> The policy of the Marshal was the following: to safeguard, defend, acquire material advantages but often at the cost of moral concessions. The Resistance had a contrary conception; it did not look to avoid immediate sacrifices. It saw moral advantages in continuing the fight.

Perhaps, *Messieurs*, in the opposition between these two theses you will see one explanation of the French drama to which I will return later on.

But the life of a State is not like the life of an individual. If it is grave for an individual to acquire material advantages at the price of moral concessions, it is not the same in the life of a state. The moral concessions that affected the honour of the leader were borne by the leader alone. But who were the material advantages for? They were for the French people.[23]

This version of the 'shield' and the 'sword' argument allowed Isorni to pay repeated homage to the Resistance, and to remind the court of the many occasions on which he had defended resisters in the Vichy courts. As for Pétain's sacrifice of his personal honour for the material interests of the French, Isorni neatly pointed out that this was exactly the choice of those magistrates who had sworn the oath to Pétain. He quoted Mornet's own reply to Blum's claim that no self-respecting magistrate would have agreed to sit in judgement at Riom:

> What would have occurred if French judges had refused to swear the oath? And it is M. le Procureur who provided the answer in his *réquisitoire*: 'the magistrature, to which I render homage, saved many French lives'. If the magistrates had resigned, others with fewer scruples would have taken their place and the French would have suffered more; the argument could be applied to all servants of the regime; to Pétain himself.[24]

Having established his argument, Isorni set about applying it to each of the policies for which the Vichy regime was criticized:

1. The STO: 640,000 workers were forced to go to work in Germany, but thanks to Vichy's efforts this figure was much lower than the Germans had wanted.
2. The LVF: it was never an official Vichy organization; it was much smaller than its Belgian equivalent, the Légion Wallone.
3. The persecution of the Jews: Pétain had resisted the imposition of the yellow star in the Southern Zone; he had refused the German demand for total denaturalization of the Jews who had acquired

nationality since 1927; the Free Zone had provided some refuge for the Jews; a much higher proportion of Jews had survived in France than Poland. 'In short, it is iniquitous to hold Marshal Pétain responsible for atrocities committed by the Germans ... It was only the action of the Marshal's government which protected them, perhaps imperfectly, but it did protect them.'

The argument on the Jews glided over many inconvenient facts, but since Isorni knew that the issue was not central to the court – indeed it had hardly figured in Mornet's *réquisitoire* – and since knowledge of it was imperfect, he was able to get away with his approximations.

When Isorni came to an issue that had greater emotional resonance for most jurors than the persecution of the Jews – the Milice's violent repression of resisters – even he fell back on the argument that the truth had been hidden from Pétain:

In the Fort of Montrouge I often talked to the Marshal about the Resistance. Yes, of course he knew about it but if you only knew how he was deceived about the reality of your action ... Really, can you believe that Marshal Pétain knew about the police brutalities?[25]

Ultimately the force of Isorni's *plaidoirie* derived less from the substance of his arguments than from his emotional conviction and complete identification with the man he was defending – a contrast with the low-key approach of Payen or the histrionics of Lemaire. *Combat* commented: 'Young, ardent, sincere, without stridency, using simple words, but possessed by a kind of compressed emotion, he was not playing a part, he was living it.' The most famous photograph of the trial shows Isorni standing behind Pétain, his hands stretched out in pleading and supplication. Madeleine Jacob had not been disappointed: 'Tall, thin, distinguished. The face of an archangel ... When later on people speak of the Pétain trial, it is the name of *maître* Isorni which history will retain from this affair.'[26]

Isorni was playing on his intuition that, despite everything, Pétain still maintained an emotional hold on the French; that the faith that had led the entire political class to shelter under his myth in 1940 had left deep traces; that if he was guilty, so was all of France – that many people would want to be persuaded that the story Mornet had told

23. Jacques Isorni pleading Pétain's case.

was not the only truth. The pathos of Isorni's *plaidoirie* reached its climax in his peroration:

> The dead have been called to bear witness. We have heard the testimony of those who were persecuted. We have been reminded of the experience of the prisoners. Now it is time for me to call to the witness stand the living. Those who were freed; those who were protected. You have heard the voices of men who were forced to go to Germany; let us also listen to the women who remained . . .
>
> But, Messieurs, if despite all that I have said, if despite the truth I believe I have expressed, you feel you must follow the Prosecutor in his merciless *réquisitoire*, if it is death that you pronounce against Marshal Pétain, then, Messieurs, that is where we will lead him. But let me tell you, wherever you find yourself at that moment, even if you are at the other end of the world, you will all be present. You will be present, *messieurs les magistrats*, bedecked in your red robes, your ermine and your oaths . . . And you will see, in the depth of your anguished souls, the death of this Marshal of France whom you have condemned. Memories of his pale face will haunt you . . . Nor must you hide behind the

clemency of another man [a nod to the idea that de Gaulle might pardon him] . . . In this moment, all our memories rise up in us, as they rise up in you, and we discern in them the image of our eternal *patrie*.

When have we ever opposed Saint Geneviève, protector of the city of Paris, against Saint Jeanne [Joan of Arc] who liberated our land? . . . Magistrates of the High Court, listen to me, hear my appeal. You are only judges; you are only judging a man. But in your hands you hold the destiny of France.[27]

PAYEN BREAKS THE SPELL

When Isorni had finished, Francine Bonitzer wrote: 'Many eyes were moist and perhaps people were ready to succumb to this desire for reconciliation that he had so eloquently proposed.'[28] The emotion seemingly affected even Mornet. Immediately after an exhausted Isorni had collapsed onto his seat, Mornet rushed up to congratulate him. According to Isorni he said: 'you have perfectly expressed everything I think'. Even more remarkably, in the short break after Isorni had finished, Mongibeaux privately asked the journalist Géo London to persuade Payen to abandon his last *plaidoirie*, arguing that it would best serve Pétain's interest if the jury was sent away to deliberate while still under the impact of Isorni's performance. But there was no chance Payen would leave the last word to this irritating young upstart. The only person in the courtroom seemingly unmoved by Isorni's performance, he shuffled his papers and looked ostentatiously at the clock.

It was now 18.15 and the court had been in session for five hours. Undeterred, Payen resumed his *plaidoirie* exactly where he had left off, almost as if Isorni had not spoken: 'Messieurs, when I handed over to my friend Isorni earlier, I had reached – perhaps you will remember – the incidents that took place between France and England over Syria . . .' As Bonitzer remarked: 'the magic was broken'.

Payen took the court methodically over familiar ground:

- He reminded his listeners of the many times the Marshal had protested against German violations of the armistice: 'protests which, of course, were made in vain but which from the juridical point of view were indispensable'. (A somewhat double-edged defence: what was the point of an armistice so easily ignored?)

– He gave examples of the many ways in which Vichy had protected French material interests – for example, only 30,000 machine tools lost out of 540,000. (After the poetic pathos of Isorni, machine-tool statistics were not liable to seize the imagination of listeners.)

– He blamed Laval: Pétain had taken him back in 1942 in the mistaken hope that 'he might as he promised put a brake on German demands. But of course M. Laval put no brake on it at all.' (In that case, why not sack him again?)

– As for the decision to stay in France after November 1942, even if Pétain's misjudgement was to have believed that he might still be able to protect the French, this decision was no crime: 'Moreover it is not by any means clear to me that he was wrong to remain.' (hardly a ringing endorsement).[29]

Whatever the arguments, the problem with Payen's performance – again – was the delivery. A journalist for *L'Humanité* reported:

> Heads were drooping, spectators nodding off, others taking out their newspapers, journalists tip-toing out, but with the nitpicking obstinacy of a country lawyer pleading the case of a partition wall, pursuing a rambling exposé that no one more than 20 metres away could hear given how weak his voice is, Payen speaks, he speaks, he speaks. 18.30, 19.20. The sun is falling, the light is fading; still Payen goes on speaking.[30]

Towards the end he rummaged in his papers to read out Ribbentrop's threatening letter of November 1943, written when Pétain had made his last fateful attempt to distance himself from Germany. The intention was to show that the Germans had considered Pétain an obstacle to collaboration. By this point even Pétain himself seemed to have had enough. He muttered under his breath, but audibly, 'We know it already.' This did not stop Payen. Once he had read the letter, Mongibeaux interrupted: 'It would be interesting to know the response.'

Pétain now uttered almost his final words of the trial: 'There was no response but the consequence was the captivity that was imposed on me.' Pétain was wrong – as Payen had to admit:

PAYEN: Perhaps there was a response.

MONGIBEAUX: It does seem that there was a response.

PAYEN: I am sure I have it . . . It is in my dossier, it will very soon be shown to you.[31]

He never showed it, but extracts had been read out by Mornet two days earlier – and they hardly supported Pétain's case. This was the craven letter with which Pétain had been confronted in the last of his pre-trial interrogations and it certainly did the defence no good for the court to be reminded of it yet again.

Finally, Payen, like Isorni, ended with a long plea for national reconciliation, offering a comparison with the trial of Louis XVI. As he finished there was some applause, and a few scattered shouts of 'Vive la France!' Mongibeaux asked the final ritual question: 'Accused, do you have anything to add for your defence?'

In the fading evening light, 'the accused' rose to his feet and read out a short statement, without glasses, that had been prepared in advance with Isorni:

In the course of this trial, I have voluntarily kept silent after having explained my reasons to the people of France.

My thought, my only thought, was to remain with them on the land of France, as I had promised, to attenuate their suffering.

Whatever happens, the people will not forget this. They know that I defended them as I defended Verdun.

Messieurs les juges, my life and my liberty are in your hands, but it is to the *patrie* that I entrust my honour.[32]

It was 21.05. The court rose. The jurors filed out to begin their deliberations.

19
The Verdict

24. The resistance jurors above, the parliamentary ones below.
France-Soir 14 August 1945.

When Payen took his seat just after nine in the evening, the journalists hurried out of the stifling courtroom eager to eat and to file their stories. The twenty-four jurors assembled in a room just behind the courtroom. They were joined by the three judges, who were there to guide their discussions but also had a vote. First everyone had to eat; the jurors had been in court continuously for eight hours. The food had apparently been specially prepared by the Préfecture de Police to prevent any last-minute attempt to poison the jurors. Lecompte-Boinet wrote:

> A meal was served in the *cabinet du président*; a piece of hake to soothe the pain of our angry stomachs. No one spoke about the trial as we ate standing up; some people told jokes ... During the meal, I said to

Pierre-Bloch: 'How can an honest man like you be favourable to unity between the Socialist and the Communist parties. Can you not see that the Communists ... are just contemptible robots in the service of a Tsar?'[1]

Once they had eaten, they gathered around a table, resisters on one side and parliamentarians on the other, Lecompte-Boinet on the same side as the Communist 'robots'.[2] Mongibeaux, looking less impressive now that he had discarded his robes, like a conjuror plucking a rabbit out of a hat, proposed finding Pétain guilty under article 80 of the Penal Code (*attentat à la sécurité extérieure de l'État*), not previously mentioned during the trial. Carrying a maximum sentence of five years, this would have made it possible for the jury to find Pétain not guilty of the more serious crime of treason. It was almost an acquittal. Since Mongibeaux had regularly been accused of being partial to the prosecution in his conduct of the trial, this opening gambit caused amazement among the jurors. Perhaps his posture in court was intended to undercut criticism of judges like himself who had sworn the oath to Pétain. Perhaps his true feelings were revealed by his attempt to persuade Payen to abandon his final *plaidoirie* so that the jurors could deliberate with Isorni's words fresh in their minds. Mongibeaux was backed up by his two co-judges, who deployed their legal expertise to convince the jurors that there was insufficient evidence to convict Pétain of treason (under article 75) or of a plot against the Republic (under article 87).

Now it was the turn of Gabriel Delattre, the spokesman for the parliamentary jurors, to address the room. Although he had not intervened during the trial, Delattre was a respected lawyer. Just before Isorni's *plaidoirie* he had told him: 'Nothing is lost. Everything rests on you.'[3] Now he spoke for forty-five minutes arguing against the death penalty, partly because it would besmirch the reputation of France abroad. His intervention was probably intimidating to those jurors who had no legal training. After he had finished, some of these tried to intervene to support the death penalty without being sure of how to justify this in law. Lecompte-Boinet writes sardonically: 'they had decided on "death" and were ready afterwards to find the juridical justifications'.

Jean Pierre-Bloch, one of the most forceful of the resistance jurors, concerned by the drift of the discussion, asked for clarification from the judges about the differences between article 75 and article 80. Broadly speaking, the answer was that for Pétain to be found guilty under article 75 there had to have been an intention to commit treason; for article 80, the treason resulted from action carried out without treasonable intent. The former carried the death penalty; the latter carried the sentence of hard labour but not for anyone aged over seventy. Pierre-Bloch proposed a preliminary vote by ballot between these two clauses. Mongibeaux agreed, providing that the vote be only indicative. By a majority of eighteen to eight (Mongibeaux was not voting at this stage) the jurors voted for article 75 – death.[4]

While the jurors deliberated, a strange atmosphere descended on the Palais de Justice. The mood was recalled by Isorni:

> There was a sudden relaxation of tension, almost an atmosphere of celebration (*kermesse*) ... The Palais's buffet, on the gloomy ground floor, was invaded by a hungry and thirsty crowd. Up to fifteen people crowded at tables normally seating only four. As the wine flowed, the hubbub grew louder. People called out to each other across the room. Military uniforms mixed with the robes of lawyers, and others in civilian dress. In the throng and the disorder, people were eating their dessert before their sausages. There were thick clouds of cigarette smoke as in a noisy and festive celebration. This was not irreverence but an inevitable moment of release that nothing could have held back.[5]

After their initial vote, the debate among the jurors resumed. Again Delattre spoke against the death penalty. This time he invoked the shock that would be caused by executing an eighty-nine-year-old Marshal of France: 'Who knows whether in a few years Pétain may not be regarded as innocent and our sons may suffer for having as fathers the men who killed him.'

The oldest of the jurors, Georges Alphandery-Lévy, declared that having been born in Alsace he was inclined to harshness, as Pétain had done nothing to prevent the annexation of his home region – but as a Jew he was grateful for the protection Pétain had offered the Jews. This was a revealing insight into the way that this issue was understood in 1945, and a sign that, here at least, the arguments of the defence had hit home. Pierre-Bloch, speaking also as a Jew, said he had no inhibitions about voting for the death penalty. He read out Pétain's craven letter of response to Ribbentrop in December 1943, which had not been read out in full during the trial.

This had a great impact. At this point, various other resistance jurors weighed in, arguing for the death penalty. As for qualms about shooting an eighty-nine-year-old man, Pierre-Bloch pointed out that everyone knew the sentence would not be carried out. The issue was to establish the principle that Pétain had committed treason.

Finally, at 1 a.m. another vote was taken. Perhaps because this was now a binding vote, the margin in favour of the death penalty had narrowed to fourteen to thirteen. Four jurors at least had changed their vote. The vote was secret, but it seems that a majority of resisters (perhaps as many as nine) and a minority of deputés (perhaps five) had voted for the death penalty. Since article 75 was carried by a margin of one vote, it was suggested after the verdict that the result might have been different if the defence had rejected the Communist juror Louis Prot at the start. But this would not necessarily have made a difference. Non-Communists also voted for the death penalty, among them Jacques Lecompte-Boinet.

In other rooms of the Palais de Justice, exhausted lawyers and journalists could be found spread out on benches to sleep. Pétain, in his little room next to the courtroom, was stretched out awake on his bed, waiting with his wife for the verdict, like everyone else. Occasionally, a bell rang and people rushed to see if the jury had finished its deliberations. These were false alarms: just a call for more cold drinks and, on one occasion, a typist.

While lights blazed through the night in the now eerily silent Palais de Justice, the sounds of celebrations were exploding in the streets outside. News had arrived that the Japanese had accepted the Allied terms for their unconditional surrender. The war was over. Fights broke out between drunken American soldiers and drunken French civilians. American jeeps raced through the streets of Paris, stars and stripes waving. Just as on the first day of his interrogation, when Pétain had heard the crowds celebrating on VE Day, so three months later the deliberating jurors could hear the crowds outside celebrating the end of the war.

Now that the decision for the death penalty had been taken, a few jurors, including Pierre-Bloch and Lecompte-Boinet, started working with Mongibeaux on drafting the '*attendus*' – the grounds for the judgement. The ever-punctilious Lecompte-Boinet was concerned to ensure that these corresponded to the crime of which Pétain was accused under the Penal Code. At about 2.30 a.m. one resistance juror (possibly Stibbe) proposed that the sentence be accompanied by the decision that Pétain should be formally stripped of his military rank (known as degradation). This time Pierre-Bloch, supported by Lecompte-Boinet, took a more moderate line, pointing out that since the sentence also carried the penalty of *indignité nationale*, Pétain would automatically lose his decorations and property. This more moderate line was supported by a majority of twenty to seven.

Although no one believed the sentence would be carried out on an eighty-nine-year-old man, the last issue to be resolved was whether or not the court would leave it to de Gaulle to exercise mercy. Who should get the credit – or blame – for this? Finally, between seventeen and twenty jurors signed a document recommending that in view of Pétain's age, the sentence should not be carried out.

Outside the courtroom the animation had died down. Joseph Kessel reported:

> The hours drag on, exhausting and unreal. Tiredness, tiredness overwhelms us. The images of the last two days merge in my memory ... I see the Marshal shooing away the photographers with his gloves. I see him suddenly turning around as his lawyers mention his name.
>
> Isorni's fragile and inspired face haunts my memory, and the cast of his features during the magnificent *plaidoirie* that has established his youthful glory at a stroke ... People are asleep in the armchairs, on the benches. The courtroom is lit up by two chandeliers, four lamps with green shades are on, lighting up the judges' bench ... Then, suddenly everyone is awake, quiet, rigid with expectation. It is 4 a.m.
>
> The judges return to their seats.
>
> Never have I experienced such an intensity of silence in this overcrowded room. An interminable silence, a silence which hardens, a silence which becomes like a presence. The presence of History.[6]

During the recess a microphone had been installed so that Mongibeaux could be clearly heard. A guard arrived in Pétain's room to escort him back into court. As the jurors filed back into the courtroom, Isorni, catching sight of a sign that one juror made to a journalist, instantly knew the verdict. For Kessel this certainty came a few minutes later when Mongibeaux started reading: 'Given that [*attendu que*] it results from the debate and the documents that have been produced, that Pétain . . .' The moment Mongibeaux omitted 'Marshal', Kessel knew the verdict. The judgement took seventeen minutes to read out to a hushed court. As Mongibeaux read, his colleague Donat-Guigne sat back as if distancing himself from the sentence that was being delivered.

Reading today the implacable litany of *attendu que* ('given that', 'given that', 'given that'), one might wonder what purpose the trial had served. The jurors in the end confirmed all of the accusations contained in the original indictment – even those tacitly abandoned by Mornet. Although, despite 'heavy presumptions', it was stated that there was insufficient evidence of a 'real plot', the allegation was still suggested by reference to the campaign around Pétain's name before 1940 and by Pétain's letter to Ribbentrop which suggested 'premeditation' and 'a political plan' that 'gambled on capitulation'. The armistice was not singled out as a crime in itself, but it was noted that Pétain's announcement that he was going to ask for an armistice had led to demoralization of the army; and that Pétain had sabotaged any move of the government abroad in the days before the armistice was signed.

The indictment had accused Pétain of having, under German pressure, promulgated 'abominable racial laws' rather than forcing the Germans to assume the opprobrium of legislation 'which went against all French tradition'. The judgement condemned the 'mass deportations of workers', 'the monstrous character of the deportations of the French', and the lack of any public protest against them. It did not specifically mention the Jews among these victims while however condemning the adoption of 'racial legislation modelled on that of Germany'. The Jewish issue remained subsidiary.

'Attendu que, attendu que, attendu que . . .' Kessel wrote: 'everyone knew the verdict towards which each of these paragraphs would lead ... Over twenty minutes we watched the verdict moving with terrible slowness towards the accused like a javelin advancing inch by inch towards its target.'

At first Pétain leaned forward in his chair to listen but soon slouched back into his usual posture, stroking his moustache, compulsively stroking the arms of his chair, occasionally cupping his hand to his ear.

Finally, Mongibeaux reached the end: '... condemns Pétain to the death penalty, *indignité nationale*, the confiscation of his property'. The only surprise lay in the final words: 'Taking account of the great age of the accused, the Haute Cour expresses the wish that the judgement not be carried out.'

There were a few cries of 'Vive la France!'; otherwise total silence. If Pétain had heard or understood, he did not show it. He remained slumped in his chair as if not comprehending what had happened. Only when Mongibeaux ordered 'Guard remove the accused' and a policeman tapped his shoulder did Pétain rise to his feet. Seemingly bemused, he turned one way and then another – perhaps temporarily blinded by the flashlights of the photographers who clustered in front of him. Looking in the direction of his lawyers, who pointed to the door, he walked out of the court.

A NEW DREYFUS AFFAIR

'So I am a Pétainicide,' wrote Lecompte-Boinet in his journal:

> This trial – this bad trial – finished at 4 a.m. on the morning of 15 August. I write bad trial because the sentence was decided in advance, because the jury was composed of partisans and because the court knew it; because the President was a *monsieur* who had no idea how to preside; because the witnesses were pitiful: because the *avocat general* had not prepared his accusation; and because the defence had Payen.

He had found the last moments painful: 'A few jackals had remained to see Pétain. I could not bear to look at him when the President said "Guards lead away the condemned man." I don't think he heard.'

Despite all this, in the end Lecompte-Boinet had no doubts about the verdict:

On re-reading the sentence, I realize how unjuridical we have been since we were saying that all the acts Pétain was reproached with had been committed with the intention of helping the enemy – which I do not believe . . .

But we could not *not* condemn him to death.

What led to my irrevocable decision was that letter to Colonel Labonne: 'you are the repository of part of our military honour . . . etc' . . . A Marshal of France could, in the pursuit of a double game, do many things; he could not do that. Nor could he say: 'I spend my time trying to convince the nation that we have been beaten.'

Exhausted by the trial, and hoping to get it out of his head, Lecompte-Boinet went to see a police thriller at the cinema. The trial caught up with him even there:

My life over the last three years has been such that no thriller could match the reality – even just the Pétain trial of which I caught a few glimpses (including myself) during the newsreels. Strange to see oneself on the cinema screen . . . I thought I was younger and thinner and not that corpulent chap leaning over a desk, head in his shoulders.[7]

Lecompte-Boinet's sense of deflation was widely shared. Public response to the verdict was muted. The prevailing sentiment was one of relief that it was finally over. On 17 August de Gaulle commuted the sentence to life imprisonment as the court had recommended – and as he had always privately intended. The Communist press predictably clamoured for the death sentence to be carried out, but otherwise few people contested the decision to spare Pétain's life.[8] The resister Jean-Louis Vigier wrote: 'The Marshal no longer has the right to divide France. We do not have the right to divide her with his blood.'[9] This was a recognition that France remained polarized and that Pétain retained much support. The trial had not diminished this; possibly the opposite.

The resuscitation of discredited Third Republic politicians had not served the interests of the prosecution. When the trial was over, one newspaper was still carrying long daily extracts from Reynaud's memoirs which had started serialization just as the trial opened. On 17 August the headline was 'Weygand Wanted to Sacrifice the Honour of France to his Army'.[10] But this harping on 1940 was a reminder that few of France's leaders had emerged unsullied by the events of that year. At one moment in court Reynaud had commented that only when reading in prison the memoirs of the former President Poincaré and of Foch and Clemenceau had he understood the true nature of Pétain. This led one journalist to mutter *sotto voce* that perhaps the solution to France's problems was to imprison France's politicians more regularly so that they could catch up on their reading.

The prosecution had never succeeded in offering a clear message. It had abandoned the idea of a plot while leaving hanging in the air an insinuation that there might have been one. As for the armistice, no witness had been ready to proclaim that it was an act of treason as de Gaulle believed. Although Mornet's *réquisitoire* had been effective, the journalist Francine Bonitzer took issue with a passage where, contesting the idea of Vichy as a 'shield', he had alleged that the Belgians, who had been directly administered by the Germans, had suffered less than the French. She pointed out that, in terms of the numbers deported, the fate of the Belgians had probably been worse. But this was irrelevant since it missed the central point by accepting the Pétainist premise of 'the lesser evil', sidelining the issue of honour: 'It needed to be demonstrated that whatever the consequences anything would have been better for France than this criminal enslavement.' France's duty had been to fight on whatever the risks, whatever the sacrifices.[11]

The defence case had been as muddled as the prosecution's. There was a tension between Payen, who argued for a *double jeu* and tried to distinguish Pétain from Laval, and Isorni, who defiantly accepted Vichy in its entirety and did not seek to explain it away. The Payen strategy was seemingly more consensual but it raised problems. Just before the trial Payen had received a letter from an ardent Pétainist. Given the atmosphere of the Liberation, the writer of this letter did not sign his name but he presented himself as a former Verdun veteran, with a son who had been taken prisoner in 1940 and who had spent the entire occupation in captivity. His long and eloquent letter to Payen was not a rant, more a cry of pain from a rank-and-file Pétainist who had *believed*, and still wanted to believe, but was disturbed by hearing that the defence might argue for a Pétainist *double jeu*:

Doubt has entered our minds and hearts and I ask myself with sadness and anguish, if I was right to serve him ... I regret nothing and whatever happens it will be the pride of my life and that of my son ... both Frenchmen who now keep piously hidden at the back of a wardrobe the portrait of the Marshal which was previously displayed in the most beautiful room in the house. Will we now have to throw it on the fire because the system of defence of the man that we passionately respected and loved is going to show that they were wrong and that he deceived us? ... How can we judge today our leader of yesterday if, at the most dramatic moment of his life, he renounces not only his words, but the solemn engagements that he repeated many times to men from whom he demanded discipline and confidence?[12]

The letter went on in this vein for six pages. For this ordinary Pétainist, it was no defence to blame Laval or to argue that Pétain had masked his secret beliefs. Pétain should be defended because month after month, year after year, his sacrifice had protected the French from a fate that would have been worse had he abandoned his people.

We do not know what the writer of this letter thought of the trial once it had started. Clearly his faith would have been more strengthened by Isorni's defence than Payen's. But the revelations during the trial about a possible *double jeu* and about the secret telegrams offered new evidence for those who wanted other reasons to continue to believe in Pétain. No one refuted Isorni's argument that Vichy had saved Jews. Only one solitary voice in the Jewish press was raised after the trial to contest this claim.[13]

And what about that procession of *fonctionnaires* who had paraded their good intentions, their patriotism, their opposition to Germany, their 'resistance', as they framed it, to Germany? The word 'treason' did not quite fit their case, even if their arguments stretched credulity. Even Xavier Vallat from his prison cell expressed a quizzical scepticism when *fonctionnaires* like Berthelot tried to convince the court that Vichy was the centre of resistance to the Germans.[14] They had presented their choices in terms of patriotism and apolitical service of the state. But there was another way of telling their story. While they had perhaps not welcomed defeat, nor harboured any sympathy for Germany, they had clearly seen political opportunities in the Vichy regime. Their 'patriotism' was not politically neutral. This led a writer in the literary journal *Lettres Françaises* to compare the Pétain trial to that of Dreyfus:

> Each is the negative and positive of the same photographic image. On one side Dreyfus is accused because the innocent man *must* be a traitor. On the other, Pétain is defended because the traitor *must* be innocent . . . This is not, in truth, an epilogue to the Dreyfus affair, but a new outbreak of that organic disease that still eats away at France. An old abscess is dormant but not dead. The Pétain trial instead of puncturing it has revealed its virulence . . . One must fear that for the Pétainists the trial remains open as it does for the anti-Dreyfusards.[15]

That fear was justified. A few months before the Pétain trial, one of the most prominent anti-Dreyfusards, Charles Maurras, had been sentenced to life in prison for his role in the Occupation. On hearing the verdict Maurras shouted out in court that it was the 'revenge of Dreyfus'. It was an article he had written in 1898 at the time of the Dreyfus Affair that had made Maurras famous. He had defended the French army officer Colonel Henry, who had committed suicide when it was revealed he had forged documents to incriminate Dreyfus. Maurras argued that the forgery was 'patriotic' since the guilt or innocence of one individual could not be compared to the importance of protecting the reputation of the army, the state and the nation. Order mattered more than justice or individual conscience. Maurras's newspaper, *L'Action Française*, was banned at the Liberation but reappeared immediately after as a semi-clandestine publication called *Documents Nationaux*. Its reading of the Pétain trial replicated Maurras's take on the Dreyfus case: the defence of honour had been erected above that of the 'good of the state', a subjective appeal to virtue and false heroism had prevailed over the objective interests of the nation, conscience over order.[16]

These interventions vindicated François Mauriac's comment after Pétain's sentence, 'a trial like this one is never over and will never end'. But in the immediate aftermath of the verdict, people had other things on their minds. Within a few days, Pétain's name had disappeared from the newspapers. For the moment, at least, France wanted to move on. The summer holidays officially began on 15 August, the

Feast of the Assumption, when Paris empties out even now, and the High Court, which had many more cases to judge, went into recess. Those who still had a taste for treason trials could follow that of the Norwegian collaborator Vidkun Quisling which was opening in Oslo. They could also read the stenographic publication of the Pétain trial, which was about to appear in twenty instalments, each costing 20 francs. Those who wanted to forget trials altogether could go out into the streets and celebrate instead the final ending of the war. On 16 August, the day after Pétain's conviction, the Eiffel Tower was illuminated to mark the victory over Japan.

Over the next few days, Paris was given over to an orgy of celebrations to mark the anniversary of the street fighting that had preceded the city's liberation the previous year when Pétain was in exile. The festivities culminated in a ceremony to commemorate the liberation of the Hotel de Ville on 20 August 1944. It was comforting to relive those heroic days when life had seemed less complicated and the future had seemed clearer. The young writer Roger Stéphane, one of a group of resisters who had taken possession of the building, commented sardonically in his diary that more people were present for the celebration than had participated in the event itself.[17] Those who had missed it were now catching up. And for those who had not yet seen it, *Les Enfants du Paradis* was still playing in Paris cinemas.

PART THREE

Afterlives

20

The Prisoner

A few hours after the sentence was read out in the early hours of 15 August, a decoy convoy of police cars, sirens blaring, set off from the Quai d'Orfèvres towards Montrouge prison. With the press off the scent, Pétain, accompanied by Joseph Simon and a doctor, was taken to the airbase of Villacoublay outside Paris where de Gaulle's personal airplane was waiting to fly him to Pau in south-western France. From Pau he was driven to the prison fortress of Portalet in the Pyrenees. A government official accompanying the flight to Pau reported that Pétain was in a strangely euphoric mood, 'very loquacious' – after three weeks of silence. Passing around the 'message' he had read out at the end of the trial, with corrections in his own hand, he was full of bile against the 'abominable Mornet' and against Payen for claiming he was old and doddery (*gateux*). He was convinced that de Gaulle had saved him from death: 'He had now understood his big mistake in not agreeing, when I proposed it, to work with me at the Liberation.' At one moment when the doctor nodded off, Pétain hit him over the head with his stick; at another he agreed to have his picture taken but before the button was pressed he thumbed his nose at the photographer. When the plane hit bad turbulence he remained calm and was amused that the other passengers seemed so easily alarmed.[1]

The choice of Portalet had a symbolic significance. It was where Vichy had imprisoned Reynaud and Mandel. Pétain was put in the cell formerly occupied by Mandel. This was to defuse Communist allegations that, once de Gaulle had commuted the death sentence, Pétain was being treated with indulgence. A cartoon in *L'Humanité* showed him sunning himself by the sea.

Even in late summer, Portalet was cold, damp and insalubrious.

25. 'The charms of imprisonment'. Cartoon in the Communist *L'Humanité* protesting that Pétain was being treated too gently.

Pétain was permitted a daily walk but this required him to ascend a long and steep staircase. Pétain's good mood did not last. On the first day he refused to eat anything. He complained: 'Now I understand why Reynaud and Blum blame me for having put them in such a sinister place.' This comment was reported by Joseph Simon, who remained Pétain's jailor for the next four years. The fifty-year-old Simon had been in the Resistance and guarding Pétain was not a role he relished. But he came to feel a grudging affection for his prisoner mixed with frequent bouts of irritation.[2] Simon incessantly lobbied his superiors to be transferred to another post, feeling that he had become in some sense Pétain's prisoner. Until he was finally transferred in May 1949, his diary provides the fullest account of Pétain's declining years.

Pétain staved off depression in the expectation that he would soon be transferred to a more agreeable location. He had hopes of the prison on the Île Sainte Marguerite off the south coast of France. His only concern was its association with Marshal Bazaine, who had been incarcerated there in 1873 though he had escaped with the aid of his wife. On another occasion, Pétain thought he might be taken to a prison near Marenne on the west coast. His wife told Simon: 'If he can get oysters, he would happily be shut up anywhere'.[3]

After an uncomfortable few months, Pétain was transferred from Portalet on 14 November. His new destination was not Sainte Marguerite but the Île d'Yeu some 20 kilometres off the west coast of Brittany. The tiny island was relatively inaccessible: it was connected to the mainland by only two ferries on a good day, but in stormy seas no ferries could operate. It was mainly inhabited by fishermen, with the occasional summer tourists. The island had had a previous brush with the conservative history of France when, in 1795, the Comte d'Artois, future King Charles X and brother of Louis XVI, had landed there with a British fleet hoping to join an anti-Revolutionary uprising in the Vendée on the French mainland. Artois arrived too late since the Vendée rising had been crushed a few weeks earlier. He left after two months, finding the climate inhospitable and the inhabitants unfriendly. No further notable events had taken place on the island. (It had, however, been an inspiration for Hergé's Tintin story, *The Black Island*.) The citadel of Pierre Levée, where Pétain was incarcerated, had been constructed in the 1850s, serving successively as a barracks and a prison. Its most recent inmates had been Communists interned there during the phoney war.

Isorni would later compare Pétain's fate on the Île d'Yeu to that of Dreyfus on Devil's Island in French Guyana, but the conditions were incomparably better. Pétain had two rooms, frugally furnished, and he could take walks around the courtyard of the fortress. The only similarity with Devil's Island was the government's hope that Pétain would be forgotten until he died. A *curé* was appointed to minister to his spiritual needs, and a local doctor to watch over his physical health. The *curé* had been like so many clergy a Vichy supporter; the doctor, Imbert, had been deported for resistance activities. He was homosexual and prone to drink but none of this stopped him getting on well with Pétain. Although Pétain's wife was not permitted to share his prison, she was allowed to visit. Otherwise she lived in their old apartment in Paris. During her stays, she took up residence in the only hotel on the island, the Hotel des Voyageurs, an establishment run by a couple, the Nolleaus, who had been pro-German during the war. Local resisters were aggrieved that Nolleau, arrested at the time of the Liberation, had not been punished. Doctor Imbert suspected it was Nolleau who had denounced him to the authorities and after Liberation he had incited a group of sailors to take the law into their own hands and ransack the hotel. The isolated little island was a perfect microcosm of the conflicts that had divided France during the Occupation.

The image of the devoted Maréchale trudging up the hill every day to visit her husband, shopping basket in arm, later became part of the Pétainist myth of exiled martyrdom. Her presence caused friction with Simon. Quite apart from her sense of rank, the Maréchale endlessly complained about the conditions of imprisonment. Simon resented her interference, and his diary is peppered with comments like 'What a bitch', 'the old witch', 'how I would like to kick her in the backside' and 'everyone hates her'.[4] If Simon is to be believed, Pétain himself looked forward rather desperately to his wife's visits but was often irritated with her when she was present.

Pétain's physical health remained amazingly good and for the first eighteen months he was mentally alert despite moments of confusion. He spent an hour each morning making his bed with military precision; he read Le Monde; started to learn English; and did some exercises. One publisher sent him three books from its recent catalogue, including one on Karl Marx (was this a joke?), and Simon wondered if he was authorized to pass these on. Simon's reports of Pétain's conversation suggest he had lost none of his acerbic cynicism. On one occasion, during a discussion about the Académie Française from which he had been expelled, his wife remarked that she had no time for that 'band of old dodderers'. Pétain replied, 'I am happy that it is a band of old dodderers. And since I am longer there, that makes one dodderer less.' Hearing that Daladier had been pelted with tomatoes in his election campaign, Pétain commented: 'I hope they were unripe. A pity he was not knocked out.' Yet he was curiously benign about Léon Blum – leading Isorni to worry that he was after all showing signs of senility.[5] One obsessive subject of conversation was de Gaulle. Pétain was convinced de Gaulle was working to have him released. His memories of de Gaulle became increasingly befuddled, and he wrongly remembered that de Gaulle had once been his pupil at the École de Guerre.[6]

The only intruder in this tense *huis clos* between Simon, his prisoner and the prisoner's wife was Isorni, who was authorized by the government to visit occasionally, sometimes with Lemaire, sometimes alone. Payen had died in January 1946, but Isorni had a final posthumous spat with him over the publication of Payen's three defence speeches with a preface distancing himself from his compromising defendant. Isorni and Lemaire took legal action to have the preface removed.

Isorni's visits to the Île d'Yeu were a test of devotion, as he suffered terrible seasickness on the crossing. He would stay at the Hotel des Voyageurs, which was becoming the centre of a little Pétainist cult. Isorni's account of his prison visits formed the last part of his book on the Pétain trial, published soon after Pétain's death. It contributed the final touches to his portrait of the Marshal as a Christ-like figure sacrificing himself for France. On his first visit, on Pétain's birthday, Isorni recounts Pétain's reaction when he presented him with a small gift of a pack of butter, saying 'a peasant whom we met on the journey handed it to us to give to you'. Pétain received the gift with tears in his eyes 'at the thought that this man who worked the soil to which he feels so attached with all his soul has been thinking about him'. He insisted that the present be shared with his guards. A conversation reported by Simon offers a different image. After Pétain complained about his menu, a guard told him that this was what Parisians had been eating for four years, to which Pétain replied: 'I couldn't care less. I need to eat.'[7]

THE HIGH COURT GOES ON

While Pétain languished in prison, the High Court, after a summer break, resumed its work. The same team of Mongibeaux, Mornet and Bouchardon remained in place; the same courtroom was used. The first case, on 3 October 1945, was that of Joseph Darnand, former head of the Milice. His trial lasted just an afternoon; he was sentenced to death and executed by firing squad a week later. Of the four trials that had so far taken place (Esteva, Dentz, Pétain, Darnand), this was the first one in which the death penalty was actually carried out.

The trial of Pierre Laval opened three days later. Even Laval's bitterest enemies agreed that his trial was a travesty. When he was actually allowed to answer questions, he ran rings around his accusers, but Mongibeaux mostly prevented him from speaking. The jurors, violently and openly partisan, interrupted the proceedings with shouts of 'bastard', 'a noose to hang him', '12 bullets in the back'. After putting up with this for three days, Laval refused to appear in court any longer, even to hear the verdict of guilty. When Bouchardon and Mornet arrived at his cell on the day of his execution, they found him semi-conscious. Laval had taken cyanide, but not enough to kill him. Bouchardon, true to his reputation, insisted the sentence be carried out, even if Laval had to be shot on a stretcher. In the end, after his stomach had been pumped out, he was dragged out to be executed, not in the fort of Chatillon but in a corner of Fresnes prison.[8]

Outrage about Laval's botched trial sparked a reorganization of the High Court. Changes would anyway have been required, because, after elections in October 1945, France had a parliament even if not yet a constitution. Since treason trials of political figures had traditionally been carried out by parliament, the provisional arrangements set up at the Liberation needed review. According to the new arrangements, all twenty-four jurors were now selected from among parliamentarians proportional to the weight of representation of each different political group. Mornet was replaced as *procureur général*. He devoted his retirement to looking after his trees and writing his fanciful memoir of the Occupation. He died in 1955. His partner in crime and justice, Bouchardon, continued to oversee the *instruction* committee. He too published his memoirs but died in 1950 before he had started the volume covering the period after 1940.

The ineffectual Mongibeaux was replaced by Louis Noguères, a lawyer, resister and former Socialist parliamentarian. Noguères threw himself into his role with great conscientiousness; he was everything that Mongibeaux had not been. Having access to the records of the High Court, he was so shocked by how many documents in the Pétain case had never been presented to it that he used them to publish a long, scrupulous and indigestible book entitled *The Real Trial of Marshal Pétain.*[9]

The Court moved to grander premises – first the Palais de Luxemburg and then Versailles. Although this was the kind of setting that people had wanted for Pétain's trial, nobody cared any longer. Noguères was frustrated at how hard it was to get the jurors to attend even when a bus was organized to take them to Versailles. The Palace proved impossible to heat in a winter of coal shortages and extreme cold. Jurors and witness were wrapped in blankets and overcoats – so different from the sweltering conditions of Pétain's trial. A new law in April 1948 halved the number of jurors. The *Commission d'instruction* was moved from the Palais Bourbon to more cramped premises in a building previously occupied by the Ministry of Agriculture. Bouchardon found himself in a cramped office next to a kitchen.[10]

Even for Brinon's trial in March 1947, the Versailles courtroom was almost deserted. He was sentenced to death and executed, the last death penalty pronounced by the court. In total, nine of those who had testified at the Pétain trial were tried by the Court. Four of them were found guilty and given sentences ranging from twenty years in prison to the lighter sentence of *Dégradation nationale*.[11] Admiral Bléhaut, who had been with Pétain at Sigmaringen, managed to escape to Switzerland before his trial where he worked as a carpenter and was sentenced to ten years in absentia. Of the other of Pétain's defence witnesses, Peyrouton was acquitted and for Weygand, Bergeret and Debeney it was decided that there was no case to answer for (*non lieu*). Since Weygand had always opposed collaboration, this judgement was logical, once it had been established at Pétain's trial that supporting the armistice was not in itself treasonable. De Gaulle never forgave Weygand for his actions in 1940, and when Weygand finally died in 1965, de Gaulle, at that time President of France, refused him a State Funeral. Reynaud was disappointed that he had been cheated of another showdown with Weygand in court.

Overall, the Court had considered a total of 108 cases. Eighteen people had been condemned to death, ten in absentia. Three death sentences had been carried out, five commuted. Eight people had died before their cases came to court, three had been acquitted, forty-two had received a *non lieu* and fifty-five had been sentenced to prison or hard labour. The Court's last case was judged on 1 July 1949. But by then no one was paying attention – certainly not the old man on the Île d'Yeu.

FRANCE ON TRIAL AGAIN

Pétain was not completely spared any further involvement in the inquest on France's wartime history.[12] One day in July 1947 he was visited by a delegation of thirteen parliamentarians who wished to interview him yet again. The previous year, parliament had set up a Commission to carry out an autopsy on the defeat of 1940. Its brief was to examine the 'totality of political, economic, diplomatic and military events which from 1933 to 1945 preceded, accompanied and followed the armistice in order to ascertain the responsibilities incurred, and to propose, if appropriate, political and judicial sanctions'. The year 1933 was chosen as a starting date because it was when the new Nazi regime had reintroduced conscription. The Commission concerned itself much more with the events leading up to the Occupation – the remilitarization of the Rhineland in 1936, the Munich agreement in 1938, the defeat and the armistice – than with the period after.

Hearings started in February 1947, and among those interrogated were many who had already testified at Pétain's trial. De Gaulle, now out of power, refused to testify with haughty condescension, saying that while 'not contesting the interest that the Commission presents for those who set it up', the debates would clearly be 'not historical but political'. Weygand was interviewed for nine separate sessions. He had lost none of his pugnacity, telling the Commission on one occasion 'I am a male and the government is a female', and on another 'there are people who have surrender in their blood' (Reynaud of course!). In his testimony, Reynaud tied himself in ever more knots about his conduct in 1940; and Louis Marin returned to argue yet again that there had never been a majority in the Reynaud government in favour of an armistice. The testimony from another one of Reynaud's former ministers, Raoul Dautry, demonstrated more honestly than anyone had done at Pétain's trial why no uncontested truth would ever emerge about the events of June 1940:

> We were there, 20 people, not sitting round a table but in complete dis-
> order in armchairs and in every corner of a room which had been set

up for a meeting of the Conseil . . . You cannot imagine the confusion of that meeting with ministers who had not slept for two days, who were no longer thinking straight, fighting furiously over improvised propositions . . . The confusion was such, people were so exhausted, so incapable of putting together arguments, that they threw words at each other like bullets rather than offering arguments and reasons.[13]

When the Commission expressed a desire to interview Pétain, Isorni urged him to refuse. In the end Pétain – or his wife – concluded that a refusal would have seemed like an admission of guilt; or perhaps he enjoyed being briefly in the limelight again. So, on 10 July 1947, a group of seasick parliamentarians arrived on the Île d'Yeu. Pétain was treated with some deference. To overcome the dilemma that it was contrary to protocol for elected representatives to rise to their feet when a condemned prisoner entered the room, they all contrived to be standing when Pétain arrived and sat down at the same time as he did.

After telling his interrogators that his memory was 'fugitive', Pétain was subjected to two hours of questions on numerous issues: military planning in the 1930s, the armistice, his relations with Laval, the events of November 1942, and so on. As far as military planning was concerned, Pétain admitted that 'from the war of 1914–18, it was over for me, my military brain was now closed'. On the Vichy occupation period he insisted there had been a Pétain–Churchill agreement and referred them to Rougier's writings for more details – but he contradicted himself a few minutes later to say that he had no recollection of any contact with the Allies between 1940 and 1944. Nor did he have any recollection of having imprisoned Blum or Reynaud. Occasionally he went entirely off-message because he no longer remembered what the message was supposed to be. Regarding the events of November 1942 he regretted not going to North Africa but said he had had no plane at his disposal. The official Pétainist defence was that he had stayed in France to sacrifice himself. When asked if he agreed that the protests he had allegedly made about German violations of the armistice served no purpose, he replied: 'Yes'.

There were occasional flashes of Pétain's caustic humour. Asked his views of Marcel Déat, he replied, 'everything you could imagine but worse'. But mostly the image he presented to his interrogators was that of an old man whose mind was slipping away. Asked why he had once declared during the Occupation that Germany was defending Western civilization, he replied sadly: 'I don't know. There was probably a reason but I don't know what it was.'[14]

It was tactically convenient for Pétain to hide behind his failing memory, but this was not just a smokescreen. Although he was mostly lucid until 1949, his memory was fading. Periods of mental confusion became more frequent and he would start reassembling fragments of his past into strange new configurations. One recurring obsession was his belief that on D-Day he had wanted to join Eisenhower in Normandy but that it had been impossible to find a plane. This was a confusion between the American landings of November 1942, when there had been some pressure on him to join the Allies in North Africa, and the D-Day landings in June 1944, when joining the Allies in Normandy would have been inconceivable. One night, Pétain refused to go to bed because he was convinced the Americans were coming to rescue him.[15]

This interrogation served no purpose. The investigators returned to the mainland none the wiser.[16] The Commission's existence automatically ceased once parliament reached the end of its term in 1951. It resulted in the publication of nine volumes of testimony but never got beyond the first volume of its report, which stopped with the events of 1936. The testimonies provided some material for future historians of the years before 1940 but otherwise the Commission's deliberations cast no more new light on the Occupation.[17]

THE OLDEST PRISONER IN THE WORLD

Nothing else happened to disturb the routine of life on the Île d'Yeu except that, for mysterious reasons, Doctor Imbert committed suicide in May 1948 – a blow to Pétain, who liked to be surrounded by familiar faces. The government was constantly picking up rumours that right-wing activists were planning to rescue the prisoner. Much alarm was caused by the Plan Bleu, an anti-Communist conspiracy uncovered in June 1947. It projected a putsch in Paris, the assassination of de Gaulle and the release of Pétain. One of those implicated was the ubiquitous conspirator Loustaunau-Lacau, who was briefly arrested. Later that year, Joseph Simon was alerted to another plan by French Canadians to launch a raid on the island.

Simon's other main preoccupation, beside fending off imaginary plots, was to ensure that no reporters could inveigle themselves into the prison to take photographs. One newspaper in June 1946 published a story headed 'I Saw Marshal Pétain on the Île d'Yeu', which was false because Simon had expelled the reporter before he could see anything. The following year, another newspaper managed to publish photographs of the interior of the fort. Simon launched an internal investigation to find the culprit. When in 1949 a tract entitled 'The

Oldest Prisoner in the World is Looking at You' appeared, with a picture of Pétain peering through prison bars, the authorities prosecuted the publishers.[18] The government wanted Pétain to be forgotten.

Isorni lobbied incessantly to improve the conditions of Pétain's incarceration. A letter he wrote to the government on the subject in June 1946 upset Simon, who noted in his diary all the things he was doing for Pétain – from listening endlessly to the same stories to smuggling in lobsters. Since the left-wing press was always on the lookout for stories about Pétain getting special treatment – Madeleine Jacob on one occasion asked to see the menus Pétain was served – Isorni's tactic of keeping Pétain's name in the news was risky unless his real objective was less to ameliorate the conditions of imprisonment than to fuel the narrative of martyrdom.

Isorni tried another ploy after the election of the venerable Socialist politician Vincent Auriol as president of France's new Fourth Republic in January 1947. It was a long tradition that a new president could accord an amnesty to some offenders on humanitarian grounds. Isorni and Lemaire were received politely by Auriol in February 1947, but even members of the government who might have been favourable accepted that public opinion was not ready for such a move. Isorni was no more successful when he wrote to the Minister of Justice to request permission for Pétain's wife to share his imprisonment. He did not help his case by comparing unfavourably the way Blum had been treated by the Nazis with the way the Republic was treating Pétain. Having failed with the government, Isorni lobbied the Académie Française, the French Catholic hierarchy, and even the Vatican. All this did as much to keep Isorni in the news as Pétain – which was probably the point.

The Pétainist faithful who had helped Isorni to prepare the trial continued to meet regularly. Sometimes the Marechale would join them 'like a queen displaced from her throne, finding in her exile her decimated court', as Isorni put it.[19] In April 1948 they formed a Committee for the Liberation of Marshal Pétain presided over by the historian and member of the Académie Française, Louis Madelin, with five other academicians, a cardinal, Pierre Mauriac (brother of the novelist), the widow of Marshal Joffre, and three generals who had testified at the trial.[20]

21

Vichy Emerges from the Catacombs

Jacques Isorni wrote of these years: 'It was as if, at the bottom of some catacomb, we were the last of the faithful celebrating a forbidden cult.'[1] Isorni was becoming its high priest. In addition to his legal career he was now in demand on the lecture circuit. Since speaking directly on Pétain was too incendiary he gave lectures on the trial of Louis XVI. Members of the audience who got the message would sometimes mix their applause with shouts of 'Long live Pétain!'

Despite Isorni's comment about the 'forbidden cult', it is remarkable how quickly Vichy apologists started to find a voice – and an audience.[2] One of the first to raise his head was Admiral Auphan, who had gone into hiding at the Liberation. His trial took place in absentia in August 1946; he was sentenced to death. Auphan had not made things easy for his defence lawyer, Maurice Garçon, with whom he was in secret contact, because he wanted to base his defence on loyalty to Pétain. Garçon tried to persuade him this was no longer viable once Pétain's trial had established that his was a treasonable government. Auphan's underground existence, protected by Catholic networks, did not prevent him producing what he later called 'samizdat', pro-Pétain tracts. When the French Constituent Assembly debated a new constitution, Auphan optimistically sent them a draft of the constitution that Pétain's advisers had drafted, but never applied, towards the end of the Vichy regime.[3]

From the end of 1945 some extreme-right publications started to emerge. Most were ephemeral but two turned out to have staying power. The first was an austere monthly review called *Écrits de Paris*, which started in 1947. The subject matter is clear from a few random selection of articles from 1956: 'General Pétain at Verdun', 'Marshal

Pétain and Alsace-Lorraine' (March), 'Marshal Pétain and the Académie Française' (April), 'Necessary Rectifications for a Proper Trial',
and so on. *Écrits* was joined in 1951 by the more pugnacious *Rivarol*,
whose circulation reached 40,000. Contributors to *Rivarol* were un-
ashamedly defending collaboration whereas *Écrits de Paris* generally
took the line that Pétain had opposed it. But hatred of de Gaulle provided common ground. These publications inhabited their own
parallel universe of rancour, resentment and victimhood; endlessly
raking over the horrors of the Liberation, depicted as a bloodbath
comparable to the massacre of St Bartholomew or the Terror; and
nursing a morbid cult of martyrology over which hovered the Christ-
like figure of Pétain.

One active centre of neo-Pétainism was Switzerland, where high-
ranking servants of the Vichy regime had taken refuge. An important
role in this community was played by Laval's former *directeur de cabinet*, Jean Jardin, a charming networker who came to be known as the
'consul' of the emigrés.[4] He put them in touch with the Nazi-
sympathizing Swiss banker François Genoud, who founded a
publishing house, Éditions du Cheval Ailé, devoted to publishing pro-
Vichyite materials. One of the first titles to appear was a defence of
Pétain and criticism of the trial by Alfred Fabre-Luce. In the interwar
years Fabre-Luce had been a brilliant and well-connected writer committed to Franco-German reconciliation. He went on to support
collaboration but acquired a serendipitous political virginity because
he had been briefly imprisoned by the Germans towards the end of
the Occupation before being arrested again at the Liberation.[5] His
book *Le Mystère du Maréchal. Le Procès de Pétain*, appearing as
early as October 1945, was the first of a flood of polemics that he
would produce over the next three decades. He argued that the 'intui-
tive genius' of the Marshal had allowed France to salvage something
from the catastrophic defeat of 1940 until the Allied victory in which
de Gaulle had played no part. Fabre-Luce was ready to acknowledge
that the positive results of collaboration up to 1942 had become
'uncertain' in 1943 and non-existent in 1944.[6]

The tenacious Professor Rougier, whose wartime activities had terminated his academic career, also published under the imprint of the
Cheval Ailé. He wrote almost a book a year endlessly revisiting – and

endlessly embroidering – his 'mission' to Churchill but also denouncing the horrors of post-Liberation France.[7] A classic text in this vein was the 1948 pamphlet *Les Crimes masqués de résistantialisme* by Abbé Desgranges, a conservative Catholic *député* from Brittany who had voted full powers to Pétain in 1940. After the Liberation he set up a confraternity (the Order of our Lady of Mercy) to aid victims of the new 'Terror'. His term 'resistantialism' became a popular neologism to distinguish those who had jumped on the resistance bandwagon at the end from 'true' resisters whom he claimed to admire. The theme of victimhood crossed the bound of good taste when Desgranges likened the new penalty of 'national indignity' to the imposition of the yellow star on Jews during the Occupation. In the one case individuals lost civic rights; in the other they often lost their lives.

Former Vichy insiders started publishing their memoirs. One of the first was by Pétain's *chef de cabinet*, Henri du Moulin de Labarthète, part of the group of Swiss refugees, who knew more secrets than anyone.[8] The portrait of Pétain that emerged was not always flattering. This was certainly not true of the book *Montoire: Verdun diplomatique: le secret du Maréchal* (1948) by Louis-Dominque Girard, who had been in Pétain's *cabinet* for the last nine months of the regime. Girard's massive tome argued that Montoire represented a victory comparable to Verdun. Montoire had come up at the trial less than might have been expected because no one was sure what had been said. The defence had suggested that Pétain had been inveigled into the meeting by Laval. But Girard boldly argued that it was Pétain who had wanted to meet Hitler and that Hitler had fallen into the trap laid for him.

Girard's starting point was a remark allegedly made by Pétain after Montoire: 'Has no one ever told you about Tilsit?' This was a reference to the famous meeting between Napoleon and Tsar Alexander I on the river Niemen in 1807, which had ended hostilities between their two countries, leaving Napoleon free to pursue his disastrous campaign in Spain. In the context of 1940, Hitler was Napoleon and Pétain was Alexander: Pétain, by reassuring Hitler that he had nothing to fear from the French in the west, left Hitler free to turn on the Soviet Union. Thus France had played the 'decisive part in the Allied victory' by precipitating the entry of the Soviet Union into the Allied camp – 'an act of strategic genius'. The policy required 'a lot of discretion even mystery' on the part of Pétain: 'What is extraordinary is the care that this 84-year-old man took to put in place all the strings of an operation that he would manipulate alone and wanted to remain entirely secret.'[9]

Even by the gymnastic standards of Vichy apologetics this was an ingenious argument. The government refused to allow the book to be displayed in the windows of bookshops, using a law usually applied to works of pornography – which of course only helped sales.

Pétain, an avid reader of Rougier's books, told Simon that he would not bother to read Girard's book because it was so long. But he seems to have relented, if a conversation reported by Isorni is to be believed:

PÉTAIN: It is a masterpiece. Girard has brought out all my ideas . . . It is a big book but not a word is wasted . . .

ISORNI: Monsieur le Maréchal, part of the book is controversial. In going to Montoire, did you really intend to turn the Germans against Russia?

PÉTAIN: I am not sure today if I did have ideas of this kind. But are they favourable to me?

ISORNI: Obviously.

PÉTAIN: In that case no need to deny them.[10]

TWO STRINGS TO FRANCE'S BOW?

France's changing political context helped Pétainist apologists find a wider audience towards the end of the decade. The unity of the Resistance had not survived the onset of the Cold War. De Gaulle's own evolution was a sign of the transformation of politics. He had resigned in January 1946 because he was unable to work with the parliament drafting a new constitution. Once that constitution was adopted, de Gaulle denounced it as replicating the worst features of the Third Republic. He launched his own new party, *Rassemblement du Peuple Français*, or RPF (Rally of the French People), to attack the constitution of the Fourth Republic and bring him back to power. De Gaulle now became violently anti-Communist and in a search for conservative voters he was ready to make a gesture of reconciliation to former Pétainists. At a press conference in March 1949 de Gaulle declared:

> Today there is an old man in a fortress. An old man who I and many others recognize has performed great services for France. We do not forget it and we must not forget it ... Why should this old man die without having been able to see again flowers, trees, friends? ... We should allow this man who has at times carried the glory of France to die with a certain dignity, a man who made a terrible mistake but is now just an inoffensive old man.[11]

De Gaulle was engaged in a delicate balancing act: winning over former Pétainists while not alienating his natural constituency. But one Gaullist ally, Gilbert Renault, a former Free French agent who had run an important resistance network under the pseudonym of 'Colonel Rémy', tipped that balance over the limit. After the war, Rémy had started publishing best-selling memoirs that made him the epitome of the cloak-and-dagger secret agent in the eyes of the public. Once Rémy had joined the RPF, he was the obvious person to write a popular biography entitled *The Unknown de Gaulle*. This work of shameless hagiography contained a passage in which Rémy remembered de Gaulle once telling him that France had needed 'two strings to her bow' – that of Pétain and of de Gaulle. De Gaulle had amended Rémy's original typescript by changing the original tense to a subjunctive – it was desirable that France '*should have* two strings to her bow' (*que la France disposât de deux cordes*), which could be read as a retrospective wish or a statement of what had actually happened. De Gaulle also inserted a qualification 'provided, of course, that both should correspond [another subjunctive] to the benefit of the nation' – leaving it ambiguous whether that condition had been fulfilled. Because few people bothered to read Rémy's saccharine propaganda, these words, even after de Gaulle's emendation, passed unnoticed.[12]

In April 1950, encouraged by de Gaulle's public remarks about Pétain, Rémy repeated the alleged remark about the two strings in the Gaullist newspaper *Carrefour* – this time omitting de Gaulle's qualification. While not repudiating his former opposition to the armistice, Rémy now seemed more exercised by the excesses of the Liberation. The next day, de Gaulle issued a terse statement denying that he had made the statement attributed to him. Rémy resigned from the RPF. Having failed to secure de Gaulle's benediction for his attempt to create a strand of Pétaino-Gaullism, he gravitated to the right.[13] Remy's semi-recantation of his past gave new publicity to the Pétain case beyond the circles of unrepentant Vichyites. Isorni and Lemaire were emboldened to publish a book together outlining their case for a revision of the verdict.[14] Pétain was back in the news.

Also in April 1950 the popular newspaper *Samedi-Soir* ran a huge banner headline: 'Pétain: Judge for Yourself'. Carrying a picture of the jurors from the trial, it invited its readers to play juror in their turn, asking: 'In their place would you have condemned Pétain?'

> 22 April: Was he right or wrong to advocate and sign the armistice? Did he carry out a coup or did he represent legitimate power?

> 29 April: Montoire: diplomatic Verdun or treason? The National Revolution: renewal or fascism?

> 6 May: North Africa: did the Marshal's policy serve the allies or the Axis?

> 20 May: Did he persecute the Israelites or protect them? Was STO slavery or protection?

The final issue on 17 June asked, 'At Simaringen was Pétain the accomplice or the prisoner of Hitler?'[15]

The newspaper was coy about its own answers – although even postulating Montoire as a 'diplomatic Verdun' was a sign of the times – but another big circulation newspaper, *L'Aurore*, played its cards more openly in a series of articles running over May and June 1950 which opened with a huge headline: 'Was Montoire the Starting Point of Treason or Was It a Diplomatic Masterstroke Whose Repercussions Were Fatal to the Nazis in the Long Term?' In case readers had not picked up the message of this loaded rhetorical question, they were provided with reasons to opt for the second alternative. Finally, an important regional newspaper, *Le Courrier de l'Ouest*, carried twenty articles between September and October 1950 under the heading rubric: 'Should the Pétain Verdict be Revised?'[16]

Another sign of the new mood was that Vichy apologists found their books accepted by mainstream publishers. The venerable publishing house Plon, which produced the memoirs of both Churchill and de Gaulle, had no compunction about publishing memoirs by four individuals who had all testified for the defence at Pétain's trial.[17] The Pétainists were well and truly out of the catacombs.

Catholic spokesmen were also emboldened to raise their heads. The Liberation had been traumatic for the Catholic Church, which had so ostentatiously supported the Vichy regime, even if a few senior clerics had spoken out against the arrests of Jews in 1942. When Pétain made his only visit to occupied Paris in April 1944, he was welcomed at Notre Dame by Archbishop Suhard, who presided two months later over a mass in the cathedral for Philippe Henriot, Vichy's Minister of Propaganda, who had been assassinated by the Resistance. When on 26 August 1944 de Gaulle ended his procession down the Champs-Elysées with a mass in Notre Dame, Suhard was locked out of his own cathedral and forbidden to officiate.

Six years later, the Church had its revenge. On 25 February 1951, Suhard's successor Cardinal Feltin celebrated a mass in Notre Dame to commemorate the anniversary of the Battle of Verdun. On the previous day, a government minister present at Verdun itself had managed the feat of never mentioning Pétain. But in Notre Dame, Feltin solemnly invoked his name: 'we know that he is suffering. Christian charity and our role as soldiers under his orders invite us to give, on his behalf, a fervent prayer to our Lord.' Twice he was interrupted by applause; the Prefect and another representative of the government walked out in protest. Feltin received a vast postbag of support for his sermon. He had clearly touched a nerve.[18]

The values of those who subscribed to this nostalgic Pétainism are revealed in the petition sent to the wife of President Vincent Auriol in 1949, asking that Pétain be released from prison. The signatories accompanied their name with commentaries:

M. Paul M. (12 children): I never doubted in him; his portraits still decorate all the rooms in my house.

M.P. (Paris): He is not forgiven for having humiliated the political elites ... To have governed without *députés*, rid the nation of the harmful division of parties.

M.E des Essarts: He succeeded in limiting the damage to a remarkable degree. Without him there would have been so many more shot and deported.[19]

The change in the political climate emboldened Pétain's supporters to form a new party, the Union des nationaux indépendants et républicains (UNIR) for the parliamentary elections of 1951. It had a predictable right-wing platform – anti-Communism, defence of the French Empire – but above all defence of Pétain's memory and an amnesty for those convicted at the Liberation. Since de Gaulle's RPF, which opposed the existence of the Fourth Republic, was viewed as a threat by mainstream politicians, the centrist government was not above giving these violently anti-Gaullist conservatives some help behind the scenes. Isorni was provided with a photograph which had never been published, showing de Gaulle shaking the hand of the Communist leader Maurice Thorez in 1945: de Gaulle's Montoire, as the Pétainists portrayed it. In the end four UNIR candidates were elected to parliament, including Isorni and Loustanau-Lacau.[20] In January 1951 they succeeded in getting parliament to approve an amnesty for those who had been sentenced at the Liberation to less than fifteen years in prison.[21]

This would not of course affect Pétain, whose health was seriously deteriorating by this point. Three doctors had been sent to the Île d'Yeu in February 1949. They recommended that Pétain be hospitalized, but the government instead opted to provide extra medical care in the prison. It also pondered what to do when Pétain died. A detailed plan was drawn up in November 1949: Pétain's death certificate would carry no mention of his career; he would be buried in the Île d'Yeu fort in civilian clothing with no military decorations. No members of the public would be admitted to the funeral ceremony. But Pétain hung on for one more year. In June 1951, as his state worsened, he was moved into a house on the island that was accredited as a military hospital. After twenty-two days, he died there on 23 July.

When de Gaulle's aide and future prime minister Georges Pompidou conveyed the news that 'Pétain is dead', de Gaulle corrected him: 'Yes, the Marshal is dead.' And when Pompidou added: 'The affair is now over once and for all', de Gaulle corrected him again: 'No, it was a great historical drama, and a historical drama is never over.'[22]

22

Keepers of the Flame

Given the inaccessibility of the island, Pétain's funeral was a low-key affair as the government had hoped. Only his lawyers and members of his family were allowed to enter the room where he had died and see the body. No photographs were authorized, and when the coffin maker was found to be carrying a camera provided for him by a newspaper, he was replaced. Isorni succeeded in having Pétain's title of Marshal included on the death certificate, but his formal request to the *préfet* that Pétain's body be transferred to the mainland for burial at Verdun was refused, as expected. At the same time, he and members of the family had secured a plot in the local cemetery. Pétain's coffin was carried there by eight veterans of Verdun, watched by a small crowd of mourners, fishermen and curious tourists. Prominent among the mourners was General Weygand. Condolences were sent by Francisco Franco from Spain and Antonio Salazar from Portugal. Masses were also said in several Paris churches.[1]

Immediately after the funeral, those who had been involved in the Committee for the Liberation of the Marshal set up a new organization: The Association to Defend the Memory of Marshal Pétain (ADMP). The Honorary President was Weygand, and its executive committee included Isorni, Lemaire, Girard and Rougier, and that recent recruit to the Pétainist cause, Colonel Rémy. Another active member was the former tennis star Jean Borotra, who had been Vichy's Minister for Youth. The association (membership 4,700 in 1954, 6,700 in 1955) published a quarterly bulletin which carried pious articles about Pétain and rebutted negative references to him in the press.[2]

The ADMP was more cult than political movement. It had a full

Nouvelle série - Nº 42 - Juin-Juillet 1964 — Prix du numéro : F. 1,00

LE MARÉCHAL

Organe de l'Association pour défendre la Mémoire du Maréchal Pétain

Direction et Rédaction : A.D.M.P., 6, rue Marengs, PARIS (1er) — C.C.P. 6459-26 PARIS — Tél. : GUT. 39-50 (poste 114)

AI-JE DONC VRAI-MENT MERITE UN TEL SORT ?

Philippe PÉTAIN

L'A.D.M.P. à VERDUN

Il s'imposait à l'A.D.M.P. d'associer en un même hommage, à l'occasion de la célébration du cinquantenaire de la guerre de 1914, les soldats de la grande guerre et leur chef victorieux, le Maréchal Pétain. Et c'est à Verdun, au point culminant de l'épopée, que le rendez-vous avait été pris.

Dimanche 14 juin, avec son strict souci du respect de la légalité, notre Association avait organisé un pèlerinage à Douaumont. Il s'est déroulé dans une ambiance d'émotion, d'espérance et d'union.

Toute liberté avait été laissée aux pèlerins de se joindre aux diverses personnalités qui s'étaient rendues à Verdun. Autour des dirigeants qui avaient entrepris le voyage, des adhérents et fidèles de l'A.D.M.P. étaient venus de très nombreux départements que nous voulons énumérer : Paris et Seine-Ouest, Meuse, Vosges, Puy-de-Dôme, Var, Hérault, Seine-Maritime, Nord, Meurthe-et-Moselle, Ardennes, Martinique, Haute-Marne, Seine-et-Oise, Morbihan, Marne, Moyenne, etc. M° Jean Lemaire, président, empêché au dernier moment, s'était excusé. Le groupe était conduit notamment par MM. Jacques ISORNI, Pierre HENRY (secrétaire général et des membres du Comité National), MM. RIVOLLET, ancien Ministre, le Capitaine de Vaisseau FEUILLADE, et MARANDE, président de la filiale des Vosges.

Dès le samedi, un groupe de la filiale Seine-Ouest avait effectué un circuit des champs de bataille de la rive gauche de la Meuse.

Le dimanche matin, après un instant de recueillement devant le monument aux Morts de la ville de Verdun, notre groupement montait en un long cortège automobile vers le fort de Douaumont.

La visite en fut faite sous la conduite de M. OLIVIER, gardien-chef du fameux monument, authentique combattant des grandes heures de la tragédie ; et chacun des visiteurs acquit la conviction que la

(Suite page 2.)

1914

Le colonel à Arras — Le général au front

HOMMAGE au Maréchal PÉTAIN

Commandant en chef de l'Armée française à l'occasion du cinquantième anniversaire de la Grande Guerre

La translation de Ph. PÉTAIN à Douaumont

Par Jacques ISORNI

D'ABORD se mettre d'accord sur les mots dont on se sert avant de discuter du fond des choses. Retenons ce l'expression trop communément employée de transfert. Transfert n'est qu'un terme de finances et de commerce. Il y a le transfert-palement et le transfert-recette. C'est aussi un changement de propriétaire d'un titre nominatif, effectué soit par endos, soit par signature d'un acte synallagmatique émanant de l'ancien proprié-

taire et du nouveau, et déposé au siège social ou transcrit sur un registre destiné à cet effet. Tandis que l'action par laquelle on transporte un objet, un individu — et un cercueil — d'un lieu dans un autre s'appelle en français une *translation*. « La translation du corps de l'homme était touchante, et tout était en pleurs, et plusieurs criaient sans pouvoir s'en empêcher. » Tel est l'exemple du Littré. Retenons-le. Il n'y aura qu'un nom à changer

dans une édition future. Il n'y aura jamais de transfert des cendres à Douaumont. Seulement une *translation*.

Si nous ne parlons de nouveau, ce n'est pas pour régler un problème de vocabulaire, c'est que le bruit circule, sans pouvoir être vérifié, que le Général DE GAULLE serait prêt, et près de l'ordonner.

Une question se pose, en dehors du Général DE GAULLE, sous forme de préalable : le Maréchal doit-il être

(Suite page 4.)

L'ANNIVERSAIRE DE LA MORT DU MARÉCHAL

Le 23 juillet prochain sera célébré le treizième anniversaire de la mort du Maréchal PÉTAIN, prisonnier à l'île d'Yeu.

Nous savons déjà que de nombreuses démonstrations se préparent, et nous demandons que, précisément, cette année où est commémoré l'anniversaire de la guerre de 1914, et alors que le souvenir du vainqueur de Verdun s'impose de plus en plus à l'opinion publique, nos filiales, et nos amis, organisent des cérémonies portant témoignage de leur fidélité.

La messe annuelle pour Paris sera célébrée le jeudi 23 juillet, à 19 heures 30 précises en l'Eglise Saint-Pierre du Gros-Caillou, 92 rue Saint-Dominique (7). Métro : La Tour-Maubourg et Ecole Militaire.

PÉTAIN ET LE POILU

Ce qu'il en a dit :

« Le soldat et l'officier français comprenant la grandeur de leur tâche, s'en acquittaient avec stoïcisme ; perdus dans un océan déchaîné, sachant que nul n'entendrait leurs signaux de détresse ils s'acharnaient à ralentir le flot qui les débordait les uns après les autres et préféraient la mort ou l'horrible captivité au salut qu'ils eussent pu trouver dans la retraite. Nos hommes souffraient et peinaient au-delà de ce que l'on peut imaginer : ils accomplissaient leur devoir avec simplicité, sans forfanterie, et, par-là, ils touchaient au sublime.

« Il y avait en eux moins d'enthousiasme que de mille détermination et leur force résidait surtout dans une volonté inflexible de défendre leurs familles et leurs biens contre l'envahisseur. Soldats dans la plus haute acception du mot, froids, résolus, ils acceptaient le danger comme la souffrance. Lorsque le moment était venu d'entrer en ligne, ils s'avançaient d'un pas ferme vers leurs destinées, n'ignorant rien du sort qui les attendait... »

« En 1917 j'ai réussi parce que j'aimais mes soldats. Je les aimais comme un chef. Je les aimais comme un frère, parce que je combattais avec eux. »

« Mon grand honneur et mon grand bonheur auront d'avoir réussi à faire pénétrer le sentiment de ses responsabilités dans l'âme du soldat français, devant lequel nous ne nous inclinons jamais assez, parce qu'il a donné sans mesurer, et quand même, et s'est librement soumis et mourir pour un idéal, supérieur toujours et quand même, et s'est libre-ment porté au premier rang des peuples levés contre l'oppression, l'injustice et la barbarie. »

calendar of celebrations: Pétain's birthday was marked by a visit to Cauchy, the village where he was born; 1 May was celebrated in memory of Vichy's Labour Charter and for its proximity to the Catholic commemoration of Saint-Philippe (3 May). But the high point of the year was the annual 'pilgrimage' to the Île d'Yeu to commemorate the Marshal's death. Prohibited from entering the fortress where he had been imprisoned for six years, 'pilgrims' gathered outside and descended the rocky path to Port Joinville – retracing his wife's 'road of the cross' as she would trudge up to the fort from the Hotel des Voyageurs. The enterprising hotelier Nolleau produced a little brochure entitled 'Île d'Yeu, Terre de Pèlerinage' and turned her room into a little museum of relics, which 75,000 people had visited by 1959. Finally, the faithful gathered at the tomb. For those who could not make the complicated journey there was also a mass in Pétain's church in Paris.

We do not know much about ordinary members of the ADMP. There were veterans of the Great War, veterans of 1940, nostalgic Vichyists, individuals who had suffered at the Liberation. Some anonymous letters to its Bulletin give an insight into their mental universe. One former veteran of 1940 wrote:

> I was 20 years old in June 1940 when I was made a prisoner. Having neither voted nor expressed yet any political opinions, I was on the margins of this disaster which overwhelmed me ... In interminable columns we marched along France's roads under a torrid sun, exhausted, dirty, hungry, watched by guards who knew that our civilian protectors had deserted us and that nothing now protected us ... No news. Villages in flames. Everywhere endless columns of unfortunate refugees, unforgettable images of sadness and abandonment.
>
> Then one night, all changed; our guardians changed their tone and told us that a glorious French Leader was seeking an armistice ...
>
> From the bottom of our hearts, exhausted by our suffering (and perhaps only those who lived through those days can understand), rose a ray of light, and we said a prayer for this great Soldier who, in the gravest crises, crowned by his Glory, had been there to protect us.
>
> Eight months later I managed to escape and I will always be grateful to the Marshal for having preserved a tiny corner of France where I could take refuge with my family.[3]

28. 'Glory and Sacrifice of Philippe Pétain Marshal of France'. Pétainist propaganda of the ADMP, beginning with Pétain's victory at Verdun in 1916 and his 'gift of his person' in 1940, and ending with his imprisonment in 1945 and his death in 1951.

As well as organizing the Pétain cult, the ADMP launched a petition demanding that Pétain's body be transferred to Verdun to lie alongside the soldiers he had commanded in the Great War. This was compared to the return of the ashes of Napoleon in 1840 – another French 'hero' who had died in enforced exile. Within two years, 38,000 people had signed the petition. The Pétain of Verdun was hugely celebrated in the columns of the Bulletin, but so too was the Pétain of Vichy. The organization emphasized especially the regime's policies of class reconciliation and the imaginary secret agreement with Churchill. There was little on Montoire (despite Girard's book); and Laval was almost never mentioned.

In 1957 an organization of former resisters tried to get the ADMP banned. The case was rejected by the courts, but a Free French journal published the eighty-four pages of their lawyer's brief under the title 'The New Pétain Trial'. In reality, there was nothing 'new' about this recapitulation of Mornet's arguments a decade earlier and only a handful of people had attended the court to hear them again. The shadow-boxing between the ADMP and the resistance organizations attracted little attention.

France was entering into the period of post-war prosperity later dubbed the '30 glorious years'. In 1951 and 1953 parliament voted amnesties for most of those convicted in the *épuration* trials; the French wanted to move on. To the extent that there was any consensus about Pétain at this time it was best represented by the history of Vichy published by the journalist Robert Aron in 1954.[4] Before the war, Aron had belonged to a group of young intellectuals later dubbed the 'non-conformists' of the 1930s. What this group shared was a deep alienation from the Third Republic, not just its ineffectiveness but its ideology of liberal individualism. They went in all kinds of political directions after 1940, some to Vichy, some to collaboration, some to the Resistance. Although he was Jewish, Aron himself had survived the Occupation thanks to the protection of Laval's aide Jean Jardin, who moved in the same intellectual circles before the war. For Aron personally, Vichy had been a 'shield'.[5]

Aron was immensely well connected and his book relied on a wealth of personal testimonies, as well as the records of the High Court, to which he was given access before they were opened. His book was not a complete whitewash, but he was inclined whenever possible to give Vichy the benefit of the doubt. It was significant that more than half of his book – a full 300 pages – was devoted to the first six months of the regime and less than a third – 180 pages – to the period following November 1942. He had six pages on the Rougier mission, and only two on the *rafle*, the round-up of Jews in 1942. His conclusion that Pétain was 'right for the short term ... and de Gaulle was right for the long term' was a repackaging of the 'sword and shield' theory. Reviews all pointed out that in his book Aron had bent over backwards to strive for impartiality. This was indeed exactly the reproach that de Gaulle made to him: 'Your book is so objective that it sometimes ends up not being so.'[6] But the ADMP did not like the book either.[7] Aron's reassuring soft Pétainism annoyed Pétainists and Gaullists in equal measure but perfectly embodied the tortured feelings so many French still harboured about their recent past.

PÉTAIN'S REVENGE

And that past was where the Pétainist faithful ADMP lived. Their publications carried few references to current politics. At the annual meeting of the ADMP in September 1954, one speaker pointed out that many of the Fourth Republican politicians now advocating reconciliation with Germany – a step towards what would one day become the EU – were the same people who had castigated the former policy of 'collaboration'.[8] Some on the left made the same point. A cartoon compared the 1951 meeting of the French Premier Robert Schuman and the German Chancellor Konrad Adenauer to that between Hitler and Pétain eleven years earlier.

One issue where the ADMP did draw parallels between past and present – to the advantage of the past, of course – was the Empire. Since 1945, French governments had been embroiled in unwinnable colonial wars. Indochina was lost after the battle of Dien Bien Phu in 1954 and after that, France had been caught up in an ever more bloody conflict to hold on to Algeria. In the heroic Pétainist narrative, the armistice had saved the Empire by keeping it out of German hands. Everything had started to go wrong when de Gaulle had launched his attack on Vichy-controlled Syria in 1941. The inevitable consequence had been Syrian independence in 1945 – the first step down the road of imperial decline. In advance of the centenary of Pétain's birth in April 1856 the ADMP portrayed him as 'the pre-server of the Empire'.[9] And it was through the Empire that Pétainist nostalgia was able to tap into a new audience after May 1958, when the crisis in Algeria exploded on to the mainland.

The European population of Algeria and the French Army were increasingly suspicious that successive French governments were not genuinely committed to the struggle against Algerian nationalism. This suspicion erupted into violence when a moderate politician, Pierre Pflimlin, became the French premier in May 1958 and tried to form a government. It lasted just two weeks. A huge demonstration in Algiers against Pflimlin was supported by the army. France seemed on the verge of a coup d'état. De Gaulle, who had been out of power for twelve years, emerged as a possible saviour. For the army in Algeria, he was the man who would keep Algeria French; for the politicians in France, he was the man who could save them from the army.

The parallels with 1940 were striking: at a moment of national crisis a providential hero emerged to save the nation. At a press conference to declare his intentions, de Gaulle was asked if he represented a threat to democracy. He replied with a quip: 'Am I going to start a career as dictator aged sixty-seven?' Many people remembered that Pétain had started such a career ... aged eighty-four. In the end, like Pétain in July 1940, de Gaulle was invested by parliament with emergency powers to resolve the crisis and draft a new constitution. As in 1940, legal forms were preserved but, as then, those who voted were acting under the pressure of forces outside parliament. In both cases, the historical legitimacy of the saviour trumped legal quibbles.

Those on the extreme right who had spent a decade ruminating on their hatred of de Gaulle faced a moment of choice. Should the hope that de Gaulle might save the Empire outweigh their memories of de Gaulle's past crimes? Four days before the vote, the cover of *Rivarol*, the most virulently anti-Gaullist publication, carried portraits of Pétain and de Gaulle. Its editorial was headed 'When De Gaulle Takes Himself for Pétain'. But two days later it saw no alternative: 'All that counts now is what use de Gaulle will make of the new – and miraculous – opportunity that he now has to save the *patrie* ... a gamble that we neither chose nor wanted to make.'[10] This was hardly a ringing endorsement. But from a publication that had lived on horror stories about 'Charles the Bad' it was remarkable step. *Écrits de Paris*, the other publication of Pétainist nostalgia, took the same line through even more gritted teeth: 'His past errors make us worry about the future. But this does not prevent us from ardently wishing for the success of his enterprise.'[11] In parliament, members of the extreme right were willing to give de Gaulle the benefit of the doubt.

Not Jacques Isorni. During the crisis, Isorni invoked the parallels with 1940. He announced a few days before the vote that he would be one of the 'eighty' – a reference to those eighty parliamentarians who had refused to vote for Pétain in 1940. As he watched how his fellow parliamentarians dropped one by one their objections to de Gaulle, he remembered the words of Léon Blum at Pétain's trial describing his experience in July 1940: 'I saw men transformed and corrupted in front my eyes, as if they had been dipped into some kind of toxic bath.'[12] Isorni was present in the Chamber on 1 June 1958 when de Gaulle attended parliament to defend his proposals. He had not seen him since that night in February 1945 when he had pleaded that Brasillach should escape the death penalty. Since then in Isorni's imagination, de Gaulle had come to assume ever more demonic form:

> I scrutinized his heavy and long silhouette. Beyond the history that he carried what did the majestic prince of equivocation represent? My forehead was running with sweat and my hands were moist. I knew that, at odds with my friends, and with my adversaries lying in wait, once he had left the podium I was going to take his place and speak against him precisely because of what he represented. I was rigid with fear. This seemed like a dream; glimmers of the present mixed with fragments of the past: the *appel* of 18 June, the division of our fatherland, the hope of which he was the voice without a face, and the bloodshed, on that winter's night when in vain I begged him to save a life [Brasillach's].[13]

Isorni could not bring himself to vote for de Gaulle, he said, because of 'memories which I am connected to, some of them stained by blood, and that no gesture and no words can eradicate'. He observed perceptively that de Gaulle had studiously avoided any commitment about keeping Algeria French. He ended: 'May God save him from himself.' Isorni's colleague Jean-Louis Tixier-Vignancour, who had briefly served in the Vichy government, tried to persuade him to vote for de Gaulle. Isorni replied: 'Louis XVI's lawyer cannot vote for Robespierre.' De Gaulle became prime minister on 1 June. In September, after his return to power, there was a referendum on whether to approve the new constitution. Isorni of course advocated a 'no' vote but curiously Pétain's widow, who had briefly turned into a fervent Gaullist, was in the opposite camp. Posters in Paris proclaimed 'Isorni says no; the Maréchale says yes.'[14] In the subsequent parliamentary elections, Isorni lost his seat and he would never sit in parliament again.

For once hatred was no obstacle to lucidity. Isorni was proved right. De Gaulle gradually came to accept the inevitability of Algerian independence, shattering the hopes of those who had imagined that he would save 'French Algeria'. For Isorni, de Gaulle's 'betrayal' was easy to explain: unlike Pétain, who believed that defending France meant defending her 'soil', de Gaulle had a purely abstract vision of France as an 'idea'. Thus he had left France in 1940; Pétain had stayed. Pétain, if he had lived, would have refused to give up the soil of Algeria, which had been French since 1830; de Gaulle had no qualms about doing so if it served his 'idea' of France.[15]

This new cleavage in French politics was not an exact replica of the previous one between Pétainists and anti-Pétainists. Some former resisters were ardent supporters of Algérie Française. The former resister Georges Bidault, President of the National Council of the Resistance in 1944, now set up a new National Council of the Resistance – this time not to defend France against Pétain but French Algeria against de Gaulle. Some of these new recruits to anti-Gaullism put their previous anti-Pétainism on the back-burner; others completely repudiated their former allegiances. Just as Isorni once joked that he had retrospectively entered into collaboration in 1944 by defending Pétain, others now became retrospective Pétainists in 1962 through their defence of French Algeria.

As the bitterness of the Algerian conflict intensified, France seemed to be slipping into another civil war. In April 1961 there was a botched military putsch in Algiers. In a parallel with the High Court of the Liberation, de Gaulle created a High Military Tribunal to judge the leaders of the operation. Of the four ringleaders, Generals Challe and Zeller gave themselves up and were sent to prison. Two others, Generals Salan and Jouhaud, went into hiding and were not apprehended until March 1962. The year that had elapsed since their attempted coup had seen the setting up of a paramilitary organization – the Organisation Armée Secrète, or OAS – to spread chaos and violence in France and Algeria. De Gaulle himself was the victim of an assassination attempt in September 1961. The stakes in the trials of Jouhaud and Salan were higher than those of their accomplices in the previous year.

Jouhaud was sentenced to death after a two-day trial in April 1962. But everyone agreed that he had been a less central player than General Salan and he benefitted from the mitigating circumstance that he had a genuine attachment to French Algeria, where he was born. For this reason everyone expected that, once Salan had been tried, de Gaulle would commute Jouhaud's sentence. Salan's case was, however, complicated because four years earlier he had played a key role in rallying the army to de Gaulle. Thus, having supported a successful putsch for de Gaulle in 1958, he had led an unsuccessful one against him in 1961. Salan's defence lawyer was Tixier-Vignancour, who was emerging as one of the most prominent figures of the extreme right, to some extent eclipsing Isorni. Born in 1907, Tixier-Vignancour was in fact four years older than Isorni. He had been elected to parliament in 1936, had voted for Pétain in 1940, and even briefly held a post in the Vichy government. Sentenced to *indignité nationale* in 1945, he had only resumed his legal career after an amnesty was voted in 1953.

Salan's trial took place in the same courtroom as that of Pétain seventeen years earlier. There were many echoes of the Pétain trial – not least that Salan opened by reading out a statement to the court:

> I am not the leader of a gang but a French general representing the army in victory, not the army in defeat. I do not need to ask forgiveness for having defended, in that France situated south of the Mediterranean, the entirety of the free world . . .
>
> I owe an explanation only to those who suffer and die for having believed in a broken promise and betrayed commitments.
>
> From here forward I will remain silent.[16]

Aside from momentary interruptions, Salan, like Pétain in 1945, refused to say another word. He too became a silent witness at his own trial, even if his appearance lacked the inscrutable nobility of Pétain's. With the fading of the orange hair dye that had formed part of his disguise in exile, he started to look like an ageing music-hall comedian.

Over sixty witnesses appeared for the defence, almost a third of them soldiers. Many appeared despite official attempts to dissuade them. Alphonse Juin, now a Marshal of France, while not attending the court in person, sent a letter of half-hearted support, as he had done for Pétain in 1945. General Pouilly, who had not joined the putschists, told the court: 'I also chose a path different from General Salan; I chose discipline, but in choosing discipline I equally chose to share with my fellow citizens and the French nation, the shame of abandonment.' One former resister, asked whether there could be 'legitimate insubordination', replied 'I think we had an illustrious example in 1940.' Other themes of the Pétain trial were played out again: where did patriotic duty lie? Could personal conscience override the duty of obedience? What was the relationship between legitimacy and legality? What were the higher interests of the nation?

Tixier-Vignancour astutely avoided any direct attack on de Gaulle, arguing that Salan had done his duty as he conceived it. His peroration was remarkably similar to Isorni's in 1945. After deliberating for three hours, the judges found Salan guilty but with extenuating circumstances. This meant he was spared a capital sentence. The courtroom erupted into cheers and the singing of the *Marseillaise*; Tixier-Vignancour collapsed into Salan's arms. Later he recorded his speech so that it could be made into a record that was distributed by the young right-wing activist (later leader of the Front National), Jean-Marie Le Pen.

This sensational verdict was a humiliating rebuff for de Gaulle. His fury surpassed anything his advisers had ever witnessed before. He resolved that, since Salan could not be executed, Jouhaud would be. In the end de Gaulle relented when his own prime minister, Georges Pompidou, threatened to resign. But his anger was understandable: as he commented in private to one politician, the verdict on Salan had been Vichy's revenge.[17]

23

Memory Wars

One of the hits of 1964 was the song 'The Two Uncles' by the French *chansonnier* Georges Brassens. He imagined an 'Uncle Martin' who had 'liked Tommies' and an 'Uncle Gaston' who had 'liked Teutons'. But none of this, he sang, mattered to the new generations of French for whom these battles over the Second World War were as remote as the Hundred Years War.

The sentiments of this song were typical of Brassens's anarchist sensibility. He may have wanted to believe that the events of the Occupation were as remote as the Hundred Years War, but in reality, between 1964 and 1966, while de Gaulle was President of France, those who believed the same as 'Uncle Gaston' were back in the public eye more than at any time since the Liberation. This was partly a coincidence of the calendar: those three years encompassed the fiftieth anniversaries of the outbreak of the Great War (anniversary 1964) and the battle of Verdun (anniversary 1966). How to commemorate these events without invoking Pétain's name? And how to deal with the fact that 1964 was also the twentieth anniversary of the Liberation?

De Gaulle's regime was doing everything possible to promote what came to be dubbed the 'Gaullist myth' of the war. According to this narrative, France was a nation of resisters and the Vichy regime had counted for nothing. The climax of this strategy was the transfer to the Pantheon of the remains of the Resistance hero Jean Moulin in December 1964. But in these same years a flurry of books appeared on Pétain. In one of them, *Pétain avant Vichy*, the best-selling right-wing journalist Henri Amouroux wrote that, while de Gaulle might currently be 'King' of France, magazine sales suggested that Pétain was more popular: 'What a revenge!'[1] *Paris-Match*, a bellwether publication of popular taste, had no fewer than three covers on Pétain in 1966, one of which was devoted to the trial.[2]

All this led *Combat* – no longer the leftist publication it had been in 1944 – to organize a new debate over Pétain at the end of 1964 under the headline: 'People are Talking about Him. People are For, People are Against. There is a New Battle over Pétain.' In fact, there was nothing 'new' about the resulting debate as could have been predicted by the participants: Isorni and Rémy for the defence; two former resisters for the prosecution; and the journalist Maurice Clavel, who had covered the trial in 1945, somewhere in the middle. For one of the resistance participants, Daniel Mayer, this interest in Pétain was factitious: his name sold magazines in the same way as stories about British royalty or serial killers.[3]

Renewed interest in Pétain was not an opportunity that Isorni could pass over. In 1964 he opportunistically published a book with the provocative title *Pétain a sauvé la France* (*Pétain Saved France*) – and he was referring not to Verdun but to Vichy.[4] All this formed part of Isorni's sacred mission to rehabilitate the Marshal's memory, but he was also cashing in on Pétain because he needed money and had time on his hands. He even found time to publish a book restaging the trial of Jesus Christ.[5] The fact is that Isorni's political and legal careers were on the rocks. He had lost his parliamentary seat in 1958 on de Gaulle's return to power, and in 1963, while acting as a defence lawyer in the last major trial of the Algerian War after another assassination attempt on de Gaulle in August 1962, he was struck from the Bar for three years. Tixier-Vignancour, boosted by his successful defence of Salan, had been awarded the plum role of defending the leader of the assassination plot, Jean Bastien-Thiry, who was found guilty and shot. Isorni, relegated to defending a less prominent conspirator, announced in advance that he would raise the case of Bonnier la Chapelle, who had assassinated Admiral Darlan in 1942 and subsequently been rehabilitated by de Gaulle – which showed, according to Isorni, that de Gaulle was not necessarily opposed to political assassination.

All this was vintage Isorni. What caused his suspension from the Bar was his reading out in court a letter impugning the integrity of the magistrates. Isorni was a master of provocation but this time he had gone too far. His breach of professional conduct was an opportunity for those wanting to muzzle him. He spewed out his rage in a book accusing de Gaulle of having connived at political assassination in the past.[6] For these accusations he was convicted in 1965 of the crime of 'offending the Head of State'.

Isorni's 1964 book on Pétain elicited a surprisingly friendly response from François Mauriac, who wrote that the book had 'neither shocked nor scandalized' him. But he rightly identified the problem with Isorni's approach. If he genuinely wanted to celebrate the Pétain of the Great War, he had to avoid turning his campaign into 'a revenge by the defeated of yesterday' seeking to overturn the trial verdict of 1945.[7] Despite this tentative olive branch, Mauriac soon found himself ferociously attacked by another Pétainist apologist. Since 1958, Mauriac had become so ardent a supporter of Gaulle that even his admirers were embarrassed. In 1965 he produced a treacly biography that prompted a ferocious response – and a much better book – from Jacques Laurent, a Vichy apologist and supporter of French Algeria. Despite having tried, in 1945, to save Brasillach from the firing squad, Mauriac was a hate figure to former Pétainists. But Laurent's polemic against Mauriac was really an attack on de Gaulle: 'Between 1940 and 1944,' he wrote, 'de Gaulle's action consisted in attributing to himself victories that he had not won . . . a heroic upheaval in which he did not participate while remaining sheltered in London.'[8] There were several hundred pages in this vein. The violence of this polemic led Laurent, like Isorni, to be prosecuted for offending the Head of State.[9]

Another violent tract hostile to de Gaulle was published in 1964 by Alfred Fabre-Luce, who had written one of the first defences of Pétain in 1945. This was the fourth of Fabre-Luce's books on de Gaulle – whom he affected to call simply 'Gaulle'. A previous book in 1962, imagining de Gaulle appearing before a High Court, caused Fabre-Luce to be convicted under the same law as Isorni and Laurent.[10] The government's liberal use of this law punishing offences against the Head of State, which dated back to 1881, allowed Pétain apologists to claim that political life in Gaullist France was more repressive than under Vichy – a wild exaggeration. The tense political atmosphere of the period – which included two narrow escapes from assassination for de Gaulle – explains why the government was so touchy.[11]

At the same time, de Gaulle was contemplating extending an olive branch to those not implacably opposed to him. In 1965 his first seven-year term as president would come to an end. As a result of a reform he had introduced in 1962, French presidents would from now on be elected by universal suffrage. It was inconceivable that de Gaulle would not win such an election if he chose to run, but the size of the victory was uncertain. Although he dominated French politics, he had accumulated many enemies. The left opposed his authoritarian style of government, moderate conservatives resented his Algerian policy, and the extreme right's rage against the 'betrayal' of Algeria was compounded by its nostalgia for Vichy. In 1963, Tixier-Vignancour had announced that he would run in the election, hoping to tap into some of this anti-Gaullist sentiment. One publicity stunt of his campaign was to charter a private plane from which he scattered flowers over Pétain's tomb.[12] Might de Gaulle find a means of throwing a few flowers in the direction of the extreme right?

The most obvious gesture would be to concede a key demand of the Pétainist faithful: that his body be taken to rest with the soldiers of Verdun in the nearby Ossuary of Douaumont some 10 kilometres away. Already when de Gaulle returned to power in 1958, members of his entourage had given some unofficial signals that he might be ready to accept a transfer of the body to Douaumont in a spirit of national reconciliation. At this moment, Isorni took it upon himself to write to de Gaulle urging the transfer of the body. For de Gaulle to be seen to be acting on a summons from Isorni was the best way to sabotage any such operation. Isorni announced that he had been informed by an emissary of de Gaulle that a transfer of the body was not possible, that de Gaulle had refused this simple gesture of reconciliation. For the moment, the matter was closed. Isorni's enemies believed that he had sought a confrontation because he did not want de Gaulle to receive any credit for such a gesture – and certainly not if it meant closing the prospect of a revision of the verdict of the trial.[13]

In 1964, six years later, with the Algerian War over, an election looming, and several key anniversaries of the First World War on the horizon, de Gaulle returned to the question. In an off-the-record comment to a Gaullist *député*, he remarked that Pétain might merit a place at Verdun as the 'man who helped France and her allies to triumph in that gigantic struggle'.[14] There were legal obstacles, to be sure. In theory, only soldiers who had fallen in combat could be buried in a national war cemetery. This ruled out burying Pétain in the cemetery of Verdun. And the Ossuary of Douaumont, a private foundation not governed by this law, was intended only for the bones of unidentified fallen soldiers on both sides. This also ruled out Pétain.[15] Doubtless it would have been possible to overcome these technicalities, but they were complicated by another question: who had the legal authority to approve the exhumation of Pétain's body? According to a law passed in 1941 – when Pétain was in power – this was the prerogative of the 'closest relative' of the deceased. Who was Pétain's closest relative?

FAMILY QUARRELS

In July 1945, while awaiting his trial at Montrouge, Pétain had drafted a new will making his wife and her descendants his legal heirs – superseding a previous will made in 1938. Thus upon the death of the Maréchale in 1962, her son by her first marriage, Pierre de Hérain – no blood relation of Pétain – became his sole legal heir. Immediately, another set of claimants presented themselves in the form of the family of Pétain's grand-niece, Yvonne de Morcourt, the granddaughter of his elder sister. Pétain had never shown much affection for his family, but he was closer to this branch of it than to any other. Yvonne de Morcourt and her daughter, Marie-Edith, had been among his few visitors on the Île d'Yeu. They now argued that the will drafted in Montrouge had no legal validity because Pétain had been a prisoner awaiting trial. The Morcourts claimed that this gave them the sole right to approve an exhumation. To complicate matters further, Marie-Édith Morcourt had in 1949 married Louis-Dominique Girard, a former member of Pétain's *cabinet* and author of the book claiming Montoire had been a new Verdun. Girard took up the cause of his new family with a vengeance.

This ensuing legal battle unhinged its participants. To complicate matters, Isorni agreed to act as lawyer for the de Hérain clan (although he could not plead the case until his ban on appearing in court ended in 1968). Girard and others tried to get the de Hérains expelled from the ADMP. This family squabble concealed a deeper rivalry between claimants for the role of guardians of Pétain's memory. As part of this battle, in 1966 Isorni published his correspondence with the Maréchale during Pétain's imprisonment. Girard fought back with a heavily documented book showing that the Marshal's 'real' family had always resented Eugénie, that she had been a sexual adventurer who entrapped the innocent Marshal and that Pétain himself had disliked his own stepson.[16] If one camp adopted one position, the other automatically took up the opposite.

In November 1965, Isorni, responding to de Gaulle's conciliatory comments about transferring Pétain's body to Verdun, announced that it might be possible to envisage this providing it was presented as a provisional step towards a burial in Douaumont. The Morcourt clan protested that Isorni was betraying the cause: nothing less than Douaumont would do. There was also the related issue of whether any transfer had to be preceded by a 'revision' of the trial or some other kind of 'rehabilitation'. Tixier-Vignancour, another rival of Isorni, rallied to the harder line. For several years the ADMP was plunged into crisis by these internecine feuds. Old Pétainist loyalists such as Admiral Auphan and Jean Borotra tried to avoid taking sides.[17] The Pétainists had presented the transfer of their hero's body as a gesture of national reconciliation to end France's civil war – but they were plunged into a civil war of their own.

While letters and memoranda were flying between lawyers, and insults were traded in the press, the 1965 presidential election had come and gone. The surprise was that de Gaulle, while coming top of the ballot, did not secure an absolute majority in the first round. Tixier-Vignancour performed respectably by coming in fourth with 1.3 million votes (5.2 per cent). A week later, in the run-off between the two best-placed candidates of the first round, Tixier's voters either abstained or transferred their votes to François Mitterrand. Mitterrand was the candidate of the left, but Tixier's supporters would have voted for Caligula's horse rather than de Gaulle. Their choice was eased by the fact that Mitterrand had a complicated Vichyite past, which no one talked about but was known to the initiated. This past would resurface nearly thirty years later in ways no one could have imagined.

In the second round, de Gaulle was re-elected with 55 per cent of the vote. Whether or not his suggestion of moving Pétain's body had ever been serious, he no longer had any compelling political reason to act. But he had to say something during the ceremonies to commemorate the fiftieth anniversary of the battle of Verdun in 1966. How to invoke that battle without mentioning the name of the man who had won it? De Gaulle's nuanced speech ended any speculation that he might support a translation of the body: 'If, in the extreme winter of his life and in the midst of terrible events, the Marshal, worn down by age, was responsible for reprehensible failures, the glory that he acquired at Verdun, and then conserved later by leading France's armies to victory, should not be contested.'[18] While de Gaulle was speaking in Verdun, Isorni was on the Île d'Yeu. After listening to the speech on the radio, he proclaimed in front of the house where Pétain had died: 'From this land of exile and martyrdom . . . I say to you, Charles de Gaulle: "Philippe Pétain, Marshal of France, will be one day transferred solemnly to the national cemetery of Douaumont."'[19] Only a handful of the ultra-faithful were assembled to hear these words. Many of them had refused to make the journey because the conflict between the two Pétainist clans was still tearing the ADMP apart.

The anniversary season ended in November 1968 with the fiftieth anniversary of the armistice that had ended the Great War. The government agency preparing the celebrations tried to erase Pétain from events altogether. Thus the liberation of Metz by General Pétain's 19th army became 'November 17th, 1968 at Metz, ceremony of the liberation of Metz', accompanied by a mention of a visit by Marshal Foch, who had passed through the city a week after Pétain.[20] Even so, on 11 November 1968, de Gaulle had wreaths placed on the tombs of all seven Marshals of the Great War – including Pétain. This was done in total discretion, with a few journalists informed at the last moment. In the aftermath of the violent upheavals of May 1968, which came close to ousting him from power, de Gaulle was making gestures to rally conservative opinion. The most spectacular of these was an amnesty for those OAS activists who were still in prison; the wreath on Pétain's tomb was another. Paris, to adapt the famous words of Henri IV, was well worth a wreath. Isorni, present on the island that day, placed a wreath of his own next to de Gaulle's. He wrote in the ADMP's bulletin: 'this gesture is a beginning'.[21]

It was not the beginning of anything. De Gaulle's successor, elected in 1969, was Georges Pompidou, his former prime minister. Pompidou, who had no resistance record, had dropped remarks suggesting he would like to draw a veil over the conflicts of the past. But he did not initiate any change of policy towards Pétain. After the flurry of nostalgia of the mid-1960s, Pétain faded from view. A scene from a 1970 comedy by François Truffaut, *Domicile Conjugal*, suggests that Brassens's hope that the Occupation would soon seem as remote as the Hundred Years War was coming to pass. The film is the third in the saga of Truffaut's young hero, Antoine Doinel. An electrician appears in the courtyard of a Paris building to repair a television set. No one answers the bell. He asks Doinel whether the person who had telephoned about the television might be out shopping:

> 'That would surprise me. He hasn't left his flat for 25 years. He is in a sort of voluntary isolation. He does not want to leave until that Marshal Thingummybob . . .'
> 'Marshal Juin?'
> 'No; an older one? The one who was in charge of France during the war?'
> 'Ah, you mean Marshal Pétain.'
> 'Yes, that's the one. He says he will not leave his flat till Marshal Pétain is buried at Verdun.'

Brassens's 'Uncle Gaston' had become Truffaut's 'Marshal Thingummybob'.

STEALING THE MARSHAL

Pétain's defenders had a new trick up their sleeve. On the morning of Monday, 19 February 1973 the municipal guardian of the cemetery of Île d'Yeu noticed that the ground around Pétain's tomb had been disturbed. Further inspection revealed that the tombstone had been secured with a new sealant. The police were summoned; the tomb was opened; Pétain's coffin had disappeared. The news hit radio and television news bulletins that day and the government immediately put up roadblocks around Verdun. There was fevered speculation as to who was responsible for the theft. Was it the extreme right or the extreme left? What was the purpose of the stunt? Had it been organized from Spain where many former Pétainists were living in exile – an idea supported by the fact that Spanish newspapers were wedged into the sealing of the tomb to hold the stone in place?

The operation had been hatched by Isorni's rival, Tixier-Vignancour. Parliamentary elections were due in March 1973 and the stunt was intended to embarrass the government and bring Pétain back into the news. The date was chosen to coincide with the anniversary of the start of the battle of Verdun. Tixier-Vignancour had visited the island in January to survey the lay of the land. To lead the operation he had recruited a right-wing activist, Hubert Massol, who assembled five helpers including a soldier who had served in Algeria and a professional stonemason. Posing as tourists, they crossed over with a van on the afternoon ferry. After dinner at the Hotel des Voyageurs, they drove to the cemetery in the small hours of the morning. As the coffin was raised the men broke into a rendition of the Vichy hymn 'Maréchal nous voilà'. After a celebratory glass of champagne at the hotel, they took the 4 a.m. ferry back to the mainland.

Then things started to go wrong. The conspirators had planned a stop at a château in the Vendée belonging to a right-wing aristocratic *député*, but no one was there to receive them – the chatelain had presumably got cold feet – and they had to continue their journey. Their original intention had been to hide the body, possibly near Verdun, reveal to the world what had occurred, and coerce the government into agreeing to a transfer to Doaumont. At the very least it was hoped that the heist would re-open the debate. This timetable was thrown into disarray when the conspirators heard on their car radio that the theft had been discovered. Arriving in Paris, they drove their van down the Champs-Elysées – a symbolic gesture to recall the memory of Pétain's descent down that avenue in 1919 and expunge the memory of de Gaulle's in 1944 – and then hid the coffin in a garage at St Ouen, a working-class suburb of Paris.

Press coverage fluctuated between amusement and outrage. Massol realized the game would soon be up. Hoping that his possession of the body would give him some bargaining power, he proposed to reveal its whereabouts if the government would agree to let it lie in Paris at the Hotel des Invalides, where Napoleon was buried, until a decision was taken about a final resting place. The plan was announced at a press conference in the afternoon of 21 February, but Massol was promptly arrested. Later that night he took the police to the garage where the coffin was hidden. The whole escapade had lasted just three days.[22]

The coffin was deposited for one night in a chapel of the main military hospital in Paris, where it received military honours. The next day a helicopter returned it to the Île d'Yeu. The coffin was received by the Prefect, but gendarmes were ordered not to salute it. Some wreaths were placed on the tomb including one from President Pompidou. The little stunt had achieved nothing except to reveal the strange fanaticism of the most ultra-Pétainist circles. They had succeeded in putting Pétain in the headlines for two days but more as a figure of comedy than reverence.

RE-OPENING THE TRIAL

All this appalled Isorni, who had a furious altercation with Tixier-Vignancour at the Palais de Justice. Isorni had a taste for provocation but not at the risk of ridicule. He was not above carrying out stunts of his own, but he had also been working for decades to obtain a revision of the verdict.

To request a re-opening of the trial verdict it was necessary to produce new evidence not available to the court in 1945. Isorni and Lemaire had prepared the ground in 1948 by publishing a collection of 'documents which formed the basis of the first formal plea for the verdict to be revised'.[23] This plea, running to 250 pages, submitted in 1950, was followed by two more supplementary pleas in 1951 and 1953 which produced further 'new documents'.[24] These comprised a patchwork of scraps culled from interviews, memoirs and diaries that had seen the light of day since the trial. Use was made of a book by the Harvard historian William Langer to whom the American government, embarrassed by its controversial Vichy policy, had offered privileged access to State Department archives to write a rationale for the policy. Langer's book, published in 1947 under the title *Our Vichy Gamble*, was an almost total whitewash of a policy that would, according to one reviewer, have been better described as 'Our Vichy Fumble'.[25]

Isorni jumped at the chance to cite an 'objective' outsider who had affirmed that 'having read every word of the trial transcript I find it hard to believe that anyone who has done likewise could regard the conviction of the Marshal as anything but a political judgement'.[26] Langer argued that Roosevelt had pursued a pragmatic policy placing the defence of Allied interests above moral considerations. In his judgement de Gaulle 'hardly offered an effective alternative' since he was just 'a hireling of the British . . . with no demonstrable following in France', while Pétain had 'maintained France as a going concern, kept the French fleet out of the enemy's clutches, and fended off the danger to North Africa, which was to serve as our gateway to Europe'. As for the inconvenient fact that Vichy forces had fired on American troops and Pétain had denounced the American attack, Langer's line was that 'this was probably meant for the record' and that Pétain had handed over his protest 'with a knowing tap on the shoulder'. The 'knowing tap on the shoulder' was Langer's version of the 'secret' messages.[27]

Isorni also took the opportunity to revisit the Montoire meeting – or, as he later put it, 'to correct errors that some of Pétain's friends, badly informed, led us to commit'.[28] Unsure how to treat Montoire, the defence at the trial had either ignored it or blamed it on Laval. But the publication of the contortionist defence by Girard (not yet Isorni's mortal enemy) offered a new approach. Isorni added other scraps of documentation which supported Girard's argument, for example an interview in 1947 with Pétain's former 'jailor' Renthe-Fink, who asserted that Montoire had been 'the greatest defeat of German policy towards France', ignoring the fact that when Montoire took place Renthe-Fink was not in France at all and had no special insights into the encounter.

Once Isorni and Lemaire had submitted their plea, the authorities needed to rule on whether it was in principle 'submissible' (*receeva-ble*): could a High Court judgement be revised? The Ministry of Justice ruled that in theory it could be – but Isorni heard no more. After de Gaulle's return to power in 1958 it was obvious that nothing was going to happen. When de Gaulle resigned in 1969, Isorni submitted a fourth revision plea.[29] But two years later the Minister of Justice, René Pleven, issued a new ruling that a revision of a High Court judgement was not admissible: the only possible revision was the judgement of history.

With a new president, Valéry Giscard d'Estaing, in power, Isorni tried again in 1978 with a fifth plea. This time the 'new' document was the photocopy from British archives of a memorandum by the British Foreign Secretary Lord Halifax in December 1940, which only showed what no one denied and everyone knew: that there had been a few unofficial contacts between Vichy and London.[30] The French government stuck to the position that revision was not admissible.

TELEVISION TRIAL

Isorni submitted three more revision pleas, but more and more he resembled a man running desperately up a downward escalator that was moving faster every year. His scraps of 'new evidence', ever more flimsy and circumstantial, hardly weighed in the scales when set against the new historical work on the Occupation that began appearing in the late 1960s.

The most important was a sensational book by the young American historian Robert Paxton, published in 1972. Paxton's work demolished Robert Aron's consensual history of Vichy which had held sway since 1954. Using German documents, Paxton showed that the Vichy regime, far from having collaboration forced upon it, had consistently sought a collaboration that the Germans rebuffed; that the first repressive policies of the Vichy regime, including the persecution of the Jews, were entirely home-grown and not the result of German pressure.[31]

Not all of Paxton's arguments were new, but his work was revolutionary in its demonstration that Vichy's internal and external policies – the 'National Revolution' and collaboration – were logi-cally interconnected. In Paxton's reading, collaboration was not so much about 'treason', as the Pétain trial had sought to argue, as it was the underpinning of a domestic political strategy, rooted both in the immediate context of defeat – finding culprits – and in a longer trad-ition of extreme right-wing politics. Paxton's book fitted in with the Zeitgeist. In the wake of the anti-Gaullist student protests of May 1968, France's younger generation was in a mood to challenge the heroic Gaullist narrative of French history. The way had been pre-pared by the 1969 documentary of Marcel Ophüls, *The Sorrow and the Pity*, which presented a dismally negative image of the French under Occupation.

Three years later, following the French publication of his book, Paxton was invited to appear on *Les Dossiers de l'Écran*, one of France's most-watched television shows. The format was to invite a panel of invited guests to debate an issue after viewing a film related to the subject under discussion. It sometimes treated social issues – homosexuality, juvenile delinquency, abortion, the death penalty – and sometimes history – the Commune, the Battle of Stalingrad, the Drey-fus Affair, Napoleon. On 25 May 1976 the subject was simply: 'Philippe Pétain'.

Compiling the panel had been laborious. Resistance organizations protested against the prospect of giving any platform to defenders of Vichy. In the end three spokesmen were found to represent the anti-Vichy position: Pierre Lefranc, who as a student had participated in a demonstration against the Occupation on 11 November 1940 and went on to become a member of de Gaulle's inner circle; Henri Fre-nay, leader of *Combat*, one of the most important resistance movements; and Pierre-Henri Teitgen, de Gaulle's Minister of Justice at the time of the Pétain trial. They were pitted against three defenders of Vichy: the former Vichy Naval Minister Admiral Auphan; Jacques Isorni (of course); and Louis-Dominique Girard. Assembling this group was a feat because only a few weeks earlier Girard had told the organizers that he would not participate if Isorni were invited.[32] In the end he relented because he hated Paxton even more than he hated Isorni. Finally, there were three historians: Paxton; Henri Michel, a former resister who had become the leading French authority on the

Occupation; and Jean Vanwelkenhuyzen, a Belgian historian and expert on the occupation of his country. At forty-four, Paxton was by the far the youngest participant; at eighty-two, Auphan was the oldest.

The Vichy camp was nervous in advance. Jean Borotra wrote to Girard offering translations of what he considered to be some of Paxton's most outrageous assertions.[33] The much-awaited debate started thirty minutes late, as the television studio was occupied by anti-Pétain demonstrators and the programme had to be moved to another studio. Once the programme had started, the show's moderator reminded the participants, like Mongibeaux in 1945, that they must conduct themselves with serenity. He rapidly proved as incapable of controlling his debate in 1976 as Mongibeaux had been of controlling his court. Within minutes the programme had degenerated into a shouting match. Auphan, whose deafness prevented him from following all the details, launched into a personal crusade to correct the slur on his reputation contained in Paxton's account of the secret telegrams of November 1942. He was incensed that someone only seven years old at the time – and an American to boot – could claim to know better than a Frenchman who had been on the spot. 'One of the two of us is a liar,' Auphan declared belligerently. Not only did Auphan take this matter personally but the secret telegrams, along with the 'double game', were, as one historian has commented, 'the heart of the Pétainist gospel'.[34]

Lefranc took the classic Gaullist line that everything stemmed from the armistice. Girard, whose arguments in defence of Montoire were too complicated for a television debate, was largely reduced to silence, and querulously complained that professional historians ignored his unreadable books. Frenay argued that Pétain's gravest crime was to have misled so many honest French citizens as to where their duty lay. He cited the case of his mother, who had believed in 1942 that it was her duty to denounce her own son to the authorities.

The debate was dominated by Isorni and Teitgen, who seemed to have been transported back to 1945, when one had been in court defending Pétain and the other had been Minister of Justice. Isorni resurrected the arguments he had been rehearsing endlessly over three decades, an exercise he could have performed in his sleep. When he moved on to the conditions under which Pétain had been convicted, the moderator finally put his foot down in exasperation, saying 'We are not here to re-run Pétain's trial.' And yet that is exactly what the participants were doing.

Paxton hardly managed to get a word in. Ten years younger than any other protagonist, and seemingly younger still, he looked like a bemused adolescent who had stumbled into a family feud of half-crazed grown-ups. Michel made many effective interventions reminding the Vichy defenders of inconvenient facts. The programme had been running for three hours when he embarked on an elaborate exegesis of the 'secret telegrams', demonstrating that even if they did exist they did not necessarily mean what Admiral Auphan believed them to have meant. It is inconceivable that anyone still listening after midnight could have followed this complicated argument any more than the jurors had followed the story of the telegrams when it was presented to them in 1945.

This debate was followed by many others over the next decade.[35] Vichy was good for viewing figures. These programmes became such a staple of French television that they were satirized in the 1983 comedy film *Grandpa in the Resistance*, which ended with a studio discussion between ageing survivors of the war locked in their eternal quarrels. The ADMP was always on hand to provide a spokesman to defend Pétain. Despite the internal quarrels, its membership peaked at about 20,000 members in 1966.[36] No sooner had some resolution been reached in the squabble between Girard and Isorni than another one broke out between Isorni and Rémy. There had always been tension between those who genuinely sought a reconciliation between Pétainism and Gaullism, and those for whom Gaullism was beyond the pale. The naively well-meaning Rémy, who genuinely sought a Pétaino-Gaullist consensus, was incensed by a grotesque parallel that Isorni had drawn between the death of the collaborator Robert Brasillach and that of the Free French resister Honoré d'Estienne d'Orves, shot by the Germans in 1941. Rémy resigned from the ADMP in 1982.

In the run-up to the presidential elections of 1981, the ADMP polled all the candidates about transferring Pétain to Douaumont. The winner of the election, François Mitterrand, promised to set up a round-table to debate the proposition. Once he was elected this promise was forgotten. Nonetheless Isorni hoped that Mitterrand might prove more sympathetic than his predecessors. Although Mitterrand was a Socialist, Isorni had known him well in the period they had both served as *députés* during the Fourth Republic. They were both anti-Gaullist in different ways and for different reasons. Mitterrand had even testified for the defence in the trial of General Salan in 1961. He had even been present in the courtroom in 1945.

Immediately after Mitterrand's election, Isorni filed yet another plea for revision – the sixth – and to his surprise the new Justice Minster, Robert Badinter, whose Jewish father had died in the Holocaust, ruled that it was 'admissible'. Not for long. Faced with an outcry from the Socialist Party, the government reverted to the previous line. Isorni submitted another plea in 1982 and still another in 1983. This (the eighth) was the last one. Mitterrand told his close aide Roland Dumas, 'Isorni is getting on my nerves . . . fob him off.'[37] Dumas took Isorni out to an expensive lunch and made some soothing noises. Nothing more happened. Mitterrand presumed the Pétain problem would fade away as the survivors disappeared: General Weygand had died in 1966, and Admiral Auphan and Louis Rougier followed in 1982. He could not have been more wrong. Over the next two decades, the Pétain affair returned to haunt France more intensely than at any time since the Liberation.

24

Remembering the Jews

In the 1976 television debate, Pierre-Henri Teitgen, recalling the fate of the Jews in Vichy France, had exclaimed that it was an 'abomination, a participation in genocide, a crime punished by the Penal Code with the most severe sanctions'. As a lawyer Teitgen must have known that there was no clause in the Penal Code in 1945 to repress such crimes. The term 'genocide', coined at the time of the Nuremberg trials, had been incorporated into the Declaration on Human Rights adopted by the United Nations in 1948. The term 'Crimes against humanity' was not used in any of the French trials after the war. But the concept was subsequently incorporated into the French Penal Code, and in 1964 the French parliament voted to lift the existing twenty-year statute of limitations in cases of crimes against humanity. This was done to ensure that Germans who had carried out atrocities in occupied France could still be pursued in the courts. It had not been envisaged that this law might also be used against French citizens.

The fate of the Jews had been peripheral to the Pétain trial. This fact came to seem incomprehensible following a major shift in public perceptions about the importance of the Holocaust. There were many reasons for this development, not unique to France. The trial in Jerusalem of Adolf Eichmann, architect of the Nazi genocide, in 1961, had an impact throughout the world. When the veteran journalist Madeleine Jacob covered the Eichmann trial it is revealing that she criticized the event for 'particularizing Jewish suffering'. Eichmann's crimes, in her view, were 'the crimes of fascism, of which anti-semitism is just one aspect'.[1] Within a few years, such a view would come to be considered anomalous. The Six Day War in 1967 between Israel and her neighbouring Arab states gave many French Jews a sense of the fragility of their existence. The following year, the student protests caused the young in France to question the historical narratives with which they had been brought up.

In the case of France, historians played a key role. In 1981, Robert Paxton co-authored a new book specifically on Vichy France and the Jews.[2] It demonstrated that the regime's first anti-semitic measures had been passed with no German pressure, that they had excited no significant public condemnation, and that the French government had helped the Germans carry out the arrests of thousands of Jews in the summer of 1942. Paxton startlingly showed that it was safer to be a Jew in the small part of France that had been occupied by the Italians during the war than in the supposedly 'free zone' of Vichy France.

Nothing contributed more to bringing the fate of the Jews under Occupation to the forefront of public attention in France than an interview in 1978 with the former Vichy Commissioner for Jewish Affairs, Louis Darquier de Pellepoix. Before the war Darquier (the 'de Pellepoix' was an affectation) had been a venal, monocle-wearing, drunken, street-brawling, professional anti-semite. He was tracked down to his exile in Spain by an enterprising French journalist whose sensational interview was published in the magazine *L'Express* under the headline, 'Only Lice were Gassed at Auschwitz'. Darquier expressed no remorse, only regret that more Jews had not been eliminated. The ravings of this deranged old man might not have mattered had he not worked officially for the Vichy regime. At Pétain's trial it had been mentioned several times that Pétain's feelings about Darquier were revealed by his calling him 'M. the torturer' – but this was a torturer whom Pétain had appointed. And Darquier claimed in his interview that Pétain had never disavowed him. The most damning passage was the revelation of the central role played in the persecution of the Jews by René Bousquet, head of the French police during the Occupation. This was not news for professional historians, but Bousquet's name had previously been unfamiliar to the general public. Unlike the fanatical Darquier, Bousquet had been at the heart of the Vichy state, directly answerable to Laval.

The Darquier interview was the catalyst for the lawyer Serge Klarsfeld to start legal proceedings against Jean Leguay, the representative of the French police – of Bousquet – in the Occupied Zone. Klarsfeld was himself a Holocaust survivor. He had only survived, along with his sister and mother, because they had hidden in a cupboard when the police had come to arrest the family. His father had died in Auschwitz. In 1979, Klarsfeld created the Association of the Sons and Daughters of Jews Deported from France (FFDJF). He painstakingly compiled his massive 'Memorial': a list of every Jew deported from France, the day of their arrest, the day of their death. Klarsfeld also published in 1987 a heavily documented study of the cooperation between Vichy and the Germans once the deportations had started in 1942. This was reviewed in *Le Monde* under the title 'Holocaust on the Seine'.[3]

With his German-born, non-Jewish wife Beate, Klarsfeld had long been active in unmasking former Nazis and tracking down individuals implicated in the Holocaust.[4] The Klarsfelds were masters of publicity, using the tactics of provocation inherited from the activists of May '68. In November 1968. Beate had famously slapped in public the German Chancellor Kurt Kiesinger, who was accused of having covered up his Nazi past. After the Darquier affair they turned their attention to France, starting with Leguay who became, in 1979, the first Frenchman indicted for crimes against humanity. Leguay died before the case could come to court, and in 1989 the Klarsfelds filed a case against Leguay's former boss, Réné Bousquet himself.

In June 1992, Klarsfeld was one of the signatories of an appeal published in *Le Monde* calling upon the President of the Republic, François Mitterrand, to recognize the responsibility of Vichy 'for persecution and crimes against the Jews of France'. This text was the initiative of the Comité du Vel d'Hiv 42, founded by a Jewish survivor who had spent the war in hiding in rural France.[5] The date was chosen in advance, for the fortieth anniversary of the notorious round-up (*rafle*) of Jews in Paris in July 1942.

Mitterrand announced that he would attend the ceremony of commemoration on 16 July – the first time a President of the Republic had done so – but two days before the event he gave an interview stating that it was not for the French Republic to apologize for the actions of Vichy: 'In 1940 there was a French State, the regime of Vichy, it was not the Republic.' Mitterrand did attend the event but the image that lingered was the spectacle of the president being booed, with shouts of 'Mitterrand to Vichy'.

NO FLOWERS FOR PÉTAIN

Klarsfeld had another card up his sleeve. On 21 July he announced that he had heard from a reliable source that Mitterrand would not be placing a wreath on Pétain's tomb, as he usually did on the anniversary of the armistice. This was completely untrue, but the intention was to force Mitterrand's hand. The first president to place a wreath on Pétain's tomb had been de Gaulle himself in 1968 on the fiftieth anniversary of the armistice; Pompidou had done the same in 1973 after the theft of the body. His successor Giscard d'Estaing did so in 1976 for the sixtieth anniversary of the Battle of Verdun and again (with all the other Great War Marshals) in 1978 for the sixtieth anniversary of the armistice. When Mitterrand met the German Chancellor Helmut Kohl at Verdun in a grand gesture of reconciliation on 22 September 1984, he again had a wreath placed on Pétain's tomb. He did the same again in June 1986 for the seventieth anniversary of Verdun. From that moment, Mitterrand continued the practice every year on 11 November. No one had paid much attention to this until Klarsfeld's intervention in 1992. What would Mitterrand do?

On 11 November 1992, Klarsfeld and some activists from the Union of Jewish Students arrived at the cemetery on the Île d'Yeu. Also present were a similar number of right-wing activists. The police kept the two groups apart. Only after both groups had caught the ferry back to the mainland did a helicopter arrive bearing a wreath in the name of the President of the Republic. It was laid on the tomb next to other wreaths, including one from Jean-Marie Le Pen, leader of the extreme right-wing Front National.[6] Klarsfeld issued a communiqué expressing outrage that 'after having honoured the victims of Pétain's anti-semitism, the President of the Republic has taken the scandalous decision once more to honour their executioner'. The next day, he laid a wreath on the site of the Vel d'Hiver sports stadium where 13,000 Jews had been rounded up (destined for Auschwitz) in July 1942, with the dedication: 'To François Mitterrand with all my gratitude, signed Philippe Pétain'. The wreath was in the shape of the *Francisque*, the medal awarded by Vichy to its servants – and one of those who had received it as a young man was Mitterrand himself.

After his initial defiance, Mitterrand was forced to backtrack. In February 1993 he signed a decree making the anniversary of the Vel d'Hiver, 16 July, an official day of remembrance for 'racist and anti-semitic persecutions committed by the de facto authority known as the "government of Vichy"'. No wreath was laid on Pétain's tomb that year by the president; and none has been laid by any president since then.

Mitterrand's tactical retreat did not end the controversy. The next year saw the publication of a book about his early years by the investigative journalist Pierre Péan.[7] The book covered Mitterrand's political formation in the 1930s, his association with Vichy, and his move into the Resistance. The cover showed two photographs: Mitterrand the resister (code name Morland) sporting a moustache as a disguise and Mitterrand (no moustache) being received by Pétain in October 1942. Mitterrand's Vichy past was not in itself a revelation. Isorni never lost an opportunity to remind people that Pétain had awarded Mitterrand the *Francisque*. But most people believed this had been a cover for his resistance activities. What was new about Péan's book was his documentation of Mitterrand's right-wing activism in the 1930s and the seriousness of his involvement with Vichy until 1942. Having escaped from a German prisoner-of-war camp in December 1941, Mitterrand worked for an organization set up by Vichy to reintegrate prisoners of war. That organization worked loyally for Vichy until it gradually moved into the Resistance.

The oddity was that Mitterrand had granted an interview to Péan and authorized friends to speak to him. Why he did this remains a mystery. Was he hoping to exert some control over the storyline? Was he engaged in a final settling of accounts, or a confession? Was he acting in a spirit of pedagogy – to show that France's history had not been written in black and white? Whatever the reasons, Mitterrand did not predict the shock his book would cause. As a fire-fighting exercise, he agreed to explain himself in a long television interview in September 1994.[8] His fourteen-year presidency had only six more months to run and he had just undergone an operation for cancer. He was known to be a dying man. Although the interview was relatively deferential, it was a strange and painful occasion. Visibly ailing, Mitterrand seemed to be clinging to life only by willpower and the desire to complete his presidency. While he had lost none of his icy hauteur, his ghostly pallor, and the skin on his face stretched like parchment under thick makeup, evoked a death mask.

Mitterrand's starting point was that it was necessary to 'put an end to this permanent civil war between the French'. This was clear from his response to a question about Klarsfeld:

> QUESTION: Today Serge Klarsfeld writes in *Libération* that historians should reveal, seek out the full nature and extent of the crimes and faults committed by the Vichy regime.
> MITTERRAND: Klarsfeld has a right to his view . . .
> QUESTION: You would not accept any attempt to rehabilitate Vichy?
> MITTERRAND: Certainly not. One does not rehabilitate what does not deserve to be rehabilitated and which even deserves some form of condemnation . . . When have you seen me doing this? I have never lifted a finger in that direction.

Then he moved on to Vichy:

> How many times do I have to say it? The first thing that was reprehensible about Vichy was to have drawn a line under the Republic. That was a truly intolerable act . . . At the beginning Vichy was bedlam (*pétaudière*), an old man around whom people who harboured an ideology succeeded in infiltrating themselves . . . I don't say that Pétain did not have an ideology but he was no thinker.

Finally, the trial:

> QUESTION: I think you were present, if what I have read is correct, for three days at the trial of Pétain. So you think he was responsible for what happened?
> MITTERRAND: Yes, I think I was at the trial of Pétain for one day. I do think, yes, that Vichy harmed French interests; that is obvious.
> QUESTION: But when you say that there were things to condemn are you saying it as President of the Republic or in a personal capacity?
> MITTERRAND: I do not need to express myself as President of the Republic. It is not for me to write the history of France.

Mitterrand's defence contained many half-truths, errors and fudges. There were also curious evasions. Among these was his supposed uncertainty about whether he had been at Pétain's trial – it was no crime to have been there – or how many times. He certainly had been there in his capacity as editor of the newspaper *Libres*, organ of the former prisoners-of-war movement. We have a photograph of him present on the sixth day of the trial; and at least one article by him reporting on another day:

> In this little room a great trial is taking place. But this great trial is attended by tiny pygmies, and so the little courtroom does not seem out of place. Everyone is *Monsieur le Président* . . . Starting with the President of the court, who does not miss an opportunity to make a little *bon mot*, right through to those former premiers who, having all failed in the face of History, try to make up for it by telling their stories. The accused remains silent; despite his deafness one feels he can hear and is listening. He plays with his *képi* or his gloves. From time to time he flushes or looks irritated . . .
>
> Each of the witnesses speaks for himself. M. Daladier recites his own defence at Riom. M. Lebrun, an honest man, asks himself questions and reaches no conclusions . . .
>
> Through a high window, one can see the spire of the Sainte Chapelle. It is outlined against the July sky, fragile and pure. In truth, if one wants to breathe, one can only do so outside this gilded and oppressive courtroom. In this trial for treason, one feels exhaustion at the number of little treasons on display. A sad regime that had for its defenders men who only know how to prate about their errors! . . . What Frenchman does not feel a secret irritation at their retrospective pirouettes? He would like to put them all into the same boat . . . the accusers and the accused.[9]

In this strange settling of accounts, it may be, as one commentator suggested, that Mitterrand was trying finally to exorcise de Gaulle as if telling the French 'he wasn't really like us, but you my friend, were very much like me'.[10] Perhaps as he neared the end of his life this narcissistic, devious, imperious and slippery personality was trying to remain faithful to the young man he had once been, gazing out of the fetid courtroom at the clear blue sky; animated by contempt for the ghosts of pre-Vichy France re-emerging from the wreckage to claim their rights; feeling indifference, perhaps pity, for the old man in the armchair, and dissolving his responsibility into a wider collective culpability.

29. The courtroom on 28 July 1945. The young François Mitterrand, looking meditative, can be spotted second from the right on the third press bench. The witness is General Doyen; Madeleine Jacob has her head turned.

VICHY ON TRIAL

The gesture Mitterrand refused to make in 1992 was accomplished three years later by his successor, Jacques Chirac, the first French president too young to have any adult memories of the war. Only two months after his election, in a solemn speech on 16 July 1995, the fifty-third anniversary of the round-up of Jews at the Vel d'Hiver stadium, Chirac proclaimed:

> Fifty-three years ago, on July 16, 1942, four hundred and fifty French police agents and gendarmes, acting under the authority of their leaders, responded to the Nazis' demands.
>
> That day, in the capital and the Paris area, nearly ten thousand [sic] Jewish men, women, and children were arrested in their homes at dawn . . .

France, land of the Enlightenment and of Human Rights, land of hospitality and asylum, France, on that day, committed an irreparable act.[11]

For the first time a French president had accepted the responsibility of 'France' in the Holocaust. Two years later, that responsibility was debated in court at the trial of the former Vichy civil servant Maurice Papon. This was the third trial for crimes against humanity staged in France. The first, in 1987, was of Klaus Barbie, the former Gestapo chief in Lyon, who had been extradited from Bolivia thanks to the Klarsfelds. The second, in 1994, was that of the former *milicien* Paul Touvier, who had gone into hiding at the Liberation and managed to escape detection until the 1970s. Both Barbie and Touvier were sentenced to life imprisonment. Papon's case was different because he had been an official of the Vichy regime. Barbie was a German and Touvier a member of a radically collaborationist organization. Papon was not a Nazi or an ideologically convinced anti-semite: he was an obedient French civil servant doing his job. After the Liberation, he had embarked upon a stellar administrative career, rising to be Prefect of Paris police between 1958 and 1966, and then a minister.

During the Occupation, Papon had been a relatively junior official. In 1943–44 he was deputy to the Prefect of Gironde in the south-west of France, where he helped organize the deportation of Jews. He was only executing orders, much less important than Leguay or Bousquet, but Leguay had died of cancer in 1989 before he could be tried; and Bousquet, indicted in 1989, had been murdered in 1993 by an unhinged publicity seeker. Papon was a Vichy surrogate; he was in court *faute de mieux*. This challenge was relished by his defence lawyer, Jean-Marc Varaut, who had a history of commitment to right-wing causes, defending the Putschist general Maurice Challe, one of the leaders of the failed coup against de Gaulle in 1961, and supporting Tixier-Vignancour's presidential campaign in 1965. Varaut had also written a book on the Pétain trial. Now he wanted his Isorni moment.

Between 1985 and 1997, France's highest court, the Cour de Cassation, modified the definition of crimes against humanity four times to make the definition fit the accused. As defined in 1945 at Nuremberg, a crime against humanity had to be part of a general 'project' of persecution. The Cour de Cassation had, in 1985, translated this idea to mean that the crimes must be committed by – or on behalf of – a state pursuing a 'policy of ideological hegemony'. This worked for Barbie who was a Nazi, but in 1992 another French court ruled that Vichy had no precise ideology and was merely a 'constellation of good intention and political animosities'. In that case Touvier's association with Vichy did not constitute a crime against humanity. A few months later another court found a jurisprudential way around this dilemma.[12] These judicial somersaults offered some openings to Papon's defence. He himself, despite being only a year younger than Pétain had been in 1945, was articulate, pugnacious, unrepentant, and fully in command of the details

The six-month trial was the longest in French history.[13] It turned into a daily media circus. Among the many lawyers representing the victims was the flamboyant Arno Klarsfeld, son of Serge, wearing blue jeans under his lawyer's robes and often arriving at court on roller skates while his father led demonstrations outside the court. Over 120 people were called to testify, half of them Holocaust survivors. Four historians, including Robert Paxton, gave evidence. Another historian of the period, Henry Rousso, refused to do so on the grounds that courtrooms were not the place to debate history. What the trial demonstrated above all was how perceptions had shifted since the Liberation. In 1945, France had wanted to celebrate resistance heroes; now the emphasis was on mourning victims. This shift was already prefigured in Barbie's trial. Barbie's original notoriety came from his role in the death of the resister Jean Moulin, but in 1987 this figured less prominently than the arrest of forty-four Jewish children from the orphanage of Izieu in eastern France in April 1944.

In Papon's case this shift in perception was even more glaring. One reason why Papon had succeeded in pursuing a successful career after 1945 was the role he was alleged to have played in helping the Resistance. When the revelations of his Vichy past had surfaced in 1981 he asked for his name to be cleared by a 'jury' of former resisters. They concluded that he had genuinely helped the Resistance. This led to a sardonic comment from Klarsfeld: 'The jury is the first resistance organism which publicly declares that the Jews of France were sent to their deaths by a French resister.'[14] During the trial a procession of venerable resisters testified in Papon's defence. Pierre Messmer, one of de Gaulle's earliest recruits in 1940, declared that 'whatever respect we owe to all victims, especially innocent ones ... I respect more those who died with weapons in their hands because it is to them that we owe our liberation'. The Gaullist Maurice Druon, who had co-written the famous resistance anthem *Le Chant des Partisans*, expressed concern that the current emphasis on the fate of the Jews was distorting perceptions:

> The trial of Vichy has already been carried out; it is over ... And now people want to start all over again ... At the Liberation we put in the same category all those who suffered from the war: the hostages, the resisters who were deported, the Jewish resisters. And now today we are creating a special category.

As for prosecuting everybody who had worked for the Vichy regime, where would it end? 'Do you want to try every gendarme who pushed people on to trains [shouts of yes]? This is turning into a trial of France; but France did not conduct herself too badly.'[15]

What the trial showed was that the historical certainties of these old resisters were out of step with the moral certainties of the end of the twentieth century. In the end Papon was found guilty of complicity in the arrest and deportation but not the murder of the Jews. He was given a ten-year sentence. This mild sentence satisfied the Klarsfelds, who had never claimed that Papon was a major player. In truth, the public prosecutor had not made a convincing case, but to have found Papon innocent would have implicitly denied Vichy's own culpability. Yet sentencing him to only ten years did seem to let Vichy off the hook symbolically. Even if Papon had essentially been a scapegoat, as one journalist remarked, 'scapegoats can be guilty'.[16]

The Papon trial triggered an outpouring of public repentance. In 1997 the Paris Bar, the French Catholic episcopate, the Order of Doctors all formally offered apologies for their complicity in anti-semitism during the Occupation; and the government set up a commission to investigate the despoliation of French Jews during the Occupation and offer them compensation.[17]

'ISORNI V FRANCE'

Isorni did not live to witness these developments. He died in May 1995, two months before Chirac's speech. In his last years, he had become an embarrassing relic where once he had been a celebrity. In 1951, when a publisher launched a series inviting personalities to write on 'my profession', Isorni was commissioned to write the volume on the law, in the distinguished company of Christian Dior on fashion and Arthur Honegger on music. He was admired as a legend in the Palais de Justice even by those who did not share his political views. But his grandiloquent style came to seem dated, and his legal career never fully recovered from his three-year ban from the Bar in 1963.

Over the years, the bravura of the Don Quixote-like figure defending a lost cause with passion had curdled into pathological anti-Gaullism. A book that Isorni published in 1973 was described by *Le Monde* as so crazed in its anti-Gaullism as to be 'burlesque'. As a young lawyer Isorni had mocked Payen's desperation to be elected to the Académie Française. Now he too was bitten by the bug. But his attempt failed disastrously in 1971. Being Isorni, he immediately wrote a book about his experience.[18]

Over the years Isorni's Paris apartment had become a shrine to Pétain. His New Year's cards carried a photograph of Pétain with the words 'Have you forgotten me?' Isorni was like a broken record; there were few days when Pétain was not mentioned in his conversation.[19] He seemed almost to relish this: 'I know that I am boring – the word is inadequate – the world. I could not care less. I will continue to bore the world. I will never give up boring the world.'[20] Isorni's last public appearance was a 1995 television interview with the biographer of Pétain, Marc Ferro. Having recently suffered a stroke, Isorni was like a waxwork and could hardly speak. Ferro tried to probe the motivations behind his lifelong crusade: 'Was it not in essence sentimental? You came to identify yourself, a little bit, as Pétain's son.' 'If that is how you view it, perhaps,' Isorni offered non-committally. Pétain had launched Isorni's career; perhaps he had partly come to see himself as Pétain's son; he had also become in some sense his prisoner. But it is only through Pétain that he will be remembered.

Three years after his death, as the wave of repentance gathered force, Isorni had a small posthumous legal victory in a case that had been trundling through the courts for years. After submitting in 1983 his last plea for the trial to be revised, Isorni tried another tack. On 13 July 1984 the ADMP took out a full-page advertisement in *Le Monde* under the banner of a famous phrase uttered by Pétain during the Occupation: 'French, you have short memories.' The text was drafted and signed by Isorni and the current President of the ADMP, François Lehideux, Industry Minister under Vichy. It contained the usual arguments of Pétainist apologists and even the allegation that 'the prosecution, with the collusion of persons in the highest authority, used forgery as in the Dreyfus Affair'. The text was published the day before President Mitterrand was to make a symbolic gesture of Franco-German reconciliation at a ceremony at Verdun with the German Chancellor Helmut Kohl. Its last line read: 'the shadow of the Marshal hovers over this encounter'. In fact, portraying Pétain as prophet of Franco-German reconciliation had not usually been a staple of Pétainist defence and it undercut the argument earlier in the same text that Pétain had been playing a double game: Rougier's visit to London is given the same prominence as Montoire.

An association of former resisters filed a criminal complaint, calling this text 'an apology for the crime of collaboration'. The case moved through the courts. In 1990 the signatories of the ADMP letter were found guilty by a Paris appeal court; the judgement was confirmed in 1993 by the Cour de Cassation. Finally, Isorni and Lehideux appealed to the European Court of Human Rights. The French government asked the court to reject their application. Now the case was designated 'Lehideux and Isorni v France'.

The government argued that claims of a Pétainist double game 'had been refuted by all historians who had made a special study of the period'. Isorni and Lehideux were also accused of sinning by omission for failing to mention the anti-semitic legislation which 'in the words of the American historian Robert Paxton was the 'blackest mark on the whole Vichy experience'. This was all to no avail. In September 1998 the majority (fifteen to six) of judges ruled in favour of Isorni and Lehideux on the grounds that article 10 of the European Convention on Human Rights guaranteed free speech. They ruled that the arguments should be considered 'a debate that is still ongoing between historians about the interpretation of the events in question', and for that reason did not come under the 'category of clearly established historical facts, such as the Holocaust, whose negation or revision would be removed from protection'. Finally, the Court emphasized the importance, in a democratic society, of debate around a figure like Pétain about whom 'different opinions had been and might be expressed'.[21]

LEGALITY VS. LEGITIMACY: WHERE WAS 'FRANCE'?

One paradox of Jacques Chirac's speech was that, although delivered by an ostensibly Gaullist president, it undermined the Gaullist narrative that between 1940 and 1944 'France' had been in London and that Vichy was a parenthesis in French history described as the 'de facto authority known as the "government of the État français"'. For this reason, Chirac's speech upset some Gaullists who were also unhappy about the Papon trial.[22] Some on the left were unhappy too, especially those so-called 'souverainistes' like Mitterrand's former minister, Jean-Pierre Chevènement, for whom accepting a continuity of the State between the Republic and Vichy implied that the members of the resistance were 'terrorists' and comforted those who claimed that 'Pétain was France'. Chevènement saw this as part of a sinister plan to dissolve the exceptionalism of France in the cosmopolitanism of the European union.[23]

Proving the illegality of Vichy had always posed a problem for the Free French.[24] In 1940 one of de Gaulle's earliest followers, the jurist René Cassin, had started elaborating the juridical arguments. These culminated in a Free French decree on 9 August 1944, a few weeks before the Liberation of Paris, ruling that 'the form of the government [of France] is and remains the Republic'; that 'legally the Republic has never ceased to exist'; that as a consequence all laws passed since 16 June 1940 were 'null and void'. This idea underpinned de Gaulle's refusal on 25 August 1944 to declare that he was restoring the Republic: one could not restore something that had never ceased to exist.

But what was the case for the illegality of Pétain's government? And why date it from 16 June? Cassin's arguments for the illegality of Vichy had been based on the irregularities of the vote of full powers to Pétain. But that vote had occurred on 9–10 July: 16 June was the day Pétain had replaced Reynaud with the intention of signing an armistice (which occurred on 22 June). The idea that everything stemmed from the armistice was de Gaulle's view, but it caused problems at Pétain's trial and only one jurist supported this line after the war.[25] For most jurists, the claims for Vichy's illegality did not stand up for the period from 16 June to 10 July. The respected jurist Georges Vedel, whose legal textbook was like a bible for generations of law students, argued that between 16 June and 10 July Pétain had been at the 'head of a regular government, both legal and legitimate'.[26] This view was supported by an important piece of case law from the Conseil d'État regarding the case of a magistrate, Charles Frémicourt, who had been sanctioned at the Liberation because he had been a member of Pétain's government formed on 16 June 1940. Ruling in June 1947, the Conseil d'État overturned the sanction because Frémicourt had resigned on 11 July.[27]

De Gaulle knew he was on thin ice when claiming that Vichy was illegal. For that reason he generally preferred to talk about legitimacy.[28] He commented once, in the 1960s: 'If legality is lacking, legitimacy must be substituted for it . . . I invoked legitimacy because legality was against the Free French.'[29] But the concept of legitimacy is slippery. For de Gaulle a government that signed an armistice allowing the occupation of part of French soil had forfeited its role as its guarantor of national interests. The legitimacy of a government can also be judged by the degree to which it commands popular consent. But that would not have offered solace to de Gaulle in 1940. After the war, the Vichy apologist Alfred Fabre-Luce asked 'where was the nation between 1940 and 1944?' His answer: 'In the aftermath of the armistice incontestably behind Pétain but on the eve of the Liberation, incontestably with the liberators'. In between those two dates, 'one had to feel one's way'.[30]

A new ruling on these philosophical debates came up before the courts twenty years after Chirac's speech, in a ruling from France's highest court of administrative law, the Conseil d'État. It was asked to adjudicate when an organization calling itself the Association du Musée des Lettres came into possession of what were supposedly original drafts of telegrams sent by de Gaulle from London during the war. The government intervened to assert its rights to ownership, claiming that since the Free French had been since 16 June 1940 the official repository of French sovereignty, the documents in question were state archives. After this claim was supported in the courts, the Association appealed to the Conseil d'État against this judgement. Ruling in 2018, the Conseil essentially supported the government on the grounds that all incarnations of the Free French since 16 June 1940 had been 'depositaries of national sovereignty and ensured the continuity of the Republic'.[31] So 'France' *was* in London after all.

But the judgement went on to say that since 'the actions of the *de facto* authority calling itself the "government of the French State" engage the responsibility of the State, documents generated by it should be considered as public archives'.

So 'France' was also in Vichy . . .

25

Judging Pétain Today

Whatever these legal niceties, no president has ever rowed back from Chirac's declaration in 1995. If anything, his successors have gone further at the risk of writing the Germans out of the story. Thus on 29 July 1997 the prime minister, Lionel Jospin, declared: 'This round-up was decided, planned, realized by the French ... Not a German soldier was necessary.' Emmanuel Macron took the same line on 16 July 2017:

> The crimes of 16 and 17 July 1942 were the work of the French police, obeying the orders of the Government of Pierre Laval, the General Commissioner for Jewish Affairs, Louis Darquier de Pellepoix, and of Prefect René Bousquet.
>
> Not a single German took part.[1]

Despite the initial criticisms from traditional Gaullists, these positions were widely supported. An opinion poll immediately after Chirac's speech showed that 72 per cent approved; and only 18 per cent thought that 'people talk too much' about the extermination of the Jews in the war.[2] Another poll three years later showed an 80 per cent approval.[3]

But there is a paradox. When people are asked in polls more generally about their view of Pétain, the results show a surprisingly indulgent view which has changed little over fifty years:

<u>May 1980:</u>
Pétain was right to sign the armistice: 53 per cent
Pétain should have gone abroad: 21 per cent
Pétain was:

A traitor: 8 per cent
An ambitious man who accepted defeat to come to power: 7 per cent
Sincerely acting in the interests of the nation but overwhelmed by events: 59 per cent
A hero who was unjustly condemned: 7 per cent

April 1993
Pétain betrayed France: 38 per cent
Pétain was mistaken but acted in good faith: 28 per cent
Pétain tried to protect the interests of France: 30 per cent

December 1994
Pétain was right to ask for an armistice: 59 per cent
Pétain was wrong to ask for an armistice: 15 per cent
Pétain betrayed France: 22 per cent
Pétain made a mistake in good faith: 24 per cent
Pétain tried to safeguard French interests: 30 per cent

March 1997
The armistice was:
A very good thing: 10 per cent
Quite a good thing: 52 per cent
Quite a bad thing: 15 per cent
A very bad thing: 7 per cent
Pétain was:
A traitor using his prestige for collaboration with Germany: 8 per cent
An ambitious man who accepted defeat to come to power: 7 per cent
Sincerely acting in the interests of the nation but overwhelmed by events: 59 per cent
A hero who sacrificed himself for France and was unjustly condemned: 7 per cent[4]

Polls need to be treated sceptically. The questions are not always comparable; and the way they are framed inflects the answers. Even so, these polls show remarkable stability. Some 60 per cent of the population were consistently supportive of the armistice and the total number who completely condemn Pétain never surpassed 20 per cent. Between 50 and 60 per cent regularly believed Pétain had genuinely sought to defend French interests.

It is hard to reconcile these findings with the general consensus on the responsibility of Vichy for the fate of the Jews. Perhaps respondents distinguish in their mind between the Vichy regime and Pétain; perhaps the complex feelings that the French have had towards Pétain ever since 1945 coexist with their more recent condemnation of what was done to the Jews. Perhaps people believe that in general the armistice was the right choice while simultaneously deploring what happened to the Jews. It may be that memories of Pétain's role in the Great War still impact on his later reputation. When in 2018, in advance of the centenary celebrations of the Great War, a poll asked the French to name the personality most associated in their minds with the Great War, Pétain came top (60 per cent) just ahead of Clemenceau (59). Since the same poll showed very sketchy knowledge of the Great War – around 25 per cent believed that it had contained the battles of Waterloo and Marignano, which took place in 1815 and 1515 respectively – their fresher memories of the 'negative' Pétain of Vichy may have helped revive memories of the 'positive' Pétain of 1916–17, whereas the other French Marshals of that war have sunk into oblivion.[5] By a similar boomerang effect, the positive memory of 1914 may have softened the negative one of 1940.

Every important anniversary of the Great War presented the French government with a conundrum, none more so than the centenary in 2018. In November of that year, President Macron, master of political triangulation, announced that it was 'legitimate' to pay homage to Pétain, alongside the other seven Marshals, during the ceremonies on 10 November. Pétain had been a 'great soldier' in that conflict even if he had made 'fatal choices' in the next one. There was a flurry of simulated outrage, and Macron's idea was rapidly dropped.

Macron's *ballon d'essai* was only a two-day wonder, but his retreat did not signify that the Pétain 'case' was closed. It was given a new airing by the extreme right-wing journalist Éric Zemmour. He is from a *pied-noir* Jewish family that left Algeria in 1952, six years before Éric was born. Perhaps because his parents moved to France before the start of the Algerian War, he never inherited the anti-Gaullism of many *pied-noirs*, and claims to be a fervent admirer of de Gaulle. His obsession is the threat of Islam. Zemmour rose to prominence through his verbal dexterity and pugnaciousness on television chat shows.

The proliferation of independent continuous news channels all ferociously competing for audiences was tailor-made for someone whose oxygen was provocation. Zemmour gloried in his various condemnations for incitement to racial hatred which allowed him to pose as the victim of a politically correct establishment muzzling minority opinions. In reality, it was almost impossible to turn on a television without coming across Zemmour or people talking about him. From 2019 he had a daily show on the C-News channel, which was positioning itself to be France's Fox News: over 1 million viewers tuned in to be provoked or titillated by him. He said aloud what many listeners believed in private. Zemmour also had footholds in more mainstream outlets such as the conservative newspaper *Le Figaro*.

In his best-selling book *Le Suicide français*, published in 2011, Zemmour charted what he saw as France's descent into decadence since May 1968: the nefarious influences of feminism, gay activism, and globalization. This was familiar terrain, but he also threw in a short chapter criticizing the *mea-culpism* of Chirac and his successors. He argued that thanks to Vichy fewer Jews had perished in Occupied France than in other Western European countries: Pétain had resisted the imposition of the yellow star in the Occupied Zone, and in 1942 Vichy had bargained with Germany to save French Jews at the expense of foreign ones. He repeated the argument in another book a few years later where he resuscitated Rougier's claims to have brokered a Pétain–Churchill deal as evidence of Pétain's 'dissimulations, double, triple, quadruple games'.[6]

It is not clear what drove Zemmour to take up the defence of Vichy. Maybe he was seeking to ratchet up the level of provocation; maybe there was a more subtle motive. Exculpating Vichy of what was now widely perceived as its most important crime opened the way to a general rehabilitation of the regime's other policies. Zemmour himself had begun advocating extensive denaturalization of French Muslims, suppressing all financial aid to foreigners and as far as possible eradicating Islam from France. He even proposed that French Muslims be required to have approved 'French' names. This is a version of Vichy's Statut des Juifs applied to Muslims. On one occasion Zemmour noted that the instructions given to the French police on the eve of the 1942 *rafle* were the same as those given to the police today when expelling foreigners without identity papers – another way of relativizing what Vichy had done.[7] As Jean-Marie Le Pen, founder of the extreme right-wing Front National, remarked sardonically, Zemmour, as a Jew, could get away with comments that would have been unthinkable for others. Nor was Zemmour daunted by the fact that Vichy's abrogation of the Crémieux Decree of 1870, giving French citizenship to Jews in Algeria, had deprived his own parents of citizenship during the Occupation – just as Isorni's view of Vichy was not affected by the fact that, as the son of an immigrant, he would have been banned from the Bar by Vichy legislation had he not secured an exemption.

Whatever his motivation, Zemmour's neo-Pétainism threw the Pétain case into the limelight once again. Historians hesitated how to respond. If they refused to debate Zemmour, they risked allowing his ideas to circulate without refutation; if they agreed to do so, they risked being steamrollered by a polemicist more at ease with the format of television debates, cavalier with facts and impervious to nuance.[8]

WHAT IF . . .

Zemmour's resuscitation of the 'shield' argument revived a question that was asked in one of the first books on the trial after 1945 by a writer sympathetic to Pétain: 'We need to weigh up which side of the scales is heavier: the concessions that were made to the enemy or the concessions that were won from the enemy.'[9] Or as Jean Schlumberger wrote: 'We will endlessly argue over what the fate of France would have been with a Quisling instead of a Pétain.'[10]

As was argued during the trial, this reading of the Occupation in terms of a balance sheet ignored issues of morality and honour. The debate was prefigured in the 1920s in a spat between de Gaulle and Pétain about a phrase the former had drafted for the book they were writing on the history of the French Army. De Gaulle had written that the Revolution had made France's generals the victims of political upheavals, depriving them 'of prestige, often of life, sometimes of honour'. Pétain amended this to 'of prestige, sometimes of honour, often of life'. De Gaulle shot back: 'It is an ascending hierarchy: prestige, life, honour.' 'Honour' or 'life' – protecting an 'idea' of France or protecting (or claiming to protect) the French – that was the nub of the conflict between Pétain and de Gaulle in 1940.

Isorni argued at the trial that Pétain had sacrificed his honour to protect the French. But Pétain's honour also implicated the French. That is why the memory of the war has been so painful in France. In Holland, Belgium or Norway, day-to-day administration was carried out by local civil servants but they were working under the authority of the occupier. Collaborators certainly existed and were punished after the war but the population did not feel their nation had been implicated. The French situation was more comparable to that of Denmark, where the Germans allowed an independent government to exist until August 1943. But although the Danish government necessarily collaborated with the Germans in some areas, it left existing political structures intact rather than carrying out an internal political revolution. It also saved its tiny Jewish population, many of whom were evacuated to neutral Sweden.

Leaving aside arguments about honour, Pétain's defenders constructed a counterfactual argument that France's fate would have been worse without the choices Pétain had made; his accusers offered their own alternative version of history. Counterfactuals have never had a good reputation with professional historians.[11] Yet any history seeking to identify a 'cause' carries hidden counterfactuals. To argue that X was 'caused' by Y implicitly asks readers to imagine an alternative outcome if Y had not occurred. Those historians who accept some validity in counterfactual history propose the rule of 'minimal rewrite', the avoidance of 'exuberant' counterfactuals and the identification of plausible ones: 'We should consider as plausible or probable,' writes Nial Ferguson in *Virtual History*, 'only those alternatives which we can show on the basis of contemporary evidence that contemporaries actually considered.'[12]

The criterion of 'plausibility' is certainly met if we imagine how history might have been different if the French government had moved to North Africa in June 1940 rather than signing an armistice. That option was favoured by many in the French government – possibly a majority according to Louis Marin – and was rejected because

Weygand and Pétain insisted there was no realistic alternative to the armistice. Were they right?

This counterfactual challenge has been taken up by a group of historians imagining an alternative French history in 1940. It started in the form of two online forums involving professional and amateur historians.[13] Three participants then published a dense volume postulating, day by day, an alternative history of 1940 if France had fought on. This was followed by another volume covering the years 1941–42.[14] A third one promised for the period 1943–44 has not been published. That is probably a good thing. The further one moves from what counterfactualists call the Point of Departure (POD) – that moment when the narrative deviates from reality – alternative scenarios become ever more speculative. Restricted to the summer of 1940, however, the exercise is plausible.

The POD chosen by the authors of this exercise was 6 June 1940, the day Paul Reynaud reshuffled his government and brought in de Gaulle. In addition to this real historical event, a fictional one is also imagined: the death in a car crash of Reynaud's mistress Madame de Portes, whom so many eyewitnesses blamed for undermining his resolve. Killing off Madame de Portes at that moment – she did in reality die a month later when the armistice had been signed – is a neat device but not necessary. Since opinions about an armistice in Reynaud's government were so evenly divided, and since Reynaud was personally in the anti-armistice camp, it is eminently plausible to imagine that he might have decided to fight on without this melodramatic scenario.

Whatever its cause, Reynaud's new sense of purpose empowers the pro-armistice members of the government. The alternative scenario plays out:

> 10 June: Weygand is sacked and replaced by General Huntziger whose orders are to slow the German advance to win time for the transfer of soldiers and equipment to North Africa.
> 11 June: Pétain protests against Weygand's sacking. Arrested for defying the government, he suffers an apoplectic fit a few days later.
> 12 June–7 August: The French armies successfully slow down the German advance.

Not until 7 August do the Germans reach Port Vendres on France's south coast. In these weeks of fighting the French, with British naval support, evacuate about 800,000 men and a large part of the airforce to North Africa. The Third Republic lives on from Algeria and North Africa remains in French hands and relies on American supplies of material. Meanwhile France is fully occupied by the Germans.

The military aspects of this counterfactual scenario are convincing. Histories of the battle of France show that, after the initial disasters, the performance of French troops in June 1940 during the fighting on the Somme and Aisne rivers was impressive. All of that changed after Pétain's speech of 17 June announcing that he was seeking an armistice: what is the point of fighting if the war is about to end? If there had been a will to do so, France's military leaders could have established further lines of defence to slow the German advance. And since German supply lines were dangerously stretched, the French might have won precious weeks to cover the transfer of troops and material to North Africa.

How would the Germans have reacted to a French government in North Africa remaining in the war alongside the British? Three possibilities are floated in the counterfactual simulation:

1. The Germans decide to finish off France by landing in Tunisia with Italian naval support.
2. The Germans decide to pursue the French into North Africa by sending troops through Spain and attacking Gibraltar.
3. Hitler decides not to risk any operation in North Africa, and turns his attention to the Battle of Britain.[15]

This alternative history opts for the third scenario. An operation from Tunisia would have been risky since the Italian navy was massively outweighed by the combined British and French navies. As for an operation through Spain, the Germans had drafted a plan on these lines, code-named 'Operation Felix'. But it was contingent upon Spanish support. Given Spain's exhaustion after the Civil War, and given the prudence Franco showed towards Hitler when they met at Hendaye in October 1940, it seems reasonable to assume he would have been equally uncooperative back in June – probably more so since at this stage France was not crushed but still in the war. For Hitler to have contemplated moving through Spain without Franco's permission would have been logistically difficult. The alacrity with which Hitler offered the French armistice terms, and squashed Mussolini's desire for tougher ones, shows that he was aware of the risks of any operation through Spain. General Noguès, the head of the French forces there, certainly believed that North Africa could hold out after the fall of metropolitan France. He only abandoned the idea out of loyalty to Pétain.

This scenario undercuts the Pétainist argument that the armistice served the interests of the Allies by preventing North Africa from falling into German hands. That argument was first put at the trial by Weygand. Over the years more extravagant Vichy apologists started to elevate the fact that North Africa had been kept out of German hands as no less important to Allied victory than the Battle of Stalingrad. There was much bad faith in this argument. Even if it turned out beneficial to the Allies in November 1942 that the Germans were not in Morocco and Algeria, this was an entirely unintentional – and unintended – outcome. In 1940, Vichy's leaders had assumed that Britain would soon be out of the war. When the Americans did attack North Africa in November 1942, Vichy's immediate response was to fire upon them. Pétainist apologists for decades clung to the idea that Vichy's true position was revealed by the famous 'secret telegrams' seemingly approving Darlan's defection. Once their existence was established, a close reading of the context demonstrates that the telegram did not mean what Admiral Auphan and others claimed – or possibly even came to believe – it meant. The telegram is a reply to one from General Noguès explaining that he and Darlan were in contact with the Americans in order to sideline the American candidate Giraud, who wanted to join the Allied war effort. In other words, the telegram was approving Darlan's desperate attempt to preserve Vichy's neutrality; it was not approving a return to war on the side of the Allies.[16]

A VICHY SHIELD?

In this alternative history where the French government moves to North Africa, what happens in France? An argument frequently repeated at the trial was that the alternative to the armistice was a France run by a 'Gauleiter' and subjected to 'Polandization'. In truth no occupied country in Western Europe was treated as harshly as Poland nor subjected to a Gauleiter. The Germans established various occupation regimes in Western Europe, but nowhere was there a Gauleiter (except Alsace with a view to its ultimate incorporation into Germany): Belgium was run directly by the German military, Holland by a civil administrator (Seyss-Inquart), Norway by a rump government (Quisling). We can only speculate what solution the Germans might have adopted in France if there had been no armistice. The only certainty is that Hitler was keen for the French to assume as much of the burden of administration as possible.

In the alternative scenario imagined above, Pétain dies a few days after his stroke; France is fully occupied by the Germans, who set up a collaborationist government headed by Laval. This would have been, as it were, a kind of French Quisling-style government lacking the moral or legal authority enjoyed by the Vichy regime. But killing off Pétain seems an easy way out. Being in remarkably good physical health, it is likely that, after the departure of the legal Reynaud government to North Africa, he would have remained on French soil and been ready to form some kind of government. Any government headed by someone of Pétain's stature, offering his protective 'body' to the French while the cowardly politicians had 'deserted', would have had more moral authority than one headed by Laval. It would not have been a 'legal' government like the Vichy regime, but Pétain's name alone would have compensated for a lot. That was Reynaud's argument at the trial: nothing he could do would have counted in the face of Pétain's opposition. Blum, on the other hand, argued in his testimony that preventing him and others from going to North Africa 'had played a decisive role in the history of the armistice'. And the lengths to which the pro-armistice faction resorted to prevent members of Pétain's government leaving France suggests that such a departure was considered a serious threat. One politician who strongly supported the armistice wrote later: 'If Marshal Pétain had remained on the quayside watching the ship take away the *emigrés* he would certainly have been surrounded with the greatest respect . . . but in his solitude he would not have been able to represent, in fact and law, the government of France.'[17]

Perhaps, then, a dissident Pétain 'government' would have enjoyed a level of acceptance and legitimacy somewhere between the Quisling government of Norway and the Vichy government that did end up governing France. How would this have changed the experience of the French people? Did the Vichy government – a technically legal government headed by a revered figure – protect the French from a worse fate?

At the time of the trial this argument was usually constructed by asking whether the proportion of French citizens conscripted to work in German factories or deported for resistance activities was higher or lower in France than in Belgium and Holland. Meaningful comparisons are difficult to make but even if the French proportion was lower, the difference was not significant enough to outweigh the humiliation represented by the Vichy regime. The sheer size of France means that no other country in Western Europe had contributed more to the German war economy than France. Today, however, the burden of the argument about Vichy as a 'shield' has shifted to the fate of the Jews.

The idea that Vichy had been a shield for the Jews is superficially supported by the incontrovertible fact that the total percentage of Jews deported to their deaths from France was significantly lower than that of other Occupied countries in Western Europe: 25 per cent in France, 50 per cent in Belgium and Norway, 73 per cent in the Netherlands.[18] For at least two decades after the Liberation most historians agreed that Vichy's existence helped explain the lower proportion of Jewish deaths in France. More recently, however, historians have preferred to invoke the role of the French people.[19] There were indeed innumerable cases where Jews were protected and rescued by individuals, by communities (especially Protestant ones), and by underground support networks. But such examples existed in every country, and it is difficult to prove that it was a determining variable in the French case. One reason people talked of a French 'paradox' is that Holland, where a higher proportion of Jews perished, was a country with a less intense anti-semitic tradition than France and where opposition to anti-semitic measures during the Occupation emerged sooner than in France. Solidarity was not lacking in Holland but it was not enough to save most Jews. Perhaps a more important variable was that France's geography (the size of the country, the numerous mountains and hills, the borders with Switzerland and Spain) made it easier for Jews to hide and allowed rescue networks to operate more effectively than elsewhere. In the light of these favourable conditions, one could invert the framing of the French 'paradox': not why so *many* Jews survived but why so *few* survived.

Other historians suggest that the rates of survival were explained by different German priorities and resources in each occupied country. Because Holland was run by a zealous Nazi civilian, the SS took control of the deportation policy from the start whereas in Belgium, run by the military, the SS only took over from May 1942. This might help explain why although Holland displayed the greatest civil opposition to measures against the Jews, it had the lowest Jewish survival rate. A pause in the rate of deportations from France occurred in the spring of 1943 because the camp of Auschwitz-Birkenau was working at full capacity to murder the Jews of Salonika. Another factor that may have weighed in the higher French rate of survival was that Liberation in France came in August 1944, while in Belgium and Holland the Occupation lasted a few weeks longer. Every day counted.[20]

In short, many factors explain different outcomes in different countries. But what difference did Vichy make? At the trial, two arguments were produced by the defence: first, Vichy's refusal in May 1942 to impose the yellow star in the Unoccupied Zone; second, Vichy's refusal in August 1943 to denaturalize all Jews who had been naturalized since 1927.[21] Regarding the rejection of the star, Vichy's true motivation was more concern about public opinion than solicitude for the Jews. Instead in December 1942 the government required the identity papers of all Jews, both French and foreign, to be stamped with the word 'Jew'. This was arguably more fateful to the Jewish population than the imposition of the star.

As for Vichy's rejection of a blanket denaturalization of Jews in 1943, the story was more complicated than the uplifting narrative of Pétain's defenders. On 11 June 1943, under German pressure, the French government had prepared a decree denaturalizing all Jews who had become citizens since 1927. But Heinz Röthke, the Gestapo officer in charge of Jewish matters in France, delayed publication until he had received a simultaneous assurance that it would be followed immediately by a massive new round-up of foreign Jews before the end of the month by the French police. The French police remained essential because the Gestapo headquarters in Berlin had just warned their representatives in Paris that they could not provide any more manpower. While negotiations were proceeding between Bousquet and his German counterparts, it was becoming increasingly evident that the tide of the war had turned. Allied troops landed in Sicily on 10 July; Bousquet had started to form those links with resistance leaders who would provide an alibi in his *épuration* trial. Against this background, Bousquet and Laval had second thoughts. On 24 August, Pétain informed the Germans that the government opposed blanket denaturalizations.[22]

Thwarted in their plan, the Germans no longer discriminated between French and non-French citizens when arresting Jews. Previously, French citizenship had provided a degree of protection. Of the approximately 75,700 Jews deported from France, 24,000 (32 per cent) were French and 51,700 foreign (68 per cent).[23] The difference can partly be explained by the fact that the integrated French Jews enjoyed more effective support networks among the French population. But the striking difference in survival rates led defenders of Vichy to draw a second conclusion: that Vichy had protected French Jews at the cost of sacrificing foreign ones. This argument was not put explicitly at the Pétain trial, but it was used by Laval at his trial and then repeated endlessly over the years by others. Since all these victims, French or non-French, were human beings, there is something morally grotesque about the argument. But since the argument forms the nub of Zemmour's defence of Vichy, it needs to be examined as a piece of unfinished business from the Pétain trial.

It was at the Wannsee Conference of January 1942 that Germany fixed the details of the so-called Final Solution. In June 1942 the head of the German police in France, Karl Oberg, demanded the arrest of a first batch of 40,000 Jews over the summer. The negotiations, conducted on the French side by Bousquet, resulted in an agreement on 2 July that French police would conduct the arrests but that only foreign Jews would be targeted. To make up the numbers it was agreed that arrests would occur in the Unoccupied Zone, a suggestion that Bousquet had made early in the negotiations. The enormity of this proposal, which initially surprised the Germans, should not be underestimated: the French government was voluntarily proposing to arrest Jews in that part of France supposedly independent and out of German reach.

The Vichy regime would never itself have initiated a policy to murder Jews. Vichy's anti-semitism was exclusionary not exterminatory, starting in October 1940 with the Statut des Juifs excluding French Jews from participation in many social and professional activities, making them at a stroke second-class citizens. The logic driving Vichy's cooperation in the *rafle* of 1942 was collaboration rather than anti-semitism. In 1942 the Germans, dissatisfied that the French police were not acting vigorously against the Resistance, were threatening to take full power over policing. The Oberg–Bousquet agreement offered a way for the French to retain authority over their police, keep collaboration alive, and preserve a key area of French sovereignty. Thus one could argue that, rather than using the sovereignty it enjoyed to save French Jews, Vichy sacrificed foreign Jews to preserve a sovereignty that was under threat. For a regime already prey to structural and embedded anti-semitic prejudices such a bargain caused fewer moral dilemmas than it might otherwise have done. In that sense there is no watertight boundary between Vichy's exclusionary policy and Germany's exterminatory one. Nowhere do the reported conversations of Vichy leaders at this time express any private expressions of regret at what was happening to the Jews. Indeed ridding the country of foreign Jews, many of them former refugees from Germany, was viewed less as a sacrifice to be endured than an opportunity to be seized. At the meeting of the French government where the Oberg–Bousquet agreement was ratified on 3 July, Laval referred to these Jews as 'garbage waste [*déchets*] sent by the Germans'. It was in the same spirit that Laval asked the Germans if children under sixteen could be included in the first deportation convoys – not because he worried about breaking up families but because he did not want the troublesome burden of caring for children with no family.[24]

What if Vichy had not agreed to this devilish bargain? The Germans would presumably have gone ahead and carried out arrests in the Occupied Zone alone. Since they lacked the manpower to perform the operation themselves, they would have ordered the French police to cooperate – as they did with the police in Holland and Belgium. But it is unlikely that the police would have acted as zealously under German orders as under French ones. Already, with the supposedly full cooperation of the French authorities, the numbers arrested on 16 July in Paris were a third below the target. Negotiating with the Germans over the arrests of Jews in the summer of 1942, Vichy, which was a nominally independent government, had agency: it could have said 'no', as it did in the summer of 1943. In 1942, before the occupation of the whole of France and the loss of North Africa, Vichy's position – the possibility of saying 'no' – was stronger than it was a year later. The change in policy between 1942 and 1943 was dictated less by moral scruple than because the arrests of 1942 had outraged public opinion – and because the tide of the war seemed to be turning. The lack of French cooperation made a big difference. In 1943 the total numbers arrested, at 23,000, were less than they had been just in the two summer months of 1942, when the French had been fully cooperative.

This raises a final counterfactual. If there had been no armistice and no Vichy regime, if France had been fully occupied, the Germans *might* have made different decisions about policing; they *might* have deployed more resources to the policing of France – although one must remember that from 1942 onwards they were suffering manpower shortages. In such circumstances it is *possible* that the fate of the Jews *might* overall have been even worse than if Vichy had not existed. We will never know. But the fact is that Vichy *did* exist; that its existence *did* allow the French a degree of independence, autonomy and agency; and that one of the regime's alleged *raisons d'être* was to use that autonomy to protect the population. But only belatedly in 1943 did it try to exert this autonomy on behalf of the Jews. Vichy therefore was guilty not only for what it did choose to do but for what it chose not to do for the Jews. According to the most unfavourable interpretation, Vichy aided the German arrests in 1942 because it saw an opportunity to rid France of foreign Jews who were widely seen as an encumbrance. According to a slightly less unfavourable interpretation, it aided the Germans because, for a regime saturated with anti-semitic prejudices, saving Jews was less of a priority than maintaining the illusion of sovereignty through the policy of collaboration. That was Vichy's crime.

And Pétain's? His trial had constantly come up against what Blum called the 'Pétain mystery'. Pastor Boegner testified that Pétain had always expressed sympathy with the plight of the Jews; the court heard that Pétain used to call Darquier de Pellepoix the 'torturer'; the unassuming Jean-Marie Roussel, who had chaired the Denaturalization Commission set up by Vichy in July 1940, testified to Pétain's support for a 'humane' policy on denaturalization. It was only after 1945 that evidence emerged to challenge this picture. Published in 1948, the diaries of Paul Baudouin, Vichy's Foreign Minister before Montoire, recorded how, in a key meeting on the Statut des Juifs in October 1940, Pétain had intervened to make the text harsher. Baudouin's diaries were doctored in different ways but this point was substantiated in 2010 by Serge Klarsfeld, who discovered a draft of the Statute with an annotation in Pétain's own hand to propose that magistrates and teachers should be added to the professions from which Jews were excluded.[25] Pétain was not directly involved in the negotiations leading up to the arrests of July 1942, but when the Oberg–Bousquet deal came up for government approval on 2 July – the meeting where Laval expressed his satisfaction at getting rid of *déchets* – Pétain spoke up to say that the distinction being made between foreign and French Jews was 'fair and would be understood by opinion'. Two weeks later the arrests began.

Epilogue: On the Pétain Trail

The crime of Vichy's complicity in the round-up of Jews is now commemorated in gold lettering on black plaques which have gone up, since 1995, on the facades of school buildings all over France. These plaques invoke the memory of Jewish children deported as 'innocent victims of Nazi barbarism and of the government of Vichy'. The tiny handful of streets still bearing Pétain's name were renamed. The last was in Belrain, a village of fifty inhabitants not far from Verdun. In March 2013 the municipal council voted to remove its Rue Maréchal Pétain. To find any Pétain streets today it is necessary to travel abroad. There is one in Singapore, another in the old French concession of Shanghai, and another in Quebec. In the United States, there were twelve at the last count, including a Pétain road in Dallas, Texas, and another in Milltown, New Jersey. A proposal to rename the latter was rejected by the city council in 2020. But Mount Pétain on the border between Alberta and British Colombia in Canada was renamed in 2022.[1]

Occasional rearguard actions were mounted against the 'de-Pétainization' of France's landscape. In 2020 a visitor to the *mairie* of a village in Normandy noticed that it contained portraits of every French Head of State since 1871. Between Presidents Lebrun (1932–40) and Auriol (1947–54) hung the portrait of Pétain. The mayor refused to remove it on the grounds that its presence had no political significance and that the village remained 'attached to its past'. He was forced by the courts to backtrack because 'the symbolic importance' of the Pétain portrait infringed the 'principle of neutrality' of public administration.[2]

Thus Pétain has progressively disappeared from the physical landscape of France. What remains? Is there any possible 'Pétain trail' for interested tourists or devotees? In Italy, visitors to the village of Predappio can visit the house where Mussolini was born and the crypt where he is buried. Tourist shops in Predappio trade in tacky fascist memorabilia – posters, key rings, fridge magnets. In October 2021 it was possible to book an eight-day Mussolini history holiday, taking in sites all over Italy, guided by an 'expert historian' and including also a 'special guest appearance by the Duce's youngest granddaughter, Rachele Mussolini'.[3] This is the phenomenon known as 'Dark tourism' motivated by a variety of impulses ranging from historical curiosity to ghoulishness, from pedagogy to nostalgia.[4]

There has always been a sensitivity in France to the cult of Pétain propagated by his devotees. When, in 1976, an auction was organized in Versailles of objects once belonging to Pétain, a local Communist politician lobbied to ban this sale of 'relics of the old traitor' and the auction was disrupted by protests from resistance associations. The auctioneer defended himself by saying that he would have been equally ready to sell Stalin's cap. In the end the sale went ahead. A Pétain walking stick was sold for 1,000 francs and the *képi* he wore in 1919 at the parade down the Champs-Élysées for 7,000 francs.[5] These were probably bought by the ADMP, which piously collects Pétain memorabilia.

Where might a Pétain tourist trail take us? One possibility might be Montoire, though trains no longer stop there. In 2003 the little station was turned into a museum. Although the tourist office website mentions the museum, it gives more prominence to other local sites such as the many local châteaux. After the war a plaque was placed in the station commemorating not the October 1940 meeting but the arrival of American troops in August 1944 – as if to exorcize what had happened four years earlier. The decision to create a museum caused some local opposition, and the evasive name 'Museum of Meetings' (Musée des Rencontres) suggests a degree of embarrassment. In 2017, after a makeover, the museum extended its remit to cover the history of the Occupation in general. But it is always closed on 22 and 24 October – the anniversary of Hitler's two 1940 meetings – to discourage visits from possible Pétainist sympathizers. In fact, these were unlikely since Pétainists tend not to be comfortable with the memory of Montoire.

As for the city of Vichy itself, it has long struggled to exorcize the memory of those four years.[6] During the war an Escoffier cookbook republished in New York changed the name of Vichyssoise soup. To move on from this kind of erasure at the Liberation, Vichy's municipal council proclaimed: 'Vichy is not the seat of a traitorous government but the Queen of spas.' Tourist guides glossed over the city's troubled past. The first Michelin guide produced immediately after the war ignored it entirely; a 1994 guide was matter of fact: 'Recently Vichy gave its name to the government of the French State, the regime led by Marshal Pétain which ruled the country under close German supervision from 12 July 1940 until 20 August 1944.'

The citizens of Vichy have long seen themselves as victims. The city's mayors campaigned for years to forbid the use of the term 'Vichy government' or 'Vichy regime' in official documents and to secure visits to the city from the President of the Republic. De Gaulle visited the city in April 1959 during one of his tours of the French regions. Commenting on his 'emotion' at finding himself in Vichy, he declared 'we are the one and single people of France. And it is at Vichy that I say it!'[7] This typically gnomic comment was perceived as a gesture of absolution, but de Gaulle's successors avoided this delicate exercise.

There is little reference to the events of the Occupation on the streets of Vichy. Two exceptions are a plaque in memory of the Jews and another in the Opéra building. The plaque to the Jews was a personal initiative of Serge Klarsfeld. It was first placed in the Hotel du Parc, where Pétain lived for four years, but after complaints from residents it was moved across the street. The other is discreetly placed in the foyer of the Opéra, whose doors are closed during the day. This was the building where in 1940 parliament voted full powers to Pétain but the plaque commemorates the eighty parliamentarians who voted 'no' – and thus 'affirmed their attachment to the Republic and their love of liberty'. It fails to tell us that most of those present voted yes, 'spinning', as one commentator has written, 'a moment of national shame into a celebration of resistance'.[8]

The Hotel du Parc did not re-open after the war and in 1956 it was turned into private residences. There is currently no museum in Vichy. In 1987 the tourist office did start organizing tours of 'Sites of the Vichy regime'. The only objection came from the Hotel de Portugal which was concerned that its clients might not want to know that the premises had once served as the headquarters of the Gestapo. The tours still run today. There is a project for a museum to open in 2026, but the local mantra is that this will cover '2,000 years' not just four.

In 1970 the ADMP bought Pétain's former apartments in the Hotel du Parc and set about reconstituting them as they were during the Occupation. Visits are only possible for select groups. The ADMP has never sought to make Vichy the centre of a Pétainist cult. They make more of Pétain's birthplace, a farm in Cauchy-à-la-Tour which it purchased and turned into a small museum. Here, on the anniversary of Pétain's birth, the ADMP organizes every year a small event for the faithful. Anyone wishing to visit at other times needs an authorization.

The main centre of the Pétainist cult has always been the Île d'Yeu, because of its association with Pétain's 'martyrdom'. Here are the *lieux de mémoire* of Pétainism: the prison where he was incarcerated, the house where he died, the cemetery where he is buried, the room where the Maréchale stayed on her visits to her husband.

The anniversary of Pétain's death has always been a high spot of the commemorative calendar, but even in the 1970s and 1980s, with luminaries like Isorni and Borotra attending, the numbers were small because the island was so inaccessible. Pétain continued to be celebrated by Jean-Marie Le Pen's Front National, but since his daughter Marine's efforts to 'detoxify' the party and brand it as the Rassemblement National, party luminaries prefer to pay homage to de Gaulle's grave at Colombey in the Haute-Marne *département* of north-eastern France. In June 2020, Marine Le Pen visited not the Île d'Yeu but another west coast island, the Île de Sein, whose entire population of fishermen had joined de Gaulle in 1940.

What about July 2021, the seventieth anniversary of Pétain's death? On this first Covid-free summer since the outbreak of the pandemic, the Île d'Yeu is crowded with holidaymakers. Numerous ferries now run between Port Joinville and the mainland. The sunshine is glorious and the beaches are packed. The former fishermen's cottages, all painted white and now rented by tourists, are evocative of a Greek island. The local newspaper carries no mention of the forthcoming anniversary. On the road leading inland from Joinville stands a house which carries a plaque: 'Here died Marshal Pétain on 21 July 1951'. This is the Villa Luco, accredited as a military hospital when Pétain was too ill to remain in prison. When the owner of the house originally put up the plaque in 1955, the government ordered it to be taken down. The affair caused a mini-controversy, now long forgotten. Today tourists pass by without even noticing the plaque.

The cemetery is only fifteen minutes by foot from Port Joinville. Pétain's grave stands apart from all the others, in front of the north wall surrounded by yew trees. The inscription reads simply: 'Philippe Pétain, Marshal of France'. On the wall a few feet away are plaques to the many fishermen who lost their lives at sea. These memorials are more embedded in the island's long history than the awkward presence of Philippe Pétain.

Every year around the anniversary of his death, the local authorities are nervous. Often the grave is defaced. But any police presence this year is so discreet as to be invisible. Certainly no one seems to think there is anything suspicious about the Englishman lurking in the cemetery for much of the week. In the days leading up to the anniversary, on Friday 23 July, a few holidaymakers heading to the beach trickle through the cemetery to look at the grave. They are there out of idle curiosity. Most remain only a few minutes; some take selfies – 'that is not done', one girl says to her friend. A few of the visitors speculate as to why Pétain's grave is turned in the opposite direction from all the others. Was it because he was condemned to *indignité nationale*? Was it because he had requested to face France?

The 'museum' in Port Joinville stands just opposite the street from the Hotel des Voyageurs. It was originally the hotel annex where Pétain's wife lodged during her visits. In pseudo-medieval script the tiny building grandly proclaims itself the 'Musée Historial de l'Île d'Yeu'. No one reading this would have any idea what was inside, and tourists passing by seem oblivious to it. The receptionist at the nearby tourist office seems surprised that anyone should be interested in visiting the 'museum'. She says that the old lady who runs it keeps no regular hours; that no one has seen her for weeks; and that there is no telephone number. The old lady is the daughter of the Nolleau couple who once ran the hotel and turned the annex into a shrine.

What about the fort of Pierre Levée, where Pétain was imprisoned?

For many decades the fort, although no longer in use, was closed to the public and it served for a time as a holiday camp for the children of army personnel. Since 1985 it has been open to the public. Cultural events are organized in its courtyard, including for several years an annual sardine and tuna festival. There is no opportunity to visit Pétain's cell – this is not Elba or St Helena – and only one of the many explanatory panels in the fort informs visitors that Pétain was incarcerated here. These panels offer more information about the forgotten history of enemy aliens interned in the fort during the Great War.

On Friday 23 July, the day of the anniversary, the cemetery seems no busier apart from the presence of two journalists lurking in the hope of a story.[9] Around midday an old couple arrive. He wears a blazer emblazoned with medals; she is carrying a huge bunch of gladioli. They seem to be carrying some fishing tackle. Are they planning to combine piety with recreation. The mystery is soon explained: the fishing rod is actually a flagpole, whose cover the gentleman unzips before unfurling his flag. This turns out to be Lieutenant Louis de Condé, a member of the ADMP. He and his wife have come over for the day from Vichy because they could not be here on Sunday, when the ADMP delegation will be visiting. They live in Vichy, where he runs a bookshop; and he also has the keys to the Pétain apartment owned by the ADMP. They seem like an old couple putting flowers on the grave of a deceased relative. In fact, Louis de Condé has a long career of militancy behind him. He is the last survivor of the 1962 assassination attempt on de Gaulle for which he was sentenced *in absentia* to life imprisonment. He was tracked down and spent three years in prison before being released in 1968. Later he stood three times as a candidate of the Front National, most recently in 2014. After the couple have paid their respects and set off on the long journey home, the cemetery is deserted again. One of the journalists hears that the museum has opened; there is not a moment to lose before it closes again.

The Musée Historial de l'Île d'Yeu must be the smallest 'museum' in France. Once the 5-euro ticket has been purchased, Madame Nolleau turns on the soundtrack, which provides an uplifting commentary. On the staircase leading to the exhibition are niches with models of 'Prehistoric Yeu', 'Merovingian Yeu', 'Norman Yeu', and so on, to

sustain the fiction that we are in a real museum. Then, after a waxwork of Pétain in his prison cell, one enters 'the chambre de souvenir',
a minute space crammed with Pétainist memorabilia. The highlight is
the suit in which Pétain died, laid out on a bed, and surrounded by
Vichy insignia. Every inch of the walls is covered with posters, photographs, banners, flags, letters. Other exhibits include a cape offered to
Pétain by shepherds from the Pyrenees; a bundle of wheat offered by
some peasants; the wooden crate sent by Franco with oranges when
he heard that Pétain was no longer eating. This is a shrine, not a
museum.

It is impossible to know what other visitors might make of this,
since there are none – apart from the two journalists. Perhaps it would
not be so different from what a *Le Monde* journalist observed in 1971
on the twentieth anniversary: 'Some move round indifferently as in
any museum; the children impatient; some are indignant; a father
pulls his son by the hand: "Don't look; that is a past that is best forgotten." Another, evidently moved, takes a handkerchief from his
pocket and dabs his eyes.'[10]

There is a visitors' book. Apparently there had already been
300,000 signatures by 1971, but only the last five years are visible. All
the entries are from the months of July and August. Most have been
penned by the faithful:

> Let Honour and Faith govern our Nation again. Let the National Revol-
> ution return. Thank you, Marshal, for your sacrifice!

> Glory to the Marshal! What sadness to see what France is today! This
> great Frenchman would be so sad!

> As every year, we renew our oath to accompany the Marshal to
> Douaumont.

A few are more neutral:

> Very instructive museum.

> Bravo for this marvellous museum which has allowed us to relive the
> history of the Island for a few minutes.

One is mysterious:

I'm Japanese. I'm Pétainist. Japan loves Pétain.

A few are downright hostile:

> Fine illustration of a sad page of French history. Liberty, Equality, Fraternity.

> Very moving museum. I will come back. Signed: François Mitterrand.

A few black-and-white postcards are on sale, but it is not possible to procure a copy of the catalogue of the museum; there are only two left and Madame Nolleau says that she does not expect ever to have it reprinted.

Back at the cemetery, the grave now has two more bouquets from the two organizations that will be visiting over the next two days.

There is now a trickle of visitors. A middle-aged man in holiday attire arrives. He stands with his head bowed for fifteen minutes in silent contemplation, crosses himself, and leaves. He is followed a few minutes later by another man, in his mid-forties, sporting a white T-shirt emblazoned with the words (in English): 'Cool to be white'.

30. A mourner at Pétain's grave, 23 July 2021.

He takes it off and slips on another proclaiming 'France for the French'. Having stood with his head bowed, he steps aways and puts the first T-shirt back on.

The next day, Saturday 24 July, it is the turn of Jeune Nation. First founded in 1949, this is the oldest existing movement of the French extreme right. The members arrive coming directly from their summer training camp in the west of France for a one-day 'March of Rehabilitation'. Their website, proclaiming Vichy as 'the only authentically counter-revolutionary experiment in France since 1789', announces a full programme: two masses, a stop at the Villa Luco, homage at the tomb, a picnic, a visit to the fort and a tour of the Museum.

Since the timings of their itinerary are vague, it proves impossible to find them until their visit to the grave has taken place. But they can be spotted later walking to the museum. There are about fifteen of them, a priest bringing up the rear. They do not look that 'young'; and those who do are not people with whom one would want to argue. A few of them post stickers protesting against Covid vaccination on lamp posts and the façade of the church.

The next day, Sunday 25 July, a delegation from the ADMP arrives on the morning ferry. Meeting point: the Hotel des Voyageurs. There

31. The right-wing organization Jeune Nation calls on its followers to remember Pétain in 2021.

are only eight of them. They include two old ladies walking with difficulty and one young man of slightly military appearance. First stop is the Villa Luco where their leader reads out a short speech. Then to the tomb, which takes a long time as the two ladies walk slowly. They unfurl their flags. The ceremony consists of an uncontroversial lecture on Pétain's interwar career. In conversation, the leader admits that they are a tiny and diminishing band. Later they can be seen tucking into seafood in the port before taking the ferry home. A pleasant day's outing for the last worshippers of what would seem to be a moribund cult.

And yet . . .

On 30 November 2021, four months after this hardly noticed anniversary and following weeks of false suspense, Eric Zemmour announced that he was standing as a candidate in the presidential election. The 'polemicist' had entered politics. This did not lead him to tone down his provocations. Quite the contrary. In one television appearance he made the extraordinary comment that Alfred Dreyfus's innocence could never be established with certainty.[11] Zemmour also continued to defend his line about Pétain and the Jews. It became even clearer than before that this was more than just a provocation: it was a key part of his strategy to build a new union of the right by overcoming the historic chasm which the memory of Vichy had created between the Gaullist right – Zemmour presented himself as a Gaullist – and the extreme right represented by the Front National. Gaullists like Jacques Chirac had traditionally refused to form electoral alliances with the Front National. Zemmour denounced Chirac's speech of 16 July 1995, saying, 'People are trying to make the French people permanently guilty so that they submit to the immigration invasion and to islamization.'[12]

Zemmour's candidacy aroused much initial excitement, perhaps because the public thirsted for novelty and did not want just a replay of the 2017 presidential run-off between Marine Le Pen and Emmanuel Macron. He called his new party *Reconquête!* – a not very subliminal reference to the Spanish *Reconquista*. His meetings generated genuine excitement among some young voters. A number of personalities defected to him from both the Gaullist right and the extreme right, seeming to indicate that he was having some success in breaching that historic divide. In the last days of his campaign, he also secured the support of Marine Le Pen's niece Marion. Having dropped the Le Pen suffix from her name, Marion Maréchal as she now calls herself had emerged as a rising star of the extreme right before quarrelling with her aunt, whom she viewed as too moderate.

For some weeks, opinion polls showed Zemmour taking large numbers of votes from Marine Le Pen. At moments there was even fevered speculation that he might be one of the two candidates to qualify for the second round of the elections along with Emmanuel Macron. In December 2021, Macron accompanied by Serge Klarsfeld visited Vichy, the first president to do so since de Gaulle. He marked a minute's silence in front of the memorial to Jews. Macron said, 'Vichy transports us back into history . . . I think we are better off respecting, studying history and allowing historians to build a historiographic truth based on evidence and documents, and let's avoid manipulating it, agitating it, revising it.' This was clearly a sign that Macron was taking Zemmour's candidature seriously – even if it would have been easier for the president to beat Zemmour in the second round than anyone else.

In the end, the Zemmour balloon burst. In the first round of the election, on 10 April 2022, he came fourth in the ballot, with only 7.7 per cent of the vote, far below both Marine Le Pen, who came second (23.1 per cent), and the third-ranked leftist candidate, Jean-Luc Mélenchon (21.9 per cent). The top-ranked candidate was Macron with 28 per cent. Marine Le Pen had held her nerve and her electors had mostly resisted the temptation of switching to Zemmour. Her policies on Europe, immigration and Islam – she proposed banning muslim women from wearing the headscarf (*foulard*) in the street – were only slightly less radical than Zemmour's, but she gave them less prominence than she did to a raft of populist social policies to deal with the cost of living. The moral would seem to be that Marine Le Pen's policy of detoxifying her 'brand' was a more successful way to win support for ideas that would once have been considered beyond the pale of normal politics than Zemmour's unapologetic embrace of the historical themes of the extreme right. Marine Le Pen had partially succeeded in detoxifying herself; Zemmour had entirely failed to detoxify Vichy. The

moral here would appear to be that while the extreme right is flourish-
ing in France – in the second round of the election Marine Le Pen
secured the historically high vote of 41.5 per cent to Macron's 58.4 per
cent – its future does not lie in invoking the memory of Pétain. The
Pétain case is closed.

Notes

INTRODUCTION: THE FATEFUL HANDSHAKE

1. Michael S. Neiberg, *When France Fell: The Vichy Crisis and the Fate of the Anglo-American Alliance* (Cambridge, MA, and London: Harvard University Press, 2021), 36

2. Henri Du Moulin de Labarthète, *Le Temps des illusions, juillet 1940–avril 1942* (Geneva: Enseigne du Cheval Ailé, 1946), 43–58; Renaud Meltz, *Pierre Laval. Un Mystère français* (Paris: Perrin, 2018), 740–41.

3. The story behind the film and photograph is actually a bit more complicated. There was a German film that did not actually show the handshake; and a German photograph that did. At the Liberation resisters produced a small documentary which added a handshake. This piece of montage did, however, show an event that had genuinely occurred!

4. Jacques Isorni, *Souffrance et mort du Maréchal* (Paris: Flammarion, 1951), 196 (22 April 1947).

5. AN 72AJ/3229, Isorni to Louis-Dominique Girard, 18 February 1948: 'Mais il me tendait la main; je ne pouvais tout de même pas cracher dedans! D'autant plus que j'étais venu lui demander le retour de nos prisonniers.'

6. Philippe Pétain, *Discours aux Français 17 juin 1940–20 août 1944* (Paris: Albin Michel, 1989), 94–6.

7. De Gaulle, *Discours et messages. I. Pendant la guerre* (Paris: Plon, 1970), 16 (13 July 1940).

8. Louis Noguères, *La Haute Cour de la Libération* (Paris: Minuit, 1965), 39.

9. For other countries, see Lise Quirion, 'La Presse québécoise d'expression française face au procès du Maréchal Pétain, 1945', *Bulletin d'histoire*

politique 7/2 (1999); F. A. Abadie-Maumert, 'La Presse norvégienne et suédoise et le procès du Maréchal Pétain', *Revue d'histoire de la deuxième Guerre mondiale* 101 (1976), 87–106.

10. *Combat*, 25 April 1945.

11. John Laughland, *A History of Political Trials: From Charles I to Saddam Hussein* (Oxford: Peter Lang, 2008); Kevin Heller and Jerry Simpson (eds), *The Hidden Histories of War Crimes Trials* (Oxford: Oxford University Press, 2013).

12. Henry Rousso, 'Juger le passé: le procès Eichmann' in *Face au passé: Essais sur la mémoire contemporaine* (Paris: Belin, 2016), 197–227, observes that all such trials are to differing degrees *'répressif'*, *'transitionnel'*, *'réconciliateur'*, *'mémorielle et historique'*.

13. Peter Novick, *The Resistance versus Vichy: The Purge of Collaborators in Liberated France* (New York: Chatto and Windus, 1968), 173.

14. Charles de Gaulle, *Mémoires* (Paris: Gallimard, 2000), 6.

15. The first was Paul Louis Michel, *Le Procès Pétain* (Paris: Éditions Médicis, 1945) (Michel was the pseudonym of a lawyer, Delzons, an old friend of the Pétain family); the second was *Les Silences du Maréchal* (Paris: Éditions nouvelles, 1948) by an anonymous author who is said to have been Donat-Guigne, one of the three judges in the trial. Other accounts of the trial are: Jules Roy, *Le Grand Naufrage* (Paris: Julliard, 1966), Frédéric Pottecher, *Le Procès Pétain. Croquis d'audience par André Galland* (Paris: J. C. Lattés, 1980), Fred Kupferman, *Les Procès de Vichy: Pucheu, Pétain, Laval* (Brussels: Complexe, 1980), and Jean-Marc Varaut, *Le Procès Pétain 1945–1995* (Paris: Perrin, 1997).

16. Louis Noguères, *Le Véritable Procès du Maréchal Pétain* (Paris: Fayard, 1955).

17. De Gaulle, *Mémoires*, 834–5.

18. Raymond Aron, *De l'Armistice à l'insurrection nationale* (Paris: Gallimard, 1945), 355–69.

19. Raymond Aron, 'Après l'événement, avant l'histoire', *Les Temps modernes* (October 1945), reprinted in *Commentaire* 96:4 (2001), 881–6.

20. *Cahiers Simone Weil* X (March 1987), 1–5.

21. Jeffrey Mehlman, *Émigré New York: French Intellectuals in Wartime Manhattan, 1940–1944* (Baltimore, MD: Johns Hopkins University Press, 2000), 101–2.

22. Robert Paxton, 'The Last King of France', *New York Review of Books*, 14 February 1985.

23. François Mauriac, *Journal. Mémoires politiques* (Paris: Bouquins, 2008), 342–3.

1. THE LAST DAYS OF VICHY

1. Anna von der Goltz and Robert Gildea, 'Flawed Saviours: The Myths of Hindenburg and Pétain', *European History Quarterly* 39:3 (2009), 439–64.
2. Bénédicte Vergez-Chaignon, *Le Docteur Ménétrel. Eminence grise et confidant du Maréchal Pétain* (Paris: Perrin/Grand Livre du Mois, 2001).
3. She is referred to either as Eugénie or Annie.
4. Bénédicte Vergez-Chaignon, *Pétain* (Paris: Perrin, 2014), 77–85.
5. Louis Noguères, *La Dernière Étape. Sigmaringen* (Paris: Fayard, 1956), 108.
6. Gilbert Joseph, *Fernand de Brinon, l'aristocrate de la collaboration* (Paris: Albin Michel, 2002), 492. Because this kidnapping was such a staged affair it was extensively documented. A good summary is in Vergez-Chaignon, *Pétain*, 838–49. See also BDIC, F delta 1832/26/3 Fonds Robert Aron, 'Dossier Pierre Henri', which has an eyewitness account by one of Pétain's orderlies, Colonel de Longeau Saint-Michel; AN F7/15549 has the account which reports Bléhaut's expletive.
7. A note of the RG 2/5/45 (AN F7/15549) mentions a film that was made but it seems to have disappeared.
8. Pétain, 'Messages', 340–41.
9. Vergez-Chaignon, *Pétain*, 849. For an example of someone finding the text on the road, see: http://jacquotboileaualain.over-blog.com/article-Pétain-au-ban-de-champagney-81066165.html.
10. De Gaulle, *Mémoires*, 582.

2. A CASTLE IN GERMANY

1. Henry Rousso, *Pétain et la fin de la collaboration. Sigmaringen 1944–1945* (Brussels: Complexe, 1984), 80–106, is the best account of these negotiations.
2. Noguères, *Dernière Étape*, 54.
3. G.-T. Schillemans, *Philippe Pétain. Le Prisonnier de Sigmaringen* (Paris: MP, 1965), 47–8.
4. Rousso, *Pétain*, 111, agrees with André Brissaud, *Pétain à Sigmaringen 1944–1945* (Paris: Perrin, 1965), 156–62, that Pétain was persuaded to modify his position by his continued obsession with the POWs; Noguères, *Dernière Étape*, 78–80, has no explanation other than Pétain tended to listen to the last person he talked to. On Pétain's confused state of mind at this time, see a report in Noguères, *Dernière Étape*, 60.

5. On the Sigmaringen episode, see Rousso, *Pétain*; Noguerès, *Dernière Étape*; Brissaud, *Pétain*. Also a dossier in AN F7/15288 which contains, *inter alia*, a 24-page detailed chronology established by the Direction Général de la Sureté Nationale, 14 September 1945.

6. Testimony of Gerard Rey in the Hoover Institution, *France during the German Occupation 1940–1944. Volume III* (Stanford, CA, 1957), 1,177.

7. Ferdinand Céline, *D'un Château l'Autre* (Paris: Gallimard, 1957), 124, 126, 133.

8. Joseph, *Fernand de Brinon*, 511.

9. Rousso, *Pétain*, 118.

10. Noguères, *Dernière Étape*, 113–14. Debeney fully supported Ménétrel's efforts to prevent Pétain from compromising himself further: see his note of 6 October to Pétain in ibid, 125.

11. Céline, *D'un Château*, 148.

12. Subsequently labelled 'Notes de Sigmaringen', this document is usefully reproduced in Benoît Klein, *J'accepte de répondre. Les interrogatoires avant le procès (avril–juin 1945)* (Paris: André Versaille, 2011), 222–36. The section on the events of November 1942 is in the form of the answer to two questions from Pétain (as if he needed to be told what his own policies had been): 'What is the situation of the French government in regards to the American and British governments in November 1942' and 'The Marshal asks to be reminded of the decisions taken by his government in November 1942 after the Anglo-American aggression [*sic*] in North Africa'.

13. Joseph, *Fernand de Brinon*, 525.

14. Noguères, *Dernière Étape*, 136–7, 204.

15. Schillemans, *Philippe Pétain*, 107–8.

16. Rousso, *Pétain*, 415–16.

17. The entire collection is in AN F7/15288.

18. Rousso, *Pétain*, 48.

3 . PARIS AFTER LIBERATION

1. De Gaulle, *Mémoires*, 614.

2. Pierre Bourdan, *Carnet de retour avec la division Leclerc* (Paris: Payot, 2014), 172–3.

3. Hervé Alphand, *L'Étonnement d'être. Journal 1939–1973* (Paris: Fayard, 1977), 181.

4. Susan Mary Alsop, *To Marietta from Paris: 1945–1960* (New York: Doubleday, 1975), 33.

5. Alphand, *L'Étonnement*, 182–3.

6. Maurice Garçon, *Journal 1939–1945* (Paris: Fayard, 2015), 655.

7. Janet Flanner, *Paris Journal 1944–1965* (London: Victor Gollancz, 1966), 13.

8. Alsop, *To Marietta*, 35–6.

9. Serge Toubiana, 'Stratégie de sortie et accueil critique des *Enfants du Paradis* en 1945', *L'Avant scène cinéma* 596, 1/12, 232–8; Jill Forbes, *Les Enfants du Paradis* (London: BFI, 1997); Denis Marion, 'Les Enfants du Paradis', *Combat*, 6 April 1945.

10. Garçon, *Journal*, 685.

11. Simone de Beauvoir, *La Force des choses* (Paris: Gallimard, 1963), 42.

12. Flanner, *Paris Journal*, 29.

13. François Rouquet and Fabrice Virgili, *Les Françaises, les Français et l'épuration* (Paris: Gallimard, 2018), and Marc Oliver Baruch (ed.), *Une Poignée de misérables. L'Épuration de la sociéte française après la Seconde Guerre mondiale* (Paris: Fayard, 2003), are now the standard reference works on the purges. Among earlier books see also Novick, *The Resistance*; Jean-Paul Cointet, *Expier Vichy. L'Épuration en France 1943–58* (Paris: Perrin, 2008); Herbert Lottman, *The Purge: The Purification of French Collaborators after World War II* (New York: Morrow, 1968).

14. *Code pénal annoté par Emile Garçon, vol. 1 (art. 1–294)* (Paris: Sirey, 1952). Once the trials were underway, defence lawyers argued that, since the armistice had ended hostilities, some of the actions for which people were being accused could not technically be seen as treason. But the Cour de Cassation found, however, with reference to The Hague Conventions, that an armistice was only a suspension of hostilities and therefore still constituted a war for the purpose of the application of Article 75 of the Criminal Code.

15. Anne Simonin, *Le Déshonneur dans la République: une histoire de l'indignité 1791–1958* (Paris: Grasset, 2008).

16. For example, Jacques Charpentier, *Au Service de la liberté* (Paris: Fayard, 1949).

17. Alain Bancaud, *Une Exception ordinaire. La Magistrature en France 1930–1950* (Paris: Gallimard, 2002); Jean-Paul Jean (ed.), *Juger sous Vichy, juger Vichy* (Association française pour l'histoire de la justice, 2018); Henry Rousso and Alain Bancaud, 'L'Épuration des magistrats à la libération (1944–1945)' in Association française pour l'histoire de la justice, *L'Épuration de la magistrature de la révolution à la Libération* (1994), 117–44; Loira Israël, *Robes noires, années sombres. Avocats et*

magistrats en résistance pendant la deuxième guerre mondiale (Paris: Fayard, 2005).

18. Garçon, *Journal*, 264.

19. Ibid, 485.

20. Israël, *Robes noires*, 168–75.

21. Jean-Paul Jean, 'Paul Didier, le juge qui a dit non au Maréchal Pétain', *Revue historique* 2022/3 (703), 543–62.

22. Jean, *Juger sous Vichy*, 16; on Rolland, see Jean-Paul Jean, 'Le Rôle de Maurice Rolland (1904–1988) et de l'Inspection des services judiciaires à la Libération' in *La Justice de l'Épuration à la fin de la seconde guerre mondiale* (Paris: Documentation Française, 2003), 133–48.

23. Jean, *Juger sous Vichy*, 378.

24. Maurice Clavel quoted by Roy, *Grand Naufrage*, 44.

25. Commission Centrale de l'Épuration de la Magistrature (CCEM).

26. Novick, *The Resistance*, 85.

27. Rousso and Bancaud, 'L'Épuration des magistrats', 117–44; Bancaud, 'L'Épuration des épurateurs: la magistrature' in Baruch (ed.), *Une Poignée de misérables*, 172–203.

28. Jacques Isorni, *Le Procès de Robert Brasillach* (Paris: Flammarion, 1946), 202–3.

29. Garçon, *Journal*, 636.

30. Camus' articles: 20 and 25 October 1944; 5 and 11 January 1945; Mauriac's: 8, 10, 13, 19, 22 September 1944, 12 December 1944, 2, 8, 12 January 1945 (reprinted in Mauriac, *Journal*, 555–61, 592–4, 606–11, 789–90, 793–5).

31. Alice Kaplan, *The Collaborator: The Trial and Execution of Robert Brasillach* (Chicago: Chicago University Press, 2000).

32. *Journal officiel*, *Débats*, 28 December 1945, 624–5.

33. Géo London, *L'Amiral Esteva et le Général Dentz devant la Haute Cour de Justice* (Lyon: R. Bonnefon, 1945), 111.

34. AN BB/18/7164/2 (Mornet to Garde des Sceaux, 11 May 1945).

4. PÉTAIN'S RETURN

1. Noguères, *Dernière Etape*, 225–6.

2. AN F7/15288.

3. Noguères, *Dernière Etape*, 239–40.

4. Charles Vallin report to de Lattre in Alain de Lattre, *Reconquérir, 1944–1945* (Paris: Plon, 1985), 231–43.

5. AN 3AG4/49. Report by Hoppenot, French ambassador to Switzerland, 24 April 1945.

6. Dominique Lormier, *Koenig. L'Homme de Bir Hakeim* (Paris: Éditions du Toucan, 2012), 305–06; 'Rapport de la police suisse sur le retour en France du Maréchal Pétain, 28 April 1945' in Jean-Raymond Tournoux, *Pétain et de Gaulle* (Paris: Plon, 1964), 482–4; BDIC F delta 1832/26/3 Fonds Robert Aron, 'Dossier Pierre Henri'.

7. AN F7/15549. 'Réaction a/s du retour du Maréchal Pétain en France', 26 April 1945.

8. Synthesis of American press reactions to the return of Pétain, 25 April 1945, NARA RG 59 A1-205H 1945–49 Central Decimal File: 851.00 6228.

9. Garçon, *Journal*, 674.

10. Mauriac, *Journal*, 306: 'L'ennemi, près de succomber, lâche sur la France le Maréchal Pétain'.

11. TNA FO371/49149 (26 April 1945).

12. Synthesis of American press reactions to the trial of Pétain, NARA RG 59 A1-205H 1945–49 Central Decimal File: 851.00 6229.

13. AN 3AG4/49. Report by Hoppenot, 24 April 1945.

14. AN 3AG4/48. Telegram from Georges Bidault (Washington) to Paris, 5 April 1945.

15. AN 3AG4/49. Note from André Bertrand, 26 April 1945.

16. Julian Jackson, *A Certain Idea of France: The Life of Charles de Gaulle* (London: Allen Lane, 2018), 91–113.

17. De Gaulle, *Lettres, notes, carnets 1905–1941* (Paris: Bouquins, 2010), 877.

18. De Gaulle, *Mémoires*, 64.

19. De Gaulle, *Discours et messages* I, 11.

20. Duhamel, *France-Illustration*, 28 July 1945; and Mauriac quoted in *Le Monde*, 2 October 1964.

21. De Gaulle, *Mémoires*, 698.

22. Tournoux, *Pétain et de Gaulle*, 347.

23. The comment was reported by Jean Auburtin, a friend of de Gaulle since the 1930s, to Louis-Dominique Girard on two occasions (24 April and 29 April 1945), AN 72AJ/3200 'Journal'.

24. Tournoux, *Pétain et de Gaulle*, 346.

25. Claude Mauriac, *L'Autre de Gaulle* (Paris: Hachette, 1970), 119.

26. AN 450AP/3. Unpublished journal of Jacques Lecompte-Boinet (8 July 1945).

27. René Benjamin, *Le Palais et ses gens de justice* (Paris: Fayard, 1919).

28. Pierre Laborie, *L'Opinion française sous Vichy* (Paris: Seuil, 1980), remains the best study of public opinion.
29. Noguères, *Dernière Etape*, 31–32; BDIC F delta 1832/26/3.
30. Pierre Bourget, *Témoignages inédits sur le Maréchal Pétain* (Paris: Fayard, 1960), 110.
31. AN F7/15549. There are innumerable examples in 'Dossier Pétain. Notes. 1945'.
32. Novick, *The Resistance*, 175; *Historia*, October 1977. These polls are not strictly comparable and some were restricted to Paris alone, but the overall pattern is striking.
33. AN F7/15549. 'Extrait des résultats d'enquêtes publiés par le service de sondages et statistiques (méthode Gallup)'.
34. *Combat*, 16 April 1945.
35. Flanner, *Paris*, 25.
36. *Combat*, 14 April 1945.
37. Henri Amouroux, *La Page n'est pas encore tournée. Janvier–octobre 1945* (Paris: France Loisirs, 1994), 223.
38. *Le Figaro*, 25 and 27 July 1945.
39. *Franc-Tireur*, 3 May 1945; *The Guardian*, 2 May 1945.
40. *L'Humanité*, 30 April 1945; *L'Humanité*, 29 April 1945: 'Le scandaleux séjour de Bazaine-Pétain à Montrouge Palace'.

5. PREPARING THE TRIAL

1. Klein, *J'accepte de répondre*, 49–50.
2. Madeleine Jacob, *Quarante Ans de journalisme* (Paris: Julliard, 1970), 172.
3. AN 72AJ/3200, Papers of Louis-Dominique Girard, 'Journal' (12 May 1945).
4. Klein, *J'accepte de répondre*, 49–50.
5. AN 3W300(2). A letter from Charpentier to Bouchardon (5 June 1945) says that Payen had offered his services.
6. Pierre Bouchardon, *Souvenirs* (Paris: Albin Michel, 1953), stops in 1940.
7. Meltz, *Pierre Laval*, 1,040.
8. Maurice Garçon, *Journal 1912–1939* (Paris: Fayard: 2002).
9. Bouchardon, *Souvenirs*, 315.
10. Jacob, *Quarante Ans*, 180.
11. AN BB 19770067/331 (Bouchardon's *dossier personnel*). This information was kindly communicated to me by Jean-Paul Jean.
12. *Je Suis Partout*, 26 June 1945. See also the anti-semitic barbs in Bouchardon, *Souvenirs*, 285.

13. Kaplan, *The Collaborator*, 175–6.

14. Isorni, *Souffrance*, 79.

15. Jean-Paul Jean, 'André Mornet (1870–1955), la justice comme une guerre', *Histoire de la justice*, 2022 (33), 269–301. Jean-Paul Jean and Jean Royer, 'Du procès Mata Hari au procès Pétain: André Mornet, un magistrat contesté', conférence Cour de cassation, 1 October 2020, www.youtube.com/watch?v=09QP5HFfAaI; Jean-François Bouchard, *André Mornet. Procureur de la mort* (Paris: Éditions Glyphe, 2020); Bouchardon, *Souvenirs*, 278–9.

16. Garçon, *Journal*, 675–6. See also similar comments in Garçon, *Journal 1912*, 233, 497–8.

17. Bouchardon, *Souvenirs*.

18. Isorni, *Souffrance*, 81.

19. Géo London, portrait of Mornet in *Carrefour*, 10 August 1945.

20. Garçon, *Journal*, 675.

21. André Mornet, *Quatre Ans à rayer de notre histoire* (Paris: Éditions Self, 1949).

22. Israël, *Robes noires*, 336.

23. AN 3W 26. *Procés verbaux de la Commission d'Instruction Haute Cour*, 24/1/45 (7th session).

24. AN 3W 26, 7/2/45 (9th session).

25. AN 3W 26, 10/1/45 (5th session).

26. Guy Raïssac, *Un Soldat dans la tourmente* (Paris: Albin Michel, 1963).

27. AN 3W 26, 21/2/45 (11th session).

28. AN 3W 26, 28/2/45 (12th session).

29. Guy Raïssac, *De la Marine à la justice. Un magistrat témoigne* (Paris: Albin Michel, 1972), 223.

30. AN 3W 26, 20 March 1945 (16th session); and Guy Raïssac *Un Combat sans merci. L'affaire Pétain-De Gaulle* (Paris: Albin Michel, 1966).

31. Noguères, *Haute Cour*, 8–11.

32. AN 3W 300(1). VIIIB: Procedure.

33. Details on the trunk appear in AN F7/5489 and 3W300(1).

34. Raïssac, *De la Marine*, 229.

35. One can follow this saga in 3W 300(1); AN BB/18/7164/2 (Dossier 3); AN F7/15549.

36. Henry Bernstein, *The New York Times*, 27 September 1941; André Schwob, *L'Affaire Pétain, faits et documents* (New York: Editions de la Maison française, 1943).

37. Schwob, *L'Affaire Pétain*, 155.

38. AN 3W 281 Dossier III A (1), pièce 5: 'Rapport d'ensemble', 31 May 1945.

39. Isorni, *Souffrance*, 40–42.

40. Klein, *J'accepte de répondre*, 35–8; BDIC Fonds Mornet, F delta rés 875 III D.7; Charles Rist, *Une Saison gâtée: journal de la guerre et de l'Occupation* (Paris: Fayard, 1983), 301–2.

41. Israël, *Robes noires*, 56–9, 143, 150.

42. Fernand Payen, *Vers le grand parti de la réconciliation? Plaidoirie pour les Français* (Paris: Centre d'études économiques et sociales, 1945).

43. Garçon, *Journal*, 664; Gisèle Sapiro, *La Guerre des écrivains 1940–1953* (Paris: Fayard, 1999), 272.

44. Jacques Isorni, *Le Condamné de la citadelle* (Paris: Flammarion, 1982), 14.

45. For Isorni's career see Gilles Antonowicz, *Jacques Isorni: l'avocat de tous les combats* (Paris: France-Empire, 2007), which gives a sympathetic but not distorted account of his subject; and also his *Isorni, Les procès historiques* (Paris: Les Belles Lettres, 2021); Jacques Isorni, *Mémoires I 1911–1945* (Paris: R. Laffont, 1984); *Mémoires II 1946–1958* (Paris: R. Laffont, 1986); *Mémoires III 1959–1987* (Paris: R. Laffont, 1987); Kaplan, *The Collaborator*, 109–21.

46. Jacques Isorni, *Je suis avocat* (Paris: Éditions du Conquistador, 1951), 11.

47. Kaplan, *The Collaborator*, 120; Isorni, *Je suis avocat*, 98–9.

48. Jean Grenier quoted by Kaplan, *The Collaborator*, 184.

49. Isorni, *Mémoires I*, 314–15.

50. In *Mémoires I*, 406–7, Isorni gives his fullest account of how he came to be chosen based on information he claimed only to have recently discovered: Henri Lémery, himself a former *avocat*, who was concerned that Payen – whom he knew well – was not up to the job, had consulted a former colleague, Jeannine Alexandre-Debray, mother of Regis, who suggested Isorni. Lémery went to see Pétain at Montrouge, who then imposed the choice on Payen.

51. Klein, *J'accepte de répondre*, 64–5.

52. Isorni, *Le Condamné*, 47–8; Aron, *Épuration*, 459–60; Isorni, *Mémoires*, 408–9.

53. *Combat*, 17 July 1945.

54. AN 72AJ/3200. Girard journal (22 May 1945).

55. Isorni, *Souffrance*, 29; *Mémoires I*, 409.

56. Isorni, *Souffrance*, 32–3.

57. Antonowicz, *Jacques Isorni*, 222.

58. Isorni, *Souffrance*, 60.

59. Ibid, 32; Joseph Simon, *Pétain mon prisonnier* (Paris: Plon, 1978), 33.

6. INTERROGATING THE PRISONER

1. He had two assistants on the case, and Lemaire and Payen had one each: Marcel Hubert, Simone Frère, Lacan, Monin.
2. All the quotations from the interrogations come from Klein, *J'accepte de répondre*, 95, 110, 73–4, 94.
3. Ibid, 92.
4. Noguères, *Véritable Procès*, 20–27.
5. Marc Ferro, *Pétain, les leçons de l'histoire* (Paris: Tallandier, 2016), 243, reports this from a Brazilian diplomat who accompanied Pétain on these visits.
6. Klein, *J'accepte de répondre*, 93.
7. Isorni, *Souffrance*, 23.
8. Alfred Naud, *Pourquoi je n'ai pas défendu Pierre Laval* (Paris: Fayard, 1948), 21.
9. Isorni, *Souffrance*, 25.
10. Ibid, 58.
11. Isorni, *Mémoires I*, 408.
12. AN 3AG/4 (report of 25 May 1945). All the reports on Pétain's health are in AN 3W 304.
13. Isorni, *Souffrance*, 52.
14. Ibid, 59.
15. Antonowicz, *Jacques Isorni*, 231.
16. Isorni, *Souffrance*, 86.
17. Vergez-Chaignon, *Le Docteur*, 326–38; Bénédicte Vergez-Chaignon, *Vichy en Prison: Les épurés de Fresnes après la Libération* (Paris: Gallimard, 2006), 98–99; Isorni, *Mémoires II*, 83; AN 72AJ/3200, Papers of Louis-Dominique Girard, 'Journal' (12 May 1945).
18. Isorni, *Souffrance*, 70.
19. TNA FO371/49139 (note on Rougier, 1 March 1945). For what actually happened on the visit see R.T. Thomas, *Britain and Vichy: The Dilemma of Anglo-French Relations 1940–1942* (London: Macmillan, 1978); François Delpla, 'Du Nouveau sur la mission Rougier', *Guerres mondiales et conflits contemporains* 178 (April 1945), 103–13.
20. Louis Rougier, *Les Accords Pétain-Churchill. Histoire d'une mission secrète* (Montréal: Beauchemin, 1945).
21. This photograph of the document is in 72AJ3219 (Dossier: Procès Pétain).
22. TNA FO371/49141 (Churchill Memorandum, 30 April 1945).
23. AN 3AG4/48 (Rougier–de Gaulle, 18 March 1945).

24. AN 3AG4/48 (Report by Burin des Rosiers, 9 April 1045).
25. TNA FO 371/49141 (20 June 1945).
26. Klein, *J'accepte de répondre*, 124. There were in fact two letters, one of 11 December, one of 18 December: see Noguères, *Véritable Procès*, 597.
27. Klein, *J'accepte de répondre*, 88–91.
28. Mornet Papers AN 72/AJ/1291 contains a file on the affair. See also the Brinon High Court dossier AN 3W/110 Dossier V, Pieces 1–32; and the Pétain dossier AN 3W/283 liasse 3bis.
29. *République française. Haute Cour de Justice. Compte rendu in extenso des audiences transmis par le Secrétariat général de la Haute Cour de Justice. Procès du Marechal Pétain* (1945), 6–9 (27 July). This was the official transcript of the trial published by the *Journal officiel*. All future citations from the trial references to the trial will come from this source, cited henceforth as *Procès Pétain*. A photographic reproduction of this was usefully republished in 1997: *Haute Cour de Justice. Procès du Maréchal Pétain* (Nîmes: C. Lacour, 1997), and another under the auspices of the Musée de la Résistance nationale in 2015 (Paris: Les Balustres, 2015). The 1997 reproduction has a preface by a lawyer not unfavourable to Pétain, and the 2015 one an afterword by a historian ferociously hostile to him.
30. TNA FO371/49142 (Report by Holman, 7 July 1945); NARA Box 6229 (Report by Caffery, 27 June 1945).
31. AN 3AG4/49; AN 3W 26, 1 June 1945.
32. *Journal Officiel, Débats*, 19 July 1945, 1,423–9.

7. FRANCE WAITS

1. For a lively description of the Palais and its workings in 1919 see Benjamin, *Le Palais*.
2. Jacques Isorni, 'Le Procès du Maréchal Pétain', *Historia* 104 (July 1955), 83–94.
3. Henri Calet, 'Les Parisiens votent', *Combat*, 30 April 1945.
4. There is a short note on the jurors by the Renseignements généraux in AN F7/15549, but it gets some names wrong.
5. Isorni, *Souffrance*, 98.
6. Lecompte-Boinet Papers, AN 450AP/3 (12 March 1945). This journal was published in 2021 as *Mémoires d'un chef de la Resistance* (Paris: Éditions du Felin, 2021), but this edition ends in August 1944 and so does not cover the Pétain trial.
7. AN 450AP/3 (24 April 1945).

8. This comment is quoted also in Isorni, *Souffrance*, as coming from Lecompte-Boinet himself.
9. AN 450AP/3 (21 July 1945).
10. *Franc-Tireur*, 22 July 1945.
11. *L'Humanité*, 24 July 1945.
12. *Combat*, 18 July 1945.
13. 'Le Régime du Pétainat', *Franc-Tireur*, 22 July 1945.
14. Cassou, 'La Justice', *Lettres Françaises*, 21 July 1945.
15. Clavel, 'Leçon de la honte', *L'Époque*, 22 July 1945.

8. FIRST DAY IN COURT

1. *France-Soir*, 24 July 1945.
2. Unlike the press benches, these were not removed after the trial and are now used for the press.
3. Pierre Scize, *Les Nouvelles du Matin*, 24 July 1945.
4. Léon Werth, *Déposition. Journal de Guerre. 1940–1945* (Paris: V. Hamy, 1992). His reports on the trial were later published in book form, *Impressions d'audience: le procès Pétain* (Parsi: V. Hamy, 1995).
5. Joseph Kessel's reports on the trial were published in book form, *Jugements derniers: le procès Pétain, le procès de Nuremberg* (Paris: Grand Livre du Mois, 1995).
6. Jean Schlumberger, *Le Procès Pétain* (Paris: Gallimard, 1949), 51.
7. Jacob, *Quarante Ans*, 328.
8. *Noir et blanc*, 8 August 1945.
9. Jacob, *Franc-Tireur*, 18 October 1944.
10. Kessel, *Jugements derniers*, 23–34.
11. Rémi Dalisson, *Les Fêtes du Maréchal* (Paris: CNRS Éditions, 2015); Pierre Servent, *Le Mythe du Maréchal Pétain: Verdun ou les tranchées de la mémoire* (Paris: Payot, 1992); and for Pétain memorabilia see also Laurence Bertrand-Dorléac, *L'Art de la Défaite: 1940–1944* (Paris: Seuil, 1993).
12. Léon Werth, *Impressions*, 27.
13. Schlumberger, *Le Procès*, 52.
14. 'Le procès', *Historia* 104 (July 1955), 83–94.
15. Francine Bonitzer, 'Impressions d'audience', *L'Aurore*, 24 July 1945.
16. Raïssac, *De la Marine*, 178.
17. Jean-Paul Jean, 'Léon Lyon-Caen (1877–1967). Soldat du droit au service de la Paix', *Delibérée* 2021/1 (no. 12), 41–9 (https://www.cairn.info/revue-deliberee-2021-1-page-41.htm). On the resistance and the Jews

see Renée Poznanski, *Propagandes et persécutions. La Résistance et le 'problème juif'* (Paris: Grand Livre du Mois, 2008).

18. AN BB 19770067/331 (Mongibeaux's dossier).

19. Jean Galtier-Boissière, *Journal 1940–1950* (Paris: Quai Voltaire, 1992), 313.

20. Noguères, *Véritable Procès*, 9.

21. Isorni, *Souffrance*, 99; on Donat-Guigne see also his reaction to the measures against Pierre Caous as recounted by Raïssac, *De la Marine*, 170, 180.

22. Flanner, *Paris Journal*, 34.

23. Werth, *Impressions*, 129; Galtier-Boissière, *Journal*, 312.

24. *Procès Pétain* 3 (23 July 1945).

25. Report of Renseignements Généraux (RG), AN F7/15549.

26. 'La Troisième République accusée, *Carrefour*, 27 July 1945.

27. Isorni, *Souffrance*, 89.

28. The phrase is crossed out in the typed-up version in AN Fonds Pétain 514MI.

29. BDIC Fonds Robert Aron F delta 1832/26/8 (Dossier Isorni) has copies of the different drafts, part of which are also reprinted in Robert Aron, *Histoire de l'épuration II: Des prisons clandestins aux tribunaux d'exception. Septembre 1944–Juin 1949* (Paris: Fayard, 1969), II, 462–5. For the final draft as read in court: *Procès Pétain* 9–10 (23 July 1945).

30. Jacob, *Franc-Tireur*, 24 July 1945.

31. 'Courtroom riots', *The New York Times*, 24 July 1945.

32. *The Daily Telegraph*, 24 July 1945.

33. A note by the RG of 24 July 1945 in AN F7/15549 supports this idea and provides the names of the ringleaders.

34. Kessel, *Jugements derniers*, 26.

9. REPUBLICAN GHOSTS

1. Roy, *Grand Naufrage*, 42.

2. Flanner, *Paris Journal*, 32.

3. *Procès Pétain*, 27–8 (24 July 1945).

4. Ibid, 24 (24 July 1945).

5. De Gaulle, *Lettres, notes, carnets*, 832 (14 May 1937).

6. Thibault Tellier, *Paul Reynaud. Un Indépendant en politique 1876–1966* (Paris: Fayard, 2005); Raymond Krakovitch, *Paul Reynaud: dans la tragédie de l'histoire* (Paris: Tallendier, 2002).

7. RG note in AN F7/15549.

8. Paul Reynaud, *Carnets de captivité (1941–1945)* (Paris: Fayard, 1997), 100.

9. Ibid, 38.

10. TNA FO371/49141 (1 May 1945).

11. Reynaud's deposition is in *Procès Pétain*, 13–24 (23–24 July 1945).

12. *Procès Pétain*, 58 (26 July 1945).

13. Georges Althusser, *Combat*, 25 July 1945.

14. AN 450AP/3 (24 July 1945).

15. Flanner, *Paris Journal*, 37.

16. Reynaud, *Carnets*, 124.

10. DEBATING THE ARMISTICE

1. Werth, *Impressions*, 39.

2. *Procès Pétain*, 46 (25 July 1945).

3. Ibid, 47 (25 July 1945).

4. Ibid, 63–70 (26 July 1945).

5. Ibid, 72 (26 July 1945).

6. Ibid, 57–60 (26 July 1945).

7. Ibid, 48 (25 July 1945).

8. This was reported by Jean Fernand-Laurent, *Un Peuple ressucité* (New York: Brentano's, 1943), in a chapter called 'La Confession de Raphaël Alibert', 85–91, based on a conversation with him in Clermont-Ferrand in 1942.

9. *Procès Pétain*, 48 (25 July 1945).

10. BDIC Fonds Mornet. F delta rés 875 III D.7 (Transcript of interview with Lebrun, 23 March 1945)

11. *The New York Times*, 26 July 1945.

12. *Procès Pétain*, 37 (25 July 1945).

13. Michel Tony-Révillon, *Mes Carnets (juin–octobre 1940)* (Paris: O. Lieutier, 1945). The other four jurors on the ship were: Lévy-Alphandery, Delattre, Dupré; and one *suppléant*: Jammy Schmidt. Delattre also published an account, 'Le Journal de bord du *Massilia*', *L'Aurore*, 3–7 October 1944.

14. *Procès Pétain*, 50 (25 July 1945).

15. Ibid, 49 (25 July 1945).

16. De Gaulle, *Mémoires*, 609.

17. Tal Bruttman and Laurent Joly, *La France antijuive de 1936. L'Agression de Léon Blum à la chambre des députés* (Paris: CNRS Editions, 2006).

18. *Procès Pétain*, 75–8 (27 July 1945).

19. Isorni, *Souffrance*, 117.

20. Werth, *Impressions*, 44, 49.

21. Jacob, *Franc-Tireur*, 28 July 1945.

11. THE DEFENCE FIGHTS BACK

1. Flanner, *Paris Journal*, 57–8.
2. Pierre Scize, *Les Nouvelles du Matin*, 25 July 1945.
3. *Procès Pétain*, 33 (24 July 1945).
4. Isorni, *Souffrance*, 110.
5. *Procès Pétain*, 39 (25 July 1945).
6. Ibid, 61 (26 July 1945).
7. Ibid, 79 (27 July 1945).
8. Isorni claimed somewhat fancifully in *Mémoires I*, 465, that Lebrun had also developed a passion for the Queen after meeting her on the State Visit to France in 1938 – such that he had even pressed her to his breast and kept a memory of an 'impossible love' – and wanted to do nothing that might upset her!
9. *Procès Pétain*, 55 (25 July 1945).
10. Ibid, 44 (25 July 1945).
11. Henri Michel, *Le Procès de Riom* (Paris: Albin Michel, 1979).
12. *Procès Pétain*, 78 (27 July 1945).
13. Isorni, *Souffrance*, 119.
14. Ibid, 101–3 (28 July 1945).
15. Ibid, 110–13 (30 July 1945).
16. Ibid, 113 (30 July 1945).
17. Ibid, 117 (30 July 1945).
18. Ibid, 40 (25 July 1945).
19. Ibid, 30 (24 July 1945).
20. Ibid, 53 (25 July 1945).
21. Ibid, 78 (27 July 1945).

12. LAST WITNESSES FOR THE PROSECUTION

1. *Procès Pétain*, 63 (26 July 1945).
2. Ibid, 108 (28 July 1945).
3. This was in fact very flimsy. Since Pétain was not even in Paris when Monzie dated the conversation, it seems more likely that it happened on 3 May when he was there.
4. *Procès Pétain*, 74–5 (26 July 1945).
5. Ibid, 104 (28 July 1945).
6. De Gaulle, *Lettres, notes, carnets*, vol. 1, 125.
7. Klein, *J'accepte de répondre*, 70, 83.
8. AN 3W/278 (IB2).

9. Isorni, *Souffrance*, 124–5.
10. *Procès Pétain*, 119–22 (30 July 1945).
11. Isorni, *Souffrance*, 124–5.
12. *Procès Pétain*, 151 (1 August 1945).
13. Ibid, 94–8 (28 July 1945).
14. Ibid, 84–8 (27 July 1945).
15. *L'Humanité*, 27 July 1945.
16. Kessel, *Jugements derniers*, 37–40.
17. Jacob, *Franc-Tireur*, 25 July 1945.
18. Gabriel Reuillard, *Depêche de Paris*, 31 July 1945.
19. Simon, *Pétain*, 50–51.
20. *Procès Pétain*, 41 (25 July 1945).
21. Ibid, 51 (25 July 1945).
22. Ibid, 91–4 (28 July 1945).
23. Francine Bonitzer, *Aurore*, 29 July 1945.
24. AN 450AP/3 (29 July 1945).
25. Alsop, *To Marietta*, 38.
26. Georges Altman, *Franc-Tireur*, 27 July 1945.
27. *Combat*, 29 July 1945. Caffery, the American ambassador, reported to Washington that seeing all these discredited former politicians was probably bolstering de Gaulle's arguments for the need for a radical constitutional change: NARA RG 59, 6229, Report, 3 August 1945.
28. Schlumberger, *Le procès*, 80.
29. Mauriac, *Journal. Mémoires politiques*, 823–4 (26 July 1945).
30. AN F7/15549 (Rouen, 30 July 1945).
31. AN 317AP/63 (Louis Marin Papers).
32. Ibid.
33. AN F7/15549 (Dossier Comptes Rendus RG, 27 July 1945).
34. London, *L'Amiral Esteva*.
35. Isorni, *Souffrance*, 111.
36. Kaplan, *The Collaborator*, 100.

13. 'YOU WILL NOT MAKE ME SAY THAT THE MARSHAL IS A TRAITOR'

1. Reynaud, *Carnets*, 303, 312.
2. Isorni, *Souffrance*, 131.
3. *Procès Pétain*, 130–36 (31 July 1945).
4. Ibid, 137–8 (31 July 1945).
5. Ibid, 166 (1 August 1945).

6. Ibid, 140 (31 July 1945).

7. Ibid, 134 (31 July 1945).

8. Ibid, 143 (31 July 1945).

9. Ibid, 147 (31 July 1945).

10. Ibid, 154 (1 August 1945).

11. Ibid, 156 (1 August 1945).

12. Neiberg, *When France Fell*, is the best recent account.

13. TNA FO371/49141 (30 April 1945).

14. William Keylor, *Charles de Gaulle: A Thorn in the Side of Six American Presidents* (Lanham, MD: Rowman & Littlefield, 2020), 117.

15. The letter can be found in AN F7/154 among many other places.

16. William Leahy, *I Was There* (London: Victor Gollancz, 1950), 531.

17. Neiberg, *When France Fell*, 110, 134.

18. NARA RG 59, 6228 does not seem to have played any role in the drafting of the reply.

19. *Procès Pétain*, 157 (1 August 1945).

20. Ibid, 175–82 (2 August 1945).

14. THE PIERRE LAVAL SHOW

1. Kessel, *Jugements derniers*, 82–3.

2. Galtier-Boissière, *Journal*, 484.

3. Meltz, *Pierre Laval*, 139.

4. Pierre Tissier, *I Worked with Laval* (London: Harrap, 1942), 39–40.

5. Ibid, 367.

6. Meltz, *Pierre Laval*, 367.

7. Ibid, 367.

8. Ibid, 871.

9. Vergez-Chaignon, *Vichy en Prison*, 112.

10. Simon, *Pétain*, 48, 134.

11. *The Daily Telegraph*, 6 August 1945.

12. In addition to the usual newspaper reports we also have eyewitness reports by Roger Stéphane, *Fin d'une jeunesse. Carnets 1944–1947* (Paris: Table Ronde, 2004), 111–15; Claude Mauriac, *L'Autre de Gaulle*, 139–42.

13. Isorni, *Souffrance*, 138–39; Simon, *Pétain*, 47–8.

14. Meltz, *Pierre Laval*, 1,046.

15. AN 450AP/3 (4 August 1945).

16. *The Guardian*, 4 August 1945.

17. Flanner, *Paris Journal*, 33.

18. *Procès Pétain*, 185 (3 August 1945).

19. Ibid, 186 (3 August 1945).
20. Naud, *Pourquoi je n'ai pas*, 12.
21. Kessel, *Jugements derniers*, 80–82; Jacob, *Franc-Tireur*, 4 August 1945; *Combat*, 4 August 1945; Lecompte-Boinet, *Journal*.
22. Werth, *Impressions*, 94.
23. *Procès Pétain*, 192 (3 August 1945).
24. Ibid, 194–5 (3 August 1945).
25. Ibid, 197–8 (3 August 1945).
26. Werth, *Déposition*, 314–15.
27. *Procès Pétain*, 200–201 (3 August 1945).
28. Ibid, 202 (3 August 1945).
29. Simon, *Pétain*, 130–31.
30. The Dieppe affair came up in the trial on several occasions – *Pétain procès*, 40–41, 207–8, 287–8 – but no certainty was ever reached.
31. *Procès Pétain*, 216 (4 August 1945).
32. Ibid, 217 (4 August 1945).
33. Flanner, *Paris Journal*, 39–40.
34. Isorni, *Souffrance*, 141.
35. *Procès Pétain*, 222 (4 August 1945).
36. Francine Bonitzer, *Aurore*, 5 August 1945.
37. AN 450AP/3 (4 August 1945).

15. GENERALS AND BUREAUCRATS

1. 'Et la France?', *Résistance*, 5 August 1945.
2. Pierre Scize, 'Journée des doublures', *Les Nouvelles du Matin*, 9 August 1945.
3. Syria was briefly discussed in the testimonies of Bergeret and Berthelot on 8 August, *Procés Pétain*, 260–64, 267–9 (8 August 1945).
4. On life in Fresnes, Vergez-Chaignon, *Vichy en prison*, 90–130.
5. Jacques Benoist-Méchin, *De la Défaite au désastre* (Paris: Albin Michel, 1984), vol. II, 374; Vergez-Chaignon, *Vichy en prison*, 132.
6. Xavier Vallat, *Feuilles de Fresnes 1944–48* (Paris: Déterna éditions, 2013), 62.
7. Ibid, 86–94; some reports in AN F7/15549 mention the showing of the trial in cinemas.
8. Isorni, *Souffrance*, 117.
9. Galtier-Boissière, *Journal*, 483.
10. Jacob, *Franc-Tireur*, 8 August 1945.
11. *Procès Pétain*, 246 (7 August 1945).

12. Ibid, 265 (8 August 1945).
13. Werth, *Impressions*, 103.
14. 'Rumeurs et longueurs', *Le Figaro*, 2 August 1945.
15. Ibid, 270 (8 August 1945).
16. Ibid, 233 (6 August 1945).
17. Ibid, 252 (7 August 1945).
18. Ibid, 234 (6 August 1945).
19. Ibid, 175 (2 August 1945).
20. Clavel, 'Antimonies', *L'Époque*, 11 August 1945.
21. Jacob, *Franc-Tireur*, 11 August 1945.
22. Schlumberger, *Le Procès*, 116–17; Werth, *Impressions*, 113.
23. TNA FO371/49141 (Cadogan note, 5 July 1945).
24. All this can be followed in TNA FO371/49139, 49140, 49141.
25. *Procès Pétain*, 248 (7 August 1945). If the prosecution had done its homework better, it could have cited a letter in the *instruction* files which undermined the scaffolding of fantasy constructed around Rougier's claims. The day before receiving Rougier for the second time, Pétain had written to Weygand mentioning that he was expecting to see Rougier on his return from London: 'he is considered here as an agent of the English'. Noguères, *Véritable Procès*, 258.
26. *Procès Pétain*, 254–6 (7 August 1945).
27. TNA FO371/49143 (Final report on the trial, 14 August 1945; marginal comment by Hoyal).
28. *Procès Pétain*, 39 (25 July 1945).
29. Rémy, 'La Justice et l'opprobre, *Carrefour*, 11 April 1950.
30. This was mentioned by Weygand (*Procès Pétain*, 139, 31 July 1945) and Bergeret (262, 8 August 1945).
31. *Procès Pétain*, 279–82 (9 August 1945).
32. Hervé Couteau-Bégarie and Claude Huan, *Darlan* (Paris: Fayard, 1989).
33. *Procès Pétain*, 280 (9 August 1945).
34. Noguères, *Véritable Procès*, 468; the Ménétrel notes are in AN 3W/298 (Dossier 3).
35. AN 3W/281 (III IA2).
36. Vergez-Chaignon, *Pétain*, 725.
37. Noguères, *Véritable Procés*, 461, 538.

16. THE ABSENT JEWS

1. Blum was not testifying 'as a Jew'.
2. Many examples are in AN 3W/302.

3. Flanner, *Paris Journal*, 36.

4. François Azouvi, *Le Mythe du grand silence. Auschwitz, les Français, la mémoire* (Paris: Fayard, 2012); Simon Perego, *Pleurons-les. Les juifs de Paris et les commémorations de la Shoah (1944–1967)* (Ceyzérieu: Champ Vallon, 2020); Philip Nord, *After the Deportation: Memory Battles in Post-War France* (Cambridge: Cambridge University Press, 2020).

5. *Droit et Liberté*, 17 May, 31 May, 31 July 1945; Poznanski, *Les Juifs en France*; Galtier-Boissière, *Journal*, 445.

6. Archives Mémorials de la Shoah, Procès Verbal (PV) of CRIF, 15 May and 9 July 1945.

7. PV CRIF 22 May, 29 May, 21 June 1945 where these incidents are discussed.

8. AN 3W/285 (III 3A2).

9. AN 3W/285 (III 3A2 Liasse 3).

10. Ibid.

11. Vergez-Chaignon, *Pétain*, 521; Jeanneney and Herriot told the court that they had refused to provide lists of Jewish parliamentarians when asked by Vichy: *Procés Pétain*, 59 (29 July 1945), 112 (30 July 1945).

12. *Procès Pétain*, 213 (4 August 1945).

13. Ibid, 125 (30 July 1945).

14. Philippe Boegner, *Carnets du Pasteur Boegner 1940–1945* (Paris: Fayard, 1992).

15. Claire Zalc, *Dénaturalisés. Les retraits de nationalité sous Vichy* (Paris: Seuil, 2016), is an exhaustive history of the workings of the Commission.

16. *Procès Pétain*, 248–50 (7 August 1945).

17. London, *L'Amiral Esteva*, 274.

18. Robert Badinter, *Un Antisémitisme ordinaire. Vichy et les avocats juifs 1940–1944* (Paris: Le Grand Livre du Mois, 1997); Jacques Charpentier, *De Vichy à la résistance* (Paris: Fayard, 1949), 152–3.

19. 'En Marge du Procès', *Le Réveil des Jeunes*, 1 August 1945.

20. These contextual details are given in *Terre retrouvée*, 25 August 1945. The role of Pétain in the deportation of the Jews was also raised in two other Jewish publications: *Droit et liberté*, organ of the Union des juifs pour la résistance et l'entreaide (UJRE), articles of 24, 31 July and 10 August 1945; and in *Le Réveil des Jeunes*, a publication in the orbit of the Bund, 1 August 1945. For an overview see: 'La presse francophone des Juifs immigrés et perception des crimes nazis dans l'immédiat après-guerre', *Archives juives. Revue d'histoire des juifs de France* 44:1 (September 2011), 123–35.

21. *Terre retrouvée*, 25 August 1945. He was to complain in *Le Monde juif* in November 1946 that too little had been said about the Jews at Nuremberg.

17. THE COUNT, THE ASSASSIN AND THE BLIND GENERAL

1. Paul Morand, *Journal de guerre. Tome 1. Londres-Paris-Vichy 1939–1943* (Paris: Gallimard, 2021).
2. *Franc-Tireur*, 10 August 1945; TNA FO 371/49143 (report on Day 14); AN F7/15549 (9 August 1945).
3. *Procès Pétain*, 285 (9 August 1945).
4. Ibid, 289 (9 August 1945).
5. TNA FO371/49143; Werth, *Impressions*, 120; *Combat*, 10 August 1945.
6. *Procès Pétain*, 290–91 (9 August 1945).
7. Ibid, 296 (9 August 1945).
8. Isorni, *Souffrance*, 136.
9. *Procès Pétain*, 299–300 (10 August 1945).
10. AN 72AJ/1921 (Mornet Papers).
11. *Procès Pétain*, 316–18 (10 August 1945).

18. *RÉQUISITOIRE* AND *PLAIDOIRIES*

1. Simon, *Pétain*, 51.
2. *Procés Pétain*, 319 (11 August 1945).
3. Clavel, *L'Époque*, 12 August 1945.
4. After Mornet had finished, the court heard a letter from Rochat which confirmed entirely what Laval had said about Pétain's response to this speech: *Procés Pétain*, 336 (11 August 1945).
5. Galtier-Boissière, *Journal*, 491.
6. Schlumberger, *Le Procès*, 130.
7. *L'Époque*, 12 August 1945.
8. Simon, *Pétain*, 50.
9. Jacob, *Franc-Tireur*, 12 August 1945; Galtier-Boissière, *Journal*, 491.
10. *Procès Pétain*, 336 (1 August 1945).
11. AN 450AP/3 (10 August 1945).
12. *Procès Pétain*, 344 (13 August 1945).
13. Ibid, 348 (13 August 1945).

14. Maurice Felut, *France-Soir*, 14 August 1945.
15. Maurice Clavel, *L'Époque*, 14 August 1945.
16. Jacob, *Franc-Tireur*, 14 August 1945.
17. Isorni, *Souffrance*, 132.
18. *Procès Pétain*, 358 (14 August 1945).
19. Ibid, 356 (14 August 1945).
20. Ibid, 364 (14 August 1945).
21. Isorni, *Souffrance*, 153.
22. Pierre Scize, *Les Nouvelles de Paris*, 14 August 1945; Antonowicz, *Jacques Isorni*, 276.
23. *Procès Pétain*, 365 (14 August 1945).
24. Ibid.
25. Ibid, 369 (14 August 1945).
26. Jacob, *Franc-Tireur*, 15 August 1945; Antonowicz, *Jacques Isorni*, 284–5.
27. *Procès Pétain*, 371 (14 August 1945).
28. *L'Aurore*, 15 August 1945.
29. *Procès Pétain*, 371–84 (14 August 1945).
30. *L'Humanité*, 14 August 1945.
31. *Procès Pétain*, 381 (14 August 1945).
32. Ibid, 384 (14 August 1945).

19. THE VERDICT

1. AN 450AP/3 (14 August 1945).
2. Regarding the deliberations of the jurors, we have a number of different accounts based on the later recollections of three jurors and the journal of Lecompte-Boinet. None of these accounts is very detailed and there are minor discrepancies, but they offer what is probably a generally accurate account of a long and confused discussion: Pétrus Faure, *Un Témoin raconte* (St Etienne: Dumas, 1962); *Le Procès Pétrus Faure. Juré au Procès du Maréchal Pétain* (St Etienne: Dumas, 1967); Pétrus Faure, *Un Procès inique* (Paris: Flammarion, 1973); Gabriel Delattre, 'J'étais premier juré au procès Pétain', *L'Histoire pour tous* 4:64, 491–9; and Pierre-Bloch, *Le Monde* (23–24 May 1976), 'Témoignage sur le procès du Maréchal Pétain', of which a slightly different version was first printed by Aron, *L'Épuration*, 514–21. A few rumours about the deliberations also filtered through to the press: 'La Grace de l'ex-maréchal Pétain', *Le Monde*, 20 August 1945.
3. Isorni, *Souffrance*, 152.

4. *Le Monde* gave the figures as 20 to 6.
5. Isorni, *Souffrance*, 158–9.
6. Kessel, *Jugements derniers*, 91–4.
7. AN 450AP/3 (16 August 1945).
8. Jean-Richard Bloch, *Ce Soir*, 16 August 1945.
9. 'Pitié pour la France', *L'Époque*, 16 August 1945.
10. *Nouvelles du Matin*, 17 August 1945.
11. 'Impressions', *L'Aurore*, 12 August 1945.
12. AN 3AG4/48. This letter found itself into the de Gaulle archives, where it was marked 'very interesting' and noted that de Gaulle had read it.
13. Charles Lederman, 'Pétain protecteur des Israélites?', *Droit et liberté*, 15 September 1945.
14. Vallat, *Feuillles*, 92, 94; the right-wing journalist E. Beau de Loménie, 'Autour du Procès Pétain', *Centre d'études économiques et sociales* (September 1945), also argued that this was not the best defence for Vichy to offer.
15. Rousseaux, 'Épilogue de l'affaire Dreyfus', *Lettres Françaises*, 25 August 1945.
16. 'Honneur et bien commun', *Documents nationaux*, November 1945.
17. Roger Stéphane, *Fin d'une jeunesse*, 115–16.

20. THE PRISONER

1. Report in AN 3AG/4/48 (16 August 1945).
2. Simon, *Pétain*, 55.
3. Ibid, 71. In addition to this diary, detailed reports on Pétain in prison, mostly by Simon, can be found in AN 3W 303.
4. Simon, *Pétain*, 68, 73, 87.
5. Ibid, 72, 76, 100.
6. Ibid, 57, 163.
7. Isorni, *Souffrance*; Simon, *Pétain*, 67.
8. Meltz, *Pierre Laval*, 1,054–99.
9. Noguères, *Véritable Procès*.
10. Noguères, *Haute Cour*, is the fullest account of the Court's history.
11. Jean Berthelot, Yves Bouthillier, Jean Jardel, Jacques Chevalier.
12. There had also been a short visit to interrogate him for the trial of Benoist-Méchin, recipient of the notorious Dieppe telegram. Pétain said, according to Isorni, *Mémoires II*, 96: 'Il ne faut jamais croire M. Benoist-Méchin même quand il dit du bien de moi.'

13. Quoted in Jean Stengers, 'Les Événements survenus en France de 1933 à 1945. Témoignages et documents recueillis par la Commission d'Enquête parlementaire', *Revue Belge de philologie et d'histoire* 30:3–4 (1952), 993–1005 (102).

14. Klein, *J'accepte de répondre*, 159–200; Simon, *Pétain*, 181–84; Isorni, *Souffrance*, 198–99.

15. AN 3W 304 (5 February 1948).

16. Pierre Dhers, 'Du 7 mars à l'île d'Yeu. Note sur quelques travaux de la Commission parlementaire d'Enquête', *Revue d'histoire de la deuxième guerre mondiale* 5 (January 1952), 17–26.

17. Jean Stengers, 'Les Événements survenus en France de 1933 à 1945'; Henri Michel, 'L'Oeuvre de la commission parlementaire chargée d'enquêter sur les événements survenus en France de 1933 à 1945', *Revue d'histoire de la deuxième guerre mondiale* 3 (June 19: 51), 94–6.

18. AN F7/15488 contains a file about a case against the revue *Réalisme*, which in November 1949 produced 5,000 tracts with this photo of the 'oldest prisoner in the world'.

19. Isorni, *Souffrance*, 87.

20. Generals Héring, Serrigny and Georges.

21. VICHY EMERGES FROM THE CATACOMBS

1. Isorni, *Souffrance*, 176.

2. Jérôme Cotillon, *Ce qu'il Reste de Vichy* (Paris: A. Colin, 2003); Vergez-Chaignon, *Vichy en prison*.

3. Paul Auphan, *L'Honneur de servir. Mémoires* (Paris: Éditions France-Empire, 1978).

4. Pierre Assouline, *Une Éminence grise: Jean Jardin* (Paris: Gallimard, 1986), 189.

5. Alfred Fabre-Luce, *Double Prison* (Montréal: Variété, 1945).

6. Alfred Fabre-Luce, *Le Mystère du Maréchal. Le Procès de Pétain* (Geneva: Bourquin, 1945). Fabre-Luce was exceptionally quick off the mark. A 21-page typed defence of Pétain by him, under the title 'Opposition', was already circulating in typed form before the trial: AN F7/15549 (25 June 1945). It circulated widely enough to be mentioned in Galtier-Boissière, *Journal*, 465 (5 July 1945).

7. Some titles of Rougier's books: *La France Jacobine* (Brussels: Diffusion du livre, 1947), *De Gaulle contre de Gaulle* (Paris: Triolet, 1948), *La Défaite des vainqueurs* (Geneva: Cheval Ailé, 1947), *Pour une Politique*

d'amnistie (Geneva: Cheval Ailé, 1947), *Les Accords franco-britanniques de l'automne 1940. Histoire et imposture* (Paris: Grasset, 1954).

8. Labarthète, *Le Temps des illusions*.

9. Louis-Dominique Girard, *Montoire. Verdun Diplomatique* (Paris: A. Bonne, 1948), 165–9, 207. On the reception of the book see the Girard Papers: AN 72AJ/3229, 3230.

10. Isorni, *Souffrance*, 209.

11. De Gaulle, *Discours et messages. Dans l'attente*, 293 (29 March 1949).

12. Rémy, *De Gaulle cet inconnu* (Monte Carlo: Raoul Solar, 1947). On Rémy's life see Philippe Kerrand, *L'Étrange Colonel Rémy* (Ceyzérieu: Champ Vallon, 2020).

13. Rémy, *Dix Ans avec de Gaulle (1940–1950)* (Paris: Éditions France-Empire, 1971).

14. *Requête en révision pour Philippe Pétain, Marechal de France* (Paris: Flammarion, 1950). In the previous year two former Pétainists had published an article-by-article rebuttal of the *acte de condamnation*: General Héring and Commandant Le Roc'h, *Revision* (Paris: Éditions Self, 1949).

15. *Samedi-Soir*, 22, 29 April, 6, 13, 20, 26 May, 5, 13, 17 June 1945.

16. All these articles, and many more, can be found in the Girard Papers: AN 72AJ/3229, 3230.

17. Marcel Peyrouton, *Du Service public à la prison commune* (Paris: Plon, 1950); Yves Bouthillier, *Le Drame de Vichy* (Paris: Plon, 1950, 1951); Jean Fernet, *Aux Côtés du Maréchal Pétain: souvenirs (1940–1944)* (Paris: Plon, 1953); Bernard Serrigny, *Trente Ans avec Pétain* (Paris: Plon, 1959).

18. Frédéric Le Moigne, 'Les Deux Corps', *Vingtième Siècle, Revue d'histoire* 78 (2003) 75–88. On the reactions to this Mass and others that took place in 1951 there is a whole dossier in AN F7/15849.

19. Vergez-Chaignon, *Épurer*, 318.

20. Isorni, *Mémoires II*, 207–15.

21. A second more generous amnesty law was passed in 1953.

22. Georges Pompidou, *Lettres, notes et portraits* (Paris: R. Laffont, 2012), 221–2.

22. KEEPERS OF THE FLAME

1. Detailed report (3 August 1951) in AN F7/15489.

2. Henry Rousso, *Vichy Syndrome*, Archives *Préfecture* de Police APP GA 511678.

3. 'Extraits de courrier', *Le Maréchal*, 2 (October 1952).

4. Robert Aron, *Histoire de Vichy 1940–1944* (Paris, Fayard, 1954).

5. Robert Aron, *Le Piège où nous a pris l'histoire* (Paris: Albin Michel, 1950).

6. Robert Aron, *Charles de Gaulle* (Paris: Perrin, 1964), 46–7.

7. *Le Maréchal*, 11 (January 1955).

8. Ibid, 9 (July 1954).

9. 'Le Maréchal, mainteneur de l'Empire', *Le Maréchal*, 14 (October 1955).

10. *Rivarol*, 25 and 29 May 1958.

11. Michel Dacier, 'Euphorie dans la confusion', *Écrits de Paris* 5–12 (June 1958).

12. Jacques Isorni, *Ainsi Passent les Républiques* (Paris: Flammarion, 1959), 155.

13. Ibid, 167–8.

14. Isorni, *Mémoires I*, 421.

15. Jacques Isorni, *Lui qui les juge* (Paris: Flammarion, 1961), 48.

16. *Le Procès Salan. Compte rendu sténographique* (Paris: Nouvelles Éditions latines, 1962).

17. Pierre Pflimlin, *Mémoires d'un européen de la IVe à la Ve République* (Paris: Fayard, 1991), 189.

23. MEMORY WARS

1. Henri Amouroux, *Pétain avant Vichy* (Paris: Fayard, 1967), 7. Other titles: Jean Plumyène, *Pétain* (Paris: Seuil, 1964); Tournoux, *Pétain et de Gaulle*; Henri Coston, *Pétain toujours présent* (Rennes: Lectures françaises, 1964); Gabriel Jeantet, *Pétain contre Hitler* (Paris: Table Ronde, 1966); Georges Blond, *Pétain* (Paris: Presse de la cité, 1966); Pierre Bourget, *Un Certain Philippe Pétain* (Paris: Casterman, 1966); René Gillouin, *J'étais l'ami du Maréchal* (Paris: Plon, 1966).

2. *Paris-Match*, 29 May, 4, 11 June 1966.

3. *Combat*, 'Philippe Pétain vingt ans après', 21 December 1964.

4. Jacques Isorni, *Pétain a sauvé la France* (Paris: Flammarion, 1964).

5. Jacques Isorni, *Le Vrai Procès de Jésus* (Paris: Flammarion, 1966).

6. Jacques Isorni, *Jusqu'au bout de notre peine* (Paris: Table Ronde, 1963).

7. François Mauriac, *Le Bloc-Notes 1963–1970* (Paris: Bouquins, 2020), 236–9 (25 September 1964).

8. Jacques Laurent, *Mauriac sous de Gaulle* (Paris: Table Ronde, 1964), 188.

9. Jacques Laurent, *Offenses au chef de l'État. Audiences des 8 et 9 octobre 1965* (Paris: Table Ronde, 1965).

10. Alfred Fabre-Luce, *Haute Cour* (Paris: Julliard, 1962); *Le Couronnement du Prince* (Paris: Table Ronde, 1964); *Gaulle Deux* (Paris: Julliard, 1958).

11. Olivier Beaud, *La République injuriée. Histoire des offenses au chef de l'État de la IIIe à la Ve République* (Paris: PUF, 2019), 325–92.

12. *Le Monde*, 16 August 1965.

13. Isorni, *Mémoires II*, 400–408; *Le Maréchal 24* (July 1958).

14. *Le Monde*, 31 May 1964.

15. Andre Passeron, 'Polémiques autour d'une tombe', *Le Monde*, 5 June 1964.

16. Louis-Dominique Girard, *Mazinghem ou la vie secrète de Philippe Pétain 1856–1951* (Paris: L.-D. Girard, 1971).

17. This interminable quarrel can be followed in detail in the Girard Papers 72AJ3202, 3206, 3207, 3221; and *Le Monde*: 21 October 1964; 11 September, 5 October, 28 October, 25 December 1966; 21 September 1968.

18. De Gaulle, *Discours et messages IV*, 40.

19. 'Me [Maître] Isorni à l'île d'Yeu', *Le Monde*, 31 May 1966.

20. Baptiste Brossard and Gary Alan Fine, 'The Problem of Pétain: The State Politics of Difficult Reputations', *Sociological Perspectives* (2021), 1–19.

21. Jean-Yves le Naour, *On a volé le maréchal!* (Paris: Larousse, 2009), 123.

22. On this extraordinary affair see: Le Naour, *On a volé*; Michel Dumas, *La Permission du maréchal: Trois jours en maraude avec le cercueil de Pétain* (Paris: Albin Michel, 2004); https://www.radiofrance.fr/franceculture/podcasts/une-histoire-particuliere-un-recit-documentaire-en-deux-parties/un-aller-retour-pour-l-ile-d-yeu-7756503

23. Isorni and Lemaire, *Après le Procès. Documents pour la révision* (Paris: A. Martel, 1948).

24. *Requête en révision pour Philippe Pétain*. For a critique see Maurice Vanino, *Le Temps de la honte, De Rethondes à L'Île d'Yeu* (Paris: Creator, 1952), who produced a demolition of the revision plea. Vanino was the pseudonym of the Jewish activist and writer Maurice Vanikoff.

25. Louis Gottschalk, 'Our Vichy Fumble', *Journal of Modern History* 20:1 (March 1948), 47–56.

26. William Langer, *Our Vichy Gamble* (New York: Alfred Knopf, 1947), 385.

27. Langer, *Vichy Gamble*, 385, 394; 348, 350.

28. Isorni, *Mémoires II*, 149.
29. *Le Monde*, 10 December 1969.
30. *Nouvelle Requête en révision* (Paris: Flammarion, 1978).
31. Robert Paxton, *Vichy France: Old Guard and New Order 1940–1944* (New York: Alfred Knopf, 1972).
32. The Girard Papers, AN 72AJ3219, have a whole file on the debate.
33. AN 72AJ/3206 (24 May 1976).
34. Rousso, *Vichy Syndrome*, 254.
35. Eric Le Vaillant, 'Le Courrier des "Enfants de Pétain"', *Vingtième siècle* 11 (July–September 1986), 110–13.
36. Archives Préfecture de Police, GA 511678 (note May 1966).
37. Antonowicz, *Jacques Isorni*, 579.

24. REMEMBERING THE JEWS

1. Philip Nord, *After the Deportation*, 51.
2. Robert Paxton and Michael Marrus, *Vichy France and the Jews* (New York: BasicBooks, 1981).
3. *Le Monde*, 6 June 1983.
4. Serge and Beate Klarsfeld, *Mémoires* (Paris: Fayard, 2015).
5. Anna Senik, *L'Histoire mouvementée de la reconnaisance officielle des crimes de Vichy contre les juifs* (Paris: L'Harmattan, 2013).
6. Klarsfeld, *Mémoires*, 798–800.
7. Pierre Péan, *Une Jeunesse française. François Mitterrand 1934–1947* (Paris: Fayard, 1994).
8. https://www.elysee.fr/front/pdf/elysee-module-8159-fr.pdf; Stanley Hoffmann, Dominique Moisi, Robert O. Paxton, Jean-Marie Domenach, Philippe Burrin and Ronald Tiersky, 'Symposium on Mitterrand's Past', *French Politics and Society* 13:1 (Winter 1995), 4–35; Claire Andrieu, 'Managing Memory: National and Personal Identity at Stake in the Mitterrand Affair', *French Politics and Society* 14:2 (Spring 1996), 17–32.
9. Mitterrand, 'Notes d'audience', *Libres*, 27 July 1945. There were other signed articles by him at this time but these are not on the trial. Péan, *Une Jeunesse*, 483–93, cites two more articles on the trial by Mitterrand, but I have not found these in *Libres*.
10. Stanley Hoffmann in Hoffmann, Moisi, Paxton, Domenach, Burrin and Tiersky, 'Symposium on Mitterrand's Past', *French Politics and Society* 13:1 (Winter 1995), 4–35.

11. https://www.elysee.fr/jacques-chirac/1995/07/16/allocution-de-m-jacques-chirac-president-de-la-republique-sur-la-responsabilite-de-letat-francais-dans-la-deportation-des-juifs-durant-la-deuxieme-guerre-mondiale-et-sur-les-valeurs-de-liberte-de-justice-et-de-tolerance-qui-fondent-lidentite-franca

12. Eric Conan and Henry Rousso, *Vichy. Un Passé qui ne passe pas* (Paris: Fayard, 1994).

13. Eric Conan, *Le Procès Papon. Un Journal d'audience* (Paris: Gallimard, 1998); Richard Golsan (ed.), *The Papon Affair: Memory and Justice on Trial* (New York: Routledge, 2000); Richard Golsan, 'Papon: The Good, the Bad, and the Ugly', *Sustance* 29:1 (2000), 139–52.

14. François Azouvi, *Français, on ne vous a rien caché. La Résistance, Vichy, notre mémoire* (Paris: Gallimard, 2020), 447.

15. Conan, *Le Procès Papon*, 30–33, 43–5.

16. Jean Daniel, 'Bouc-émissaire et coupable', *Nouvel observateur*, 11 November 1997.

17. Julie Fette, 'Apology and the Past in Contemporary France', *French Politics, Culture & Society*, 26:2 (Summer 2008), 78–113.

18. Jacques Isorni, *La Fièvre verte* (Paris: Flammarion, 1975).

19. Antonowicz, *Jacques Isorni*, 576.

20. Isorni, *Lettre anxieuse au Président de la République au sujet de Philippe Pétain* (Paris: Albatros, 1975), 17.

21. 'Lehideux and Isorni v. France', https://www.cambridge.org/core/journals/international-legal-materials/article/abs/european-court-of-human-rights-lehideux-and-isorni-v-france/4DB45B2FF5C77FD45E2E3E6B8FED0B4E.

22. 'La droite est partagée sur l'analyse du régime de Vichy', *Le Monde*, 23 October 1997.

23. Chevènement, 'Vichy pas coupable mais responsable', *Le Monde*, 12 December 1992.

24. Blandine-Kriegel, 'Vichy, la République et la France', *Le Monde*, 8 September 1995.

25. Marcel Waline, *Manuel élémentaire du droit administratif* (Paris: Sirey, 1946), 31.

26. Georges Vedel, *Manuel élémentaire du droit constitutionnel* (Paris: Sirey, 1949), 280–81; Maurice Duverger, 'Contribution à l'étude de la légitimité des gouvernements de fait', *Revue du droit publique et de la science politique en France et à l'étranger* (January–March 1945), 88–9. These issues are discussed in François Azouvi, *Français*, 261–9.

27. 'Le Premier Président Charles Frémicourt', *Revue internationale de droit comparé* (1967), 965–6.

28. Joseph Vialatoux, *Le Problème de la légitimité du pouvoir* (Paris: Editions du livre français, 1945).

29. Alain Peyrefitte, *De Gaulle parle* (Paris: Gallimard, 2002), 440–42.

30. Azouvi, *Français*, 261.

31. https://www.conseil-etat.fr/decisions-de-justice/dernieres-decisions/conseil-d-etat-13-avril-2018-association-du-musee-des-lettres-et-manuscrits-et-autres; see also this commentary on the ruling: https://www.revuegeneraledudroit.eu/blog/2018/08/10/une-histoire-de-france-par-le-conseil-detat-a-propos-de-la-qualification-darchives-publiques-des-telegrammes-du-general-de-gaulle/

25. JUDGING PÉTAIN TODAY

1. https://www.elysee.fr/en/emmanuel-macron/2017/07/18/speech-by-the-president-of-the-republic-emmanuel-macron-at-the-vel-dhiv-commemoration

2. https://www.ipsos.com/fr-fr/vichy-et-les-juifs

3. 'Les Français face à la mémoire de Vichy et de la Shoah', *Le Monde*, 27 November 1998.

4. *Figaro Magazine*, 17 May 1980; https://www.ipsos.com/fr-fr/Pétain; https://www.ipsos.com/fr-fr/le-regime-de-vichy; https://www.ipsos.com/fr-fr/le-marechal-Pétain; Olivier Duhamel, 'Vichy expurgé par l'opinion', *Le Genre humain*, 1996/1 (30–31), 303–06, comments on a Soffres poll of 1994 which is almost identical to the IPSOS one. Astonishingly, the IPSOS poll of 1997 produced almost identical results to the Soffres one of 1980.

5. https://www.bva-group.com/sondages/francais-centenaire-de-larmistice-de-1918

6. Zemmour, *Destin français* (Paris: Albin Michel, 2018), 514.

7. See Laurent Joly's analysis of Zemmour's not so hidden *arrières pensées*: 'Introduction. Vichy, les Français et la Shoah: un état de la connaissance scientifique', *Revue d'Histoire de la Shoah* 212 (2020/2), 11–29.

8. Some of these issue were aired in a debate at the Memorial de la Shoah in January 2021, https://www.clionautes.org/vichy-Pétain-et-la-shoah-la-these-du-moindre-mal-de-1945-a-nos-jours.html. Examples of where Zemmour certainly wrong-footed his opponents who were not up to the job, and of his many pieces of misinformation on this occasion, are

detailed by Laurent Joly: https://www.clionautes.org/vichy-Pétain-et-la-shoah-la-these-du-moindre-mal-de-1945-a-nos-jours.html

9. Michel, *Le Procès Pétain*, 294.

10. Schlumberger, *Le Procès*, 35.

11. Richard Evans, *Altered Pasts: Counterfactuals in History* (London: Little Brown, 2014).

12. Niall Ferguson, *Virtual History: Alternatives and Counterfactuals* (London: Picador, 1996), 86; Martin Bunzl, 'Counterfactual History: A User's Guide', *The American Historical Review* 109:3 (June 2004), 845–58, offers a reasoned defence of counterfactualism.

13. https://www.1940lafrancecontinue.org; https://forum.sealionpress.co.uk/index.php?threads/lets-discuss-france-fights-on-a-k-a-the-fantasque-time-line.450

14. Jacques Sapir, Frank Stora and Loïc Mahé, *1940. Et si la France avait continué la guerre* (Paris: Tallandier, 2010); *1941–1942. Et si la France avait continué la guerre* (Paris: Tallandier, 2012).

15. André Truchet, *L'Armistice de juin 1940 et l'Afrique du Nord* (Paris: PUF, 1955); Alphonse Goutard, 'La réalité de la "menace" allemande sur l'Afrique du Nord en 1940', *Revue d'histoire de la Deuxième Guerre mondiale*, 44, octobre 1961; Albert Merglen, 'La France pouvait continuer la guerre en Afrique française du nord en juin 1940', GMCC 168 (October 1992), 143–64; Louis-Christian Michelet, 'Pouvait-on réellement, en juin 1940, continuer la guerre en Afrique du Nord?', *Guerres mondiales et conflits contemporains*, 174 (April 1994), 143–60; Christine Levisse-Touzé, *L'Afrique du Nord dans la Guerre, 1939–1945* (Paris: Albin Michel, 1998), is sceptical because no proper planning had taken place.

16. Maurice Schmidt, *Le Double Jeu du Maréchal. Mythe ou réalité* (Paris: Presse de la cité, 1996); Robert Paxton, 'Darlan, un amiral entre deux blocs', *Vingtième siècle* 36 (1992), 3–20.

17. Jean Montigny, *Toute la Vérité sur un mois dramatique de notre histoire* (Clermont-Ferrand: Mont-Louis, 1940), 27.

18. If Vichy is compared to the two other Western European countries that also had independent governments, Vichy emerges less favourably: in Italy 'only' 16 per cent of Jews were murdered, in Denmark almost all survived.

19. Jacques Semelin, *Persécutions et entraides dans la France occupée: comment 75% des Juifs en France ont échappé à la mort* (Paris: Seuil, 2013); *La survie des Juifs en France: 1940–1944* (2018).

20. This is the line of Marrus and Paxton, *Vichy France and the Jews*. Pim Griffioen and Ron Zeller, 'Comparing the Persecution of the Jews in the

Netherlands, France and Belgium, 1940–1945: Similarities, Differences, Causes' in Peter Romijn, *The Persecution of the Jews in the Netherlands, 1940–1945. New Perspectives* (Amsterdam: Amsterdam University Press, 2012); Pim Griffioen and Ron Zeller, 'Anti-Jewish Policy and Organization of the Deportations in France and the Netherlands, 1940–1944: A Comparative Study' in *Holocaust and Genocide Studies* 20:3 (2006), 437–73; Bob Moore, *Victims and Survivors* (London: Hodder, 1997), 91–100.

21. The estimate was that 23,600 Jews had been naturalized since 1927. Some 9,039 cases had been dealt with by the Commission; and 7,055 had been withdrawn. This left another 14,601 cases. See Laurent Joly, *Vichy dans la solution finale. Histoire du Commissariat général aux questions juives (1941–1944)* (Paris: Fayard, 2006), 727.

22. Joly, *Vichy dans la solution finale*, 716–28.

23. This represented about 12 per cent of the French Jewish population and 41 per cent of the foreign Jewish population.

24. Joly, *Vichy dans la solution finale*, 118. The figures of 'French' Jews who died needs also to be adjusted upwards: (i) About one in six of the Jews deported in the summer of 1942 were children who had been born in France and this made them technically French citizens; (ii) There were also those Jews who had been French citizens in 1940 but were denaturalized under Vichy.

25. 'Découverte du texte original établissant un statut pour les juifs sous Vichy', *Le Monde*, 4 October 2010.

EPILOGUE

1. https://www.nytimes.com/2010/03/08/nyregion/08towns.html

2. *Le Monde*, 27 October 2010; another case at Verdun, *Le Monde*, 3 February 1988; https://www.senat.fr/questions/base/1988/qSEQ8802 09702.html

3. https://www.theculturalexperience.com/tours/mussolini-history-tour

4. John Lennon and Malcom Foley, *Dark Tourism: The Attraction of Death and Disaster* (London: Continuum, 2000).

5. *Le Monde*, 16 November 1976.

6. The following two paragraphs draw on: Audrey Mallet, *Vichy contre Vichy. Une capitale sans mémoire* (Paris: Belin, 2019); Bertram Gordon, *War Tourism: Second World War France from Defeat and Occupation to the Creation of Heritage* (Cornell: Cornell University Press, 2018); Eric Conan, 'Vichy Malade de Vichy', *Express*, 26 June 1992; John Campbell,

'Vichy, Vichy, and a Plaque to Remember', *French Studies Bulletin* 60.1 no. 68 (2006), 2–5.

7. De Gaulle, *Discours*, https://cierv-vichy.fr/wp-content/uploads/2021/12/17-avril-1959-La-visite-du-général-de-Gaulle-à-Vichy.pdf

8. Campbell, 'Vichy, Vichy', 4.

9. Their visit gave rise to a book, Philippe Collin, *Le Fantôme de Philippe Pétain* (Paris: Flammarion, 2022), and a series of radio programmes: https://www.franceinter.fr/emissions/le-fantome-de-philippe-Pétain

10. 'Île d'Yeu, 20ème anniversaire de la mort du Maréchal', *Le Monde*, 24 June 1971.

11. Marc Knobel, 'Lorsqu'Eric Zemmour jette le soupçon sur l'innocence d'Alfred Dreyfus', *Revue des Deux Mondes*, 22 October 2021, https://www.revuedesdeuxmondes.fr/lorsqueric-zemmour-jette-le-soupcon-sur-linnocence-dalfred-dreyfus

12. Laurent Joly, *La Falsification de l'histoire. Eric Zemmour, l'extrême droite, Vichy et les juifs* (Paris: Grasset, 2022), 20.

Sources

UNPUBLISHED

Paris

Archives Nationales (AN)

<u>3W Haute Cour de Justice</u>
3W 26: PV of Commission d'Instruction
3W 277–286: Instruction of Pétain trial
3W 287–297: Documents collected by the court (Malle Pétain, Ménétrel notes, etc)
3W 301: Dépositions
3W 302: Messages received during the trial
3W 303: Requêtes en révision
3W 304–306: Imprisonment of Pétain
3W 307–309: Petitions (mostly calling for Pétain's death)

<u>F7 Ministère de l'Intérieur</u>
F7/15288 (Sigmaringen)
F7/15488, 1489, 15549 (Reports on public opinion; RG reports on trial; revision; etc)
15549 (Dossier Pétain)

<u>Ministère de la Justice</u>
BB/18/7164/2
19770067/331 (Mongibeaux dossier)

<u>72AJ Comité d'histoire de la deuxième guerre mondiale</u>
72AJ/1796, 1797: On the Rougier affair (correspondence, etc)
72AJ/250: Material on Rougier collected by Henri Michel

72AJ/1291: Mornet files

Papers of Louis-Dominique Girard
72AJ/3202, 3203, 3206, 3207
72AJ/3219: On the trial and after (revision, the stealing of the body, dossiers de l'écran, etc)
72AJ/3200: 'Journal' 21/2/45–1/6/45; and 'Journal' 20/10/64–21/12/66
72AJ/3220, 3221: ADMP
72AJ/3229: Press reactions to *Montoire*
72AJ/3221: Press reactions to other books

Presidential Archives
3AG4/48: Archives de Gaulle

Private Papers
74AP/25 Paul Reynaud 74AP/25 (mostly press cuttings on the trial and some correspondence)
450AP/3 Jacques Lecompte-Boinet (unpublished journal covering the trial)
317AP/63 Louis Marin (mainly press cuttings but also some letters)
415AP/3 (514Mi) Pétain (miscellaneous documents on the trial)
415AP/4 (on the 1944 'kidnapping')

Contemporaine Nanterre (ex-BDIC)

Fonds Robert Aron
F delta 1832/26/8 (Isorni Dossier)
1832/26/3 (Dossier Pierre Henri)

Fonds Mornet
F delta rés 875 III (a few documents on the trial)

Centre de documentation juive contemporaine
(Mémorial de la Shoah)

Archives du CRIF

Archives de la Préfecture de Police

EA 158 (press dossier on the Pétain trial)
BA 1979 (dossier on the Pétain trial)

SOURCES

Washington

NARA

RG No. Entry No. Title Box Nos. Location
59 A1-205H 1945–49 Central Decimal File: 711.51 3318 250/36/13/5
59 A1-205H 1945–49 Central Decimal File: 851.00 6228–6234 250/38/3/1
59 A1-205H 1945–49 Central Decimal File: 851.00 6296–6297 250/38/4/4

London

National Archives

FO371/49139: Mostly on Rougier
FO371/49140: On preparations for the trial
F371/49141: Mostly on Rougier
FO371/49142–43: Reports on the trial

AUDIOVISUAL SOURCES

Film of the trial (INA)
https://www.ina.fr/ina-eclaire-actu/video/afe86003186/ouverture-du-
    proces-Pétain
https://www.ina.fr/ina-eclaire-actu/video/afe86003196/le-proces-Pétain
https://www.ina.fr/ina-eclaire-actu/video/afe86003213/le-proces-Pétain
https://www.ina.fr/ina-eclaire-actu/video/afe86003224/la-fin-du-proces-
    Pétain
https://www.ina.fr/ina-eclaire-actu/video/afe03000001/le-proces-Pétain-
    rushes
(this link contains one hour of 'rushes' that were not shown in cinemas)

PUBLISHED

Press

French Daily Press (1945) (with the names of the main writers covering the
    trial in brackets)

L'Aube (Georges Bouyx)

L'Aurore (Francine Bonitzer, Paul Bastid)
Ce Soir (Géo London, Jean-Richard Bloch)
Cité-Soir (Germaine Picard-Moch)
Combat (Albert Camus, Georges Altschuler, occasionally Georges Bernanos)
Depêche de Paris
L'Époque (Maurice Clavel)
Le Figaro (Jean Schlumberger, François Mauriac)
La France-Libre. Le Grand Quotidien d'Information
Franc-Tireur (Madeleine Jacob, occasionally Georges Altmann, Albert Bayet)
France-Soir (Joseph Kessel)
L'Humanité (Paul Viannay, Ferdinand Bonte)
Libé-Soir
Libération (Fernand Pouey)
Le Monde (Rémy Roure)
L'Ordre (Georges Salvago, Etienne Buré)
Les Nouvelles du Matin (Pierre Scize)
Paris-Presse Intransigeant
Parisien Libéré (André Ancel)
Le Populaire (Jacques Vico)
Resistance (Léon Werth)

The press articles of three commentators were also published in book form:
Jean Schlumberger, *Le Procès Pétain* (1949)
Joseph Kessel, *Jugements derniers: le procès Pétain, le procès de Nuremberg* (1995)
Léon Werth, *Impressions d'audience: le procès Pétain* (1995)

French Weekly Press (1945)
Le Canard enchaîné
Carrefour
Lettres Françaises
Regards

French Jewish Press (1945)
Droit et Liberté
Reveil des Jeunes (missing issues 1 July and 15 July)
La Terre retrouvée

British/American Press (1945)
The Daily Mail

The Daily Telegraph
The Manchester Guardian
The New York Times
The Times

Post-Liberation Anti-Gaullist Press
Ecrits de Paris (founded 1947)
Rivarol (founded 1951)
Le Maréchal (founded 1952)

Trial Debates

All direct quotations from the trial in this book come from the published stenographic record: *République française. Haute Cour de Justice. Compte rendu in extenso des audiences transmis par le Secrétariat général de la Haute Cour de Justice. Procès du Maréchal Pétain* (1945). A very slightly abridged version of the trial was published by Maurice Garçon in two volumes in 1949: Maurice Garçon, *Le Procès du Maréchal Pétain* (Paris: Albin Michel, 1949)

Other accounts of the trial are: Paul Louis Michel, *Le Procès Pétain* (Paris: Éditions Médicis, 1945); *Les Silences du Maréchal* (Paris: Éditions nouvelles, 1948); Jules Roy, *Le Grand Naufrage* (Paris: Julliard, 1966); Frédéric Pottecher, *Le Procès Pétain. Croquis d'audience par André Galland* (Paris: J.-C. Lattès, 1980); Fred Kupferman, *Les Procès de Vichy: Pucheu, Pétain, Laval* (Brussels: Complexe, 1980); Jean-Marc Varaut, *Le Procès Pétain 1945–1995* (Paris: Perrin, 1997); Philippe Saada and Sébastien Vassant, *Juger Pétain* (Paris: Glénat, 2015)

Benoît Klein, *J'accepte de répondre. Les interrogatoires avant le procès (avril–juin 1945)* (Paris: André Versaille, 2011), contains in full the interrogations of Pétain during the *instruction*

On other related High Court trials in 1945:
Géo London, *L'Amiral Esteva et le Général Dentz devant la Haute Cour de Justice* (Lyon: R. Bonefon, 1945)
Jacques Isorni, *Le Procès de Robert Brasillach* (Paris: Flammarion, 1946)

Speeches/Letters

De Gaulle, *Discours et messages* I (Paris: Plon, 1970)

De Gaulle, *Lettres, notes, carnets 1905–1941* (Paris: Bouquins, 2010)

Philippe Pétain, *Discours aux Français 17 juin–20 août 1944* (Paris: Albin Michel, 1989)

Journals and Memoirs

Hervé Alphand, *L'Étonnement de l'être. Journal 1939–1973* (Paris: Fayard, 1977)

Susan Mary Alsop, *To Marietta from Paris: 1945–1960* (New York: Doubleday, 1975)

Robert Aron, *Le Piège où nous a pris l'histoire* (Paris: Albin Michel, 1950)

Amiral Auphan, *L'Honneur de servir. Mémoires* (Paris: Éditions France-Empire, 1978)

Simone de Beauvoir, *Dans la Force de l'Age* (Paris: Gallimard, 1960)

Jacques Benoist-Méchin, *De la défaite au désastre* (Paris: Albin Michel, 1984)

Philippe Boegner, *Carnets du Pasteur Boegner 1940–1945* (Paris: Fayard, 1992)

Pierre Bouchardon, *Souvenirs* (Paris: Albin Michel, 1953)

Pierre Bourdan, *Carnet de retour avec la division Leclerc* (Paris: Payot, 2014)

Jacques Charpentier, *De Vichy à la résistance* (Paris: Fayard, 1949)

Michel Dumas, *La Permission du maréchal: Trois jours en maraude avec le cercueil de Pétain* (Paris: Albin Michel, 2004)

Janet Flanner, *Paris Journal 1944–1965* (London: Victor Gollancz, 1966)

Jean Galtier-Boissière, *Journal 1940–1950* (Paris: Quai Voltaire, 1992)

Maurice Garçon, *Journal 1939–1945* (Paris: Fayard, 2015)

Charles de Gaulle, *Mémoires* (Paris: Gallimard, 2000)

Jacques Isorni, *Souffrance et mort du Maréchal* (Paris: Flammarion, 1951)

Jacques Isorni, *Je suis avocat* (Paris: Éditions du Conquistador, 1951)

Jacques Isorni, *Le Condamné de la citadelle* (Paris: Flammarion, 1982)

Jacques Isorni, *Mémoires I: 1911–1945* (Paris: Laffont, 1984); *Mémoires II: 1946–1958* (Paris: Laffont, 1986); *Mémoires III: 1959–1987* (Paris: Laffont, 1987)

Madeleine Jacob, *Quarante Ans de journalisme* (Paris: Julliard, 1970)

Serge and Beate Klarsfeld, *Mémoires* (Paris: Fayard, 2015)

Alain de Lattre, *Reconquérir, 1944–1945* (Paris: Plon, 1985)

William Leahy, *I Was There* (London: Victor Gollancz, 1950)

Claude Mauriac, *L'Autre de Gaulle* (Paris: Hachette, 1970)

François Mauriac, *Journal. Mémoires politiques* (Paris: Bouquins, 2008)

Jean Montigny, *Toute la Vérité sur un mois dramatique de notre histoire* (Clermont-Ferrand: Mont-Louis, 1940)

Paul Morand, *Journal de guerre. 1. Londres-Paris-Vichy 1939–1943* (Paris: Gallimard, 2021)

Henri Du Moulin de Labarthète, *Le Temps des illusions, juillet 1940–avril 1942* (Geneva: Enseigne du Cheval Ailé, 1946)

Alfred Naud, *Pourquoi je n'ai pas défendu Pierre Laval* (Paris: Fayard, 1948)

Georges Pompidou, *Lettres, notes et portraits* (Paris: Laffont, 2012)

Guy Raïssac, *Un Soldat dans la tourmente* (Paris: Albin Michel, 1964)

Guy Raïssac, *Un Combat sans merci. L'affaire Pétain-De Gaulle* (Paris: Albin Michel, 1966)

Guy Raïssac, *De la Marine à la Justice. Un magistrat témoigne* (Paris: Albin Michel, 1972)

Remy, *Dix ans avec de Gaulle (1940–1950)* (Pars: France-Empire, 1971)

Paul Reynaud, *Carnets de captivité. 1941–1945* (Paris: Fayard, 1997)

Charles Rist, *Une Saison gâtée. Journal de guerre et de l'occupation* (Paris: Fayard, 1983)

Louis Rougier, *Les Accords Pétain-Churchill. Histoire d'une mission secrète* (Montréal: Beauchemin, 1945)

G.-T. Schillemans, *Philippe Pétain. Le Prisonnier de Sigmaringen* (Paris: MP, 1965)

General Serrigny, *Trente ans avec Pétain* (Paris: Plon, 1959)

Joseph Simon, *Pétain mon prisonnier* (Paris: Plon, 1978)

Roger Stéphane, *Chaque homme est lié au monde* (Paris: Table Ronde, 1946)

Pierre Tissier, *I Worked with Laval* (London: Harrap, 1942)

Michel Tony-Révillon, *Mes Carnets (juin–octobre 1940)* (Paris: O. Lieutier, 1945)

Jean Tracou, *Le Maréchal aux liens* (Paris: A. Bonne, 1949)

Xavier Vallat, *Feuilles de Fresnes 1944–48* (Paris: Déterna, 2013)

Léon Werth, *Déposition. Journal de Guerre. 1940–1945* (Paris: V. Hamy, 1992)

Post-War Pro-Pétainist/Anti-Gaullist Writings

Alfred Fabre-Luce, *Le Mystère du Maréchal. Le Procès de Pétain* (Geneva: Bourquin, 1945); *Double Prison* (Montréal: Variété, 1946); *Gaulle Deux*

(Paris: Julliard, 1958); *Haute Cour* (Lausanne: JFG, 1962); *Le Couronnement du Prince* (Paris: Table Ronde, 1964)

Louis-Dominique Girard, *Montoire. Verdun diplomatique* (Paris: A. Bonne, 1948); *Mazinghem ou la vie secrète de Philippe Pétain 1856–1951* (Paris: L.-D. Girard, 1971)

Général Héring, Commandant Le Roc'h, *Révision* (Paris: Éditions Self, 1949)

Jacques Isorni (with Jean Lemaire), *Après le procès: Documents pour la révision* (Givors: André Martel, 1948); *Requête en révision pour Philippe Pétain, Maréchal de France* (Paris: Flammarion, 1950); *Ainsi passent les Républiques* (Paris: Flammarion, 1959); *Lui qui les juge* (Paris: Flammarion, 1961); *Jusqu'au bout de notre peine* (Paris: Table Ronde, 1963); *Pétain a sauvé la France* (Paris: Flammarion, 1964); *Lettre anxieuse au Président de la République au sujet de Philippe Pétain* (Paris: Albatros, 1975); *Nouvelle requête en révision* (Paris: Flammarion, 1978)

Jacques Laurent, *Mauriac sous de Gaulle* (Paris: Table Ronde, 1964)

Louis Rougier, *La Défaite des vainqueurs* (Geneva: Cheval ailé, 1947); *La France jacobine* (Brussels: Diffusion du livre, 1947); *Pour une politique d'amnistie* (Geneva: Cheval Ailé, 1947); *De Gaulle contre de Gaulle* (Paris: Triolet, 1948); *Les Accords franco-britanniques de l'automne 1940. Histoire et imposture* (Paris: Grasset, 1954)

Index